Korean Studies of the Henry M. Jackson
School of International Studies

James B. Palais, Editor

Korean Studies of the Henry M. Jackson
School of International Studies

Over the Mountains Are Mountains:
Korean Peasant Households and Their
Adaptations to Rapid Industrialization
by Clark W. Sorensen

Cultural Nationalism in Colonial Korea, 1920–1925
by Michael Edson Robinson

Offspring of Empire: The Koch'ang Kims
and the Colonial Origins of Korean
Capitalism, 1876–1945
by Carter J. Eckert

Confucian Statecraft and Korean Institutions:
Yu Hyŏngwŏn and the Late Chosŏn Dynasty
by James B. Palais

Peasant Protest and Social Change
in Colonial Korea
by Gi Wook Shin

The Origins of the Chosŏn Dynasty
by John B. Duncan

THE ORIGINS *of the*
Chosŏn Dynasty

John B. Duncan

UNIVERSITY OF WASHINGTON PRESS
Seattle and London

This publication was supported in part by the Jackson School
Publications Fund, established through the generous support
of the Henry M. Jackson Foundation and other donors, in
cooperation with the Henry M. Jackson School of International
Studies and the University of Washington Press.

Library of Congress Cataloging-in-Publication Data   .
Duncan, John B.
    The origins of the Choson dynasty / John B. Duncan.
        p. cm.— (Korean studies of the Henry M. Jackson School of International
    Studies)
    Includes bibliographical references and index.
    ISBN 0-295-97985-2
    1. Korea—Politics and government—935-1392.   2. Korea—Politics and
    government—1392-1910.   3. Korea—Officials and employees—History.
    I. Title: Choson dynasty.   II. Title.   III. Series.
    JQ1725.A7 D86   2000   951.9'02—DC21   00-029876

For Kay

Contents

Tables

Genealogical Charts

Acknowledgments

I have many to thank for inspiration, guidance, and assistance in the preparation of this book. My interest in premodern Korean history dates back to my years as an undergraduate at Korea University. I owe much to the faculty there, for their patience and understanding in dealing with a struggling foreign student and for sensitizing me to the problems of constructing historical interpretations in a post-colonial society. I am particularly indebted to Kang Chin-ch'ŏl and Kang Man-gil of the Department of History and Kim Ch'ungnyŏl of the Department of Philosophy. Those men not only taught me much about Korea, but also inspired me and my classmates with their personal and intellectual courage in the face of an oppressive military government.

I also owe a great deal to Hugh Kang of the University of Hawaii, where I received my master's degree. It was his patient insistence on thorough documentation and exhaustive research that enabled me to compile the data on the early Koryŏ aristocracy that provided much of the basis for chapter 2 of this book.

I would be remiss if I did not mention the contributions of several of my colleagues, including Ned Shultz of the University of Hawaii at West Oahu; Carter Eckert and Peter Bol of Harvard University; Robert Buswell, Ben Elman, and Peter Lee of UCLA; Michael Rogers of the University of California at Berkeley; and Park Yong-woon, Min Hyun-ku, and Kim Hyun-koo of Korea University, who have been generous of their time and expertise in discussing various aspects of the work. In particular, I am grateful to Martina Deuchler of the University of London for her meticulous review of an earlier version of the manuscript, which enabled me to avoid many embarrassing errors. I also owe much to Lorri Hagman at the University of Washington Press for a superb job of editing what must have been a difficult manuscript.

My greatest debt, however, is to James Palais of the University of Washington. It was under his guidance that I completed the Ph.D. dissertation upon which this work is based. His trenchant reviews of the dissertation and of the revised manuscript did much to formulate my thinking and sharpen my focus. There is no way I can repay him for his generosity with his time, his insistence on rigor, and his confidence in my ability; I can only hope to pass on to my own graduate students a fraction of what he has given me.

I must also recognize my parents, Roscoe and Edith Duncan, for their emotional support when, as a youth, I set off for Korea on what must have seemed to them like a hopelessly quixotic adventure. Last, but certainly not least, I must thank my wife, Kay, whose unflagging support and patient tolerance of the many evenings and weekends I have spent locked away in my study made this work possible.

The Origins of the Chosŏn Dynasty

Introduction

In the seventh month of 1392 the 474-year-old Koryŏ dynasty came to an end, its place as ruler of the Korean Peninsula taken by a new dynasty, the Chosŏn. Dynastic changes were rare, this being the only one in the thousand years preceding Japanese colonization in 1910. It has, as a consequence, attracted a great deal of scholarly attention.

The Koryŏ did not meet its doom at the hands of foreign invaders, as did the Sung (960–1279) and the Ming (1368–1644) in China. Neither did it fall to provincially based rebel movements, as did China's Han (206 BCE–CE 220) and Yüan (1279–1368) dynasties or Korea's Silla (?–935). The dynasty, which survived serious revolts in the early twelfth century, a military coup in 1170, conquest by the Mongols in the mid-thirteenth century, and the deposal and assassination of many of its kings throughout its five centuries, was in the end done in by its own officials.

A variety of assessments of this event has been advanced within larger schemes of historical interpretation. Traditional Confucian views emphasized the moral depravity of the final Koryŏ kings and the ethical virtues of Yi Sŏng-gye, the founding monarch of the new dynasty. In the early twentieth century historian-apologists for imperial Japan argued, as part of an effort to depict Korea as a backward and historically stagnant society in need of enlightened (Japanese) leadership, that the Koryŏ-Chosŏn change of dynasties was a mere palace coup of no real historical significance. The main thrust of the imperialist view was that Korea had not followed the proper ancient-medieval-modern path of historical development that had supposedly been taken by the "advanced countries" (J. *senjinkoku*, K. *sŏnjin'guk*) of Western Europe and, of course, Japan. Various aspects of Korea's past were depicted in negative terms: political subservience to China and lack of autonomy; socioeconomic stagnancy and omission of the feudal stage of development; and cultural imi-

Unless noted otherwise, transliterated terms are Korean. "K." (Korean), "J." (Japanese), and "Ch." (Chinese) distinguish multiple transliterations.

tation of China and lack of creativity. In short, the Japanese applied to Korea the same notion of an unchanging traditional order that Western imperialist powers used against non-Western, "pre-modern" societies.

Korean scholars struggled to rebut the imperialist view throughout the colonial period. Men such as Sin Ch'ae-ho, Pak Ŭn-sik, and Chŏng In-bo, referred to as "nationalist historians" (*minjokchuŭi sahakcha,*) sought to define the Korean nation in terms of a unique spirit, the recovery of which would enable Koreans to free themselves of the shackles of foreign domination and to revitalize their country.[1] Another group, known as "positivist historians" (*silchŭng sahakcha,*) included men such as Yi Hong-jik and Yi Pyŏng-do who were trained at Japanese universities and strove to counter imperialist depictions of Korean history, particularly the ancient period, through rigorous use of documentary evidence.[2] A third group, usually called "socioeconomic historians" (*sahoe kyŏngje sahakcha*), was influenced by leftist ideas. In their efforts to refute Japanese contentions of stagnation, men such as Paek Nam-un and Yi Ch'ŏng-wŏn eschewed Marx's idea of an Asiatic mode of production and applied instead a Stalinist interpretation, claiming that Korea, too, had passed through ancient slave and medieval feudal stages of development.[3] Although these colonial era scholars labored under great political difficulties, their work laid down the foundations of modern Korean historiography and, in terms of basic approaches, still provides points of departure for scholarship in the late twentieth century.

These early efforts not withstanding, it was not until after Japan withdrew in 1945 that Koreans were free to engage in the study of their past. Historical scholarship since 1945 has devoted much energy to refuting the stagnation theory. North Korean scholars have generally followed the lead of Paek Nam-un in applying a Stalinist model of historical analysis that seeks to fit the Korean past into slave, feudal, and capitalist stages of historical development. Their interpretation, however, does not assign great significance to the founding of the Chosŏn dynasty because they see it as essentially a reconsolidation of feudal institutions within a lengthy medieval period that began with the rise of the Three Kingdoms (Silla; Paekche, ?–660; Koguryŏ, ?–668) nearly two thousand years ago and ended in the nineteenth century.[4]

South Korean historical scholarship has been more diverse. The immediate post-1945 period saw a perpetuation of all three main colonial era approaches. There were the "new nationalists" (*sin minjokchuŭija*), such as Son Chin-t'ae, who contended that the Korean nation (*minjok*) had been formed in prehistoric times and who sought to define the nation in terms of its unique cultural and spiritual aspects, arguing that the singularity of the Korean historical experience meant that it could not and should not be forced into either Western European or Marxist models.[5] A number of socioeconomic historians, such as Chŏn Sŏk-tam, continued the effort to fit Korean history into a Stalinist model.[6] Positivist historians such as Yi Pyŏng-do and Yi Sang-baek, who were ensconced in history departments at major universities at the time of liberation, criticized both the nationalist and the socioeconomic historians for their excessive devotion to abstract theory. As a result of the Korean War and the postwar political climate, positivist historians came to dominate the field in South Korea during the 1950s and 1960s.

By the mid-1960s positivists came under increasing criticism for their excessive devotion to digging out facts without providing a conceptual framework for interpretation. By the end of the decade there was a growing tendency, informed—perhaps unwittingly in some cases—by Stalinist analytical categories, to view Korea's history as a process of developmental stages propelled by the rise to power of successive new socioeconomic classes, although the South Korean scholars usually avoided the term "class" (*kyegŭp*) in favor of politically less sensitive terms such as "ruling stratum" (*chibae ch'ŭng*). Cognizant of the difficulties inherent in trying to force Korea's history into the three-stage model,[7] these scholars applied a modified periodization to Korean history that focused on such events as the Silla-Koryŏ transition, the mid-Koryŏ ascendancy of great central official descent groups, the military coup of 1170, the rise of the rusticated literati *(sarim)* in the sixteenth century, and the advent of reform Confucianism, commonly known as Practical Learning (Sirhak), in the late Chosŏn and argued that these phenomena reflected the rise of new socioeconomic forces.

This approach, known as the "internal development theory" (*naejaejŏk palchŏn non*), was given its classic formulation in Lee Ki-baik's influential book *Han'guksa sillon* (translated into English as *A New History of Korea*).[8] I can still remember the keen sense of excitement I felt when I read Professor Lee's book for the first time as an undergraduate. Here, at last, I believed, was a way to reconcile the unique aspects of Korean history with universalistic models.

As I proceeded in my graduate studies, however, I became increasingly skeptical of the internal development theory. In part, I was influenced by the new "people's history" (*minjung sahak*)[9] of the 1980s, which, while clinging to the notion of Korean history as a process of linear development, criticized mainstream historians because their emphasis on ruling classes, rather than the people, as the prime movers of history legitimated the capitalist establishment in contemporary South Korea and provided an ideological prop for the developmentalist state of Park Chung Hee and Chun Doo Hwan.[10] Although I tend to sympathize with the *minjung* historians' criticisms of mainstream scholarship, especially because I am uncomfortable with the internal development theory's implication that the rise of the capitalist system is a natural consequence of the internal logic of Korean historical development, I have found their approach to be of limited value for my purposes because of the almost total lack of information on nonelite social groups in the Koryŏ and early Chosŏn periods and, perhaps more importantly, because I, like many Western scholars in the second half of the twentieth century, have become skeptical of depictions of history as a linear developmental process leading inexorably towards modernization. My apprehension regarding the specific applicability of the internal development approach to Korean history has been bolstered by the findings of several of my more empirically oriented colleagues, both in the West and in Korea, who have demonstrated that continuity, rather than radical change, in the ruling class was a central feature of Korea's historical experience during the Koryŏ and Chosŏn periods.[11]

These valuable studies not withstanding, there has been no comprehensive critical examination of the issue of change and continuity in the Koryŏ-Chosŏn change of dynasties, which, according to the advocates of the internal development theory, was the consequence of the rise of a new class of scholar-officials (*sinhŭng sadaebu*) who were medium and small landowners of rural petty official (*hyangni*) backgrounds, whose ideology was Ch'eng-Chu Neo-Confucianism (Chŏngjuhak, Ch. Ch'eng-Chu Hsüeh), and who advocated a pro-Ming foreign policy.[12] They are believed to have came to power by overthrowing an old ruling class composed of capital-based aristocrats who were the absentee owners of large landed estates, who found ideological support in Buddhism, and who pursued a pro-Yüan diplomatic course. It was clear to me, however, that a number of features of the Koryŏ-Chosŏn transition could not be explained by the "new scholar-official" interpretation. One was the large number of men from prominent old Koryŏ descent groups, such as Cho Chun of the P'yŏngyang Cho and Min Yŏ-ik of the Hwangnyŏ Min, who continued to hold high offices after 1392. A second was that ownership of large landed estates by high-ranking central officials continued to be an important feature of Korean society. Yet another was that the "old aristocrats," such as Yi In-im, who dominated the government in the second half of the fourteenth century, actually pursued a flexible, pragmatic diplomatic course that sought to build solid relations with the Ming and turned to the Yüan Mongols only when they were rebuffed by the Chinese.[13]

In my own doctoral dissertation at the University of Washington, therefore, in order to test the "new scholar-official" theory, I chose to reexamine the social and economic backgrounds of the men who held high office in the early years of the Chosŏn dynasty.[14] What I found—the wholesale survival of the old ruling class into the new dynasty—only deepened my suspicions about the usefulness of the internal development theory. If my dissertation demonstrated the weaknesses of the "new scholar-official" argument, however, it failed to provide a satisfying reinterpretation of the forces that led to the change of dynasties. Indeed, to the extent that it focused on continuity in the official class, it could even be seen as supporting the old imperialist contention that the founding of the Chosŏn was nothing more than a palace coup. I have, as a consequence, spent the last few years conducting additional research into various aspects of the Koryŏ-Chosŏn transition and rethinking my approach to the issue. Part of this effort has gone into expanding the scope of my research on the bureaucracy back earlier into the Koryŏ and later in the Chosŏn, but my primary focus has been on the institutional debilities of the late Koryŏ and how the reforms that accompanied the founding of the Chosŏn addressed those problems.

The late Koryŏ suffered from a weak kingship, erosion of state control over material and human resources, and powerful aristocratic elements fighting with the throne and with each other over resources and political power. Seeking an alternative theoretical perspective that would allow me to explore those institutional problems, I turned to S. N. Eisenstadt's classic study of historical bureaucratic polities, *The Political Systems of Empires*. Although this work seems—in its depiction of historical bureaucratic societies as occupying an intermediate stage between less sophisticated patrimonial and feudal systems and more highly developed modern systems—to share some of the assumptions of modernization theory, it is based primarily on analysis of such non-Western societies as Ottoman Turkey, Sassanid Persia, and China and does not depict modernization as an inevitable outcome of historical change. Eisenstadt's analysis of the relationship between the extent of social differentiation and the amount of free-floating resources and generalized power available to rulers of historical bureaucratic polities is relevant to the study of a society such as Koryŏ and early Chosŏn Korea, which combined the trappings of bureaucracy with strong aristocratic tendencies.

Eisenstadt depicts China, which is the closest analogue to Korea, as a polity that was able to maintain itself over a long period of time because the major types of change were marginal—rebellious and dynastic changes that became reintegrated into the basic framework of political institutions. He treats the institutional problems that appeared in the later years of Chinese dynasties as the result of rulers' exploitative policies, which put excessive pressure on the free strata, leading to a decline in the amount of free-floating resources available to the state. In short, he appears to subscribe to a fiscally oriented dynastic-cycle theory such as that described by Edwin O. Reischauer and John K. Fairbank in *East Asia: The Great Tradition.*

I have found in Korea, however, that the institutional difficulties of the late Koryŏ were not simply manifestations of the declining phase of a dynastic cycle. Rather, they were deeply rooted in the nature of the early Koryŏ political settlement. The tenth-century Koryŏ kings, seeking to expand their political power and put their dynasty on a firm foundation, imported the institutions of centralized bureaucratic rule from China. The society on which they sought to impose those institutions, however, was a poorly differentiated one with strong aristocratic tendencies and a tradition of particularistic local autonomy. The result was a compromise between centralized bureaucracy and local aristocracy that left political roles embedded in ascriptive social groups and left the dynasty dependent on hereditary local elites (who came to be called *hyangni*) to provide its officials and to administer the bulk of the prefectures and counties throughout the country. Lack of distinction between political and social roles enabled those recruited to serve in the dynasty's government to develop a powerful new central aristocratic bureaucracy whose interests were no longer compatible with those of the local elite stratum. At the same time, reliance on hereditary elites for local administration meant that the state depended on cooperation of the *hyangni* and maintenance of the traditional local social order for access to material and human resources. Thus conflict between central and local interests and between the interests of the throne and the central aristocratic bureaucrats (who came to be known as *yangban*) was inherent in the early Koryŏ political settlement.

Despite fundamental tensions deriving from the rise of a powerful central aristocratic bureaucracy in a system designed to protect the interests of local elites, the Koryŏ polity might have been able to limp along had it not been subjected to great pressure in its later years as a result of foreign invasions. These invasions not only drained the state of resources, but also disrupted the *hyangni*-centered traditional local social order, a situation that was aggravated by increasing penetration of the countryside by economic interests of the central *yangban*. Consequences of the breakdown of local society were twofold: intensification of the state's fiscal problems and emigration of disembedded local elites to the capital in search of opportunity, threatening the power of the central *yangban*.

The late Koryŏ kings, facing an entrenched central *yangban* aristocracy and lacking the resources and prestige to carry out basic reforms, attempted to deal with the deteriorating situation through methods—including offsetting *yangban* power by investing political authority in foreigners and eunuchs and rewarding *hyangni* for military service by granting them official status—that only aggravated the threat felt by central aristocratic bureaucrats and ultimately deepened the crisis.

Endangered by an institutional structure that no longer served their needs and that alienated them from their sovereigns, reform-minded *yangban* eventually allied themselves with a relative newcomer, the military strongman Yi Sŏng-gye, who had the armed might needed to push through reforms against conservative opposition. The subsequent political struggle culminated in the overthrow of the Koryŏ in 1392. Reforms implemented by the founders of the new dynasty were designed in part to redress the balance of power between throne and officials, but, more importantly, to reduce competition for political power and buttress the position of the *yangban* as the country's social and political elite.

The establishment of the Chosŏn dynasty, therefore, came about as tensions were worked out between an imported centralized bureaucracy that presumed a comparatively high degree of social differentiation, and a locally particularistic native tradition in which resources and political roles remained embedded in ascriptive social groups. The institutional reforms carried out at the time of the Koryŏ-Chosŏn transition represented a reorganization of the country's sociopolitical system around the interests of the central *yangban* class and thus constituted a break with the old order which, despite some degree of centralization, was based primarily on the interests of the local strongman class of the late Silla–early Koryŏ period. In short, what we see is a shift—still within the broad outlines of the historical bureaucratic society—from a strongly aristocratic system (in which the dominant social group was a locally based elite) to a mixed aristocratic-bureaucratic system (in which the dominant social group derived its power and prestige from ancestral traditions of service in the state bureaucracy). Whether this represented historical "progress" seems to me to be very much an issue of teleological judgment. But of one thing I am certain: it was not stagnation.

Finally, I would like to note that in the past few years a new generation of Korean scholars, inspired in large measure by older positivist historians who have not accepted the premises of the mainstream, has begun to challenge the conclusions of the internal development theory regarding the late Koryŏ-early Chosŏn period.[15] These historians include Kim Kwang-ch'ŏl, who has demonstrated the underlying continuity between the early Koryŏ ruling class and that of the late Koryŏ;[16] Kim Tang-t'aek, who has taken issue with the "new scholar-official" versus "old aristocrat" dichotomy,[17] and Chŏng Tu-hŭi, who has shown that the rusticated literati and the meritorious elite of the early Chosŏn came from the same social class.[18] It is no small comfort to me, as a Westerner studying Korean history, to know that I have colleagues in Korea who, while they might find shortcomings in my scholarship, share my misgivings about imposing Western-derived models—models that inevitably privilege the "modern" Western experience—on Korea's rich historical heritage.

1 / The Koryŏ Political System

The Koryŏ dynasty's political system was at one time conventionally described as a replica of that of T'ang China. Indeed, if one relies solely on the description of political institutions in the "Monograph on Officials" (Paekkwan chi) of the dynastic history, the *Koryŏsa* (History of the Koryŏ), it is hard to come to any other conclusion. Recent studies have shown, however, that the way in which the Koryŏ government actually worked was quite different.[1]

Although these studies have piqued scholarly interest in Koryŏ political institutions, research in this area has been carried out almost in a vacuum. Historians drawing contrasts between Korea in the Koryŏ period and China have usually proceeded from the assumption that the Chinese dynastic histories describe the actual structure and operation of Chinese institutions. Furthermore, there has been virtually no effort to interpret findings on the Koryŏ in light of what is known about premodern polities in other parts of the world, aside from one or two attempts to use Max Weber's work on bureaucracy. Even those efforts, however, have been almost universally rejected because of the strongly aristocratic nature of Koryŏ society.[2] Thus while studies on Koryŏ political institutions accumulate, we have very little sense of how the Koryŏ system compares with the political systems of other countries.

The classic comparative study of historical bureaucratic societies is S. N. Eisenstadt's *The Political Systems of Empires*. Eisenstadt's conclusions, which point to the existence of substantial aristocratic elements as an important variable in determining the nature of traditional bureaucratic polities, are drawn from an examination of several major societies, including Sassanid Persia, Ottoman Turkey, Byzantium, and China. Koryŏ Korea was smaller than those polities, but it shared many of their features and grappled with similar problems. A reconsideration of Koryŏ institutions in the light of Eisenstadt's findings should give us a better understanding of how the Koryŏ system worked and what it shared with other historical polities, as well as in what ways it was different.

Eisenstadt sees the historical bureaucratic society as a type of polity that falls between feudal and patrimonial systems and "modern" political systems. Feudal and patrimonial systems arise in poorly differentiated societies where material and human resources remain embedded in various ascriptive descent or territorial collectivities. Modern political systems, on the other hand, form in highly differentiated societies with large amounts of free-floating resources that can be used by the state in pursuit of its political goals. In the historical bureaucratic society, with its limited degree of social differentiation, free-floating resources—those not tied up in feudal fiefs or estates, freely alienable and subject to taxation by the state—coexist with resources still embedded in traditional ascriptive groups. Maintenance of the historical bureaucratic polity is dependent on the continuing coexistence of both types of resources. Failure to preserve some degree of free-floating resources will result in the regression, in Eisenstadt's terms, to a feudal or patrimonial type, while a predominance of free-floating resources will lead to the demise of the historical bureaucratic polity in favor of "modern" democratic or totalitarian regimes. By the same token, many of the differences among historical bureaucratic polities can be explained by the extent of social differentiation. Less differentiated societies, where social and economic roles are embedded in traditional ascriptive groups, produce fewer free-floating resources and thus tend to have weaker political systems, while more differentiated societies tend to have stronger, more complex political systems. The Koryŏ was a relatively poorly differentiated society, in which rulers struggled constantly with ascriptive elites for access to resources.

Initiative for the formation of bureaucratic societies, Eisenstadt argues, comes from rulers, whose aim is to create a more centralized and unified system in which they can monopolize decision making without being bound by traditional aristocratic or tribal entities. He notes that opposition to rulers comes from groups, typically landed aristocrats, who feel threatened by centralizing activities. To overcome such opposition, rulers find allies among groups who are opposed to the old aristocrats and have something to gain from the establishment of a centralized polity. Institutionally, rulers seek to establish administrative organs whose budgets they can control and which they can staff with loyal and qualified personnel, thereby making administrative bodies as independent as possible from traditional groups. As we will see, the tenth-century Koryŏ rulers attempted to use newer social elements while implementing institutional changes designed to enhance their control over the political process.

Eisenstadt cites a number of factors that limited the power of the rulers of historical bureaucratic polities. Among those factors was the legitimization of rulers by traditional religious beliefs, which tended to bind the new rulers within the old nexus of power relations. The founding of the Koryŏ was legitimized in large measure by Buddhist and geomantic ideas that were part and parcel of the legitimating ideology of the dominant social groups.

Other important factors were the extent to which political roles were not distinguished from basic societal roles and traditional ascriptive units still performed crucial political functions. These were closely linked to the low level of differentiation in Koryŏ society, which is revealed most clearly in its system of local administration. The dynasty did not exercise direct rule over most of the countryside; instead routine administration of the vast majority of the country's prefectures and counties remained the hereditary prerogative of local elites upon whom the dynasty relied to maintain order and mobilize resources. The descent groups of these local elites formed a hierarchical territorial status system that was the constitutional foundation of the Koryŏ polity.

Eisenstadt points out that the continuing importance of ascriptive and particularistic criteria in the structure and composition of elite groups was another major limiting factor on the power of the rulers.[3] The tradition of hereditary privilege in the powerful descent groups that dominated local society in ninth- and tenth-century Korea was carried over into the capital-based official descent groups that emerged out of the local elites to become the dominant political stratum in the eleventh and twelfth centuries. This tradition not only sanctioned the ascriptive privileges of elite groups, both local and central, but also greatly limited the amount of resources available to rulers, thus forming conditions that engendered and shaped struggles between kings and elite social groups over resources and political power.

Eisenstadt also notes that value orientations of rulers constituted a major variable in determining the nature of the polity. He defines two major types of value orientations in historical bureaucracies. One is a political-collective orientation, in which the primary goal is strengthening of the state through territorial expansion. This orientation leads rulers to pursue policies that enhance their access to resources and undermine the balance between free-floating and traditional embedded resources that is essential for existence of the polity. The other is an orientation toward the maintenance of culture in which the primary goal is to ensure perpetuation of the polity through diffusion and maintenance of cultural values. Societies oriented thus, of which China is a classic example, tend to be much more stable, maintaining or recreating themselves over long periods of time.[4]

Manifestations of both orientations can be found in the Koryŏ. The dynasty's original name of Later Koguryŏ expressed the founders' irredentist aspirations for the lost territories of Koguryŏ in the northern reaches of the Korean Peninsula and Manchuria. Although the Koryŏ did enjoy some early success in expanding its borders, particularly in the northwestern region, where it reached all the way to the Yalu River, any further expansion in the northeastern reaches of the peninsula or across the Yalu into Manchuria was blocked by the rise of the powerful empires of the Khitan Liao (907–1125) and the Jurchen Chin (1115–1234). By the time the Koryŏ worked out a settlement with the Liao in the late tenth and early eleventh centuries, it had already begun to shift to a cultural maintenance orientation. This was challenged in the mid-twelfth century by the nativist war party of the monk Myoch'ŏng (d. 1135), but Myoch'ŏng was defeated by Kim Pu-sik (1075–1151), a Confucian scholar-official whose primary concerns were creation of a Silla-based political identity and diffusion of Confucian social values.[5] Thereafter, continuing pressure from the Jurchen Chin and the eventual incorporation of Korea into the Mongol Yüan (1260–1368) empire effectively precluded any resurgence of expansionist sentiment until very near the end of the dynasty.[6]

What, then, was the essential nature of the Koryŏ political system under the cultural maintenance orientation? Winston Lo, in his discussion of the cultural maintenance orientation of Sung China, argues that the main functions of the state were "protecting the realm from its domestic and foreign enemies and maintaining the social hierarchy and the traditional lifestyle to which the different social strata were accustomed."[7] This statement seems to apply generally to the Koryŏ as well, especially in the middle and later centuries when reform efforts were designed primarily to maintain or restore the status quo. Such a cultural maintenance orientation would seem to be particularly well suited to a poorly differentiated society with strong ascriptive tendencies.

CENTRAL POLITICAL INSTITUTIONS

The Koryŏ lasted nearly five hundred years, but few would have predicted such longevity when Wang Kŏn established the dynasty in the early tenth century. The authority of Korean kings had long been constrained by powerful aristocratic constituents, and coups d'état had been the order of the day in late Silla as various aristocratic descent groups took turns seizing the throne. Wang Kŏn was hampered by the same problems that had plagued the late Silla monarchy. He himself rose to the throne via a coup, and his new regime was essentially a confederation of powerful warlords within which he was little more than *primus inter pares.*[8] The most pressing problems, therefore, for the early Koryŏ kings were legitimating themselves, enhancing the prestige and power of the throne, and creating bureaucratic institutions through which they could carry out their political aims.

The Kingship

We can gain some sense of the magnitude of the problems faced by the Koryŏ founders from a brief overview of the difficulties that plagued their Silla predecessors. The dominant center of political power in the early Silla state was the aristocratic Hwabaek Council, which exercised a broad range of powers, including choosing kings, deliberating on major policy questions, and executing policy decisions. As competition for domination of the Korean Peninsula among the three kingdoms of Koguryŏ, Paekche, and Silla began to heat up in the sixth and seventh centuries, the balance of political power shifted from the Hwabaek Council toward the throne, reaching a peak during the first hundred years after Silla's victory. The kingship became the hereditary prerogative of the descendants of King Muryŏl (r. 654–61), who came to the throne by overturning a Hwabaek Council decision in favor of another man. Muryŏl's descendants carried out a number of bureaucratizing reforms, including a change in office nomenclature designed to enhance the bureaucratic subordination of government officials and replacement of the stipend village (*nogŭp*) (a grant that allowed its high-ranking recipients to collect land rents and corvée services from residents of a fixed area) with a monthly stipend system.[9]

Despite these changes, the Silla polity remained a poorly differentiated system in which political roles were closely linked to social status. Silla's caste-like Bone Rank system, which took shape in the sixth century, allocated political offices on the basis of social status. Only persons belonging to the Holy Bone (Sŏnggol) caste or—later, after the demise of the Holy Bone line in the early seventh century—the True Bone (Chin'gol) caste, could occupy the throne, and only men born into the Holy or True Bone caste could sit on the Hwabaek Council or rise to high political office. Below the True Bone caste were the sixth, fifth, and fourth headranks (*tup'um*). Men born into the various headrank strata were limited to functionary positions in the bureaucracy, with the highest-ranking group, the sixth headrank, allowed to rise only to mid-level posts. Thus a major feature of the Silla political system was the high degree to which political roles were embedded in ascriptive collectivities.

When the reforms of the seventh and eighth century Silla kings began to impinge on True Bone privileges, an inevitable aristocratic backlash began in the mid-eighth century with the reversal of some of the most important bureaucratizing reforms of King Kyŏngdŏk (r. 742–65), including a revival of the stipend village system, and soon led to a series of revolts that culminated in the assassination of King Hyegong (r. 765–80). Hyegong's death marked the end of hereditary succession in Muryŏl's line and opened the door for free-for-all competition for the crown among the True Bone aristocrats of the capital. No fewer than 20 different individuals sat on the throne during the last century and a half of the Silla as segments of the Kim and Pak descent groups fought for power, each believing that its True Bone status gave it a valid claim to the throne.

Although the material base of True Bone power in earlier years appears to have been control over traditional tribal resources, the caste lost much of its tribal power base as a result of the centralizing bureaucratic reforms of the seventh and eighth centuries.[10] After the revolts of the mid-eighth century, however, True Bone elites began to amass large landed estates (*chŏnjang*) and became, in effect, a landed aristocracy.[11] The revival of aristocratic power resulted in the ninth-century rebirth of council politics in the Chŏngsadang.[12]

Aristocratic preoccupation with power struggles in the capital led to neglect of the routine business of governing, especially in the provinces. This opened the way for local strongmen (*hojok*), who referred to themselves as generals (*changgun*) or as lords of walled towns (*sŏngju*), to assemble private military forces throughout the peninsula. Over time many of these strongmen joined forces, either by alliance or subjugation, as they sought to bolster power and increase territory. By the beginning of the tenth century, their alliances coalesced into two large entities capable of challenging Silla: Later Paekche and Koryŏ.[13]

These local warlords appear to have been of diverse social origins. Some of the most prominent were disaffected aristocrats who had relocated to the countryside, such as the Silla prince Kungye and the descendants of Kim Chu-wŏn in Myŏngju (modern Kangnŭng). Others included rebellious local officials, members of Silla's border defense units, and even village chiefs. Another significant group were men of obscure backgrounds who were active in maritime trade.[14] The rise of such elements suggests that Silla underwent a process of social differentiation that produced new social groups, such as maritime traders, who could contest the True Bone landed aristocracy's domination of Korean society, and that practical power replaced hereditary privilege as a primary determinant of social status.[15]

Under the leadership of Wang Kŏn, a man of maritime trading origins who ousted Kungye as king in 918, the Koryŏ eventually succeeded in establishing unified rule over the Korean Peninsula, accepting Silla's surrender in 935 and defeating Later Paekche on the battlefield in 936. Wang Kŏn used a variety of ideological elements to legitimate his rule. It is clear from his reign title, "Heaven-given" (Ch'ŏnsu), that he sought to justify his overthrow of Kungye in Confucian terms by claiming to have received the Mandate of Heaven. This was the first time a Korean ruler is known to have made use of the Mandate and would appear to have given Wang Kŏn a powerful new means of legitimation while constituting a sharp break from Silla's ascriptive Bone Rank tradition.

There were restraints, however, on the authority Koryŏ kings could derive from the Mandate of Heaven. Silla had recognized the suzerainty of the T'ang emperor, and thus the theory that only China's Son of Heaven could claim the Mandate, for nearly two and one-half centuries. The weakness of the Mandate as a means of enhancing royal power in Korea is underscored by the fact that Wang Kŏn himself eventually recognized Chinese suzerainty in 933 when he adopted the reign title of the Later T'ang (923–936) emperor Ming-tsung and that all his successors (except for Kwangjong during the years 960–63) recognized Chinese, Khitan, Jurchen, or Mongol emperors as their suzerains, accepted letters of investiture from those emperors, and used Chinese, Khitan, Jurchen, and Mongol reign titles.

Additional evidence of the limits of Wang Kŏn's use of the Mandate of Heaven as herald of a new, more meritocratic social order can be found in the dynastic history's claim that Wang Kŏn had a Holy Bone general among his ancestors.[16] Although this assertion is found in a twelfth-century document, Kim Kwan-ŭi's *P'yŏnnyŏn t'ongnok* (Comprehensive records arranged by year), which has been preserved in the "Dynastic Geneology" (Segye) of the *Koryŏsa*, there seems to be no reason to doubt that its emphasis on Silla aristocratic ancestry reflected tenth-century attitudes, especially in light of evidence that the official rank system of early tenth-century Koryŏ was based on the Silla system.[17] Thus, even though the formal Bone Rank system came to an end with the fall of Silla, new elements that were rising to share in political power still sought to legitimate themselves in terms of Bone Rank status. Furthermore, as Hugh Kang has demonstrated, Wang Kŏn pursued a policy, necessitated by both the strength of ascriptive tradition and the near monopoly enjoyed by Silla aristocrats on practical administrative experience, of actively wooing aristocratic support for his regime.[18] Bloodlines remained a primary determinant of social and political status in Korea.

Additional evidence of Wang Kŏn's inability to transcend the interests of traditional ascriptive groups can be found in several of the famous Ten Injunctions (Hunyo Sipcho) he left behind as guides for his descendants. Scholastic Buddhism (Kyo), as represented by the Hwaŏm (Ch. Hua-yen) school had been closely identified with True Bone interests in Silla. Not only did Silla rulers use the ideal of the Buddha-king to bolster the monarchy, but Silla aristocrats justified their caste privileges on the basis of the doctrine of transmigration of souls, establishing many Hwaŏm temples, which they used for ancestor worship. The meditational (Sŏn, Ch. Ch'an, J. Zen) school, on the other hand, developed out in the provinces. Its Nine Mountains were closely allied with local strongmen, who found justification for their resistance to central authority in meditational Buddhism's emphasis on individual effort toward enlightenment.[19] Furthermore, the doctrines of geomancy, which held that land forms influenced human affairs, were used to justify the ascendancy of local strongmen in their various locales.[20]

Wang Kŏn's first injunction states, "The success of every undertaking of our state depends on the favor and protection of Buddha. Therefore, the temples of both the meditational and scholastic schools should be built and monks should be sent out to those temples to minister to Buddha." The fifth injunction begins, "I achieved the great task of founding the dynasty with the help of the elements of mountain and river of our country." Admonitions regarding Buddhism and geomancy also appear in several other injunctions, including the sixth, which states that the purpose of the Yŏndŭng festival was to worship Buddha and that of the P'algwan festival was to worship the spirits of heaven and of the major mountains and rivers.[21] These injunctions indicate that Wang Kŏn was ultimately unable to find a source of legitimization that would free him from the constraints of the dominant social groups—both the scholastic-oriented True Bones and the meditational/geomantic-oriented local strongmen—of his time.

The structure of the confederation that Wang Kŏn led to victory also presented thorny problems for the new dynasty in its effort to consolidate power. The Wang family itself does not seem to have been numerically strong: sources mention only two cousins who were politically or militarily active.[22] This compares poorly with some of the more powerful descent groups in the confederation, such as the Kangnŭng Kim, who had several members in prominent political and military positions.[23] We should note that Wang Kŏn's confederation also included many men of Silla True Bone backgrounds. Some of these aristocrats were from the Silla capital at Kyŏngju, but others, including the Kangnŭng Kim, were descendants of True Bone aristocrats who had relocated to the provinces,[24] where they were able to use their Bone Rank status to establish themselves as dominant local powers and develop private military forces.[25] Thus Wang Kŏn had to deal with allies whose military power and social prestige were equal to, or even greater than, his own.

One strategy Wang Kŏn employed was to ally himself with other powerful and prestigious descent groups through marriage ties. He contracted marriages with no fewer than 29 daughters of important strongmen and old Silla aristocrats. Although Wang Kŏn appears to have been motivated by a desire to bolster his numerically small family, it seems probable that he also sought support from powerful descent groups throughout the peninsula.[26] Royal in-laws came from such strategically important regional centers as Tongju and P'yŏngju in the northwest, Chŏngju and Kwangju in the west, Naju in the southwest, Kangnŭng in the east, Kyŏngju and Hapchu in the southeast, and Hongju and Ch'ungju in the center. Some of Wang's in-laws were local warlords of uncertain origins, such as Yu Ch'ŏn-gung of Chŏngju, whose forebears are described in the *Koryŏsa* as wealthy local village heads.[27] Others were maritime traders, such as the Naju O, but many were landed aristocrats of Silla True Bone origins, such as the Kangnŭng Kim, P'yŏngsan Pak, and Kyŏngju Kim.[28] Wang Kŏn's incorporation of descent groups of varying social origins from throughout the country into his central alliance was a break from the Silla monopoly of power by Kyŏngju-based True Bone aristocrats. At the same time, however, inclusion of several True Bone descent groups among his marriage alliances is an indication of the continuing prestige of the old aristocracy.

Wang Kŏn's strategy of putting together a broadly based alliance seems to have enabled him to achieve his immediate goal of ensuring the short-term survival of the dynasty. At the same time, however, it helped create the conditions for fierce struggles among royal in-laws that erupted during the reigns of his immediate successors, Kings Hyejong (r. 943–45) and Chŏngjong (r. 945–49). It also set an unfortunate precedent for royal reliance on powerful in-laws, which brought great grief to the dynasty in later years. For our immediate purposes, however, the most significant aspect of Wang Kŏn's reliance on marriage ties with powerful descent groups is its illustration of his inability to transcend the aristocrat/warlord confederation.

The initial task for Wang Kŏn's successors on the Koryŏ throne was to check the power of the military confederates who dominated capital politics and society in the first half of the tenth century. The way was paved, in part, by struggles among different groups in the confederation that resulted, as Hugh Kang has shown, in the elimination during Chŏngjong's reign of a group of strongmen with maritime trading interests by a group of old aristocrats and new strongmen who shared common interests as landed elites.[29] Although eradication of maritime traders had important long-term ramifications for the Koryŏ polity, its immediate effect was to weaken the central confederation, preparing the way for the first real sustained effort to assert the royal prerogative during the reign of King Kwangjong (r. 949–75). That strong-minded ruler introduced a number of bold measures to reduce the power of the confederation, including the Slave Investiture Act (Nobi An'gŏm Pŏp) of 956, which not only cut away at the economic base of the warlords, but also deprived them of much of the manpower in their private military forces.[30] Near the end of his reign Kwangjong's suppression reached a climax in a bloody purge that virtually eradicated the old confederation. Some sense of the extent of this purge can be gained from Ch'oe Sŭng-no's lament that only 40 old officials (*kusin*) were still alive when Kyŏngjong succeeded to the throne in 975.[31] Although Kwangjong has been disparaged by Confucian historians for his ruthlessness, he effectively put an end to the era of confederation and set the young dynasty on a much firmer foundation.[32]

The Creation of a Central Bureaucracy

Kwangjong's efforts to solidify the kingship were not limited to destruction of the military confederation. He took symbolic measures to legitimate his autocratic policies and elevate himself above his constituents, styling himself "emperor" (*hwangje*) and designating the Koryŏ capital at Kaegyŏng as the "imperial capital" (*hwangdo*).

Kwangjong also took a number of concrete steps to enhance the authority and prestige of the kingship, foremost among which was replacement of members of the old central confederation with new men drawn from the countryside. A forerunner of this was Chŏngjong's creation, in response to the threat posed by the Khitan, of the Light Army (Kwanggun), a large military force directly under royal command, which was made up of young men recruited from the provinces.[33] It seems almost certain that without such a force to back him up, Kwangjong would not have been able to break the back of the old central coalition. Kwangjong and his successors subsequently began to remold Koryŏ political institutions along more bureaucratic lines. The first step was Kwangjong's 958 implementation of the government service examination system with the help of a Chinese advisor. This reform was significant because it established the principle that merit, as well as heredity, was a qualification for positions of power and because it asserted the dynasty's right to regulate recruitment procedures.[34] The examinations were held eight times during Kwangjong's reign, producing a total of 27 literary licentiates and six classics licentiates. We know the names of only 13 of these 33 graduates, and we know the status of the immediate forebears of only four. Two had fathers or grandfathers who held high office in the central government, but the other two were the scions of local strongman descent groups, men who were the products of provincial qualifying examinations.[35] The presence of these men indicates that Kwangjong was using the examination system to recruit new blood from the countryside. He and his successors had a number of reasons for bringing in such men: to replace the old confederation; to solidify the loyalty of local strongman descent groups by bringing their sons into the dynastic government; and to create a cadre of officials personally loyal to the throne.[36]

There was, however, a real limit to the Koryŏ kings' ability to create a bureaucracy independent of traditional ascriptive groups. Although tenth-century Koryŏ society appears to have been more highly differentiated than was Silla's Bone Rank order, social differentiation had not proceeded to the point where there had come into being significant urban, merchant, or other groups from which rulers could recruit bureaucrats. Maritime trading elements had played an important role in the very early years of the dynasty, but their destruction by landed interests in Chŏngjong's reign meant that the early Koryŏ kings could turn only to local strongmen to offset the central confederation. But this group, whose ranks included many men of True Bone backgrounds, formed a hereditary landed elite as representatives of descent groups that had exercised autonomous control over their locales generation after generation. Thus even the new blood brought in through the examination system to counterbalance the old confederation was drawn from ascriptive territorial descent groups with landed interests. As a consequence, there was inherent from the very beginning a strong aristocratic tendency in the Koryŏ bureaucracy.

The high point of the effort to consolidate and bureaucratize the early Koryŏ regime was the 983 reorganization by King Sŏngjong (r. 981–97) of the central government along the lines of the Tang (618–907) Chinese Three Department–Six Board (Samsŏng Yukpu) system.[37] The three departments were the Secretariat (Chungsŏsŏng), which drafted policy; the Chancellery (Munhasŏng) which, reviewed policy; and the Executive Department (Sangsŏsŏng), which implemented policy through subordinate boards of personnel, war, revenue, rites, punishments, and civil works. Other key centers of bureaucratic authority included the Security Council (Chungch'uwŏn), modeled after the Sung dynasty institution responsible for coordinating military affairs and transmitting documents between the throne and the bureaucracy; the Finance Commission (Samsa), which handled financial affairs and accounting; the Hallim (Ch. Hanlin) Academy, which drafted royal edicts; the Office of the Inspector General (Ŏsadae), an independent surveillance agency that acted as the eyes and ears of the king in ferreting out official misbehavior; and the mid-ranking censorial officials of the Secretariat and the Chancellery, known collectively as the remonstrance officials (*nangsa* or *kan'gwan*), who not only protested incorrect policy decisions and improper royal behavior, but also exercised, in conjunction with the surveillance officials, the important power of ratification of personnel actions and policy measures (*sŏgyŏng*).

Despite the martial origins of the Koryŏ dynasty, the military held a decidedly inferior position in the reorganized institutional structure. Officials of the central government were organized in two branches, the civil branch (*munban/ tongban*) and the military branch (*muban/sŏban*). The civil branch featured an eighteen-grade structure, from the senior first grade down to the junior ninth grade. The senior first grade, however, was used only for honorary purposes; the highest active civil official, the chancellor (*munha sijung*), held the junior first grade. In contrast, the highest ranking military official, the supreme general (*sang changgun*), held only a senior third-grade post. Military affairs were, as mentioned earlier, handled at the highest level by the civilian Security Council, and it was common practice in times of war or internal revolt to give supreme military field command to high-ranking civil officials.

The emergence of the civil branch as the power center of the government in the second half of the tenth century was a mark of the Koryŏ's success in curbing the military strongmen who had dominated the government in the early tenth century. This did not mean, however, that the Koryŏ kings enjoyed autocratic power.

One of the major criteria Eisenstadt uses to analyze the political systems of historical bureaucratic societies is the extent to which major political activities were organized in special roles and to which those roles were differentiated from each other.[38] Another major feature of such systems was the development of organs of political struggle—typically councils or representative institutions of some sort—through which the demands of various social groups were aggregated and articulated. Rulers attempted to create and maintain generalized power for enhancing their own authority by giving these organs some degree of autonomy and using them to provide for the needs of the social groups upon whose support the dynasty depended. A major problem for rulers was that of keeping control of these organs away from traditional aristocratic groups. This the rulers sought to do by making membership in councils contingent on their own approval or by investing the councils in reliable social groups.[39]

The new political system adopted by Sŏngjong seems to have provided for substantial specialization and differentiation of political roles. Not only were the civil and military officials organized in separate branches, but the internal structure of the civil branch provided for significant differentiation of functions, with separate organs for policy formulation, review, and execution, as well as for finances and surveillance. The Secretariat and the Chancellery, with their respective roles of policy formulation and policy review, formed the supreme organs of political struggle. The separation of functions between these agencies potentially allowed rulers to play the two against each other. Also, participation in the organs of political struggle was contingent on office holding in the regular bureaucracy, rather than on membership in an ascriptive status group.

These separations of functions were more apparent than real. The new political system underwent modification as soon as it was introduced. The Secretariat and the Chancellery formed a combined Secretariat-Chancellery (Chungsŏ Munhasŏng) under leadership of the chancellor. The top posts at the Executive Department were left vacant or filled only as honorary appointments, while the Six Boards were directly subordinated to the Secretariat-Chancellery, whose first- and second-grade officials held concurrent appointments as supervisory heads of the Six Boards (Yukpu *p'ansa*) as well as of other key organs such as the Finance Commission and the Hallim Academy. The handful of first- and second-grade officials of the Secretariat-Chancellery in whose hands this power was concentrated formed an elite group within the central bureaucracy known as the *chaesin*. Their preeminence, especially in political struggle, was reflected in the king's regular consultation with them on major political issues or policy decisions.[40]

These modifications suggest that there was a much lower degree of political role specialization in Korea than in China at this time. The secondary literature on T'ang and Sung central political institutions, however, describes a process of consolidation similar to that which took place in the Koryŏ. The Chinese Secretariat and Chancellery also merged to form one agency, and the top-ranking officials of the combined Secretariat-Chancellery held concurrent appointments over the Six Boards.[41] Winston Lo attributes this de facto consolidation of bureaucratic authority to the need for efficiency.[42] In the case of Koryŏ Korea, one can postulate that a smaller country with fewer resources would have had even more incentive to streamline the bureaucracy. On the other hand, however, because of the importance of ascriptive privilege in both T'ang China and Koryŏ Korea, we cannot rule out the possibility that the limited differentiation of political roles was related to the low level of social differentiation.[43] Whatever the reason, consolidation of the functions of both political struggle and bureaucratic administration in a small number of top-ranking officials in the Secretariat-Chancellery represented a weakening of the checks and balances built into the formal system.

Despite considerable consolidation of authority in the combined Secretariat-Chancellery, there was another potential center of bureaucratic power. This was the Security Council, the agency responsible for transmitting documents between the throne and the bureaucracy and for coordinating military affairs. In China it was routine practice to fill the positions of the Security Council with eunuchs.[44] Chinese emperors, from the Later Han (C.E. 25–220) on, had regularly used eunuchs, men of nonelite social origins who could not produce descendants, to counter the power and influence of imperial in-laws and other aristocratic elements. The presence of large numbers of eunuchs in high positions in the Chinese Security Council suggests that emperors may have used that agency as a counterbalance to aristocratic power in the Secretariat-Chancellery.

In the Koryŏ the five junior second-grade officials who headed the Security Council were known as *ch'usin*. In addition to transmitting documents and coordinating military affairs, they routinely received concurrent appointments to supervisory posts in the Office of the Inspector General and to *nangsa* censorial positions.[45] The surveillance and censorial officials frequently acted in concert under the combined name *taegan*. Such joint action is usually explained in terms of similarity of function,[46] but we cannot ignore the possibility that *ch'usin* coordinated the activities of both entities. In effect, this pattern of concurrent appointments implies de facto consolidation of the important censorial and surveillance functions under the Security Council.

It is clear, therefore, that the Koryŏ Security Council represented a substantial second center of political power, much as did its Chinese counterpart. In Korea, however, all the men who held office in the Security Council were members of the regular bureaucracy. Eunuchs never held bureaucratic posts, nor did they exercise significant political power until quite late in the dynasty. It appears, therefore, that similar modifications of the formal bureaucracy had different ramifications in the two countries. Whereas consolidation of political functions in China occurred within a system where emperors maintained checks on aristocratic power, in Korea kings lacked an effective institutional counterbalance to aristocratic domination of the bureaucracy.

The Koryŏ transformation of the bureaucratic system was not limited to these late tenth- and early eleventh-century changes. A new trend toward broader sharing of power at the first- and second-grade levels developed in the late eleventh and early twelfth centuries as a consequence of growing competitive pressures within the official class.[47] This sharing of power took three forms, which together represented further diminishment of specialization and differentiation in political roles.

One of the changes was an increase in the number of men appointed to *chaesin* and *ch'usin* posts. Although the *Koryŏsa* "Monograph on Officials" mentions no increase in the number of slots allocated for those posts during the late eleventh or twelfth centuries, there is strong evidence that de facto expansion of the upper ranks was taking place. The "Monograph on Officials" calls for only one junior second-grade state councillor (*ch'amji chŏngsa*), but on several occasions, such as in the fifth month of 1093[48] and the third month of 1122,[49] two or three men received simultaneous appointments to this post. The same phenomenon occurred in the junior second-grade royal undersecretary (*chi Chungch'uwŏn sa*) and associate royal undersecretary (*tong chi Chungch'uwŏn sa*) posts. Although the "Monograph on Officials" indicates only one slot for each of these, in 1117 two men were made royal undersecretaries; in 1102 and again in 1125 simultaneous multiple appointments were made to the associate royal undersecretary post.[50] Although it is difficult to measure the extent of this de facto expansion of the upper ranks, it appears to have been confined to junior second-grade posts.

Another form of broadening political participation was the delegation of greater authority to junior second-grade officials. The junior first-grade chancellor and the four senior second-grade assistant chancellors (*chungsŏ munha sirang, chungsŏ munha sirang p'yŏngjangsa*) formed an upper stratum within the *chaesin* from the late tenth through the mid-eleventh century. Not only were they of higher rank than their junior second-grade colleagues, but they also enjoyed a monopoly over appointments to the important Six Boards superintendent and Finance Commission superintendent (*p'an Samsasa sa*) posts.

As table 1.1 shows, however, in the late eleventh and early twelfth centuries junior second-grade officials gained a greater share of the power exercised through concurrent appointments. Junior second-grade officials of both the Secretariat-Chancellery and the Security Council received concurrent appointments to posts that had been monopolized by junior first-grade and senior second-grade officials in earlier years. The trend began in 1081 with the appointment of a state councillor to be superintendent of the Board of War (Pyŏngbu *p'ansa*) and grew more pronounced as time passed, with 80 percent of the junior second-grade appointments to Six Boards superintendent posts coming after 1123.[51] Junior second-grade *chaesin* of the Secretariat-Chancellery were not the only beneficiaries of this shift. *Ch'usin* (all junior second grade) of the Security Council, who had not held any of the concurrent superintendent posts in the table during the early period, accounted for 10 of 14 known concurrent appointments to the Finance Commission superintendent post along with one appointment as Hallim Academy superintendent in the later period. Also, the *ch'usin* gained greater involvement in the regular administration of

TABLE 1.1

Concurrent Appointments, 981–1069 and 1070–1146.

Concurrent Post (Rank)	Appointee's Rank	981–1069	1070–1146
Six Boards Superintendent (1b)	1b	4	9
	2a	12	26
	2bs	1	24
	2br	-	-
Finance Commission Superintendent (1b)	1b	1	-
	2a	2	1
	2bs	-	3
	2br	-	10
Hallim Academy Superintendent (1b)	1b	-	-
	2a	-	-
	2bs	2	6
	2br	-	1
Six Boards Chiefs (3a)	1b	-	-
	2a	-	-
	2bs	19	17
	2br	7	30

2bs designates the junior second-grade officials of the Secretariat-Chancellery and 2br the junior second-grade officials of the Security Council.

government through increased appointments to Six Boards chief posts. Thus the increase in the number of junior second-grade posts and the delegation of greater authority to those who filled them tended to blur differentiation between *chaesin* and *ch'usin*.

The third way in which power sharing was broadened was closely related to the rise in status of junior second-grade officials. Throughout the Koryŏ dynasty the first- and second-grade officials of the Secretariat-Chancellery and the junior second-grade officials of the Security Council were known collectively as *yangbu* (lit., "two departments") or *chaech'u* (contraction of *chaesin* and *ch'usin*). Prior to 1070 these terms were rarely used except in conjunction with ceremonial occasions, such as in the eleventh month of 1048 when

King Munjong feasted the high officials of the *yangbu* and the middle-ranking officials of all agencies.[52] During the early twelfth century, however, these terms appear with increasing frequency in connection with important issues of the type that had once been the sole preserve of *chaesin*. For example, in 1105 the king called the *chaech'u* together to discuss border affairs at a time of high tension between the Koryŏ and the Jurchen.[53] In 1109 the king consulted with the *chaech'u* on the critical question of amnesty for Yun Kwan and other officials who had been punished for their conduct of the Jurchen campaign.[54] In 1122 the king, on his deathbed, summoned the *chaech'u* to discuss the crown prince's succession to the throne,[55] and in 1130 the king discussed political affairs with the *chaech'u* late into the night.[56] These examples make it clear that participation in what was perhaps the most important and prestigious function of the bureaucracy, *chaesin* deliberations with the king on important matters, was broadened to include the *ch'usin* of the Security Council in the twelfth century. In short, what we see here is the expansion of the supreme organ of political struggle to include larger numbers of officials.

Inclusion of *ch'usin* in high-level deliberations came about because of the rise in status of its junior second-grade and because of the increasing overlap in *chaesin* and *ch'usin* authority. Implications of the formation of the *chaech'u* as a joint consultative body, however, went far beyond issues of bureaucratic streamlining. Despite amalgamation of more-or-less separate domains of bureaucratic authority under the *chaesin* and *ch'usin*, Koryŏ kings hoped to maintain some semblance of a check on official power as long as the Secretariat-Chancellery (which was responsible for policy formulation and execution) and the Security Council (which potentially controlled surveillance and censorial functions) remained distinct entities. But the practical merger between the two bodies in the early twelfth century meant that there was no longer a clear separation of functions within the bureaucracy. The throne had lost important leverage in its effort to control the aristocrats who staffed the bureaucracy.

The rise of the *chaech'u* as a bastion of bureaucratic power in the late eleventh and early twelfth centuries came within the context of the growth of great hereditary civil official descent groups at the Koryŏ capital. In its early effort to create a cadre of personally loyal bureaucrats, the dynasty tried to assure the allegiance of its officials by granting them a number of special privileges, such as the protection privilege (*ŭm*, Ch. *yin*), which allowed higher ranking officials to have their children, grandchildren, or other relatives appointed to posts in the central government; and enrollment, without qualifying preliminary tests, of sons of incumbent officials in state schools that prepared students for government service examinations.[57] While these provisions may have been intended to enhance the status of central officials vis-à-vis the rest of society and thus to ensure their loyalty, they also reflect the strong sense of ascriptive privilege that characterized Korean society.

Thus although the dynasty replaced the warlord confederacy with a civil bureaucracy, it was able to do so only by creating a new hereditary class of central officials. The lines of descent established at the capital by such recruits from the countryside as Yi Cha-yŏn of the Kyŏngwŏn (Inch'ŏn) Yi and Ch'oe Ch'ung of the Haeju Ch'oe developed into great civil-official descent groups by the late eleventh century. It was at this time that members of these groups, such as the Kyŏngwŏn Yi, began openly to challenge royal authority. Examples can be found in Yi Cha-ŭi's effort to depose King Hŏnjong (1094–95) in favor of a royal prince who was his grandson, and in Yi Cha-gyŏm's effort to seize the throne for himself in 1126.[58] Thus a little over a century after Kwangjong's and Sŏngjong's reforms, the Koryŏ kings found themselves once again faced with powerful capital-based hereditary descent groups who had institutional means of dominating government and politics, and who threatened the viability of the dynasty itself. Within this context, the rise of the *chaech'u* as the supreme organ of political struggle represented further diminishment of the specialization and differentiation in political roles provided for in the Chinese political model. Furthermore, to the extent that the ranks of the *chaech'u* were filled by members of the great civil-official descent groups, it also represented a signal setback for the Koryŏ kings in their fight to keep the organs of political struggle free of the control of the dominant social group. It appears, therefore, that even though the early Koryŏ rulers may have enhanced their power through implementation of a bureaucratic system, they were ultimately unable to overcome restraints derived from the low level of social differentiation. Because important political roles remained embedded in ascriptive groups, the kings were unable to maintain a high level of generalized power.

Institutional Innovations under the Military

The evolutionary process of concentrating political power in the hands of aristocratic civil-official descent groups was interrupted by the military coup of 1170, which was sparked, at least in part, by military resentment of the increasing arrogance and high-handedness of the civil branch. Yet even as the era of military rule put an end to civil officials' domination of government, it did not bring about a revival of royal authority.

It is difficult to discern significant institutional trends during the chaotic years immediately following the 1170 coup, a time when various generals were vying for dominance. But once Ch'oe Ch'ung-hŏn (1149–1219) seized power in 1196 and established some semblance of order, the military began to create a number of extrainstitutional entities through which they ruled the country. These included the General Military Council (Tobang), through which the Ch'oe house coordinated the activities of its private military forces; the Directorate-General for Policy Formulation (Kyojŏng Togam), through which the Ch'oes made policy decisions; and the Personnel Authority (Chŏngbang), an agency that handled personnel affairs and was staffed largely by civil supporters of the Ch'oes.[59]

The creation of these private agencies in the Ch'oe house meant a corresponding loss of authority on the part of regular dynastic institutions. The *chaech'u* lost their role as supreme policy makers to the Directorate-General for Policy Formulation; the Security Council yielded its military coordination role to the General Military Council; and the boards of Personnel and Military lost their power over personnel matters to the Personnel Authority. That does not mean that the old dynastic institutions were abolished, however. The military rulers continued to use the existing institutional structure to implement their policies. There were also instances of the *chaech'u* gathering to discuss important issues during the Ch'oe era, but those sessions were invariably convened at the order of the Ch'oe rulers at their private residence, which indicates that the *chaech'u* were brought together to provide counsel and symbolic sanction for the Ch'oe, not to make independent policy decisions.[60] In short, although the regular dynastic institutions, which were still staffed primarily by civil officials, were left intact, their function now was largely limited to administering the policies made in the private agencies of the Ch'oe house and to legitimating Ch'oe rule.[61]

The military rulers of the mid-Koryŏ overshadowed the throne to an unprecedented degree. They routinely deposed kings—including Ŭijong in 1170, Myŏngjong in 1197, and Hŭijong in 1211—and replaced them with other members of the royal family whom they favored, effectively reducing the kings to puppets. Although the rise of military rulers in the mid-Koryŏ is usually seen as constituting a sharp break in Koryŏ political history, to the extent that the Ch'oe and their supporters were officials of the dynastic government, their dictatorial regime can be seen as a culmination of the trend toward official domination of the throne that had been developing prior to the 1170 coup.

THE SYSTEM OF LOCAL ADMINISTRATION

After the Koryŏ dynasty had put in place a civil-dominated bureaucratic regime at the capital in the late tenth century, it directed its attention to the problem of establishing greater control over the countryside. Kwangjong's mid-century destruction of the leading members of the military confederation may have secured, for the time being, the position of the royal family in the capital, but local elite descent groups still enjoyed virtual autonomy in the countryside and presented a major obstacle to the creation of a centralized polity.

The Local Sociopolitical Order

The problem the Koryŏ dynasty faced in the countryside had its genesis in the Silla system of regional governance. In the early centuries before unification, Silla's local administration appears to have been based on traditional tribal territorial boundaries and political structures. After unification, however, Silla found itself in possession of a greatly expanded realm, some of which was populated by potentially hostile peoples. The initial Silla response to this challenge was to dispatch True Bone aristocrats accompanied by military forces to important locales (mostly in newly conquered territory) designated as lesser capitals (*sogyŏng*) or protectorates (*ch'onggwan*, later *chu*). While this sufficed as a transitional measure, for the long run the kingdom needed to put its local administration on a firmer institutional basis.

The model Silla used was the Chinese prefecture-county (*kunhyŏn*, Ch. *chün-hsien* or *chou-hsien*) system, which featured a regular hierarchy of administration in which a number of villages formed a *hsiang* (K. *hyang*) a number of *hsiang* formed a county, and a number of counties reported to a single prefecture, which in turn reported to a higher central authority.[62] In the mid-eighth century when Silla's royal power was at its zenith, King Kyŏngdŏk carried out a major reorganization of local administration, apparently to make the Silla system conform more closely to the Chinese model. This entailed reshuffling various prefectures and counties and introducing Chinese-style place names. The *Samguk sagi* (History of the Three Kingdoms) "Monograph on Geography," which depicts the system after Kyŏngdŏk's reforms, tells that the nine protectorates of Silla administered a total of some 450 prefectures and counties.[63] The "Local Official" (Oegwan) section of the *Samguk Sagi* "Monograph on Officials" (Chikkwan chi) describes Silla's posting of centrally appointed officials: prefects in 115 prefectures (*t'aesu*, Ch. *t'ai-shou*) and magistrates (*hyŏllyŏng*, Ch. *hsien-ling*) in 201 counties. The prefects had relatively large staffs, including 14 secretaries and assistants who held central official ranks and a large number of lesser functionaries whose ranks were unknown and who may have been local men assigned to supplement the prefects' staff.[64] We do not know when these prefectureships and magistracies were established, nor the size or composition of the subordinate staffs of the magistrates. Nonetheless, on the basis of the information contained in the *Samguk Sagi,* it appears that during its heyday Silla had a substantial central presence in the countryside. This impression is strengthened by Hatada Takashi's analysis of Silla village documents recently discovered in Japan showing strong government control over individual villages for purposes of collecting land taxes and corvée.[65]

As a consequence of the political instability of the late eighth and ninth centuries, however, the Silla prefecture-county system collapsed. Although various locales continued to be known as prefectures or counties, centrally appointed prefects and magistrates were no longer posted throughout most of the realm and the countryside fell under the control of local strongmen. The more powerful of these expanded the territory under their sway by subordinating the leading descent groups of neighboring prefectures and counties. These strongmen created their own local regimes with elaborate administrative systems, including such organs as tax and military bureaus, through which they usurped the central government's powers of taxation and policing. They expressed their autonomy by bestowing upon their subordinates ranks and titles identical to those of the Silla central government.[66] These locally autonomous regimes, which constituted the building blocks of the warlord confederations of the tenth century, formed a unique system of local governance in which control prefectures (*chugun*) controlled subordinate prefectures (*sokkun*) and subordinate counties (*sokhyŏn*), and control counties (*chuhyŏn*) controlled other subordinate counties.[67]

Thus the new Koryŏ dynasty confronted a well-entrenched local sociopolitical order dominated by strongman descent groups. The central regime had no choice but to rely on the cooperation of the strongmen of the control prefectures and counties in order to carry out even the most basic governmental functions, such as coordinating local defense and police forces and collecting taxes. These strongmen, in turn, leaned on the top descent groups of their subordinate prefectures and counties to mobilize forces and collect taxes in those areas.[68]

This system appears to have been closely related to the ancestral seat (*pon'-gwan*) system, which identified descent groups by geographic place of origin rather than by Bone Rank surname, as had been the case in Silla. The generally accepted interpretation of the genesis of this system holds that as the Bone Rank system began to unravel in late Silla, locally dominant descent groups began to identify themselves by their locales.[69] Thus, for example, the Kim group that controlled the Kangnŭng area referred to themselves as the

Kangnŭng Kim, and the Pak group that held a dominant position in P'yŏngsan called themselves the P'yŏngsan Pak. This represented recognition that real power was shifting away from True Bone aristocrats in the Silla capital to strongmen out in the countryside.

The ancestral seat system was not only acknowledged but even encouraged by the new dynasty. The *Koryŏsa* contains several examples of early Koryŏ kings' granting surnames to locally prominent individuals and even designating ancestral seats for Chinese and other foreigners settling in Korea.[70] While this may have been simply imitation of Chinese practice, it seems likely that it was more a reflection of the advantages the ancestral seat system offered to both the dynasty and the local strongmen. The central government gained a readily identifiable locus of responsibility for each area as well as assurance of continuity among regional authorities, while local elites gained dynastic sanction of their privileged position. The ancestral seat system was the linchpin of the early Koryŏ prefecture-county system, the crucial element that enabled the new dynasty to establish a measure of stability in the countryside. But at the same time the two systems formed a well-integrated local sociopolitical order that presented a significant impediment to strong central rule.

There appears to have been a close relationship between local status and central office holding. Historians have noted that high officials of the early Koryŏ government came from protectorates (*tohobu, todokpu*) and district shepherdships such as Kyŏngju, Ch'ŏngju, and Suju that were high in the local administrative hierarchy.[71] Access to power seems to have broadened, as might be expected, after Kwangjong's implementation of the examination system. Men of prefecture and county origins, such as Sŏ Hŭi of Ich'ŏn Prefecture and Yi Cha-yŏn of Kyŏngwŏn County (at the time a subordinate county), were apparently able to pass the examinations and rise in the bureaucracy without hindrance.

A recent study focusing in on the elite descent groups of the prefectures and counties has found that Koryŏ *hyangni* were ranked according to their family traditions (*kap'ung*) in a classificatory scheme that determined both how high they could rise in the *hyangni* hierarchy and which government service examinations they could take. According to this study, Koryŏ *hyangni* comprised three major categories: men in the first category, who had the highest family tradition, started service in local offices at the second level as assistant township headmen and were qualified to sit for civil service examinations; those in the second category, with less distinguished family traditions, began in local offices at the sixth grade, but could rise to headman positions and thus could also take the civil service examinations; those in the third category, with the least illustrious family traditions, were limited to the lower four levels of local offices and could sit only for technical examinations, such as the physician examination (*ŭi kwa*).[72] It appears, therefore, that the Koryŏ sociopolitical order was essentially a territorial-based status system in which there was a close relationship between a descent group's local status and the level to which its members could rise in the central government.

The best evidence we have regarding the relationship between court status and local administrative status is found in the biography of Yu Ch'ŏng-sin, a high-ranking official of the early fourteenth century who became a royal favorite because of his skill in the Mongol language. The biography states that he

> was a man of Koi *pugok* of Changhŭng district. His forebears had all been *pugok* officials [*i*, Ch. *li*]. According to the dynasty's system [*kukche*,] a *pugok* official, even though he had merit, could not rise above the fifth grade. . . . King Ch'ungsŏn issued an edict saying, "Ch'ŏng-sin went with Cho In-gyu, did his utmost, and achieved merit. Even though his family background limits him to the fifth grade, I authorize him for the third grade and also I elevate Koi *pugok* to be Kohŭng County."[73]

Freed from the limitations of his descent group's relatively low status in the local hierarchy, Yu Ch'ŏng-sin went on to hold a series of second-grade posts before finally rising to become chancellor under King Ch'ungsŏn.

Pugok[74] in the Koryŏ belonged to a level of local administration below that of prefectures and counties and composed of special administrative districts known as *so, chang, ch'ŏ*, and *hyang*, and ferry and post stations (*chin and yŏk*). These units typically were located within prefectures and counties.[75] At one time historians generally agreed—based on the knowledge that *hyang* and *pugok* had existed since Silla times and that Koryŏ legal codes discriminated against people from those areas by prohibiting their entering government schools and taking government service examinations, and requiring that the offspring of mixed marriages between people from prefectures or counties and people from *pugok* take *pugok* status—that they were special administrative units for hereditary groups of servile people.[76]

Recent studies of actual living conditions and social organization of *hyang* and *pugok* in Koryŏ Korea have shown, however, that people living there were not unfree: as in the case of prefectures and counties, the bulk of their populace was self-cultivating commoner peasants under the control of hereditary *hyangni* descent groups.[77] Thus the *hyang* and the *pugok* should be seen not as special areas of servile people, but rather as lower-level administrative units roughly analogous to the *hsiang* of T'ang China.

Restrictions against people from the *hyang* and *pugok* applied not to the populace at large, but rather to their *hyangni*. The promulgation of regulations permitting sons of prefecture and county township headmen and assistant township headmen to sit for government service examinations implies that lower ranking *hyangni* and commoners were not allowed to take the examinations. The top-ranking officials of *hyang* and *pugok* were not considered peers of the top-ranking *hyangni* officials of the prefectures and counties: whereas the top *hyangni* of the prefectures and counties bore the title "township headman" (*hojang*), the top *hyangni* of the *hyang* and *pugok* were denied that title and called simply "head" (*chang*). The prohibitions against *pugok* officials' sons entering government schools, taking the government service examinations, or rising above the fifth grade should thus be seen as a reflection not of unfree social status but rather of the relatively low position of the *pugok* official descent groups in the local sociopolitical hierarchy. Yu Ch'ŏng-sin was the offspring of just such a hereditary *pugok* official descent group.

It may be that the late Koryŏ restrictions against men of *pugok* official descent groups were merely vestiges of a more comprehensive early Koryŏ system, but the fact is that such restrictions were still an issue in the fourteenth century. Furthermore, when faced with objections to Yu Ch'ŏng-sin's *pugok* official background, the king, rather than brushing the objections aside or simply declaring the restrictions invalid, chose to legitimize Yu Ch'ŏng-sin's rise by elevating his native *pugok* to county status. This indicates the enduring strength of the basic principles underlying the local hierarchical status system and its relationship to central office holding.

The social status of local descent groups was closely connected to central office holding in medieval China also. During the interregnum between the Han and T'ang dynasties, the Eastern Wei (534–550) ranked the clan status of all the great *shih* descent groups into surnames of the nation, commandery surnames, prefecture surnames, and subprefecture (county) surnames.[78] At first glance, this would appear to be very similar to the Koryŏ hierarchy, but in reality there existed substantial differences between the two systems. Medieval China featured the Nine Rank Impartial and Just (Chiu-p'in Chung-cheng) system, under which the population was classified by prefectural officials into nine ranks. These ranks were supposedly based on talent and character and determined the level at which men could enter the central government. In practice, however, it was not merit that determined ranking, but rather family status. Although the prominent local clans in China were known as commandery or prefecture surnames, the prestige they enjoyed stemmed not from hereditary leadership of their locales, but rather from a family tradition of holding office in the central government.[79] This was markedly different from Koryŏ Korea, where a man's qualification to hold central office was determined by his descent group's status as hereditary local elites, that is, descendants of powerful local warlords of the ninth and early tenth centuries.

Thus it appears that the constitutional basis of the Koryŏ political system was the territorial status system that had come into being during the late Silla period. The entrusting of local governance to hereditary descent groups and the relationship between a descent group's position in the local administrative hierarchy and the limits to which its members could rise in the central government illustrate the relatively low level of differentiation in Koryŏ society.

The Attempt to Establish Intermediary Provincial Offices

In its early years, the Koryŏ dynasty kept strongmen in line by maintaining a military presence in the protectorates it established in such strategic areas as Chŏnju (Annam *tohobu*) and Sangju (Andong *todokpu*). It was, however, many decades before the Koryŏ could establish even a semblance of regular bureaucratic administration in the provinces. In the early years, the most it could do was periodically send out officials for specific temporary purposes such as coordinating tax collection[80] For day-to-day implementation of its policies, the dynasty found it necessary to rely on local elites, and appointed powerful men as local inspectors general (*sasimgwan*) of their home districts, as seen in the case of Kim Pu, the last king of Silla, who was made local inspector general of Kyŏngju.[81] The local inspector-general system was instituted in tandem with a hostage (*kiin*) system, under which appointees' sons were brought into the capital (ostensibly as advisors on local conditions) to serve as guarantors of the inspector generals' good behavior.[82]

In 995 the Koryŏ attempted to replicate the T'ang system of provincial administration, establishing ten circuits (*to*, Ch. *tao*) with the same names as their T'ang counterparts and appointing civil governors (*kwanch'alsa*, Ch. *kuanch'a shih*) and military governors (*chŏltosa*, Ch. *chieh-tu shih*) for each. This system failed to take root, undergoing several revisions before finally being abandoned 30 years later.[83]

What emerged in lieu of a functional circuit system as the primary intermediary provincial office were regional centers. According to the "Monograph on Geography," there were 14 of these centers, including three regional cap-

itals (western, southern, and eastern), four military protectorates and eight
district shepherds (*moksa*).[84] The Western Capital at P'yŏngyang was established under Wang Kŏn, the Eastern Capital at Kyŏngju under Sŏngjong, and
the Southern Capital at Yangju during the reign of Munjong (1046–83). The
Western Capital's government was almost a replica of that at Kaegyŏng, but
its administrative authority was greatly curtailed after the rebellion of
Myoch'ŏng in the 1130s.[85] The Eastern and Southern capitals were headed
by third-grade officials who oversaw small administrative complements of
just seven men each.[86] Protectorates—whose actual numbers and locations
fluctuated—were established at various times in such locations as Anbuk at
Yŏngju and Anbyŏn at Tŭngju in the north, Andong at Kyŏngju in the southeast, Annam at Kobu (later Chŏnju and Suju) in the south, and Haeju in the
west. Like regional capitals, protectorates were thinly staffed with only seven
officials each.

The district shepherds were first established under Sŏngjong, who set up
twelve in various locations in the central and southern regions, although their
number was reduced to eight by Hyŏnjong's (r. 1009–31) time. District shepherds were third-rank officials who headed small administrative staffs of five
centrally appointed officials.

These centers appear primarily to have been bastions of government military power. Although the *Koryŏsa* is silent regarding the numbers of soldiers
stationed at these locations, Lee Ki-baik has shown that close relationships
existed between the protectorates and the Light Army formed in Chŏngjong's
reign, and between the 12 district shepherds and 12 armies of Sŏngjong's time.[87]
Given the military confederation origins of the dynasty and the existence of
powerful warlords throughout the peninsula, it is not surprising that the tenth-
century system of local administration was primarily military in character.[88]
The Koryŏ began to move toward a civil-based local administration with the
reforms of Hyŏnjong in the early eleventh century, although the defensively
important northern border regions remained under military administration
throughout the dynasty.

Even after the shift toward civil administration, regional centers appear to
have exercised little administrative authority over the prefectures and counties beneath them. Generally speaking, routine civil administration, including
tax collection and corvée labor, was not conducted through these centers. Their
functions seem to have been largely limited to the presentation of congratu-
latory memorials, administration of local government service examinations,
and inspection of local penal facilities.[89] This limited role is reflected in their
meager staffing of centrally appointed officials. Thus while the existence of

these regional centers as standing representatives of the dynastic government marked a significant advance over the situation at the beginning of the dynasty, when there were no standing officials at all, in the eleventh century the Koryŏ still had very tenuous administrative control over the countryside.

A revised circuit system was set up early in the twelfth century and lasted without major change until the end of the dynasty. This system featured two military border districts (Pukkye and Tonggye) in the north, a capital district (Kyŏnggi) around Kaegyŏng, and five circuits (Kyoju, Yanggwang, Kyŏngsang, Chŏlla, and Sŏhae) in the southern two-thirds of the country. Each circuit was headed by a commissioner (*anch'alsa*, Ch. *an-ch'a shih*) whose duties the *Koryŏsa chŏryo* (Essentials of Koryŏ history) describes as reviewing the performance of prefects and magistrates, inquiring into the welfare of peasants, administering justice and punishments, collecting taxes and corvée, and overseeing military affairs.[90] While this appears to describe a vigorous circuit administration, the commissioners (like their counterparts in early T'ang China) in fact played a very limited role.[91] They were chosen from relatively low-ranking fifth- or sixth-grade officials, were appointed for brief six-month tours of duty, and had no standing staffs. Furthermore, even after the creation of these circuits the lesser capitals, protectorates, and district shepherds continued to play the same roles as before.[92] The reality was that the system of intermediary provincial administration had little administrative authority. For most purposes, prefectures and counties continued to report directly to agencies of the central government.

Control of Prefectures and Counties

The weakness of intermediary levels of provincial administration meant that the real test of the dynasty's centralization policy lay in establishing a standing official presence in the prefectures and counties, which formed the basic units of local administration. As a consequence of the collapse of the Silla system in the late eighth and early ninth centuries and the early Koryŏ reliance on military force to control the countryside, there were no prefects or magistrates in the prefectures and counties in tenth-century Korea. Although potentially subject to intervention by centrally controlled military forces, warlords continued to control their locales through the autonomous governing systems they had established during the final decades of Silla.

Throughout the late tenth and eleventh centuries, the dynasty implemented a series of measures designed to weaken the power of the local strongmen. The centerpiece was the replacement in 983 of the old system of local office nomenclature with a new *hyangni* system designed to reflect subordination to the center.[93] Prior to this time the heads of local regimes had referred to themselves by the old Silla central-official titles of *tang taedŭng* and *taedŭng* and used central bureaucratic names—such as Board of War (Pyŏngbu)—for their local organs of government. After 983 the top *hyangni* were known as township headmen and assistant township headmen (*pu hojang*), and all other local titles and agency names were also changed. Other measures included an order in 987 for the collection of weapons from local authorities (which suggests the probable demise of local private military forces),[94] a decree in 996 limiting the number of local superintendents in each region,[95] and an enactment in 1051 calling for the implementation of standard procedures for the appointment and promotion of *hyangni*.[96] It appears that throughout the late tenth and early eleventh centuries the dynasty made steady, if gradual, progress in bringing the countryside under some degree of central control. Although these reforms entailed the formal incorporation of the countryside into a unitary system of local administration, local elite descent groups continued to enjoy a number of privileges, including hereditary succession to the top posts in their locales and institutionalized routes of access to central offices, which left them with considerable power and prestige and effectively included them in the dynasty's ruling class.[97]

Although these administrative reforms were important steps in bringing the countryside under central control, they did not deal with the more fundamental issue of breaking up, or at least limiting, the system of local alliances embodied in the control-subordinate prefecture-county system. The process by which the dynasty tackled this problem had two overlapping phases. The first, carried out between 940 and 1018, featured subordination (presumably to areas headed by politically reliable strongmen) of large numbers of previously independent prefectures and counties and reassignment of already subordinate prefectures and counties to new control prefectures or counties. The second phase, which began in 1005, entailed posting centrally appointed prefects and magistrates as permanent overseers of local administration.

Conventional interpretations of Koryŏ's unique system of control and subordinate counties and prefectures find its origins in the late ninth- and early tenth-century collapse of the Silla's prefecture-county system and the rise of local warlords. While Hatada Takashi's analysis of the local power structure leaves no doubt about the proposition that the tenth-century arrangement of control and subordinate prefectures and counties reflected the local hierarchies of power formed in the final decades of Silla, the earliest origins of the system can be found in certain limitations of the Silla system of local administration.

Although the *Samguk sagi* states that Silla had over 450 prefectures and counties, a tabulation of the individual prefectures and counties listed in the *Samguk sagi* "Monograph on Geography" yields a total of 408 (121 prefectures and 287 counties). The number of prefectures is close to the number of prefects (115) that the *Samguk sagi* says Silla had appointed; the difference perhaps arose from unrecorded changes in the status of a few prefectures. But the number of counties exceeds the number of magistrates (201) by a margin too great to explain away without investigation. The *Samguk sagi* offers no explanation for the discrepancy; all 287 counties are listed simply as counties controlled by specific prefectures or protectorates. A typical example is the entry for Kobu Prefecture:

Kobu Prefecture was originally Paekche's Kosaburi Prefecture; King Kyŏngdŏk changed the name. The current name is the same. It controlled three counties. Puryŏng County was originally Paekche's Kaehwa County; King Kyŏngdŏk changed the name. The current name is the same. Hŭian County was originally Paekche's Hullyangmae County; King Kyŏngdŏk changed the name. It is now known as Poan County. Sangjil County was originally Paekche's Sangch'il County; King Kyŏngdŏk changed the name. The current name is the same.[98]

The *Koryŏsa* "Monograph on Geography" gives a similar brief administrative history of each locale, often providing information not found in the *Samguk sagi*. For example, the *Koryŏsa* entry for Kobu Prefecture offers the following information regarding Poan and Puryŏng counties:

Poan County was originally Paekche's Hullyangmae County; King Kyŏngdok changed the name to Hŭian County, and brought it in and subordinated [*naesok*] it to Kobu Prefecture. The Koryŏ changed it to the current name and kept it subordinate . . . Puryŏng County was originally Paekche's Kaehwa County; King Kyŏngdŏk changed it to the current name, brought it in, and subordinated it to Kobu Prefecture. The Koryŏ kept it subordinate.[99]

Whereas the *Samguk sagi* makes no mention of subordinate counties, the *Koryŏsa* shows a total of nineteen subordinate counties in the Silla period; the actual number may have been higher since there are many locales for which the *Koryŏsa* gives no Silla-period administrative history. It seems likely, therefore, that the discrepancy between the number of individual counties listed in the *Samguk sagi* and the number of county magistrates established by Silla can be accounted for by the existence of subordinate counties to which no magistrate was posted. It also seems probable that subordinate counties existed at least as early as the mid-eighth century reign of King Kyŏngdŏk.

The existence of subordinate counties in mid-eighth century Silla calls into question the idea that the irregular control-subordinate prefecture-county system came into being as a consequence of the rise of local strongmen in the final decades of Silla. It does not, however, necessarily invalidate the argument that the control-subordinate system reflected the hierarchy of local strongman descent groups. On the contrary, it may mean that the ninth- and tenth-century local strongman hierarchy represented the reemergence, after the collapse of central authority, of an older, established pattern of local power relations.

The *Koryŏsa* "Monograph on Geography," apparently based on the situation that obtained under Hyŏnjong, indicates that there were 129 prefectures and 335 counties.[100] This total of 464 prefectures and counties is close to the 450-some stipulated by the *Samguk sagi* and the 444 listed in the *Veritable Records* (Sillok) of the early Chosŏn dynasty. Thus although the numbers may have varied somewhat throughout the dynasty due to occasional combining of prefectures and counties and downgrading or upgrading of various units, it seems safe to use 450 as a working estimate of the number of prefectures and counties in the Koryŏ period.

The *Koryŏsa* "Monograph on Geography" uses two different terms to describe the subordination of prefectures and counties to other units of local administration: "subordinated as is" (*ingsok*) and "brought in and subordinated" (*naesok*). *Ingsok* apparently refers to situations where the prefecture-county alignment of the old Silla System was continued unchanged. In some cases, such as those of Poan and Puryŏng, it signified a continuation of the old subordinate relationship; in most cases, however, it meant that a county that had once had a centrally appointed magistrate under Silla was now subordinated to the same prefecture whose prefect had once supervised the county's magistrate. An example is the case of Chinwi County. According to the *Koryŏsa*, "Chinwi County was originally Koguryŏ's Pusan County. King Kyŏngdŏk changed its name and made it a county controlled by Susŏng Prefecture. The Koryŏ subordinated it as it was [*ingsok*], but later established a lesser county magistrate [*kammu*]."[101] *Naesok* appears to apply either to situations where a previously independent unit was subordinated and reassigned to a different prefecture or county or where an already subordinate prefecture or county was reassigned to a new control unit. Chŏngŭp County provides an example of *naesok*: "Chŏngŭp County was originally Paekche's Chŏngch'ŏn County. King Kyŏngdok changed the name from Chŏngch'ŏn to the present name of

Chŏngŭp and subordinated it to Taesan Prefecture. Reaching the Koryŏ, Chŏngŭp was brought in and subordinated [*naesok*] to Kobu Prefecture."[102]

These terms are used for 336 of the 464 prefectures and counties listed in the *Koryŏsa* "Monograph on Geography." In 136 cases the actions appear to have been taken at the beginning of the dynasty, being dated variously as "at the beginning of the Koryŏ" (Koryŏ *ch'o*), "reaching Koryŏ" (*chi* Koryŏ), or simply "Koryŏ" as in "The Koryŏ subordinated it as it was" (Koryŏ *ingsok*). These 136 cases include 47 prefectures and counties whose subordination was continued (*ingsok*), and 89 whose subordination was reassigned (*naesok*). It is interesting to note that nearly three-fourths (66 of 89) of the reassigned prefectures and counties were located in territory that had been controlled by Later Paekche. Unlike Silla, which had voluntarily submitted to the Koryŏ, Later Paekche resisted to the end and was ultimately defeated on the battlefield. Whereas Wang Kŏn must have been wary of alienating his Koryŏ confederates or losing the cooperation of the leading descent groups of what had been Silla territories, he had, as a consequence of the destruction of Later Paekche's military force, an opportunity to break up the old regional alliances of Later Paekche. Not able, with his limited resources, to establish a system of direct central administration, he chose to accomplish this goal by realigning prefecture and county relationships and subordinating the bulk of Later Paekche's prefectures and counties to a handful of strategic locales such as Naju, Chŏnju, Namwŏn, and Yŏnggwang.[103] That the reordering of local relationships occurred primarily in the militarily subjugated areas of Later Paekche bears out our earlier observations on the essentially military nature of early Koryŏ control over the countryside, but at the same time the lack of reorganizing changes in other areas underscores the tenuous nature of the dynasty's control over the country as a whole.

During the next hundred years 12 more subordinate prefectures and counties were reassigned, but the next major realignment didn't come until 1018, when King Hyŏnjong changed the status of 200 subordinate prefectures and counties. Only 15 of these changes took place in old Later Paekche territory, with the rest occurring in what had been Koryŏ lands or in the southeastern territories that had still been under Silla rule in the tenth century. Again the bulk of the prefectures and counties affected were assigned to a relatively small number of major regional centers, such as Sangju, Andong, Kyŏngju (the Eastern Capital), and Hongju.[104] Thus it was nearly a century after the Koryŏ reunified the peninsula before the dynasty felt strong enough to break up the system of local alliances that had originally brought it to power. The way for this major change was no doubt prepared by Sŏngjong's reorganization of the *hyangni* system and his confiscation of arms from local warlords, but another background factor that cannot be overlooked is the tense military situation that existed between the Koryŏ and the Khitan in Hyŏnjong's time. Without the stimulus for internal unity provided by the Khitan invasions, it is unlikely that Hyŏnjong would have been able to carry out such a wide-reaching restructuring of the local sociopolitical power structure.

The second phase of the consolidation of central control over the countryside was the posting of centrally appointed officials to prefectures and counties. This began in 1005, when a small number of county magistrates, probably fewer than 20, were established in unspecified control counties.[105] Another posting came in 1018, when King Hyŏnjong appointed 56 prefecture supervisors (*chi chu or kun sa*) and an additional 20 magistrates.[106] These numbers come from statements in the *Koryŏsa chŏryo;* the *Koryŏsa* "Monograph on Geography" allows us to identify only a small proportion of the prefectures and counties affected. On the basis of what information we do have, it appears that these appointments were made to locales throughout the country. Several of the prefecture supervisor posts were established in places to which large numbers of subordinate prefectures and counties were assigned, including Andong, Kyŏngsan, and Tongju. Sporadic appointment of a few new prefecture supervisors and magistrates continued even after King Hyŏnjong's reign, but the overwhelming majority of the prefectures and counties remained subordinated to control prefectures and counties.

The first major attempt to establish a dynastic presence in subordinate prefectures and counties came under King Yejong (r. 1105–22), who established 27 lesser magistrates in subordinate prefectures and counties belonging to major regional centers in 1105 and 40 more in 1108.[107] The next posting came in 1143, when King Injong (r. 1122–46) posted six magistrates and eight lesser magistrates to subordinate prefectures and counties.[108] The final spate of appointing new county magistrates came immediately after the military coup of 1170. Between 1172 and 1176, 69 new lesser county magistrates were posted.[109] By this time, the central government had placed its officials in approximately half of the country's prefectures and counties.

The establishment of a position for a prefecture supervisor or county magistrate clearly meant that the prefecture or county was no longer subordinate to other units of local government, but was this also true for the posting of lesser county magistrates? The case of Ogya County, a subordinate county of Chŏnju (a district shepherd in the southwest) is instructive in this regard. According to the "Monograph on Geography," "Ogya County was brought in and subordinated at the beginning of the Koryŏ. In 1176 King Myŏngjong posted a lesser county magistrate there, but Ogya was later brought back and subordinated again."[110] This indicates that the establishment of a lesser county magistrate did entail abrogation of the subordinate relationship and brought the lesser county under direct central control. Thus the posting of lesser county magistrates represented another step forward in the creation of a centralized system of local administration.

Prefectures and counties with centrally appointed officials had even skimpier staffs than protectorates or district shepherds. The prefecture supervisors were fifth-grade officials and were accompanied to their posts by only a single executive assistant (*p'an'gwan*) while the seventh-grade magistrates were assisted by a single eight-grade assistant magistrate (*hyŏnwi*). With such a limited complement of centrally appointed assistants, the prefecture supervisors and magistrates were even more reliant than their Chinese or Silla counterparts on the cooperation of local elites to carry out their duties, both in the control prefectures or counties to which they were posted and in subordinate counties.

By the end of the twelfth century the dynasty had been able to bring roughly half of the country's prefectures and counties under direct central control. The effort had proceeded in gradually expanding stages, and although the dynasty's centralization policy was clearly making progress both in increasing the proportion of the countryside under direct central supervision and in improving its techniques for doing so, its presence in the countryside was painfully thin and it remained very much dependent on the cooperation of local strongman descent groups.

THE STRUGGLE OVER RESOURCES

Further evidence of the relatively low degree of differentiation in Koryŏ society can be found in the country's economic order. The Koryŏ was an agrarian society. Destruction of maritime trading elements by landed interests in Chŏngjong's reign, which may indicate the shallow roots the traders had in society, seems to have marked the effective end of mercantile power in Korea. Commerce, to say nothing of industry, was so poorly developed that repeated efforts to maintain money in circulation failed, and rice and cloth remained the principal media of exchange. The primary economic resources were land and its products. Struggle between the dynasty and various elite groups for control of land and its yield formed a major theme of Koryŏ history and has been the source of much scholarly controversy.

The Field and Woodland Rank System

Evidence on the nature of land tenure in the early Koryŏ period is scant. Nonetheless, what evidence there is has given rise to an extended and somewhat convoluted debate, centered on the effort to demonstrate progressive socioeconomic change, that has probably done as much to obscure as to enlighten.[111] Much of the controversy has swirled around the Field and Woodland Rank system (Chŏnsi Kwa) implemented in 976 by Kwangjong's immediate successor, King Kyŏngjong. The Field and Woodland Rank system established two major categories of land: *kongjŏn* was land whose tax receipts went to the central government treasury, while *sajŏn* was prebendal land whose receipts went to men belonging to the various classes of persons—including civil and military officials, clerical functionaries, and soldiers—who provided services to the state. Although prebendal rights returned to the state after the recipient's death, the system also included inheritable rights (which provided for families of deceased officials) to collect tax receipts from smaller areas of land known as protected fields and woodlands (*kongŭm chŏnsi*). Officials' prebends were supplemented by salaries (*nokbong*), paid in rice on a quarterly basis.[112]

Early interpretations of this system argued that private ownership of land had not developed at the time of the founding of the Koryŏ dynasty and asserted instead, based on interpretations of T'ang China's equal field (Ch. *chün-t'ien*) system, that all land in Korea belonged to the throne. According to this king's-land theory (*wangt'o sasang*), the basic pattern of land tenure in Korea evolved from the collective ownership of primitive communism in prehistorical times to a system of royal ownership by the time of Unified Silla.[113] The system fell into disarray with the weakening of state power in the late Silla, allowing local warlords to exercise autonomous control over the lands in their districts until royal ownership was restored and systematized under the Field and Woodland Rank system. This interpretation held that under the Field and Woodland Rank system land was distributed to the entire population of the kingdom, from the highest minister to the lowliest peasant, with land to revert to the state for redistribution upon the death of the recipient. But after state power began to weaken near mid-dynasty, the great official descent groups were able to convert their Field and Woodland Rank prebends into private landholdings, leading to the rise of great landed estates (*nongjang*) and the eventual demise of the system in the late Koryŏ.

However, contradictory evidence highlights a number of weaknesses in the king's-land theory as applied to Korea. First, casting serious doubt on whether the Silla state ever actually controlled all the land in the country, is documentation of private ownership of *chŏnjang* estates[114] and the late Silla land deeds (*chŏn kwŏn*), which show buying and selling of land in 891.[115] Second is evidence that the Koryŏ state did not exercise control over all the country's land: the Field and Woodland Rank system as described in the dynastic history provided grants only to select groups that provided services to the state (such as central civil and military officials, *hyangni*, and soldiers) and did not contain provisions for allocating land to the whole population.[116] Finally, the king's-land theory's assumption that a very strong central government had direct control over the whole country was hard to sustain for the early Koryŏ in light of evidence that the dynasty was able to govern most of the country only through the cooperation of the dominant descent groups of each locale. As a result of these interpretive problems, by the 1950s scholars began to turn away from this theory.

The rejection of the king's-land theory did not, however, lead directly to a theory of private ownership of land. The lack of evidence (such as documents recording buying and selling of land) of private ownership in tenth-century Korea led some theorists to posit the existence of a different primary mode of land tenure: the village commune (*ch'ollak kongdongch'e*). According to proponents of this theory, who see the power base of late Silla and early Koryŏ elites as consisting of control over people rather than ownership of land, the commune was made up of socially undifferentiated village residents who held land collectively.[117]

According to this theory, the strongmen maintained control over the people and land of their districts up to the time of the establishment of the Field and Woodland Rank system, which in effect converted their traditional rights to prebends.[118] The assertion that the Field and Woodland Rank system represented conversion to prebends of lands already controlled by strongmen would seem to indicate an acceptance of the notion that private ownership of land existed from the late Silla on. This does not loom as a major problem to the proponents of the village commune theory because of their view of the nature of strongman control over land. This was typified in the stipend village of Silla and very early Koryŏ and the tax village (*sigŭp*) of both Silla and Koryŏ, where, "instead of ownership of a given area of land and receipt of the products from that land, control was exercised over the population of a specific territory or a specific number of households."[119] Thus a strongman could exercise effective control over an area of land through his personal subordination of the residents of that land. Like advocates of the king's-land theory, proponents of the village commune theory assert that descendants of strongmen and great central official descent groups eventually took advantage of weakening royal power to convert prebendal lands into private holdings, setting a precedent for the formation of the large *nongjang* estates of the late Koryŏ.

More recently a third interpretation has been set forth by scholars committed to depicting Korean history as a narrative of linear progress driven by the rise to power at critical junctures of successive new socioeconomic classes. Evidence of private ownership not only in the late Silla period but even earlier, in the Three Kingdoms era (c. C.E. 3rd–mid-7th cent.),[120] suggests that the rise of the village-commune mode of land tenure represented regress rather than progress. Thus scholars citing the late Silla evidence and records of private estates from the twelfth century on argue that the full right to private ownership of land existed throughout the Koryŏ dynasty. Proponents of this view avoid the issue of central control over the countryside since they do not assume powerful central intervention in local economy and society. They merely grant that various social strata, including powerful descent groups, of pre-1170 Koryŏ owned their own lands and that the government made no attempt to interfere with that ownership. This ownership-rights theory presents the Field and Woodland Rank system as simply a means by which the regime used lands under its control to compensate officials, petty functionaries, and soldiers, thereby ensuring their loyalty.[121]

The argument that full-fledged private ownership rights existed throughout the Koryŏ and earlier may avoid the issue of regression, but it also brings the linear-progress interpretation to the brink of self-destruction. The idea that untrammeled private land-ownership rights existed from Silla times on leaves no substantial basis, in the absence of any radical changes in the means and relations of production, for distinguishing the economic foundations of the various social class movements that purportedly informed the development of Koryŏ history. Nonetheless, as James Palais has pointed out, the ownership-rights interpretation provides the best accounting, with limitations regarding the legal defensibility of property rights, for the extant evidence on land tenure.[122]

The evidence and argumentation reviewed to this point indicates that what Eisenstadt calls "free-floating resources" existed in the early Koryŏ. There was private ownership of land—land that could be bought and sold. Furthermore, the Field and Woodland Rank system suggests that the state had direct control over land, or at least the yield of land, some of which was allocated as prebends; the rest (*kongjŏn*) was taxed for support of the state.

We cannot, however, rule out the possibility that the Field and Woodland Rank prebends may have been a legal fiction—nothing more than state confirmation of the private landholdings of elite social groups—or, more likely, that the prebends constituted de facto tax exemptions on a portion of the lands owned by elites, exemptions granted in return for service to the state. But there is evidence to the contrary in the circumstances of the implementation of the system and in some of its features. First, the system was established shortly after Kwangjong's purge of the old confederation, suggesting that it was lands freed from the control of Kwangjong's victims that were reallocated as prebends. Second, the system was put in place at the time when the Koryŏ kings were attempting to create a bureaucracy personally loyal to the throne; the granting of prebends, as an additional source of income for men recruited from the countryside, would have been not only an attractive incentive to service in the dynastic government, but, to the extent that the prebends provided for the livelihood of their recipients, they were probably seen by rulers as a means to enhance independence of the bureaucracy from dominant social groups. Third, the system provided small inheritable prebends to support the widows and children of deceased officials, a feature that would hardly have been necessary if the prebends merely recognized extant private landholdings. Finally, the system made detailed provisions for different sized prebends according to the rank held by the recipient—from 110 *kyŏl* (a measure of land ranging from 2.25 to 9.0 acres, depending on fertility) of fields and 110 *kyŏl* of woodlands for the officials of the senior first grade to 32 *kyŏl* of fields and 25 *kyŏl* of woodlands to officials of the junior ninth grade, along with varying smaller prebends for other classes of individuals who performed services for the state, including central clerks, soldiers, and *hyangni*. Prebend sizes were adjusted downward in two subsequent revisions in 998 and again in 1076 so that the highest ranking officials received 100 *kyŏl* of fields and 50 *kyŏl* of woodlands, apparently because of increasing pressure on resources as a consequence of growth of the central official class.[123] It seems unlikely that the state would have established or revised such detailed provisions if prebendal grants were merely fictive devices for recognizing lands already owned by its officials.

Other Landed Resources

If the state had direct control over the lands it granted as prebends to those serving in the central bureaucracy, what, then, of the prebends it granted to other social groups, such as *hyangni* local elites? It is highly improbable that the dynastic government, with its limited presence in the countryside, controlled significant tracts of land in each county and prefecture that it could distribute as prebends to *hyangni*. It seems more likely that in this case the state simply recognized as prebends a portion of the lands owned by *hyangni* descent groups, in effect granting tax exemptions to the owners as part of the state's policy of winning support from local elites. This reasoning implies, of course, that the remainder of the *hyangni*-owned lands were subject to taxation, most probably as *kongjŏn*. I am skeptical, however, of the state's ability effectively to tax *hyangni*-owned lands since the *hyangni* themselves acted as the state's agents in tax collection. It seems likely, therefore, that significant resources remained embedded in ascriptive social groups in the early Koryŏ, even after promulgation of the Field and Woodland Rank system.

Finally, we should consider the relationship between the dynasty's multi-tiered structure of local administration and its system of exacting resources. Whereas the lands of the prefectures and counties were classified either as prebendal *sajŏn* or general revenue *kongjŏn*, the lower levels of administrative units such as the *hyang* and *pugok* seem to have served specific economic and financial purposes. As is well known, *so* were locales that produced items of special economic importance (such as gold, silver, paper, and, of course, the famous Koryŏ celadon), while *chang* and *ch'ŏ* were agricultural lands that supported the royal family. *Hyang* and *pugok* were also agricultural areas, and their lands appear to have provided resources for specific governmental functions, such as special military installations, schools, and certain government agencies.[124] That the state was able to set aside certain locales for funding specific government activities might seem to suggest fairly strong state control over resources. It seems to me, however, that it was the state's inability to secure access to large amounts of free-floating resources that prompted creation of special collectivities for support of vital governmental functions. The comparatively low status of the descent groups that headed these collectivities may have been a result of their inability to maintain a significant degree of autonomy vis-à-vis the central regime. It is also possible that higher-ranking local strongmen sought to keep them from using their connections with the center to enhance their social and political position, which would have undermined the foundations of the territorial status system. At any rate, the existence of these special, hereditarily defined collectivities constitutes further evidence of the low level of differentiation in Koryŏ society.

SUMMATION

This examination of the Koryŏ political system has shown that during the dynasty's first century, when the political-collective orientation was more prevalent, major steps were taken toward establishing a centralized, bureaucratic polity of the type Eisenstadt describes as enabling the rulers to make policy decisions free of traditional aristocratic domination. Those steps included implementing merit-based recruitment procedures, establishing a regular governmental financial system, importing centralized bureaucratic institutions, and attempting to extend central control over the countryside.

We have also seen, however, that a number of the factors Eisenstadt specifies as limiting the ability of rulers to arrogate policy authority also applied to the Koryŏ kings. One was the strength of traditional legitimizing ideologies. The Koryŏ kings' recognition of Chinese suzerainty and their acceptance of letters of investiture from the emperor may have provided them with external sanction, but at the same time it consequently undermined any claims to ultimate authority deriving from Heaven. The Koryŏ rulers had no choice but to seek additional legitimization in traditional ideologies such as Buddhism and geomancy, which were closely linked to landed Silla aristocratic and local warlord interests.

Perhaps the most important limiting factor was the dynasty's ultimate inability to separate societal and political roles. Although the Bone Rank system, under which political roles were rigidly defined in terms of social caste, came to an end with the demise of Silla and there was some degree of upward social mobility in the later Three Kingdoms period, ascriptive social privilege for landed elements remained an important feature. This was true both at the center, where men of True Bone backgrounds continued to enjoy high prestige and play important political roles, and in the countryside, where the bulk of the country's prefectures and counties remained under the semiautonomous control of hereditary *hyangni* descent groups. Within this ascriptive climate, the dynasty gave important concessions, such as the protection privilege, to the men it recruited to fill the top posts in its bureaucracy. Even eligibility to sit for the merit-based government service examinations was determined by hereditary social status. A consequence of this was the rise of a new central aristocratic-bureaucratic elite. By the late eleventh and twelfth centuries powerful descent groups producing generation after generation of officials emerged to dominate the dynastic bureaucracy. As a result high office became increasingly the hereditary domain of these aristocratic descent groups, who constituted a landed elite within Koryŏ society.

As the great descent groups established themselves at the capital, the dynasty shifted from a political-collective to a cultural-maintenance orientation. This change manifested itself in various ways: diplomatically, in acceptance of Liao and Chin suzerainty and abandonment of efforts to recover old

Koguryŏ lands; culturally, in Kim Pu-sik's grounding of Koryŏ's legitimacy in Silla; and politically, in loss of impetus towards institutional reform, especially in local administration. While this shift no doubt originated in the rise of powerful Manchurian states that blocked Koryŏ's irredentist aspirations, it also went hand-in-hand with the rise of the great central-official descent groups. Thus government policy from the mid-twelfth century on was conservative, primarily concerned with defending the dynasty and maintaining an ascriptive social order dominated by landed interests.

The Koryŏ political system featured many points of similarity with that of T'ang China. Both used the Three Department–Six Board system and made similar modifications, combining the Secretariat and the Chancellery into one policy-making organ that controlled the administrative activities of the Six Boards through concurrent supervisory appointments. The Koryŏ kings, however, seem to have had a considerably weaker hold over the political process than did the T'ang and Sung emperors. Whereas the Chinese rulers enjoyed an unparalleled source of legitimatization as emperors sanctioned by the Mandate of Heaven and were able to make use of extrabureaucratic elements (such as eunuchs) to counter the power of the Chinese aristocracy, the Koryŏ kings were hampered by weaker sources of legitimization and the Korean tradition of royal marriage alliances with powerful and prestigious descent groups.

The Koryŏ kings found it particularly difficult to maintain control over the organs of political struggle. Although the *chaech'u* who formed a joint consultative body in the twelfth century were officials of the dynastic bureaucracy, their status as representatives of powerful landed descent groups lent a strongly aristocratic tinge to the political process. Although *chaech'u* were relegated to ceremonial duties after the 1170 coup, they were replaced by new organs of political struggle that were created and dominated by the Ch'oe house dictators during the military era.

In local administration, both the T'ang and Koryŏ used the prefecture-county system and featured relatively weak governorships, at least until the rise of powerful autonomous governors in the late T'ang. Similarities in local governance are more apparent than real, however. Whereas the T'ang prefecture-county system formed a regular administrative hierarchy based on the posting of centrally appointed prefects and magistrates, the Koryŏ system was an irregular patchwork of control and subordinate prefectures and counties based on local social status with only a limited central presence. Rather than approximating the T'ang prefecture-county setup, the Koryŏ system bears closer resemblance to the highly aristocratic and decentralized system of interregnum China. But even this comparison must be qualified by noting that whereas a family's prestige in medieval China seems to have stemmed from its history of central office holding, status in Koryŏ, while enhanced by central office holding, ultimately derived from a tradition of local autonomy.

Given the limited extent of social differentiation in the Koryŏ, as reflected in the prevalence of landed aristocratic interests, frailty of the kingship, and weakness of state control over the countryside, one wonders why Koryŏ did not devolve into a decentralized system such as the several competing states of interregnum China or the various domains of Ashikaga Japan (1336–1573). It seems certain that external sanction of the dynasty by Chinese, Liao, Chin, and especially Mongol emperors helped prop up the Koryŏ rulers. Also, the presence of the aggressive Khitan and Jurchen states in Manchuria appears to have provided Koreans with extra stimulus toward unity. It seems likely, however, that important causes also lay within Korea itself. One factor must have been the country's smaller geographic size; potential rebels could not rely on vast distances to protect themselves from dynastic retaliation. Another important element may have been the steps the dynasty took—as seen in Wang Kŏn's marriage policy and use of the examination system to recruit men from the provinces—to incorporate leading descent groups from throughout the country into its central bureaucracy. As long as local elites felt that their interests were being served by the dynasty and as long as they had access to positions in the central government, they would have had little incentive to break away and form independent regimes.

The ability of the dynasty to survive, even in such a weakened state, should not blind us to the stresses that wracked the Koryŏ, stresses that derived primarily from the rulers' inability to overcome limitations presented by landed aristocratic groups. Despite its major overhaul of central political institutions and the subsequent century-plus of domestic peace, the Koryŏ was ultimately unable to establish a strong kingship. By the late eleventh century the central bureaucracy came under the domination of powerful central-official descent groups who developed landed estates of their own. From that time on, Koryŏ's kings found it increasingly difficult to maintain a substantial degree of generalized power and to keep resources from falling under aristocratic control.

2 / The Rise of a Central Bureaucratic Aristocracy

The rise of a hereditary central bureaucracy is one of the most salient features of Koryŏ history. This would appear, on the surface of things, to be yet another area of affinity with T'ang China, with its great aristocratic clans. Indeed a reading of current East Asian scholarship on the ruling strata of the Koryŏ and of medieval China will leave the reader with the impression that there were great similarities. Historians emphasize how Korean and Chinese elites distinguished themselves from the rest of the populace by surname (sŏng, Ch. hsing) and ancestral seat identifiers.[1] Historians also regularly use identical terminology—such as munbŏl (Ch. men-fa, J. monbatsu) and kwijok (Ch. kuei-tsu, J. kizoku)—for the ruling strata of both societies.

Despite these historiographical conventions, however, there existed significant differences between medieval China and Koryŏ Korea. The elites of both countries did use surnames and ancestral seats, but beyond that the terms they used to identify themselves were quite different. Although the great clans of China routinely called themselves men-fa and kuei-tsu, the Koryŏ elites rarely, if ever, used the terms munbŏl or kwijok.[2] The use of these terms in reference to the Koryŏ is a twentieth-century innovation. Such usage can perhaps be justified on the grounds that those terms have come to have wide currency as generic terms for "powerful families" (munbŏl) and "aristocracy" (kwijok). Nonetheless, to the extent that they are applied to suggest parallels between medieval China and Koryŏ Korea caution is necessary.

The problem of terminology is not limited to munbŏl and kwijok. That medieval Chinese elites commonly identified themselves by such terms as shih, shih-tsu, and shih-ta-fu suggests that office holding was an important component of their group identity.[3] Koryŏ elites did not use these terms (except occasionally sadaebu (shih-ta-fu) to denote incumbent officials) until very near the end of the dynasty;[4] throughout most of the Koryŏ period they referred to themselves by such terms as taejok ("great descent group," Ch. ta-tsu), myŏngjok ("famous descent group," Ch. ming-tsu), or hyŏnsŏng ("illustrious surname," Ch. *hsien-hsing*), which do not suggest the same degree of identi-fication with office holding as the Chinese *shih* or *shih-ta-fu*.[5]

Second, whereas the great clans of T'ang China were organized on patri-lineal principles, the kinship organization of Korean elites was, as Martina Deuchler has shown, more complex and inclusive, embracing patrilateral, matri-lateral, and affinal relatives.[6] The people of the Koryŏ traced their descent along both male and female sides and maternal descent continued to be an impor-tant factor in the actual organization and functioning of the elite kinship group throughout the dynasty, as seen, for example, in inclusion of the maternal grand-father among the "four ancestors" examination candidates were required to list, as well as in provisions for succession to property and in eligibility for the *ŭm* privilege.[7] Nonetheless, tombstone inscriptions show that by the mid-eleventh century central political elites had begun to place greater emphasis on paternal ancestry, identifying themselves primarily as members of a descent group defined by surname and ancestral seat, and specifically as members of a line of descent traced back through father, grandfather, and great-grandfather.[8] We have no evidence to tell us whether the same trend was developing out in the countryside, but central elites commonly listed *hyangni* among their ances-tors and continued to use their *hyangni* antecedents' surnames and ancestral seats. This not only reflects an awareness of their origins in the local strong-man class, but also indicates that they retained a sense of kinship with rural relatives. Broadly speaking, therefore, the ancestral seat surname identifier used by the Koryŏ central elites was a complex entity embracing both central and local segments. But what we will deal with here is a more narrowly defined centrally based group that is depicted in the sources as an essentially paternal line of descent.

The issues are not merely pedantic questions of proper terminology and pre-cise description of kinship organization, but that the use of T'ang terminol-ogy and concepts to describe Koryŏ elites implies some sort of parallel social evolution. The great aristocratic clans that had dominated interregnum and early T'ang China lost much of their power and prestige as a consequence of the increasing importance of the examination system and widespread provincial rebellions so that, by the late T'ang, they no longer existed as a self-conscious collective entity. Conventional interpretations of Koryŏ history argue that the civil aristocracy of the early Koryŏ lost much of its power and pres-tige in the military coup of 1170 and that vestiges of the aristocratic system were undermined by recruitment of new elements through the government ser-vice examinations in the second half of the dynasty. This chapter shows that local strongmen who were recruited to serve in the bureaucracy in the early dynasty developed by the late eleventh century into a powerful central bureau-cratic aristocracy that perpetuated itself through the revolts, coups, and inva-sions of the twelfth and thirteenth centuries and reemerged in the late Koryŏ with a strong sense of itself as a collective political and social ruling class dis-tinct from the local elite class from which it had sprung.

THE CENTRAL BUREAUCRACY IN THE EARLY KORYŎ

A number of excellent studies—such as Fujita Ryosaku's examination of the Kyŏngwŏn Yi and Pak Yong-un's studies on several other descent groups—have examined specific groups who dominated the central government in the early Koryŏ.[9] There has been, however, no comprehensive study of the posi-tion of these descent groups within the central bureaucracy as a whole. This section assesses the relative importance of the great descent groups in terms of numbers and political power and sheds further light on the sociopolitical nature of the great descent groups through an examination of how they attained power and how they kept it.

The Great Descent Groups of the Early Koryŏ

Who were the great central-official descent groups of eleventh and twelfth cen-tury Korea? To what extent were they able to dominate the dynastic govern-ment, and what kind of political power did they exercise? The answers to these questions depend on a study of the actual structure and composition of the central bureaucracy. To that end, I have compiled data on the careers of all men known to have held office in the central government from 981, when under King Sŏngjong the dynasty adopted the T'ang system of government, through the end of King Injong's reign in 1146. Claims of office holding for various individuals can be found in such sources as genealogies and local gazetteers, but in order to maximize reliability I have limited my consideration to appointments that can be found in the dynastic histories.[10] I have also com-piled data on the social origins of all officials for whom such information can be found, using the biographical information in the dynastic histories, tomb-stone inscriptions, local gazetteers, and, to a limited extent, genealogies. While the data for the early Koryŏ is skimpy compared to that for later periods, there is enough to allow us to draw some conclusions about the power structure of the Koryŏ before the military coup.

A total of 1,140 men appear in the dynastic histories as officials of the cen-tral government during the 981–1146 period, including 959 civil and 181 mil-

TABLE 2.1.

Descent Structure of the Central Bureaucracy, 981–1146.

Total known officials	1,140
Officials of known descent	257 (23%)
Total known *chaech'u*	234
Chaech'u of known descent	143 (61%)
Total descent groups	87
Descent groups with only one known official	45 (52%)
Most powerful descent groups*	29
Officials from most powerful descent groups	169 (15%)
Chaech'u from most powerful descent groups	94 (40%)

* Groups with four or more total officials or two or more *chaech'u* noble titleholders

itary officials. Since the total number of regular military and civil posts in the two branches (civil and military) of the Koryŏ central government, according to the *Koryŏsa* "Monograph on Officials," was 4,358,[11] it is obvious that our 1,140 men represent only a small proportion of those who held office during those years. Furthermore, these 1,140 individuals hardly constitute a representative sample of the bureaucracy, since the *Koryŏsa* almost totally neglects lower-level officials. Nearly 70 percent (3,014 of 4,358) of the posts in the central bureaucracy were ninth-grade positions, yet officials known to have held that grade make up less than 1 percent (12 of 1,140) of known officials; in contrast, first- and second-grade *chaech'u* of the Secretariat/Chancellery and the Security Council (also known as *chaesang*) account for less than one-half of 1 percent (12 of 4,358) of central government offices, but 21 percent (234 of 1,140) of known officials.[12] This means that, while we may not be able to speak authoritatively about the bureaucracy as a whole, it may be possible for us to draw some conclusions about the highest echelon of the dynastic government—the echelon that exercised real political power.

Descent groups (surname plus ancestral seat) can be identified for 257 (23 percent) of the 1,140 men in table 2.1, including 245 civil and 12 military officials. The 257 men of known origins were spread out among 87 separate descent groups. The majority of these groups (45), however, accounted for only one official each, suggesting fairly broad representation in the central government.

The most important revelation of the data in table 2.1, however, is the degree to which relatively few descent groups dominated the central bureaucracy. It is impossible to know for certain the number of elite descent groups eligible to hold central government offices in the Koryŏ. One source, based on early Chosŏn materials, puts the number at 2,181.[13] But even if we use the conservative estimate that there was only one elite descent group for each of the 450-some prefectures and counties and if we disregard the fact that major regional centers such as Andong, Kyŏngju, and Ch'ŏngju had multiple elite descent groups, the data in table 2.1 would indicate that only 6 percent (29 of 450) of the kingdom's elite descent groups accounted for 15 percent (169 of 1,140) of all known officials and over 40 percent (94 of 234) of known *chaech'u* during the 981–1146 period. This indicates that while a relatively large number of descent groups held offices in the dynastic government, a small number enjoyed a disproportionate share of power.

Who were those few powerful descent groups? We have no sources such as the state-sponsored lists of great clans found for medieval China that would allow us to identify the great descent groups of the Koryŏ period.[14] Thus we must determine great descent-group status on the basis of actual office holding in the central government. Table 2.2 presents the numerical ranking of descent groups known to have produced significant numbers of officials in the early Koryŏ, revealing that a very few—particularly the Kyŏngwŏn Yi, Kyŏngju Kim, and the Haeju Ch'oe—held dominant positions in the central bureaucracy, greatly overshadowing other groups. The data in table 2.2, which is compiled from names appearing in the dynastic histories, probably understates the actual representation of many descent groups. If we were to take into consideration data from tombstone inscriptions, for example, the numbers for the Ich'ŏn Sŏ would increase to seven total officials and four *chaech'u,* and the number of total officials for the Hwangnyŏ Min would expand to seven.[15] Thus while the Kyŏngwŏn Yi clearly stands above all other descent groups, the gap in numbers between such groups as the Kyŏngju Kim and Haeju Ch'oe on the one hand and the Hwangnyŏ Min, Ich'ŏn Sŏ, and Chŏngju Yu on the other was probably somewhat smaller than the data in table 2.2 indicates.[16]

Table 2.2 reveals other interesting aspects of the composition of the early Koryŏ central bureaucracy. One is that those of Silla True Bone backgrounds, such as the Kyŏngju Kim,[17] Kangnŭng Kim, and P'yŏngsan Pak, were among the most powerful descent groups of the early Koryŏ. This contradicts the conventional notion that the central aristocracy of the eleventh and twelfth centuries was primarily made up of descendants of Silla sixth Bone Rank officials and local strongmen of nonaristocratic origins.

TABLE 2.2

Most Powerful Descent Groups, 981–1146

Descent Group	Total Officials	Chaech'u
Kyŏngwŏn Yi	27	12
Kyŏngju Kim	14	10
Haeju Ch'oe	13	8
Kyŏngju Ch'oe	9	6
Kangnŭng Kim	9	5
Tanju Han	7	2
P'yŏngsan Yu	7	2
Kwangyang Kim	6	5
P'yŏngsan Pak	5	2
Kaesŏng Wang	5	2
Suju Ch'oe	5	2
P'ap'yŏng Yun	5	2
Pongju Chi	5	2
Kongam Hŏ	4	2
Chŏngan Im	4	4
Namp'yŏng Mun	4	3
Ch'ŏngju Kwak	4	2
Hwangnyŏ Min	4	1
Tongnae Chŏng	4	1
Ich'ŏn Sŏ	3	3
Ch'ogye Chŏng	3	2
Okku Im	3	2
Yŏnggwang Kim	3	2
Ch'ŏngju Yi	3	2
Suju Yi	3	2
Ch'ungju Yu	3	2
Yŏngch'ŏn Hwangbo	3	2
Ansan Kim	2	2
Chŏngju Yu	2	2
Total: 29	169	94

Another feature is that the great official descent groups came from all over the peninsula, from Kangnŭng on the eastern coast to Ch'ogye and Yŏngch'ŏn in the southeastern corner and Kwangyang, Namp'yŏng, Yŏnggwang, and Okku in the southwest. This rebuts the argument that the early Koryŏ was dominated by descent groups from the north-central region and that outlying areas did not gain significant representation until late Koryŏ period.[18] Given the dynasty's need, as seen in Wang Kŏn's marriages, to win the support of local strongmen throughout the country, it is not surprising that the geographic distribution of leading descent groups covers the whole peninsula.

Finally, it is important to note that the great descent groups of the early Koryŏ did, in fact, serve in the civil branch of government. Only five (2 percent) of the 169 men identified as belonging to the great descent groups were military officials: two from the P'yŏngsan Yu, two from the Kyŏngwŏn Yi, and one from the Kangnŭng Kim. The two military officials from the Kyŏngwŏn Yi belong to a segment that Fujita Ryosaku has identified as a military branch of the descent group, but military branch members of the Kyŏngwŏn Yi do not appear to have been politically active and never rose to hold *chaech'u* posts.[19] The one member of the Kangnŭng Kim who served in the military branch did rise to *chaech'u* posts as a consequence of his pivotal role in suppressing the Yi Cha-ŭi rebellion in the late eleventh century. That man was Wang Kung-mo, a member of a segment within the Kangnŭng Kim that was given the royal surname Wang at the beginning of the dynasty.[20] These few examples suggest that at least some of the great descent groups included lines of military officials, but their numbers were few and their political roles (with the exception of Wang Kung-mo) limited. Members of the great official descent groups of the early Koryŏ were civil bureaucrats.

These civil official descent groups were closely related. Fujita Ryosaku's findings on their marriage relations show that the great descent groups of the early Koryŏ central bureaucracy were intermarried with each other as well as, in many cases, with the royal family.[21] The Kyŏngwŏn Yi, for example, married their daughters to royal princes no fewer than 10 times, while also marrying with the Haeju Ch'oe four times and with the Kyŏngju Kim, Kangnŭng Kim, and Kwangyang Kim three times each. It is often noted that the marriages these descent groups contracted with the royal family facilitated their domination of the throne in the twelfth century, but we should also recognize that these marriages represented the building of alliances among powerful descent groups. The pattern of multiple unions within a small number of descent groups suggests that civil aristocrats tended to form a closed elite at the top of the Koryŏ sociopolitical order.

Origins of the Great Descent Groups

Discussing the origins of the great descent groups of his time, the fifteenth-century scholar and official Sŏng Hyŏn stated, "All of our country's great descent groups arose from among the leading descent groups of the prefectures and counties."[22] Sŏng Hyŏn's contention is borne out by the source materials for the Koryŏ period, which are rife with examples of the scions of local elite descent groups taking posts in the dynastic government and then remaining in the capital to establish hereditary lines of central officials.[23]

It appears that while a few of the descent groups in table 2—groups such as the Kyŏngju Ch'oe, Kyŏngju Kim, Kangnŭng Kim, and P'yŏngsan Pak, whose ancestry can be traced back to Silla sixth Head Rank and True Bone origins—were active in the central government from the very beginning of the dynasty, the majority arose from the local strongman stratum after implementation of the government service examination system in the mid-tenth century. Central official descent groups whose post-950 local origins can be demonstrated include the Ich'ŏn Sŏ,[24] Kwangyang Kim,[25] Suju Ch'oe, Kyŏngwŏn Yi,[26] Haeju Ch'oe, Tanju Han,[27] P'ap'yŏng Yun,[28] and Tongnae Chŏng.[29] One particularly well-documented example can be found in the Suju Ch'oe descent group, which appears to have established itself in the capital in the mid-tenth century. An 1160 tombstone for a prominent member states that his eighth-generation forebear was a Suju *hyangni* who had two sons, the younger of which "entered the service of the court, reached the rank of chancellor and first resided at the capital; his descendants have all been men of the capital."[30] Another well-known example from the eleventh century is the great scholar and official Ch'oe Ch'ung. Ch'oe, the son of a Haeju *hyangni*,[31] rose to the top of the central bureaucracy in the eleventh century; his sons, grandsons, and great grandsons all went on to hold high office.[32] The segments established by men such as Ch'oe Ch'ung and Yi Cha-yŏn of Kyŏngwŏn formed the nucleus of the central official class of eleventh- and twelfth-century Korea.

The rise of these great descent groups must be understood in relation to the early Koryŏ policy of political centralization. Although the original means of entry of the founders of several of these central official segments are not clear, many—such as Ch'oe Ch'ung, Yi Cha-yŏn, Kim Ch'aek of the Kwangyang Kim, Hŏ Hyŏn of the Kongam Hŏ, Chŏng Pae-gŏl of the Ch'ogye Chŏng, Han An-in of the Tanju Hah, Yun Kwan of the P'ap'yŏng Yun, and Chŏng Mok of the Tongnae Chŏng—first gained central offices through the examination system established by King Kwangjong in order to recruit men from outside the central confederation to fill the ranks of the central bureaucracy.[33]

Another important factor behind the rise of these great official descent groups was the internal structure of the Koryŏ descent group. Local elite descent groups tended to marry with other regional elite descent groups. The rise of a group facilitated the rise of its marriage partners, but under the Koryŏ system, in which descent was traced along female as well as male lines, this must have been more pronounced. Yi Su-gŏn has noted that "it was a general phenomenon that once a descent group from a locale established itself at the center, other descent groups from the same locale would follow."[34] The Kyŏngwŏn Yi provide a good example. Although the founder of the capital branch of this descent group, Yi Cha-yŏn, first entered the central bureaucracy through the examination system, his spectacular rise and his descendants' success owed much to marriage ties with the Suju Ch'oe and the Ansan Kim, two powerful descent groups from the same region whose appearance at the capital preceded the Kyŏngwŏn Yi's.[35]

It seems, therefore, that the initial rise of the centrally based segments of these descent groups came about as the consequence of both royal efforts to create an independent bureaucracy and the internal structure of the elite descent group. These factors helped maintain and strengthen the central bureaucratic stratum and preserved the privileged status of local elite descent groups.

Recruitment Systems and Social Elites

The Koryŏ dynasty employed a variety of means to recruit its central officials. The preface to the Koryŏsa "Monograph on Recruitment" (Sŏn'gŏ chi) states that in addition to the examination system and the ŭm privilege, men could advance into the regular bureaucracy from palace clerical and attendant posts (namban/naesi), palace guard (sŏngjungaema) posts, and miscellaneous technical (chamno) posts, such as those of astronomer or physician. This wide variety of recruitment mechanisms would seem to indicate potential for substantial social mobility. The evidence, however, suggests that these mechanisms primarily served the interests of the dominant social groups, both central and local.

The ŭm protection privilege was a very important method by which central aristocrats maintained their family's presence in the bureaucracy. It allowed higher-ranking officials to have their sons, grandsons, or other relatives—including sons and grandsons through their daughters, maternal nephews, and sons-in-law—appointed to posts in the central government. There were two general types of ŭm appointments: those regularly made to the sons, grandsons, nephews, and sons-in-law of officials of the fifth grade or higher, and those made on special occasions (such as the enthronement of a new king) for the descendants of merit subjects of earlier reigns. The first type, which undoubtedly accounted for the appointment of many more officials than the second, involved an oral test on the Confucian *Analects* (Lun-yü) and *The Classic of Filial Piety,* (Hsiao-ching), which apparently was conducted four times a year.[36] Given this degree of frequency, it is not difficult to imagine that thousands benefited from the protection system throughout the Koryŏ dynasty. Because neither the *Koryŏsa* nor any other source tells how many men received protection appointments, we must once again rely on biographies, tombstones, and literary collections. The 191 *ŭm* beneficiaries for the Koryŏ period that these sources identify obviously represent a minuscule proportion of the total number of individuals who held office.[37] What data does exist indicates that the *ŭm* privilege was widely used by central aristocrats of the early Koryŏ. Among the descent groups active at the capital from the beginning of the dynasty, the Kyŏngju Ch'oe are known to have used the *ŭm* privilege four times and the Kyŏngju Kim three times during the years prior to the military coup in 1170. During the same period, newer descent groups of recent local strongman origins also made active use of the privilege once they had established themselves at the capital. Examples include the Kyŏngwŏn Yi (with twelve known *ŭm* beneficiaries) and the Suju Ch'oe and Haeju Ch'oe (with five each).[38] Furthermore, the importance of maternal ancestors' *ŭm* has been demonstrated by No Myŏng-ho, who has found its use among such well-established descent groups as the Suju Ch'oe and Kongam Hŏ.[39] In the early Koryŏ period *ŭm* beneficiaries typically received appointments to central clerical (*sŏri*) posts, from which they advanced to offices in the regular bureaucracy.

While this suggests that capital-based descent group segments had a distinct advantage over their local counterparts, the sons of top-ranking local elites—the men holding township headman and assistant headman posts— were also guaranteed access to central clerk positions. These posts often were granted to *ŭm* appointees.[40]

The other major recruitment system, the government service examination, embraced the same dual approach to recruitment, giving substantial advantages to established capital-based descent groups, but also ensuring that local elites would have access to posts in the central bureaucracy. The Koryŏ examination system was two-tiered: students had to pass a qualifying examination before sitting for higher examinations. For capital-based elements, the preferred way to qualify for the examinations was to pass the Royal Confucian Academy examination (Kukchagam *si*), but important exceptions existed. Incumbent officials below the sixth grade could take higher examinations without going through preliminary examinations, as could students from the Royal Confucian Academy or, after the late eleventh century, the 12 famous private schools in the capital, if their academic performance was deemed excellent.[41] Since entrance into the central schools that prepared students for the examinations was restricted to the children of incumbent officials,[42] this system appears to have discriminated heavily in favor of established central bureaucratic descent group segments. On the other hand, however, the examination system also provided for qualifying examinations to be held in the countryside. Eligibility to sit for such examinations was, as in the case of appointment to central clerical posts, limited to the sons of holders of the top two local offices.[43]

The literary examination (*chesul kwa*) and the classics examination (*myŏng-gyŏng kwa*) were higher examinations. Although both were given throughout the dynasty, the literary examination carried much more prestige and produced the overwhelming majority of examination graduates. The *Koryŏsa* "Monograph on Recruitment" tells only the date of each examination, the number of successful candidates, and the name of the man who scored highest. Since the number of passers per examination ranged from eight or nine in the tenth century to between 25 and 30 in the eleventh and twelfth, the names of top scorers given in the "Monograph on Recruitment" obviously account for only a tiny fraction of early Koryŏ examination graduates. Using a variety of supplementary sources; including *Koryŏsa* biographies and tombstone inscriptions, Pak Yong-un has identified 334 literary examination graduates for the years up to 1146, roughly 15 percent of the 2,089 successful candidates during that period.[44] While such scanty data make it difficult to gauge the overall effect of the examination system, we can get some insight into the significance of the system for our top 28 central-official descent groups. First, 25 of the 28 groups are known to have had at least one examination graduate, and together account for 102 of the 334 known examination graduates.[45] Second, several of the great central-official descent groups made extensive use of the examination system to perpetuate themselves in power: the Kyŏngwŏn Yi and Kyŏngju Kim produced nine examination graduates each; the Haeju Ch'oe, eight; the Kangnŭng Kim, seven; and the Kwangyang Kim, P'yŏngsan Pak, and Suju Ch'oe, six each. Third, the examination system was more prestigious than the *ŭm* system: a number of men passed the examinations even after they had already acquired posts via the *ŭm* privilege.[46]

The prestige of the examination system becomes even clearer when we focus on the very top ranks of the bureaucracy. Fifty-seven men held the junior first-grade chancellor and senior second-grade assistant chancellor (*chungsŏmunha sirang p'yŏngjangsa*) posts of the Secretariat-Chancellery during the years from 1070 to 1146. Using the Koryŏsa biographies, tombstone inscriptions, and the "Monograph on Recruitment," I have determined that 24 (42 percent) of these 57 men were examination passers; five (9 percent) were *ŭm* beneficiaries; and another five were from military, clerical, or palace attendant backgrounds. Ten of 23 men of unknown means of entry served as examiners (*chigonggo*) or associate examiners (*tong chigonggo*), a duty they would not have been given had they not been examination graduates themselves. When we take these 10 additional men into consideration, it seems probable that nearly 60 percent (34 of 57) of the chancellors and assistant chancellors of the 981–1146 period were products of the government service examination system. This is comparable to the situation that prevailed in the first 75 years of the Chosŏn, a period usually considered much more bureaucratic than the Koryŏ, when 65 percent (40 of 61) of top-ranking officials were examination graduates and 23 percent (14 of 61) were *ŭm* appointees and indicates that passing the government service examinations was an important key to official success in the early Koryŏ period.[47]

That the dynasty's recruitment systems, taken as a whole, preserved ascriptive social privilege supports our observation about the limits of social differentiation in the Koryŏ period. At the same time, the dual nature of the recruitment systems reveals that the ruling stratum had developed into a two-tiered structure. The great central-official descent groups constituted a highly privileged and prestigious upper tier in the capital. At the same time, the local township headman and assistant headman descent groups of the prefectures and counties formed a second tier, which continued to manage local affairs with a substantial degree of autonomy and enjoyed institutionalized means of access to central bureaucratic posts, in effect forming a socially qualified reservoir of talent for recruitment.

Career Patterns in the Central Bureaucracy

One of the hallmarks of a bureaucracy is the existence of professional officials organized in a regular hierarchy and carrying out specialized functions under impersonal and uniform rules and procedures. We have already seen that there was little effective specialization of function at the very top levels of the Koryŏ bureaucracy. That does not, however, rule out the possibility of substantial functional specialization in the myriad lower-level agencies staffed by mid- and low-ranking officials. Unfortunately our lack of descriptions of daily official routine makes it impossible to gauge to what extent day-to-day business was conducted according to bureaucratic rules and procedures.

One possible approach, however, is to examine the information we have on official careers of prominent officials to determine whether they rose through the bureaucratic hierarchy in a regular fashion or enjoyed accelerated advancement due to descent group. Although the *Koryŏsa* "Annals" (Sega) often contain dozens, and in some cases hundreds, of entries on individual officials, they typically mention an official only after he has risen to mid- and high-ranking positions, leaving us with no information on which to judge his early career. The *Koryŏsa* biographies are little better—occasional brief statements about officials' early careers are never sufficiently detailed for us to trace their paths to the top.

There are other ways to approach this problem, however. Han Ch'ung-hŭi has shown that men whose fathers and grandfathers held high office in the early Koryŏ tended to rise faster and higher in the bureaucracy, regardless of whether they entered office through examinations or the *ŭm* privilege. But Han's data also shows that it typically took officials over 30 years from the time they first entered the bureaucracy to rise to *chaech'u* posts.[48] Han's research is based primarily on information culled from the *Koryŏsa*, but his findings can be corroborated by data from tombstone inscriptions, some of which contain substantial detail of the decedents' careers.

One of the more detailed early Koryŏ tombstones is that of Yi Cha-yŏn of the Kyŏngwŏn Yi. Yi Cha-yŏn passed the government service examinations in 1024, at the age of 22. He then held a variety of lower and middle rank posts before receiving appointment to his first *chaech'u* post in the Security Council in 1040, sixteen years after he received his first appointment.[49] While Yi Cha-yŏn's progress up the official ladder was somewhat faster than the typical case as described by Han Ch'ung-hŭi, his was one of the most brilliant careers of the early Koryŏ and it is thus not surprising that he advanced quickly. Another detailed tombstone is that of his son, Yi Chŏng, who entered the bureaucracy at age 20 through the *ŭm* privilege, and held a series of low and middle ranking posts (including a three-year tour in the provinces) before rising to a *chaech'u* post at age forty.[50] Men from less illustrious descent groups progressed more slowly. Im Ŭi of Chŏngan, for example, passed the government service examination in 1070 at the somewhat advanced age of 32; he subsequently held a variety of low and middle ranking literary posts while doing two tours of duty in the provinces before finally receiving his first *chaech'u* appointment as state councillor at the age of 68 in 1106, 36 years after he entered official service. Chŏng Hang of Tongnae passed the government service examination in 1103 at the age of 23; he was first posted to a provincial post, after which he went on to hold a number of low and middle rank central posts before becoming a *chaech'u* in 1136, 33 years after he passed the examinations. These examples suggest that early Koryŏ officials followed a regular path of career advancement and generally confirm Han Ch'ung-hŭi's conclusions. Although members of the Kyŏngwŏn Yi descent group, the most powerful of the time, seem to have advanced more quickly, even they had to put in 15 to 20 years in low and middle rank posts before gaining appointment to *chaech'u* positions. This indicates that the early Koryŏ system functioned, at least in the area of personnel administration, according to regular bureaucratic procedures. Considered in conjunction with the apparent importance of a government service examination background for the top levels of the bureaucracy, this suggests a surprisingly strong meritocratic tendency in the early Koryŏ central bureaucracy.

The Flourishing of the Great Descent Groups

Important changes took place in the Koryŏ bureaucracy as a consequence of the growth of the great descent groups, changes that had the ultimate effect of enhancing the power of the bureaucracy vis-à-vis the throne. One was a tendency for prominent descent groups to place more of their members in high offices. A related change was expansion of the top ranks of the bureaucracy, apparently in response to growing competitive pressures.

The great central-official descent groups did not all flourish at the same time. Some, including the Kyŏngju Kim and the Suju Ch'oe, placed men in office throughout the 981–1146 period. Others, such as the Kyŏngju Ch'oe, were most powerful during the late tenth and eleventh centuries, while several, such as the Chŏngan Im, did not become active until the late eleventh or twelfth century.

These descent groups display three basic patterns of office holding. One was a simple father-to-son succession within one line, with one known official per generation, as seen for example in the Ich'ŏn Sŏ[51] and the Ch'ŏngju Kwak.[52] A second pattern, where multiple officials from different branches of descent groups held central offices at the same time, can be found in the Kyŏngju Ch'oe and Kyŏngju Kim.[53] The third pattern, where several brothers held high offices, often simultaneously, developed among the Kyŏngwŏn Yi, Haeju Ch'oe, Kyŏngju Kim, Chŏngan Im, and several other descent groups.[54] The emergence of the third type of office-holding late in the reign of King Munjong resulted in a shift in the balance of power between throne and bureaucracy.

There are some indications that prior to King Munjong's ascension capital-based families were able to place more than one son in office. The tombstone of Ch'oe Sa-wi, a Suju Ch'oe who was a leading official under King Hyŏnjong, states that all six of his sons held posts in the central government.[55] That appointment to office can be confirmed in the histories for only one is not surprising. The histories routinely record appointments and activities of high-ranking officials, but mention low-ranking men only in unusual circumstances. It seems probable that the other five never rose above the lower ranks. In this regard, it is worth noting that in the first verifiable instances of two or more brothers in office—the Kyŏngwŏn Yi[56] and the Haeju Ch'oe[57] in the 1070s—the men in question held first- and second-grade posts. The absence of verifiable cases of brothers holding offices in the 981–1069 period indicates that office holding by brothers before 1070 was probably limited to low-ranking posts. After 1070 this began to occur at the highest levels of the bureaucracy.

How widespread was this practice during the late eleventh and twelfth centuries? Some sense can be gained from table 2.3, which lists descent groups known to have placed siblings in office during the 1070–1146 period. The rank column shows the highest rank held, and the year column indicates the year or reign when that rank was achieved. Table 2.3 confirms that during the 1070–1146 period it was common practice for two or more brothers to hold offices, with siblings from 12 descent groups accounting for a total of 51 office-holders. It also confirms that these men tended to be high-ranking officials, with 55 percent (28) attaining first- or second-grade posts. Additionally, it indicates that the trend toward simultaneous office holding among brothers increased as time passed, with over 60 percent (31) of the known instances occurring during the 1123–46 period.

Some indication of the impact of this change in the pattern of office holding can be seen in table 2.4, which compares the aggregate power of the leading descent groups of the 981–1069 period with those of the 1070–1146 period. The data in table 2.4 indicates that the first- and second-grade posts, where real power resided in the Koryŏ central government, came under increasing domination by a small number of descent groups during the late eleventh and early twelfth centuries. During the 981–1069 period the most powerful descent groups accounted for 20 percent (11 of 56) of all descent groups known to have members in central offices; this proportion increased slightly, to 25 percent (19 of 75), during the 1070–1146 period. A similarly modest increase from 11 percent (40 of 356) to 13 percent (102 of 788) occurred in the proportion of all known officials accounted for by the most powerful descent groups. In the years after 1070, however, the increase in the proportion of

TABLE 2.3
Descent Groups with Multiple Sons in Office, 1070–1146

Descent Group	Father	Rank	Sons	Ranks	Years
Chŏgan Im	Ŭi	2a	Wŏn-gae	2a	1134
			Wŏn-jun	2a	1137
			Wŏn-suk	3a	1141
Haeju Ch'oe	Ch'ung	1b	Yu-sŏn	1b	1073
			Yu-gil	1b	1077
	Yu-gil	1b	Sa-ryang	2b	1087
			Sa-ch'u	1b	1103
	Sa-je	2a	Yak	3a	1105–21
			Yong	2b	1105–21
Kangnŭng Kim	Sang-gi	2a	In-jon	1b	1126
			Ko	2a	1123
Kwangyang Kim	Yang-gam	2a	Ŭi-wŏn	2b	1126
			Yag-on	2a	1123
Kyŏngju Kim	Kŭn	3b	Pu-ch'ŏl	2b	1136
			Pu-il	2a	1127
			Pu-p'il	5a	1102
			Pu-sik	1b	1136
Kyŏngwŏn Yi	Cha-yŏn	1b	Chŏng	1b	1076
			Chŏk	2b+	1046–83
			Sŏk	4a	1075
			Ŭi	2b+	1081
			Hŏ	ă	1046–83
	Chŏng	1b	Cha-in	3a	1088
			Cha-ŭi	2b	1094
			Cha-hyŏn	5a	1084–94
	Ho	5a	Cha-ryang	2a	1123
			Cha-gyŏm	1b	1124
	Cha-gyŏm	1b	Chi-mi	2b	1124
			Chi-on	4a	1124
			Chi-bo	5a	1124
			Chi-yun	6b	1124
			Chi-wŏn	7a	1124
	Cha-sang	2a*	Ye	2b	1095
			O	2a	1103

TABLE 2.3   (continued)

Descent Group	Father	Rank	Sons	Ranks	Years
Namp'yŏng Mun	Ik	3a	Kong-mi	2b	1131
			Kong-yu	2b	1136
			Kong-wŏn	5a	1136
P'ap'yŏng Yun	Kwan	1b	Ŏn-i	2b	1146
			Ŏn-min	6a	1146
			Ŏn-sik	4a	1136
P'yŏngsan Pak	Il-lyang	2b	Kyŏng-in	2b	1117
			Kyŏng-baek	5a	1107
			Kyŏng-san	4a	1134
Suju Yi	Chŏng-gong	1b	Suk	2b	1128
			Wi	1b	1116
Tanju Han	Kyu	4a	An-in	2a	1123
			An-jung	3a	1124
Tongnae Chŏng	Mok	2a*	Chŏm	5b	1132
			Taek	4b	1134
			Hang	3a	1135

* Posthumous honorary appointments

chaech'u accounted for by the top descent groups jumped sharply, from 25 percent (24 of 97) in the 981–1069 period to 43 percent (58 of 134) in the later period. Twelve of the 19 descent groups listed for the 1070–1146 period in table 2.4 are also among the 12 descent groups with two or more brothers in office shown in table 2.3. It is clear that the practice of placing multiple sons in office enabled a small number of descent groups to achieve a dominant position in the central bureaucracy in the late eleventh and twelfth centuries.

While these groups were entrenching themselves at the capital, there was no letup in the influx of local elites from the countryside. In fact, two of the segments contained in table 2.4, the Tanju Han and Tongnae Chŏng, were late eleventh- or early twelfth-century arrivals. Han Kyu was a product of the local qualifying examinations[58] and Chŏng Mok was the son of a Tongnae township headman.[59] Other notable twelfth-century new arrivals included Ch'oe Yu from Kangnŭng,[60] Ch'oe Ch'ŏk-kyŏng from Chŏnju,[61] and Yi Chunyang, also from Chŏnju.[62] Because of the limited number of first- and second-grade posts (eight in the Secretariat-Chancellery and five in the Security Council), the combination of proliferating central descent-group segments and

TABLE 2.4

Comparison of Descent Groups, 981–1069 and 1070–1146

981–1069			1070–1146		
Group Name	Total Officials	Ranks 1–2	Group Name	Total Officials	Ranks 1–2
Kyŏngju Ch'oe	7	4	Kyŏngwŏn Yi	24	11
Kyŏngju Kim	6	3	Haeju Ch'oe	12	7
P'yŏngsan Yu	5	2	Kyŏngju Kim	9	6
Kaesŏng Wang	3	2	Kangnŭng Kim	7	5
Yŏngch'ŏn Hwangbo	3	2	Kwangyang Kim	5	3
Ich'ŏn Sŏ	3	2	P'yŏngsan Pak	5	2
Ch'ungju Yu	3	2	P'ap'yŏng Yun	5	2
Iwangnyŏ Min	3	1	Tanju Han	5	1
Ansan Kim	2	2	Namp'yŏng Mun	4	3
Haeju Ch'oe	2	2	Chŏngan Im	4	3
Kwangyang Kim	2	2	Tongnae Chŏng	4	1
			Suju Yi	3	3
			Ch'ogye Chŏng	3	2
			Suju Ch'oe	3	2
			Ch'ŏngju Han	3	1
			Yŏnggwang Kim	2	2
			Kongam Hŏ	2	2
			Chŏngju Yu	2	2
Totals: 11 groups	39	24	18 groups	102	58
All Officials: 56 groups	352	97	75 groups	788	138

continuously arriving new blood created tremendous competitive pressures in the civil branch.[63] These pressures, especially the tension between older and newer groups, were an important factor in the political instability that led up to the military coup of 1170.[64]

THE GREAT DESCENT GROUPS IN THE LATE KORYŎ

There has been a general assumption that the military coup of 1170, which purged many civil officials, resulted in major restructuring of the Koryŏ ruling stratum. Advocates of the internal development theory argue that the rise of the military to power in post-1170 Korea entailed the destruction, as a group, of the civil aristocracy that had dominated the central regime in the eleventh and twelfth centuries. According to Pyŏn T'ae-sŏp, the real significance of the military coup as a historical turning point "lies in the transformation of the status system that was the foundation of the Koryŏ dynasty and in the destruction of the aristocratic [*kwijok*] order."[65] This view holds that the military coup of 1170 was carried out by a military branch of mixed social origins, resentful of its second-class stature and incensed at the arrogance of civil officials, that erupted to slaughter many civil aristocrats and drive many more into hiding. After the generals were firmly in power, however, they discovered that they needed administrative experience and proceeded to fill that need by recruiting in large numbers a group assumed to have been largely frozen out during the early Koryŏ era, the *hyangni*.[66]

Edward J. Shultz has shown, however, that there was substantial continuity in the ruling stratum between pre- and post-military-coup Koryŏ. Officials of the military branch, due to their activities in suppressing the rebellions that broke out in the late eleventh and early twelfth centuries, had begun to take a more active political role several decades prior to the 1170 coup. Furthermore, because of their alliances with the military, many old civil aristocrat descent groups managed to survive and even prosper under the military. The Chŏngan Im, for example, continued to provide royal consorts throughout much of the military period, and members of such notable civil-official descent groups as the P'ap'yŏng Yun, Kyŏngju Kim, Kyŏngwŏn Yi, and Namp'yŏng Mun continued to hold high offices.[67] Recruitment of new civil talent from the provinces through the government service examinations, generally seen as a phenomenon of the post-1170 period, also was actually a continuation of pre-1170 practices. The persistence of civil official descent groups and the continuation of established patterns of recruitment is prima facie evidence that the coup, while shifting power from the civil to the military branch, did not destroy the established sociopolitical order.

Furthermore, there is, in contradiction to the conventional view, considerable evidence that the military rulers sought to bolster their status and prestige by allying themselves with elements of the civil aristocracy. Not only did the Ch'oe military rulers continue to promote men of civil branch origins to high positions, but they actively sought out old official descent groups, including the Chŏngan Im and the Kyŏngju Kim, as marriage partners.[68] This suggests that the new military rulers of Korea needed to win the support and cooperation of the great civil official descent groups in order to rule the country.

The survival of the old civil aristocracy was in part due to their practical administrative skills, but it was also clearly a consequence of the social pres-

TABLE 2.5

Descent Structure of the Central Bureaucracy, 1260–1392

Total known officials	2,660
Officials of known descent	1,303 (49%)
Total known *chaech'u*	800
Chaech'u of known descent	455 (57%)
Total descent groups	199
Groups with only one known official	108 (54%)
Most powerful descent groups*	22
Officials from most powerful descent groups	375 (14%)
Chaech'u from most powerful descent groups	187 (23%)

* Ten Groups with ten or more total officials or six or more
chaech'u/noble titleholders

tige they enjoyed. As a group, however, they had been displaced as the supreme political decision makers by the military and found themselves relegated largely to administrative functions as they bided their time, awaiting a chance to reassert their traditional political prerogatives.

Although many of the old civil-aristocrat descent groups managed to survive, and even prosper, during the century of military rule, the three decades of Mongol invasion and the overthrow of the Ch'oe house in 1258 provided opportunities for new elements to rise and alter significantly the makeup and nature of the central bureaucracy. Indeed, conventional interpretations depict the late Koryŏ elites as being composed of military elements that first rose after the 1170 coup, protegés of the Mongols, and a few descendants of old civil aristocrats.

I will test this proposition by examining the structure and social composition of the late Koryŏ bureaucracy and by inquiring into the functioning of the bureaucracy's means of recruitment, career patterns, and the *kwŏnmun sejok/sadaebu* issue.

The Late Koryŏ Central Bureaucracy

The "Annals" of the *Koryŏsa* mention 2,660 individuals who held office in the central government between 1260 and 1392, as seen in table 2.5. Although we have considerably more data for the late Koryŏ (2,660 officials in 132 years, as opposed to 1,140 for 165 years in the early Koryŏ), our known officeholders still represent only a small proportion of the total central bureaucracy.[69] Furthermore, table 2.5 shows that, as for the early Koryŏ, the *Koryŏsa* almost totally neglects lower-level officials in favor of those in the top ranks.[70] Once again, the higher levels of the bureaucracy hold out the greatest promise for analysis.

Table 2.5 shows that the overall descent-group structure of the late Koryŏ bureaucracy was very similar to that of the early Koryŏ. There was fairly broad representation, with 199 descent groups known to have placed men in official positions. Although the increase in the number of such groups—from 87 in the early Koryŏ to 199 in the late Koryŏ—seems to indicate much broader participation, this may simply reflect better source materials for the later period. At any rate, 108 (54 percent) of those descent groups had only one identified official, whereas the most powerful 22 (11 percent) (detailed in table 6) accounted for 14 percent of all officials and 23 percent of *chaech'u.* In other terms, these 22 descent groups, which again represent less than 1 percent of all Koryŏ elite descent groups, accounted for 14 percent of all known late Koryŏ officials and nearly one-fourth of all *chaech'u.* As in the early Koryŏ, we see a relatively small number of descent groups holding a dominant position in the central bureaucracy.

Table 2.6 lists the 22 most powerful official descent groups, those having 10 or more officials or six or more *chaech'u,* of the late Koryŏ.[71] The number of *chaech'u* posts gradually increased throughout the late Koryŏ. The figures in the *Koryŏsa* specified for various times suggest an approximate working average of 50 *chaech'u* posts for the late Koryŏ period as a whole. Based on an average tenure in *chaech'u* posts of 8.7 years,[72] I estimate that 758 men held *chaech'u* posts between 1260 and 1392. Our 689 known men thus account for 91 percent of all *chaech'u,* meaning that we should be able to get a fairly reliable picture of the upper ranks of the late Koryŏ bureaucracy.

Included in the 689 *chaech'u* are two other categories of status holders that were important in the late Koryŏ: noble titleholders and military commanders-in-chief. Noble titles, such as *kong* ("duke," Ch. *kung*), *hu* ("marquis," Ch. *hou*), or *paek* ("count," Ch. *po*), were usually given after long and distinguished service in the government. There are, however, 34 men with noble titles who are not recorded in the histories as having held *chaech'u* posts. Whether they ever actually held such posts is unclear, but because noble titleholders are known to have frequently participated in court politics, it would seem prudent to include these men among the political elite. There are an additional 34 men in commander-in-chief military posts who do not appear in the histories as

TABLE 2.6
Most Powerful Descent Groups of the Late Koryŏ

Descent Group	Total Officials	Chaech'u
Namyang Hong	28	18
Kwang San Kim	27	16
Kaesŏng Wang	25	9
Kyŏngju Yi	24	6
Andong Kwŏn	22	12
Sŏngju Yi	21	12
Kongam Hŏ	19	7
Hwangnyŏ Min	18	7
P'ap'yŏng Yun	18	9
P'yŏngyang Cho	17	8
Andong Kim	17	11
Chŏnju Ch'oe	16	7
Sunhŭng An	15	9
Ch'ŏngju Han	15	7
Tanyang U	14	5
Chuksan Pak	13	6
Kyŏngju Kim	13	7
Munhwa Yu	12	6
Onyang Kim	12	8
Kyŏngju Ch'oe	11	3
Wŏnju Wŏn	10	7
P'yŏnggang Ch'ae	8	7
Total	375	187

chaech'u. The continuous security crises (particularly the Red Turban invasions and the Wako raids) of the mid- and late-fourteenth century endowed the military branch with greater than usual importance. This was reflected in the emergence of new levels of command, both in the center under the Samgunbu (Consolidated Army Command) and in the field under various commanders-in-chief (*to chihwi* or *to anmu sa*). Since these posts were usually held concurrently by *chaech'u,* it seems appropriate to include these commanders in the *chaech'u.*

The descent groups in table 2.6 show strong continuity with the early Koryŏ. Six of the 22 leading groups were among the most powerful of the early Koryŏ:

the Kyŏngju Kim, Kyŏngju Ch'oe, P'ap'yŏng Yun, Hwangnyŏ Min, Ch'ŏngju
Han, and Kongam Hŏ; the Kaesŏng Wang (as members of the royal family)
can perhaps also be included. Nine others—the Munhwa Yu, Namyang Hong,
Chŏnju Ch'oe, Chuksan Pak, Andong Kim, Andong Kwŏn, Kyŏngju Yi, Wŏnju
Wŏn, and Sŏngju Yi—also are known to have had members in high office
during the early Koryŏ. Several of the most powerful early Koryŏ descent
groups that do not appear in table 2.6—including the Kyŏngwŏn Yi, Ich'ŏn
Sŏ, and Namp'yŏng Mun—maintained a viable, if somewhat diminished, presence in the late Koryŏ bureaucracy.[73] Furthermore, the declining fortunes of
the great early Koryŏ descent groups not in table 2.6 appear to have more to
do with factional politics and fertility than with fundamental restructuring
of ruling elites. The Kyŏngwŏn Yi descent group was already in decline as a
consequence of the political infighting of the early twelfth century, well before
the military coup of 1170, and, as Yi Su-gŏn has pointed out, the Tanju Han,
which continued to prosper under the military, came to an end when Han
Kwang-yŏn (d. 1267) died without producing any sons.[74] The evidence as a
whole suggests substantial continuity in the ruling elite between the early and
late Koryŏ.[75]

The actual situation, unfortunately, is not so simple. In a number of descent
groups—such as the Kyŏngju Yi, Kyŏngju Ch'oe, Ch'ŏngju Han, Sŏngju Yi,
Andong Kim, and Andong Kwŏn—prominent late Koryŏ members appear not
to have been directly descended from their putative early Koryŏ kin. We also
know that by the late Koryŏ some of the numerically large descent groups
were subdividing into branches (*p'a*) that were only remotely related to each
other. Thus, we cannot automatically assume continuity between the late and
early Koryŏ simply on the basis of descent groups. We must instead verify
blood ties among the top-ranking officials of the two periods.

Although genealogies—the earliest of which date from the fifteenth century—
of the historically prominent (and sometimes not-so-prominent) Korean
descent groups invariably depict an unbroken line of high office holders from
the early Koryŏ on, the genealogies also tend to depict descent groups as
single, direct lines of patrilineal descent during the Koryŏ, which subdivided
into several branch lines only after the rise of the Chosŏn. Our confidence in
genealogies is undermined, however, by the existence of a number of officials
clearly identified in contemporaneous sources as belonging to certain descent
groups who are nowhere to be found in the genealogies. Furthermore, certain
descent groups are known to have included multiple segments during the Koryŏ
dynasty, typically bifurcating into local and capital-based segments.[76] The unre-
liability of genealogies, along with the limited nature of information in the

dynastic histories, makes it difficult, if not impossible, to reconstruct the ancestry of most late Koryŏ notables, even when we know their descent groups. Despite these difficulties, for a number of our 22 descent groups ancestry of men in central official posts can be traced by supplementing information in the *Koryŏsa* with biographical data from tombstone inscriptions and other primary sources, such as recently uncovered old documents (*komunsŏ*).

The top 22 late Koryŏ descent groups can be broken down into two types, based on their initial appearance in the central bureaucracy. The first is made up of 11 descent groups with segments that first emerged as officeholders prior to the military coup of 1170. Nine of these have direct lines of paternal descent that continuously held central offices beginning in the early Koryŏ: the P'ap'yŏng Yun, Munhwa Yu, Hwangnyŏ Min, Kongam Hŏ, Kyŏngju Kim, Chŏnju Ch'oe, Chuksan Pak, Kaesŏng Wang, and P'yŏnggang Ch'ae. In six of these cases all members who held high office in the late Koryŏ were direct descendants of one prominent official of the early Koryŏ.[77] In the other three cases of demonstrable continuous office holding—the Chuksan Pak, Kyŏngju Kim, and P'yŏnggang Ch'ae—high-ranking late Koryŏ members belonged to two or more segments, one traceable to early Koryŏ ancestors and another appearing to originate after 1170.[78] The other two descent groups—the Namyang Hong and Wŏnju Wŏn—have ancestry traceable to the early Koryŏ, but their continuous presence in the central bureaucracy cannot be verified for all generations.[79] Thus half of the top 22 late Koryŏ descent groups can be traced back to premilitary coup Koryŏ. It is interesting to note that seven of these 11 groups were on King Ch'ungsŏn's list of great *chaesang* (*chaech'u*) families that were considered prestigious enough to marry with the royal family.[80] These 11 descent groups suggest a remarkable degree of continuity in bloodlines at the top levels of the central bureaucracy, through such major upheavals as the military coup and the Mongol invasions, for a period of over three centuries.

The second type is composed of the 11 prominent late Koryŏ descent groups whose direct ancestors cannot be found in the early Koryŏ central bureaucracy. These seem to have been just as powerful as the older descent groups: whereas the older groups accounted for a total of 180 officials in the late Koryŏ, with 84 *chaech'u*, the newer descent ones tallied 195, with 103 *chaech'u*.

Like the older descent groups, these later arrivals were composed of one or more segments descended from prominent individuals. Six of the nine newer groups had single segments, as seen in the case of the P'yŏngyang Cho, all of whose members in office were descended from Cho In-gyu.[81] The remaining three comprehended two or more segments whose relationships with each other are not clear, as seen for example in the three segments found in the Kwangsan Kim.[82] At any rate, it is evident that the new descent groups, like their older counterparts, achieved prominence in the bureaucracy through individual segments that produced generation after generation of high-ranking officials.

Marriage patterns represent yet another area of similarity between the newer and older descent groups. Like the great descent groups of earlier times and their late Koryŏ descendants in the Namyang Hong,[83] Kongam Hŏ,[84] and Kyŏngju Kim,[85] the new descent groups entered into marriage relations with the royal family. The *Koryŏsa* biographies show, for example, that women from the Kyŏngju Yi,[86] P'yŏngyang Cho,[87] and the Andong Kwŏn[88] became royal consorts. In addition to marrying into the royal family, the new descent groups intermarried closely with older descent groups and with each other. The Kyŏngju Yi, for example, married five times with the Andong Kwŏn, four times each with the Munhwa Yu and Ch'ŏngju Han, three times each with the P'ap'yŏng Yun and P'yŏngyang Cho, and twice each with the Hwangnyŏ Min and Sunhŭng An. The Sunhŭng An and Tanyang U were also part of this closely intermarried group: the Sunhŭng An entered into marriage relations twice each with the Kwangsan Kim, Kyŏongju Yi, and P'yŏngyang Cho and once with the Wŏnju Wŏn, while the Tanyang U joined itself with such descent groups as the Kyŏngju Kim, Chuksan Pak, Andong Kwŏn, Chŏnju Ch'oe, and even the royal family.[89]

This treatment of descent groups has focused on paternal lines because that is the form in which descent is depicted in the *Koryŏsa* biographies and tombstone inscriptions. We know that Koreans of the Koryŏ and early Chosŏn periods also traced descent on the female side, as seen in the structure of early Chosŏn genealogies such as those of the Andong Kwŏn and Munhwa Yu.[90] Tracing of descent along female as well as male lines in the Koryŏ period is reflected most concretely in the scope of application of the *ŭm* protection privilege, which allowed higher ranking officials to have relatives appointed to office. In the Koryŏ, normally the *ŭm* was allowed not only for sons and grandsons (sons' sons), but also for the sons of daughters and granddaughters, as well as for sons-in-law and nephews (sisters' sons).[91] Application of the *ŭm* privilege to men related to the benefactor only through his female relatives (daughters and sisters) shows clearly that maternal relatives were an integral part of the functional family unit of Koryŏ elites.

A source from the early fourteenth century allows us to reconstruct maternal ancestry—the household register (*hogu tanja*) of the Kwangsan Kim. The most common primary sources for ancestry in the Koryŏ are tombstone inscriptions, which typically list three or more ancestors in the male line but limit mention of the female side to only the fathers of the decedent's mother and wife. In contrast, this household register lists three generations of the mother's male ancestors and, more importantly, also the mother's mother and maternal grandfather. This allows us to recover maternal ancestry to a degree not possible with other sources. Analysis of these maternal lines can give us a better sense of the extent to which Koryŏ elite descent groups were intermarried.

The wives of Kwangsan Kim men shown in the register come from the following descent groups: the Nŭngsŏng Cho (daughter of Cho Si-jŏ, early thirteenth-century military official,[92] Sunhŭng An (An Hyang's granddaughter), Andong Kwŏn (Kwŏn Chun's daughter), Wŏnju Wŏn (Wŏn Kwan's daughter), Chuksan Pak (Pak Wŏn's daughter), and Namyang Hong (Hong Chaban's great-granddaughter). The mothers of these wives came from the Hadong Chŏng, Andong Kim (Kim Pang-gyŏng's daughter), Namyang Hong (Hong Kyu's daughter), Yŏnan Yi, and Kwangju Yi. These descent groups were prominent in the central bureaucracy during the late Koryŏ period, and six are among the 22 great official descent groups of the late Koryŏ. Thus when we look at the central official class from a point of view that takes into consideration maternal descent, we find the great descent groups to be even more closely bound by marriage ties than we can see by examining simply paternal lines.

The Kwangsan Kim household register's depiction of ties between the Kwangsan Kim and Namyang Hong also allows us a fascinating glimpse into the close interweaving of great descent groups through marriage. Kim Kwang-ni's wife was a Wŏnju Wŏn, and her mother was a Namyang Hong, the daughter of Hong Kyu; Kim Kwang-ni's daughter in turn married Pak Tŏng-nyong of Chuksan, whose mother was also a Namyang Hong, the daughter of Hong Kyŏng (Hong Kyu's nephew), while Kwang-ni's brother Yŏng-ni also married a Namyang Hong, the granddaughter of Hong Kyŏng. It is not difficult to imagine how these intertwining marriage relations created, in effect, a largely closed social stratum, much like that seen in the great descent groups of the early Koryŏ.

The evidence we have reviewed indicates a strong degree of continuity between the early and late Koryŏ in the upper stratum of the central bureaucracy. Several prominent descent groups maintained a continuous presence in office since the early Koryŏ. Furthermore, groups in the late Koryŏ intermarried with the older groups and conformed to the established pattern of hereditary access to power through one or more segments. It seems safe to say that the newer descent groups did not constitute a new, qualitatively different social element. On the contrary, they appear to be new recruits to the old central official establishment.

Recruitment

Before we can draw more definitive conclusions about the nature of the late Koryŏ central bureaucracy, we should consider how the men who held posts in the dynastic government acquired their offices and by what route they advanced to the top, as well as whether significant differences exist between the old and new descent groups in the means used to gain and keep power.

Looking first at the issue of branch affiliations, we find that the older descent groups were originally of civil-branch origins and that they continued to prefer civil offices throughout the late Koryŏ.[93] Four of the five new descent groups—the Kwangsan Kim, Andong Kim, Andon Kwŏn and Ŏnyang Kim—that first appeared in the central bureaucracy during the military era, initially rose to prominence through the military branch.[94] As Yi Su-gŏn has noted, however, after the fall of the military all switched over to the civil branch to maintain their power.[95] The other seven descent groups—the Ch'ŏngju Han, P'yŏngyang Cho, Tanyang U, Kyŏngju Yi, Kyŏngju Ch'oe, Sŏngju Yi, and Sunhŭng An—that rose to prominence after the fall of the military regime all did so through the civil branch, although the P'yŏngyang Cho did maintain a presence in the military branch.[96] The P'yŏngyang Cho is the only one of the top 22 descent groups that appears to have gained power through connections with the Mongols.[97]

Domination of the government by the civil branch in the late Koryŏ does not appear to have been as complete as in the early Koryŏ. The discriminatory grade structure of the early Koryŏ, which limited military officials to the third grade and below and thus precluded a military official from becoming a *chaech'u* unless he changed over to the civil branch, was maintained throughout the late Koryŏ, but it was more common for prominent military officials to switch to the civil branch and rise to *chaech'u* posts in the late Koryŏ. Examples include such famous men as Ch'oe Yŏng, Im Kyŏn-mi, and Yi Sŏng-gye.[98] Nonetheless, despite the continuing military emergencies of the fourteenth century, only 11 percent (79 of 689) of late Koryŏ *chaech'u* began their official careers in the military branch. On the whole, the evidence indicates that service in the civil branch of the bureaucracy was still the preferred route to power and prestige, just as it had been in the early Koryŏ.

The primary means of gaining entry to the central bureaucracy in the late Koryŏ period continued to be the examination system and the *ŭm* system. An inquiry into these should give us a better understanding of the nature of the late Koryŏ central official class and of how the great descent groups maintained themselves in power.

The literary examination was held 64 times during the 132 years from 1260 to 1392 (nearly once every two years), producing 2,024 graduates. During the same period the classics examination was held 13 times, yielding 31 graduates. Thus we have a total of 2,055 graduates of higher civil service examinations in the late Koryŏ. This means examination graduates would have accounted for less than 5 percent of our estimate of 52,800 individual officials. That estimate is, however, based on both branches; if we exclude the military branch, the estimated number (following the same criteria as before) of individual civil officeholders in the late Koryŏ becomes 6,336, and our 2,055 higher civil-service examination graduates would account for roughly one-third of civil officials.

As in the case of the early Koryŏ, the *Koryŏsa* "Monograph on Recruitment" gives only total numbers of graduates and the name of the top scoring passer of each examination. Although the Chosŏn dynasty *Kukcho pangmok* (Roster of examination graduates) includes what appear to be complete rosters of examination graduates for the last 30 years of the Koryŏ dynasty, we are still able to identify about 10 percent of late Koryŏ examination graduates. The other sources to which we can turn—such as the *Koryŏsa* biographies, tombstone inscriptions, and literary collections—allow us to fill in the picture somewhat. Combined with other sections of the *Koryŏsa* and the *Kukcho pangmok*, they allow us to identify 43 percent (886) of the 2,055 graduates of the higher examinations from the reign of Wŏnjong to the end of the dynasty.

What, then, can this data tell us of our 22 top descent groups? How important was the examination system in maintaining them in power? Was there any difference between our old and new descent groups?

Table 2.7 shows that the top 22 official descent groups account for 167 officials who are known to have successfully passed the government service examination. The 167 examination passers represent approximately 44 percent of the 375 officials belonging to the top 22 descent groups. This is a much higher proportion than that of examination passers in the bureaucracy at large (one-third) and suggests that the great descent groups of the late Koryŏ relied to a relatively high degree on the government service examinations to maintain themselves in power.

On the basis of the data in table 2.7, it appears that the newer descent groups made greater use of the examination system than did the older groups. Slightly over half (102/195) of officials from the newer descent groups are

TABLE 2.7

Examination-Graduate Officials, 1260–1392

Descent Group	Graduates	Descent Group	Graduates
Kyŏngju Yi	16	Kyŏngju Kim	7
Sunhŭng An	14	Ch'ŏngju Han	7
Hwangnyŏ Min	13	Namyang Hong	7
Kwangsan Kim	12	Chŏnju Ch'oe	6
Andong Kwŏn	11	Chuksan Pak	4
Sŏngju Yi	11	Munhwa Yu	3
Kongam Hŏ	11	Kyŏngju Ch'oe	3
Tanyang U	10	Wŏnju Wŏn	3
Andong Kim	9	Kaesŏng Wang	2
P'ap'yŏng Yun	7	P'yŏnggang Ch'ae	2
P'yŏngyang Cho	7	Ŏnyang Kim	2

SOURCE: Data from Pak Yong-un, *Koryŏ sidae ŭmsŏje wa kwagŏje yŏn'gu*, 328–557. Only men who can be confirmed as officeholders are included.

known to have passed the examinations, as compared to slightly over one-third (65/180) of those from the older descent groups, although the latter rises to 41 percent if we exclude the royal family, which produced only two examination passers among its 25 officials. Newer descent groups particularly prominent in the examination system included the Sunhŭng An, with 14 examination passers out of 15 officials, and the Tanyang U, with ten examination passers out of 14 officials. On the other hand, the descent group with the second highest proportion of examination graduates among its officials was the older descent group of the Hwangnyŏ Min, with 13 of 18 officials passing the examinations, while the Kongam Hŏ also registered a high proportion of examination graduates, with 11 out of 19. Thus while the newer descent groups showed a somewhat greater tendency to pass the examinations, descent groups of both types made extensive use of the examination system to maintain themselves.

As for the early Koryŏ, data on the protection system is meager. Although the frequency with which *ŭm* appointments were given would suggest that large numbers of men benefited, only 61 *ŭm* recipients can be identified for the late Koryŏ, accounting for just 2 percent of our 2,660 known officials. A similar percentage of known protection appointees prevails in *chaech'u*-level officials (including nobles and military commanders-in-chief): 26 out of 789, or roughly 3 percent. Nineteen of these 26 *chaech'u*-level *ŭm* beneficiaries belong to our top 22 descent groups, accounting for slightly over 10 percent of the 179 top-ranking officials from those groups. Once again, we do not know whether the higher percentage indicates heavy reliance on the protection system, or whether it merely reflects better source materials. Seven of the top 22 descent groups had no known protection beneficiary *chaech'u*. On the other hand, two—the Andong Kim and Wŏnju Wŏn—had three each, while the P'yŏngyang Cho and Ŏnyang Kim had two each. Interestingly, three of the descent groups that made the widest use of the examinations—the Sunhŭng An, Andong Kwŏn, and Sŏngyu Yi—also used the protection system, each having one *chaech'u* who first entered the bureaucracy through the *ŭm* privilege.

The paucity of information on beneficiaries of protection appointments makes it difficult to assess with certainty the extent to which late Koryŏ elites used the protection system, but it seems likely that it was an important means for descent groups to perpetuate themselves in office. As in the early Koryŏ, there was a tendency for men with *ŭm* appointments to sit for the government service examinations. Sixteen of the 61 identified late Koryŏ beneficiaries of the protection privilege are known to have subsequently taken and passed the examinations. Included in these 16 are eight *chaech'u* from the top 22 clans.[99] The willingness of these already successful entrants into the bureaucracy to subject themselves to the rigors of the examination process suggests, as in the early Koryŏ, that examination graduates enjoyed greater prestige than men who entered the bureaucracy through other means.

Unlike the early Koryŏ, for the late Koryŏ we have at least scattered fragments of evidence that members of prominent descent groups entered the regular bureaucracy through clerical, guard, and technical posts. An Hyang's father, for example, is said to have originally been a physician before rising to a senior third-grade post,[100] while one member of the Ŏnyang Kim began service as a palace attendant for King Kongmin before eventually rising to a senior second-grade post,[101] and, of course, there was King Kongmin's notorious youth guard (*chajewi*), filled by the young sons of such great descent groups as the Namyang Hong.[102]

Evidence regarding avenues of recruitment suggests that the prominent descent groups of the late Koryŏ used a wide variety of means to reproduce themselves. The examination system appears to have been the most important and prestigious. This, of course, would be a natural corollary to the restoration of power to the civil branch, but it also implies, as for the early Koryŏ, a meritocratic bent that modified an otherwise strongly ascriptive social order.

Career Patterns

One additional aspect of the late Koryŏ bureaucracy that bears investigation
is career patterns. We have already seen that officials of the early Koryŏ typically followed a regular route of advancement that took them from 20 to 30
or more years to reach *chaech'u* posts. As was the case in the early Koryŏ, the
dynastic histories do not provide sufficient information for us to reconstruct
official careers. However, a comparatively large number of detailed tombstone
inscriptions for late Koryŏ officials exist. There are 20 late Koryŏ inscriptions
that contain substantial information about the decedent's official career.
Eleven of these men belonged to our top 22 descent groups; the other nine
also belonged to descent groups that were well-represented in the dynastic government. Analysis of these men's careers may yield insight into the extent of
bureaucratic procedure in the late Koryŏ.

Fifteen of these 20 men rose to hold first- and second-grade *chaech'u* posts;
the remaining five rose to third-grade positions. Thirteen rose through the civil
branch[103] and seven through the military branch.[104] Fourteen were examination graduates (including one military branch official), seven were protection
appointees (including four who later passed the examinations), one began his
career as a common soldier (despite comparatively illustrious descent-group
origins), and three had unspecified means of entry.[105]

The generally accepted view of the late Koryŏ as a corrupt aristocratic order
implies that powerful descent groups were able to manipulate the official personnel system at will. Evidence of this can be expected to be found, for example, in cases where men with illustrious descent group backgrounds but little
or no practical experience were able to achieve high position at young ages and
where influential men were able to leapfrog their way up the career ladder.

The military branch, with its opportunities for quick promotions through
service in the field and its lack of educational requirements, would seem to
have offered the best avenue for rapid advancement. The seven men who rose
through the military branch seem to present something of a mixed bag. One
case which seems to suggest social mobility is that of Chŏng In-gyŏng of
Ch'ŏngju, who began his service as a common soldier. His military exploits
were rewarded with appointment to a junior ninth-grade military official post,
from which he eventually rose to hold a series of junior second-grade *chaech'u*
posts before retiring. Chŏng's case, however, is not as unusual as it may seem,
since both his father and maternal grandfather had held office in the central
bureaucracy.[106] Another interesting case is that of Cho Yŏn-su of P'yŏngyang.
Cho's first office was an *ŭm* appointment to a juvenile post. He later moved

over to the military branch, where he became a junior ninth-grade recorder (*noksa*). But after passing the civil service examination at the age of seventeen he went back to the military branch where, at 20 he was given a senior fourth-grade appointment as general. After this he held a variety of military and civil literary posts, often concurrently, before achieving *chaech'u* rank at 31.[107] Cho Yŏn-su, with his quick rise to the top and his military branch affiliation, seems to substantiate the conventional view of the late Koryŏ aristocracy, but Cho's was an exceptional case.

The other five military men started from low-ranking posts and rose gradually through the military branch, receiving concurrent appointments to civil branch posts as they neared the top of the military ranks and, in all but two cases, eventually gaining *chaech'u* appointments. A typical example is Wŏn Sŏn-ji of the predominantly civil Wŏnju Wŏn descent group, who began his career with a protection appointment to a civil-branch post in the provinces. At the age of 17 he moved over to the military branch, where he received a senior eighth-grade appointment. At 27 he had risen to the senior sixth grade, and at 28 he was made an acting (*sŏp*) senior fourth-grade general. The next year he was given a junior third-grade civil appointment in the Security Council. Sometime after the age of 44, he rose to hold a junior second-grade *chaech'u* post concurrent with the post of grand general.[108] Despite the prestige of Wŏn's descent group and his youthful beginnings as a protection beneficiary, it ultimately took him nearly 30 years to rise to a *chaech'u* post. The careers of Wŏn and the other four military men seem to represent a bureaucratically ordered route of advancement.

The 13 men who rose through the civil branch also seem to have followed regular routes to the top. Although five held official posts of some sort prior to passing the examinations, all followed one of two general paths of advancement afterward. The ages at which they passed the examinations ranged from 17 to 28, with the average being 23. All the new examination passers started off with low-ranking literary posts, usually in the Royal Confucian Academy, Office of Historians, or other literary offices such as the Royal Archives (Pisŏsŏng). After several years of such service their paths diverged. The most common path, taken by ten of these men, led to service at low- and mid-ranking civil posts in the provinces for one to four tours of duty before they were recalled to the capital to serve in mid-ranking posts as censors, remonstrance officials, or scholars prior to appointment to *chaech'u* positions.[109] Men taking this route included both the scions of such great late Koryŏ descent groups as the Andong Kim, Wŏnju Wŏn, and Ŏnyang Kim and men of less prominent groups, such as the Chŏnŭi Yi and Ŭisŏng Kim.

Typical of this career path is the experience of Kim Pyŏng of Ŏnyang, who passed the examination in 1268 at the age of 21. The next year he was given the seventh-grade post of Royal Confucian Academy scholar, and the year after he was transferred to another seventh-grade post, before rising to a senior fifth-grade post in the Board of Rites, at which time he accompanied the crown prince to the Mongol court in 1271. After his return from China he held a variety of local posts before being appointed to a third-grade post at the age of 38 in 1285. Subsequently he filled a number of third-grade slots in the Security Council, the Office of the Inspector General, and various scholarly agencies before gaining appointment to a *chaech'u* post in 1299, the year he died at the age of 53.[110]

Another example of this career path comes from a less illustrious descent group: Kim Tan of Ŭisŏng, who passed the examination in 1260 at age 26 while holding a clerical post. In 1266 he was given a ninth-grade post in the Office of Historians, followed by a seventh-grade post in the Hallim Academy in 1268. Two years later he was posted to a mid-ranking local position in Kŭmju for one year, before being brought back to the capital to serve as a senior fifth-grade official in the Board of Rites. In 1273, at the age of 39, he was transferred to a post in the Office of the Inspector General, and later that year was given a concurrent appointment as provincial inspector. Two years later he rose to a fourth-grade post before running afoul of some powerful enemies and being forced out of office for a year. In 1276 he was recalled to the capital to fill a fourth-grade slot in the Royal Confucian Academy, where he served until he experienced another reversal of fortunes and was again forced out of office in 1278. He was not recalled until 1288, when, at the age of 54, he was restored to his former position. He held several third-grade scholarly positions thereafter, until finally being promoted to *chaech'u* in 1296, 36 years after passing the examinations. The next year he resigned due to ill health, and died eight years later.[111]

The other career path was taken by Yi Chon-bi (early name Yi In-sŏng) of Kosŏng, Hŏ Kong of Kongam, and Kwŏn Pu of Andong.[112] Men on this route to the top did not hold any local posts, remaining instead in the capital for their entire careers. Typical of this career track is Kwŏn Pu, who passed the examination in 1279 at the age of 20 while holding a clerical position. He then moved to a ninth-grade academician post in the Royal Confucian Academy, after which he held a seventh-or eighth-grade (rank not certain) scholar post. He next gained appointment to a sixth-grade post in the combined Secretariat-Chancellery, followed by promotion to a fifth-grade post in the same agency. In his late thirties and forties he held third-grade posts in two academic offices before finally becoming a *chaech'u* at the age of 50. He served another decade in various *chaech'u* posts and finally rose to the highest position in the government in 1320, at the age of 61.[113] Why Kwŏn did not serve in any local positions is a matter of speculation; perhaps it was because of his outstanding literary and scholarly abilities. The same may hold true for Hŏ Kong and Yi Chon-bi, both also renowned for their learning.

In short, the career patterns of these 20 officials—from both military and civil branches, from both prominent and not so prominent family backgrounds—indicate that whatever role heredity or descent-group stature may have played in facilitating entry to the bureaucracy, once men were in office they were subject to bureaucratic procedures of service and promotion. Only one of 20 rose to the top of the bureaucracy at an unusually early age; all had to start at or near the bottom and work their way up the ladder, putting in their time in low- and mid-ranking positions on the way. Descent-group origins may have been a prerequisite for entry into the bureaucracy, but heredity alone did not guarantee a quick and certain rise to the top.

If climbing the bureaucratic ladder was the way to achieve high office in the late Koryŏ, what then do we make of the many men holding noble titles who are known to have participated in dynastic political decision making?[114] I have been able to identify 197 men, exclusive of the royal family, who held noble titles in the late Koryŏ. Over 80 percent of these titles appear to have been granted after long service in the dynastic government. For example, the *Koryŏsa* first refers to Yi Saek by the noble title Lord of Hansan (Hansan Kun) in 1377, after he had served in the central bureaucracy for over 24 years and had held *chaech'u* posts for six.[115] Hong Ŏn-bak was first called by the noble title Lord of Namyang in 1353, again after more than 20 years of official service and several years of holding *chaech'u* posts.[116]

Of 34 noble title holders who do not seem to have earned their titles through long service in the dynastic government, eight were foreigners and six were eunuchs, leaving only 20—roughly 10 percent of all known noble title holders—for whom we cannot determine the source of their elevated status. While this suggests the existence of a nobility independent of service to the dynastic government, several of these 20 men, such as Hŏ Chong of Kongam and Cho Ch'ung-sin of P'yŏngyang, belong to prominent descent-group segments and clearly owe their titles to their forebears' service to the dynasty. That, plus the fact that over 80 percent of known noble title holders received their titles only after holding office for long periods of time, leads me to believe that in the late Koryŏ noble titles generally were given to reward men for their service in the government and that the titled nobility existed primarily as an adjunct to the central bureaucracy.

The Kwŏnmun Sejok/Sadaebu *Issue*

Twentieth-century scholars, drawing on the terminology used by late thirteenth- and fourteenth-century reformers, usually refer to the dominant social group of the late Koryŏ by the name *kwŏnmun sejok* ("powerful houses and hereditary families" or "powerful houses and strong families," depending on the Chinese character used for *se*). This appellation is a generic for a variety of similar terms: *kwŏnmun sega* (same meanings as *kwŏnmun sejok*), *kwŏnsega* (powerful and strong families), and *kwŏnsin* (powerful officials). *Kwŏnmun sejok* are usually juxtaposed against *sadaebu* (scholar-officials), a term that also first came into wide usage in the late thirteenth and fourteenth centuries and which is generally believed to mark the rise of a new social element.

A leading spokesperson for this interpretation is Yi U-sŏng, who states: "As [Pak Chi-wŏn] says, 'the scholar is called *sa* and the administrator is called *taebu.*' The *sadaebu* were scholar-officials and it was this newly rising [*sinhŭng*] class of scholar-officials that established a political and social base in the late Koryŏ and became the main force in the founding of the Chosŏn dynasty."[117] Yi U-sŏng links the advent of the term *sadaebu* with what he believed was the initial appearance in the central bureaucracy of men of *hyangni* backgrounds who rose through the examination system and were "skilled at both letters and administration" (*nŭngmun nŭngni*). We have already seen, however, that the recruitment of *hyangni* through the examination system occurred regularly throughout the Koryŏ dynasty. Furthermore, we have seen that is it very difficult to distinguish between older and new members of the late Koryŏ central bureaucracy on the basis of means of recruitment, marriage patterns, or success in attaining high offices. All this casts doubt on whether the late Koryŏ bureaucracy can be seen as composed of two discrete social groups.

Kim Tang-t'aek, in an important recent study of the political conflict that arose between established official descent groups and men of humble origins, such as the slaves and eunuchs who were brought in and given high posts by King Ch'ungyŏl as a counterbalance to bureaucratic power, has demonstrated that the established central-official descent groups began to use such terms as *sadaebu* and *sajok* (Ch. *shih-tsu*) to distinguish themselves from new elements of low social origins. Kim concludes that the descent groups who called themselves *sajok* or *sadaebu* in the late Koryŏ were those who had been in power since early Koryŏ. The significance of the new terminology was that the rise of slaves and eunuchs in the Mongol period caused the official descent groups to redefine themselves as a social and political group in opposition to men of more humble origins.[118]

This brings into question the use of the term *kwŏnmun sejok* for the late Koryŏ ruling stratum. Twentieth-century historians, assuming that the term denoted the ruling class, conventionally assert that the Todang (*chaech'u* deliberative council) was dominated by the *kwŏnmun sejok.*[119] In fact, however, it was frequently the Todang that criticized the *kwŏnmun sejok,* as in 1345 when a Todang memorial attributed stipend shortages to excessive land amalgamation by the *kwŏnmun sega.*[120] Kim Kwang-ch'ŏl, in a thorough analysis of the use of the various terms subsumed under the catchall *kwŏnmun sejok,* has demonstrated that the words *kwŏnmun* and *sejok* (meaning "hereditary families") were almost never used together. Terms emphasizing power, such as *kwŏnmun, kwŏnsin,* and *kwŏnsega* (*se* meaning "power") were invariably used in a pejorative sense to indicate particular families or individuals, such as the Ch'oe dictators of the military era, whose arrogation of power violated the principle of power-sharing among the elites. On the other hand, terms indicating heredity, such as *sejok* or *sega* (using the Chinese character for "heredity"), were used for descent groups whose ancestors had held *chaech'u* posts. Kim Kwang-ch'ŏl's analysis suggests that much of the criticism directed towards *kwŏnmun* or *kwŏnsega* (using the character for "power") in the late Koryŏ was targeted not at the central bureaucracy as a whole, but either at individual members of the bureaucracy whose power and ambition exceeded acceptable norms or at powerful individuals who arose from outside the established descent groups of the central bureaucracy.[121]

The findings of Kim Tang-t'aek and Kim Kwang-ch'ŏl indicate the advent of nonaristocratic elements in the late Koryŏ, but they point out that these elements were not accepted by the established official descent groups. In essence, they support our conclusion that there was no significant alteration in the structure and makeup of the central aristocratic-bureaucratic establishment in the late Koryŏ period. I would, however, take Kim Tang-t'aek's conclusions one step further and point out that not only did the great official descent groups redefine themselves in the late Koryŏ, but the terms they used to do so—*sajok* and *sadaebu*—indicate that they had begun to see themselves as deriving their status primarily from family traditions of office holding in the central bureaucracy, rather than from their more remote forebears' positions as autonomous local strongmen.

At about this time the central aristocrats also began to refer to themselves as *yangban*. Yangban, which literally means the "two branches" (civil and military) of the central bureaucracy, was a natural appellation for members of the class whose primary source of power and status was a family tradition of holding office in the dynastic government. In this sense, the term seems freely interchangeable with *sadaebu* and *sajok*. Yi Sŏng-mu has noted that by the late Koryŏ the term *yangban*, which is usually applied only to elites of the Chosŏn period, no longer simply denoted officials of the two branches of the central government; it had become a term with wide social connotations. Yi quotes a late fourteenth-century letter from Chŏng Mong-ju introducing the wife of a certain official and discussing her admirable qualities: "Ch'oe Tam's wife's family are true *yangban*." This is a clear instance of pre-Chosŏn use of the term *yangban* to denote social status.[122] Further evidence that the term *yangban* connoted an elite stratum with a special sense of self can be found in a 1395 entry in the *Veritable Records*. In the seventh month of that year, the king ordered the Tadang to rescue people who were starving as a result of excessive rainfall. The Tadang ordered the inspectors-general of each province: "Have the prefects and magistrates estimate the distances between villages on all sides and the number of villages in order to establish aid stations. Choose meticulous, dignified men from among the former officials now in the provinces to be supervisors. Have the prefects and magistrates periodically check to discover and help those who are too ill to eat and those who, as *yangban*, are ashamed to come to the aid stations."[123] That fourteenth-century *yangban* felt it inappropriate for persons of their status to seek help indicates that they already had a sense of social standing.

The often-cited Chosŏn criterion for *yangban* status is that one of a person's four ancestors (father, grandfather, great-grandfather, maternal grandfather) must have held office in the dynastic government.[124] Although this was never actually codified, the four-ancestor criterion was used in the sixteenth century to determine who was eligible, as *sajok*, for the *ŭm* privilege and exemptions from certain punishments.[125]

A similar criterion for elite status appears to have been applied in medieval China: clans that for three generations failed to place members in office were threatened with loss of their privileged status.[126] But in the case of Korea, where descent groups continued to identify themselves as descendants of prominent officials or scholars for hundreds of years, it seems unlikely that descent groups really lost *yangban* status after three generations. Nonetheless, it is clear that by the late Koryŏ elite status was, as in medieval China, defined in terms of a family history of office holding in the central bureaucracy. The use of the term *yangban* by late Koryŏ elites to refer to themselves as a discrete social entity appears to be a natural consequence of the great official descent groups' awareness that the source of their prestige lay in their history as central office-holders. The advent of *sadaebu* and *yangban* as general terms for great descent groups marked a major change in the central bureaucratic aristocracy's view of itself and its relationship with other social groups. The use of such terminology was designed not only to distinguish the established central descent group segments from nonaristocratic elements, but to set the central bureaucrat aristocrats apart from the local aristocracy from which they had sprung.

ECONOMIC FOUNDATIONS OF THE CENTRAL DESCENT GROUPS

The rise of great estate holding by capital-based aristocrats is a central feature of mid- and late Koryŏ history. Although this is usually seen as having begun during the military era and as constituting a sharp break in the socio-economic structure of Korean society, evidence suggests that it began well before the military coup and developed as a consequence of the rise of the great central-official descent groups.

Early Koryŏ

The capital-based officials seem to have had two major sources of wealth in the tenth and eleventh centuries. One was the substantial private landholdings of powerful local strongman descent groups. It seems probable that central official branches of these local-strongman descent groups continued to enjoy access to the wealth of their ancestral seats, at least for the first few generations in the capital. The other was the salaries and prebends provided by the Field and Woodland Rank system, which included both regular prebends to be returned to the state upon the death of the recipient and the smaller inheritable protected field and woodland prebends.

The Field and Woodland Rank system appears to have worked reasonably well during the late tenth and eleventh centuries. The system was revised in 998 (in order to bring it in line with the new system of offices and ranks established under King Sŏngjong) and 1076. While the latter revision included some changes in the categories of people authorized to receive prebends, a noteworthy feature was reduction in the size of prebend grants and total elimination of woodland grants for lower-ranking individuals.[127] This reduction foreshadowed problems to come.

The growth of the central official class in the eleventh and twelfth centuries put the Field and Woodland Rank system under great pressure. The prebends and salaries provided by the system may have been sufficient to maintain an official and his immediate family, but, because the prebends, including the inheritable protected field and woodland, were ultimately controlled by the state, they would not have provided a solid, permanent economic foundation for an official and his family. Furthermore, it is unlikely that the dynasty, with its tenuous control over the countryside, ever had at its disposal sufficient lands to provide the entire central bureaucracy with enough hereditary prebendal grants to ensure an affluent lifestyle for all. At any rate, the store of lands available for distribution as inheritable prebends must have been exhausted with the growth of the central official class. To make matters worse, it appears that the passage of time made it more difficult for established central segments to rely on the resources of their ancestral seats. The fact that at the time of the military coup many civil officials sought refuge in temples and areas close to the capital rather than in their ancestral seats suggests considerable alienation between central and local segments of prominent descent groups by the late twelfth century.[128] Even in the halcyon days of the Koryŏ dynasty, therefore, central-official descent group segments had to deal with the problem of putting together secure, independent material bases for themselves.

Let us consider the case of the Kyŏngwŏn Yi. The proximity of the Yi ancestral seat in what is now Inch'ŏn to the Koryŏ capital (less than 40 miles) probably enabled the group's members in the capital to rely on the resources of its ancestral seat, at least until the very success of the group in producing large numbers of high-ranking central officials over several generations eventually presented the capital-based Yi with the need to create new bases of material wealth. In the almost totally agrarian Koryŏ society, landed estates would have been the answer, and the fact that Yi kinsmen such as Yi Cha-ryang (fl. early 12th cent.) and Yi Cha-gyŏm (d. 1126) are among the very first known owners of private estates suggests that this is exactly what happened.[129] It seems likely that other central official descent groups followed the Kyŏngwŏn Yi's lead to create independent economic bases for themselves.

We have very little evidence as to what kinds of lands were incorporated into the estates of the pre-1170 central-official descent groups. Some may have been Field and Woodland Rank prebends, both regular and inheritable, that central officials converted to de facto private landholdings. But it is certain that some capital-based descent groups seized control over lands owned or controlled by other persons. Evidence that this was widespread can be seen in an 1188 edict confiscating such lands and returning them to their original owners: "Everywhere wealthy and strong central officials [*yangban*] have used usury to seize the lands that have always belonged to the people [*paeksŏng*]. As a result, the people have lost their livelihood and become impoverished. Do not allow the wealthy to take over and carve up their lands. Return those lands to their original owners."[130] This measure, which was promulgated shortly after the military coup, may have been designed to dispose of the estates held by old civil official groups. How effective it was, or whether is was intended to apply to all central officials, including the military and their allies, is questionable, given the subsequent growth of private *nongjang* estates throughout the military era.

We have little information regarding the laborers who cultivated the estates created by capital-based officials. We suspect that they may have been slaves, because, as James Palais has argued, the existence of early Koryŏ legal codes providing for hereditary slavery shows that slavery almost certainly was an important part of the economic wealth of elites.[131] It also seems likely that estate owners used tenants, as is suggested by the terminology appearing in a number of royal decrees. One example is an 1111 decree on the collection of rent [*cho*] that uses terms such as *chŏnju* (lit. "field lord") and *chŏnho* (cultivating household), which indicate landlord-tenant relations of the type associated with estate holding in later periods.[132]

At any rate, it seems probable that private estates cultivated by slaves and tenant farmers formed a major part of the economic foundations of the great central-official descent groups of the pre-military-coup period. The growth of these estates in the late eleventh and twelfth centuries came about as a direct consequence of the establishment of powerful central-official descent groups who were no longer able to rely on the resources of their ancestral seats or on government prebends and needed new, independent sources of wealth.

The Late Koryŏ Period

The late Koryŏ period saw accelerated growth in the central elites' ownership of large landed estates, known by that time as *nongjang*. The military rulers of late twelfth- and thirteenth-century Koryŏ formed large *nongjang* for themselves, largely by appropriating lands owned by peasants or other persons. Generally these estates were composed of several parcels of land in various locales throughout the country, although some, such as those owned by the Ch'oe house at Chin'gang (Chinju) appear to have been made up of large, contiguous tracts. *Nongjang* proliferated in the late thirteenth and fourteenth centuries, with some so large that they encompassed entire counties.[133] The great landed estate had become a primary source of economic power for central *yangban* in the late Koryŏ period.

There is a smattering of evidence to suggest that some members of the late Koryŏ ruling class had commercial interests. One prominent *yangban,* writing in 1342, complained about high-ranking officials neglecting their duties in favor of talking about their profits in rice and salt market prices.[134] Whether these particular men belonged to established *yangban* descent groups or were palace favorites of non-*yangban* merchant backgrounds is not clear. I have been unable to find further indications of commercial activity before the final few years of the dynasty. In 1391 a censorate official presented a memorial requesting that officials be forbidden to engage in commerce.[135] Seven months later a high-ranking member of a prominent *yangban* descent group was stripped of his post and banished after being accused of trading while on an official mission to the Chinese Ming court.[136] Although we cannot rule out commercial activity as part of the economic base of the late Koryŏ ruling class, the very paucity of evidence for commerce—particularly in contrast with the abundance of that regarding landholding—suggests that it was not commerce but landed resources that formed the economic mainstay of the late Koryŏ *yangban.*

Slaves formed a major proportion of the *nongjang* estate labor force in the late Koryŏ period.[137] In 1289 the law making children of commoner-slave liaisons follow the status of the mother was abandoned in favor of a provision treating the offspring of all mixed matings as slaves,[138] a modification that seems designed to increase the number of slaves.[139]

At any rate, as Sudo Yoshiyuki has shown, litigation related to slaves was an important feature of the late Koryŏ period.[140] The two major issues were the restoration to commoner status of persons who had been forced into slavery and disputes over ownership of slaves. This suggests that the wealthy and the powerful of the late Koryŏ were actively trying by any means possible to obtain as many slaves as they could. That they were able to do so is probably less a sign of some sort of fundamental change in socioeconomic structure than of the increasing problems the dynasty encountered in keeping resources (in this case human) from falling under *yangban* control.

Even though *yangban,* as a collective entity, were successful in gaining control over landed and human resources, we should not assume that all the descent groups of the late Koryŏ central bureaucracy were wealthy land and slave owners. Evidence to the contrary can be found in Yi Saek's description of the modest circumstances of a segment of the Ch'ŏngju Kwak:

The Kwak family had fields and paddies at Ch'udong in Ch'ŏngju. They had a house built among the fields and farmed to provide the expenses needed to entertain guests and conduct marriages, funerals, and ancestor worship. They were satisfied with barely enough for breakfast and supper, without wishing for more. When the Kwak went to the royal court to hold office, they never looked back, even if their fields went to ruin. But when they left office they took their wives and children back to Ch'udong, where they farmed while reading and writing poetry. They enjoyed talking and laughing with woodgatherers and old farmers, forgetting about power and authority.[141]

This land at Ch'udong was, according to Yi Saek, given to the Kwak by the king near the end of the thirteenth century when a member of the family died while on a mission to Japan. Although Yi Saek's description of the Kwak's way of life appears somewhat idealized, it suggests that they were not wealthy landowners.

The Andong Kwŏn was another *yangban* descent group of modest circumstances. According to his *Koryŏsa* biography, Kwŏn Tan had an early desire to become a Buddhist monk, but his father, the Hallim Academy academician Kwŏn Wi, forcibly detained him and requested the court to give him a recorder post in the Chancellery. Kwŏn Wi risked the ruin of the family in providing his son's expenses, so Kwŏn Tan had no choice but to take the post.[142] While this anecdote does not provide any information about the landholdings of this branch of the Kwŏn, it does suggest that Kwŏn Wi was of modest circumstances.

Before we conclude that all the members of the Kwak and the Kwŏn were impoverished or that a large proportion of the central *yangban* class was of limited means, however, we should note that one member of the Kwak descent group, Kwak Ch'u, is known to have had a *nongjang* estate in P'yŏngju in the late fourteenth century.[143] We should also look at another piece of anecdotal evidence about the Andong Kwŏn. In his essay "Descriptions of the Cloud Brocade Tower," Yi Che-hyŏn writes of how Kwŏn Yŏm (1302–40), smitten with the view from a certain location on a lake near the capital, bought a piece of land and erected a tower some 16 feet tall and 30 feet across, where he feasted his family and friends. According to Yi, "Lord Hyŏnbok [Kwŏn Yŏm] carries the seal of a myriarch ("leader of 10,000," *manho*) and belongs to a family that married into the royal house. He is still under 40 years of age. Whether in deep sleep or a drunken dream, he will enjoy fame, wealth, and honor."[144] Yi Che-hyŏn does not tell us how large Kwŏn Yŏm's lands were or how wealthy he really was, but it is clear that he had substantially more assets at his disposal than did his relative Kwŏn Wi. Kwŏn Wi, however, was a member of only the second generation of the Andong Kwŏn to hold central office; Kwŏn Yŏm was Kwŏn Wi's great-great-grandson and a member of the sixth generation in the central bureaucracy. This suggests that at least some members of the Andong Kwŏn had been successful, over the generations, in parlaying their status as central officials into substantial wealth.

This anecdotal evidence is a poor substitute for quantitative data on the economic circumstances of officials, but it indicates that the late Koryŏ official class included men of both wealthy and modest circumstances. To the extent that some officials were of limited means, the prebends and stipends they received as compensation for their services to the dynastic government would have been important sources of economic sustenance. The Field and Woodland Rank system, which had provided prebends and salaries in the early Koryŏ was, however, near collapse by the end of the military period. As a result, shortly after returning to the capital from Kanghwa Island, in 1271 the dynastic government promulgated the Salary Rank Land (Nokkwajŏn) system, which set aside certain lands in the capital district for allotment to government officials in lieu of salaries.[145] This stopgap measure seems to have worked until the 1340s, when the state began to lose control over these prebends as well.[146]

Although certain segments of the bureaucracy were undoubtedly dependent on government salaries for their livelihood, it seems probable that the majority of the great central *yangban* descent groups of the late Koryŏ had substantial landholdings. It also seems likely that ownership of large landed estates and large numbers of slaves were not qualitatively new developments, but rather outgrowths of a pattern of estate holding by the great central-official descent groups of pre-1170 Koryŏ and an old tradition of slave ownership reflected in early Koryŏ legal provisions for hereditary slavery.

SUMMATION

After King Kwangjong's destruction of the old military confederacy and the implementation of bureaucratizing reforms in the second half of the tenth century, a relatively small number of civil aristocrat descent groups rose to dominate the dynastic government. A few, such as the Kangnŭng Kim and Kyŏngju Ch'oe, had been active in dynastic politics from the beginning of the tenth century, but the majority were later recruits from the local-strongman stratum that ruled over prefectures and counties throughout the country. By the early twelfth century, they developed into a hereditary central bureaucracy, facilitated by the ascriptive tradition in Koryŏ society and the privileges they received as inducements to serve in the central government. They consolidated their social and political position by intermarrying closely among themselves and with the royal family and by placing large numbers of their members in high political offices. Although in earlier years they appear to have been largely dependent on the prebends and salaries they received from the state, and perhaps on resources controlled by their kin in their ancestral seats, by the twelfth century they had begun to develop independent economic bases for themselves by amassing large privately owned estates.

They managed, despite the purge of some of their members and the loss of much of their political power, to maintain themselves as a social and administrative elite through the military era. The mid-thirteenth century deposal of the last of the Ch'oe military dictators and the abolition of the house political organs through which the Ch'oe had ruled the kingdom opened the door for the civil-aristocrat descent groups to reassert their claim to political predominance. The military exigencies of the late Koryŏ guaranteed that military officials would continue to play significant political roles, but the civil branch of the government once again became the center of bureaucratic power, as indicated by the civil origins of nearly 90 percent of late Koryŏ *chaech'u.*

The pre-1170 civil-aristocrat descent groups formed the nucleus of the late Koryŏ bureaucracy. Half of the most powerful descent groups of the late Koryŏ were direct descendants of early Koryŏ civil officials. Although the other half were descent groups new to the central government, they did not, as a group, represent the rise of qualitatively different, "new" social forces. On the contrary, with one or two exceptions, they represented a continuation of the early Koryŏ practice of recruiting local elites through the examination system. Furthermore, once these newer descent groups were ensconced at the capital, they too established hereditary lines of civil officials and intermarried closely with the older descent groups, in effect becoming new recruits to the old central civil establishment. In addition, the ownership of private landed estates by the late Koryŏ descent groups was less the advent of a new economic system than elaboration of the pattern of estate owning that had been developing prior to the 1170 coup. In sum, the great descent groups who dominated the bureaucracy in the late Koryŏ represented a substantial continuation of the pre-1170 civil branch–dominated system.

Many of the characteristics the political elites of the late Koryŏ shared with their early Koryŏ counterparts smack strongly of aristocracy. The great capital-based descent groups produced generation after generation of high-ranking officials, enjoying hereditary access to office through the protection privilege. They owned great landed estates and were closely intermarried, forming what appears to have been a largely closed stratum of political, social, and economic elites. At the same time, however, we must note that the great descent groups of both the early and late Koryŏ also displayed certain bureaucratic tendencies. The examination system was apparently the preferred means of entry to government service. As is indicated by the large number of protection beneficiaries who subsequently passed the higher examinations, it endowed greater prestige than other ways of gaining official posts. Also, our inquiry into the career patterns of prominent officials has shown that, regardless of descent-group background, they followed regular paths of advancement that took 20 or more years of service to rise to the *chaech'u* level, where real political power was exercised. Thus, contrary to the widely accepted depiction of the Koryŏ as a corrupt aristocracy, the picture that emerges here is one of a mixed system where meritocratic principles and bureaucratic procedures were applied within a generally aristocratic framework.

The balance between aristocratic and bureaucratic tendencies in the Korean ruling class has been pointed out by James Palais. Palais argues that this balance came about after the founding of the Chosŏn, largely as a result of Neo-Confucian influences and the increased importance of the government service examination system.[147] The evidence we have reviewed here, however, reveals that the Koryŏ ruling class also displayed a mix of aristocratic and bureaucratic attributes. Although bureaucratic tendencies may have been more pronounced in the Chosŏn period, at least with regard to the proportion of high-ranking officials who passed the government service examination, it seems to me that Palais's idea of an aristocratic bureaucracy applies to the Koryŏ as well, perhaps as early as the twelfth century and certainly by the late thirteenth century.

How does this compare with medieval China? In interregnum and T'ang China ascriptive social status was a prerequisite for gaining high office in the dynastic government and, taken as a group, the Chinese great clans appear to have succeeded very well at reproducing themselves, dominating society and politics for nearly five centuries. The Chinese clans kept genealogies and received official recognition of their preeminent status in the great clan lists that were compiled and promulgated during the T'ang. The great descent groups of the Koryŏ neither kept genealogies (though they maintained family records from perhaps the twelfth century on) nor were their names compiled into official lists, except perhaps in the case of the 15 great ministerial families designated as royal marriage partners by King Ch'ungsŏn.[148]

The existence in medieval China of officially sanctioned lists of great clans suggests that the ruling class there may have been a more formally constituted aristocracy than the great descent groups of Koryŏ. But there is controversy over whether the Chinese great clans actually were an aristocracy. Peter Bol argues, based on the primacy of birth as a qualifying factor for high office, that the great clans of the T'ang were essentially aristocratic.[149] David Johnson, on the other hand, rejects aristocracy on the grounds that there was no juridical definition of the great clans as aristocrats and that the social status that qualified one to hold office, including the ranks assigned under the Chinese Nine Rank Impartial and Just system, derived directly from the clan's past record in central office holding.[150] In the case of Koryŏ dynasty Korea, hereditary social status determined eligibility for entry into the central bureaucracy and for some, such as the *pugok hyangni,* even determined the level to which an individual could rise. Unlike in medieval China, however, this inherited social status appears to have stemmed from a descent group's origins in the autonomous local strongmen of the ninth and tenth centuries. This ascriptive status was given juridical definition by the various legal provisions regulating marriage among persons of different social strata and guaranteeing members of dominant local-strongman descent groups the right to sit for government service examinations and take entry-level jobs in the central clerical ranks leading to regular bureaucratic posts. It appears, therefore, that the base level—the strongman/*hyangni* stratum—from which the great central-official lines of descent of the Koryŏ dynasty were drawn constituted a local aristocracy. The essential independence of high social status from the central regime not only marks a significant difference between Koryŏ Korea and medieval China, but also underscores the extent to which political roles were embedded in social roles in the Koryŏ. Indeed, to the extent that the central bureaucracy can be seen as having been made up of capital-based segments of local-strongman kinship groups, one might be justified in saying that the centralizing and bureaucratizing reforms of the tenth century did little to alter the country's basic sociopolitical structure.

Such, however, was not the case. By the late thirteenth century, if not earlier, the capital-based descent group segments had begun to redefine themselves in a way that put greater emphasis on their histories as central officeholders. It is at this point that they begin to look more like the medieval Chinese great clans, whose primary source of status was their record of producing central officials. This change in the central bureaucrat-aristocrats' view of themselves and their relationship to the rest of society came about nearly two centuries after they emerged as the dominant social and political stratum. Why it took so long to manifest itself is not clear. Perhaps the vicissitudes of the military era delayed the development of a new self-image, or perhaps the tradition of the old prefecture-country aristocratic order was simply too strong to overcome. But in retrospect, it seems to have been an eventual certainty. Many of the capital-based descent groups no longer maintained close ties with their ancestral seats in the countryside; they used their status and power as central government officials to develop independent bases of economic power in their private estates; they had been marrying primarily with each other; and they had, in many cases, been placing members in central offices generation after generation for over two hundred years. At any rate, the central *yangban's* recognition of the gulf separating them from the *hyangni* out in the prefectures and counties was a turn of events whose ramifications greatly influenced the development of Korean sociopolitical history in the fourteenth and fifteenth centuries.

3 / The *Yangban* in the Change of Dynasties

The foregoing investigation showed substantial continuity in individual Koryŏ central-official descent groups and in the structure of the central-official class as a whole from the eleventh century down to the end of the dynasty. How, then, did the central *yangban* fare in the change of dynasties between the Koryŏ and the Chosŏn? Did the establishment of the new dynasty in 1392 entail significant change in the composition and structure of the ruling stratum, or did the old Koryŏ elites continue to dominate politics and society?

This chapter analyzes the composition of the bureaucracy at the beginning of the dynasty, from 1392 to 1405, and examines the origins of the most powerful descent groups of those years. Examination of the central bureaucracy in the mid-fifteenth century shows substantial continuity in both composition and structure of the ruling stratum between the late Koryŏ and the early Chosŏn.

THE BUREAUCRACY AT THE BEGINNING OF THE CHOSŎN

The first Chosŏn reigns, of T'aejo (1392–98) and Chŏngjong (1398–1400), were years of transition marked by political instability, but by the time of T'aejong's ascension to the throne in late 1400 the political situation had stabilized. Thus I examine the central bureaucracy in two periods: one covering the reigns of T'aejo and Chŏngjong from 1392 to 1400, and the other the first five years of T'aejong's reign. This allows us to identify who carried out the change of dynasties and who was left in power after things settled down in 1400.

Research in support of the hypothesis that the Chosŏn dynasty was founded by new social forces has tended to focus on select individuals.[1] This approach may have merit, to the extent that the men chosen for study were important leaders, but it offers little to assure us that its subjects are representative of the ruling stratum as a whole. In a recent effort toward a more comprehensive study, Chŏng Tu-hŭi examined the backgrounds of the merit subjects of the first three reigns of the Chosŏn dynasty and found them to be from a variety of backgrounds, both military and civil, in the old dynasty. Chŏng concedes that some, such as Cho Chun, could be considered, "in the broad sense," to be Koryŏ aristocrats, but he argues that they were at most minor aristocrats who succeeded on their own merit.[2]

The argument that such men as Cho Chun were distinct from a late Koryŏ aristocratic class because they rose through their own efforts and ability lacks persuasiveness, since it ignores the meritocratic aspects of the Koryŏ ruling class and assumes that hard work and talent were a monopoly of nonaristocratic elements. There is, however, another drawback with this study: it does not deal with the bureaucracy as a whole for either the late Koryŏ or the early Chosŏn, making it difficult to assess the relative importance of the early Chosŏn merit subjects and to accept the contention that descent groups represented in both late Koryŏ and early Chosŏn ruling circles—such as the P'yŏngyang Cho, Hwangnyŏ Min, and Sŏngju Yi—were not important members of the Koryŏ official establishment. In short, without an examination of the origins of all men known to have held offices in the dynastic government during the late Koryŏ and early Chosŏn, we cannot judge whether there was any significant change in the ruling stratum during the Koryŏ–Chosŏn transition.

The Central Bureaucracy, 1392–1400

Although Chŏng Tu-hŭi's study may not provide a definitive answer regarding the social origins of the early Chosŏn ruling stratum, it does reveal the broad outlines of the new dynasty's power structure. Chŏng found that merit subjects fall into two major categories—Yi Sŏng-gye's military allies and men of central official backgrounds.[3]

There can be no question of the importance of Yi Sŏng-gye's military coalition in the early Chosŏn. The northeastern military not only supplied the muscle to overthrow the old dynasty; it also provided the new royal family. Although it would be easy to dismiss the dynastic bureaucracy as a collection of essentially powerless individuals serving the military coalition, the evidence indicates otherwise.

The power of the northeastern military coalition was centered in the Consolidated Army Command (Samgunbu), created by Yi Sŏng-gye in 1391 to provide a joint command for the existing government central military forces and the private military forces of his coalition. Although this was an essentially military entity, the highest position in the Command, high commissioner (*to ch'ongje*), was to be filled by a concurrently appointed official of chancellor rank, and the other commissioners were also usually concurrently appointed *chaech'u*.[4] This suggests that the new royal family of the Chosŏn felt compelled to continue the Koryŏ tradition of structural subordination of military authority to the civil branch, even if many of the *chaech'u* appointed to Consolidated Army Command posts were originally of military branch origins.

Old Koryŏ political institutions continued to play important roles at the beginning of the Chosŏn. Evidence of this can be found in the activities of the Todang (usually called Top'yŏngŭisasa in the early Chosŏn), the civil branch's supreme organ of political struggle of the late Koryŏ. The *Veritable Records* are replete with examples of Todang political activity in the early dynasty, such as in the second month of 1394 when the Todang considered reform of procedures for selecting border region military officials, reform of the land and stipend system, and prohibition of falcon hunting;[5] or the first month of 1400, when the king deferred to the Todang on the vexatious issue of ratification (*sŏgyŏng*) of the king's appointment of high-ranking officials.[6] The central role of the Todang in politics was summed up by Kwŏn Kŭn in the fourth month of 1400: "The number of various *chaech'u* now exceeds 40. They all sit in the Todang to deliberate on state affairs."[7] These examples show that despite the rise of a new royal family of military origins, substantial political power continued to reside in the civil branch of the central government.

During the reigns of its first two kings the new dynasty maintained the old institutional structure. A decree issued shortly after the founding of the dynasty in 1392 shows the total of official posts to have been 4,749, a number similar to that of the late Koryŏ.[8] This number seems to have changed little in the early years of the dynasty: a 1400 memorial from the Chancellery stated that there were about 520 civil officials and over 4,170 military officials.[9] Table 3.1 shows the distribution of grades in the civil and military branches of the Chosŏn government according to the 1392 decree. The grade structure reflected here does not differ significantly from that of the Koryŏ government, although it does reflect the general overall increase in first- and second-grade civil officials that occurred in the late Koryŏ. One significant feature is that the military branch still occupied a position inferior to that of the civil branch. In the early Chosŏn men of military branch origins regularly gained appointments to the highest civil posts, but bureaucratic power resided in the civil branch, particularly in the first- and second-grade *chaech'u* offices, as in the Koryŏ.

TABLE 3.1

Grade Structure at the Beginning of the Chosŏn

Grade	Civil Posts	Military Posts
Senior First	4	
Junior First	3	
Senior Second	15	
Junior Second	23	
Senior Third	51	10
Junior Third	37	20
Senior Fourth	30	50
Junior Fourth	22	
Senior Fifth	11	150
Junior Fifth	27	
Senior Sixth	34	300
Junior Sixth	65	
Senior Seventh	29	300
Junior Seventh	52	
Senior Eighth	25	400
Junior Eighth	49	
Senior Ninth	20	1000
Junior Ninth	22	2000
Total	519	4230

The *Veritable Records* for the years 1392–1400 contain the names of 750 men, excluding slaves and others of evident nonofficial status. Some, such as Cho Chun, who is listed as an officeholder 47 times, appear repeatedly, but the majority appear only once or twice. Table 3.2 shows the distribution of ranks according to highest office held in this period. This array of officials reveals two significant things. First, in spite of the 8:1 ratio of military to civil posts, six civil officials appear in the *Veritable Records* for every military man. Although the predominance of the civil branch in the histories might, to some degree, reflect a bias on the part of the civil official compilers of the *Veritable Records,* it does support the finding based on analysis of grade structure that the center of bureaucratic power lay in the upper ranks of the civil branch. Second, although the first and second grades accounted for less than 8 percent of civil posts, first- and second-grade officials (the men who sat in the Todang) constituted nearly 38 percent of all civil officials appearing in the

TABLE 3.2
Distribution of Officials by Branch and Grade, 1392–1400

Grade/Status	Civil	Military	Other/Unknown
Senior First	13		
Junior First	17		
Senior Second	35		
Junior Second	95		
Senior Third	78	7	
Junior Third	31	21	
Senior Fourth	16	17	
Junior Fourth	31		
Senior Fifth	14	4	
Junior Fifth	24		
Senior Sixth	10	8	
Junior Sixth	23		
Senior Seventh	2	4	
Junior Seventh	7		
Senior Eight	0	5	
Junior Eighth	0		
Senior Ninth	1		
Grade unknown[a]	43	2	
Subtotal	440	68	
Provincial officials[b]	66	21	
Other status[c]	39		
Noble titleholders			14
Status unclear[d]			102
Total	545	89	116

[a] Men identified only by type of post, such as remonstrance officials (*kan'gwan*) and attendants.

[b] Governors (*kwanch'alsa, chŏljesa*), local military officers (*manho, ch'ŏnho*), county magistrates, etc.

[c] Examination graduates, emissaries to China whose posts are not specified, honorary appointees, etc.

[d] Men identified as members of certain factions, men of unspecified posts who were exiled, etc.

TABLE 3.3
Descent Structure of the Central Bureaucracy, 1392–1400

Total known officials	750
Officials of known descent	374 (49%)
Total known *chaech'u*	165
Chaech'u of known descent	138 (84%)
Total descent groups	158
Groups with only one known official	81 (51%)
Most powerful descent groups*	34
Officials from most powerful descent groups	174 (23%)
Chaech'u from most powerful descent groups	92 (56%)

* Groups with four or more officials or three officials including two *chaech'u* noble titleholders.

Veritable Records. Like the *Koryŏsa*, the *Veritable Records* show bias in favor of higher ranking officials, providing another reliable view of the uppermost ranks, where real power resided.

In table 3.3, which shows the descent-group structure of the bureaucracy in the early Chosŏn, we see substantial similarities between the early Chosŏn and the late Koryŏ. The proportion of officials with known descent origins remains the same (49 percent; see table 2.5) and the proportion of descent groups producing only a single known official is similar (51 percent in the early Chosŏn, 55 percent in the late Koryŏ). But the percentage of *chaech'u* of known descent increases greatly in the early Chosŏn (from 57 to 84 percent) and the proportion of *chaech'u* accounted for by top descent groups more than doubled (from 23 to 56 percent). This suggests that rather than ousting the old aristocracy and opening the bureaucracy up to a more widely constituted elite class, the change of dynasties resulted in greater concentration of power in a few select descent groups. This would seem to be the natural result of the new royal family's reliance on a small number of politically reliable groups, but at the same time it belies the conventional assumption of a broader, less aristocratic ruling stratum for the new dynasty.

While we cannot rule out the possibility that the 50 percent of officials of unknown descent origins represented new social elements, the fact that the proportion of men of unknown backgrounds remains the same from late Koryŏ to early Chosŏn seems to argue against it. At any rate, it would be dangerous

TABLE 3.4

Most Powerful Descent Groups under T'aejo and Chǒngjong

Descent Group	Total Officials	Chaech'u
Chǒnju Yi	15	11
Hwangnyǒ Min*	10	5
Andong Kwǒn*	9	4
P'ap'yǒng Yun*	9	1
Munhwa Yu*	8	3
Kyǒngju Yi*	8	1
P'yǒngyang Cho*	6	5
Ch'ǒngju Han*	6	4
Hanyang Cho*	6	4
Chinju Kang	6	3
Chǒnju Ch'oe*	6	2
Ch'ǒngju Yi	5	5
Kyǒngju Kim*	5	3
Chuksan Pak*	5	3
Ŭiryǒng Nam	5	3
Andong Kim*	5	3
Ch'angnyǒng Sǒng	5	2
Miryang Pak	5	2
Tongnae Chǒng	5	1
Kwangsan Kim*	4	3
Sunhŭng An*	4	2
Tanyang U*	4	1
Haeju Ch'oe	4	1
Sǒngju Pae	4	1
Yǒngch'on Hwangbo	4	1
Paekch'ǒn Cho	3	3
Andong Chang	3	3
Sǒngju Yi*	3	2
Ch'ǒngju Kyǒng	3	2
Yǒngil Chǒng	3	2
Ponghwa Chǒng	3	2
Ch'ǒngju Chǒng	3	2
Ch'ǒngsong Sim	3	2
Kosǒng Yi	3	2
Total	180	94

* Late Koryǒ powerful *yangban* descent groups (see table 2.6).

to conclude that 50 percent of officials did not belong to any of the established descent groups or that they were of such low origins as to not belong
to any recognized descent group. As Edward Wagner has pointed out, the mid-
and late Chosŏn compilers of genealogies tended to favor politically prominent segments to the neglect of those historically less prominent.[10]

Who, then, were these 34 descent groups that held such a dominant position at the beginning of the Chosŏn?

A quick glance at table 3.4 reveals some descent groups familiar to the student of late Koryŏ history—groups such as Hwangnyŏ Min, Andong Kwŏn,
P'ap'yŏng Yun, and Munhwa Yu. Sixteen, or nearly half, of the most powerful descent groups of the immediate post-foundation years were among the
most powerful *yangban* descent groups of the late Koryŏ. Several others had
produced multiple *chaech'u* in the late Koryŏ (1260–1392): the Chinju Kang,
Kosŏng Yi, and Miryang Pak with five each; and the Haeju Ch'oe, Ch'angnyŏng
Sŏng, and Ch'ŏngju Yi with four each. Viewed from the other perspective,
nearly three-quarters (16 of 22, 73 percent) of the great *yangban* descent groups
of the late Koryŏ were among the most powerful descent groups of the early
Chosŏn. Thus it appears, at least on the basis of descent-group affiliation, that
there was a great deal of continuity at the top of the bureaucracy during the
Koryŏ–Chosŏn transition.

The Bureaucracy under T'aejong, 1401–1405

If the great descent groups of Koryŏ managed to maintain access to power
during the transitional period from 1392 to 1400, what then of the post-1400
years? Is it possible that the new royal family temporarily tolerated the old
elites while it was consolidating its hold on the country? Were the old *yangban* descent groups weakened or destroyed in the political upheavals of the
late 1390s as the Yi princes fought among themselves for power? Were the
old groups eliminated once T'aejong, one of the strongest monarchs in all of
Korean history, took the throne at the end of 1400? In order to answer these
questions, we need to analyze the bureaucracy under T'aejong.

During his first five years on the throne, T'aejong carried out a major restructuring of central political institutions. The centerpiece of this reorganization
was replacement of the Todang with the much smaller State Council (Ŭijŏngbu).
T'aejong, however, took a gradual approach, allowing the old institutions to
continue alongside the new State Council until 1404. This means that there
was probably little reduction in the number or political importance of first-
and second-grade positions as a whole until late in the 1401–1405 period.

TABLE 3.5
Descent Structure of the Central Bureaucracy, 1401–5

Total known officials	325
Officials of known descent	153 (47%)
Total known *chaech'u*	78
Chaech'u of known descent	59 (76%)
Total descent groups	96
Groups with only one known official	60 (63%)
Most powerful descent groups*	19
Officials from most powerful descent groups	63 (19%)
Chaech'u from most powerful decent groups	34 (44%)

* Groups with three or more officials or two officials including one
chaech'u or noble titleholder.

Table 3.5 shows that descent-group structure of the central bureaucracy during the first five years of T'aejong's reign generally conforms to that of the
1392–1400 period. All proportions are slightly down compared to the earlier
period, except for the percentage of descent groups with only one known official, which rose from 51 to 63 percent. This could reflect the purge of groups—
such as the Ponghwa Chŏng of Chŏng To-jŏn—as a result of political infighting
in the first two reigns, but it also suggests some broadening of political participation under T'aejong. Nonetheless, the tendency toward greater domination of the upper ranks of the bureaucracy by a small number of powerful
descent groups continued into the early years of T'aejong's reign.

Was there any significant change in the composition of the most powerful
descent groups? Table 3.6 lists the 19 most powerful descent groups of the
first five years of T'aejong's reign. A quick glance reveals that over three-quarters (15 out of 19) of the most powerful descent groups of T'aejong's early
reign were among the most powerful groups of the 1392–1400 period. It is
interesting to note that the new royal family, the Chŏnju Yi, does not appear
among the top official descent groups of T'aejong's early reign. This no doubt
reflects the outcome of the princes' revolts of the 1390s and of T'aejong's determination to not tolerate any rival claimants for the throne. Four descent groups
do not appear among the most powerful groups of the preceding eight years.
However, two of those—the Kyŏngwŏn Yi and Namyang Hong—were well-
established *yangban* descent groups of the Koryŏ.[11] The Hamyang Pak was

TABLE 3.6
Most Powerful Descent Groups under T'aejong, 1401–5

Descent Group	Total Officials	Chaech'u
Andong Kwŏn*	9	2
Hwangnyŏ Min*	5	3
P'ap'yŏng Yun*	5	2
P'yŏngyang Cho*	4	4
Munhwa Yu*	4	3
Kyŏngwŏn Yi	4	2
Chinju Kang*	3	3
Kwangsan Kim*	3	3
Hanyang Cho*	3	2
Kyŏngju Yi*	3	2
Tanyang U*	3	2
Kongam Hŏ*	3	1
Hongju Yi	2	2
Namyang Hong	2	2
Hamyang Pak	2	1
Ch'angnyŏng Sŏng*	2	1
Ch'ŏngju Han*	2	1
Ch'ŏngju Yi*	2	1
Sŏngju Yi*	2	1
Total	63	38

* Descent groups in table 3.4

also an important central-official descent group of the late Koryŏ, accounting for two *chaech'u* and nine officials overall; this group had three officials, including one *chaech'u* during the 1392–1400 period. The Hongju Yi were not among the great descent groups of the late Koryŏ, but even they had some late Koryŏ predecessors, with one *chaech'u* in the military period and another in the late Koryŏ.[12] In sum, there was no significant difference, except for the decline of the royal family, in the structure or composition of the central bureaucracy between the transitional years of 1392–1400 and the first five years of T'aejong's reign.

If we combine the data for the 1392–1400 and 1401–1405 periods, we get a total of 38 great *yangban* descent groups in the early Chosŏn, as shown in table 3.7. All of these groups had members holding office during the late Koryŏ

TABLE 3.7

Most Powerful Descent Groups, 1392–1405

Descent Group	Total Officials	Chaech'u
Chŏnju Yi	15	11
Hwangnyŏ Min	12	7
Andong Kwŏn	12	5
P'ap'yŏng Yun	9	2
Munhwa Yu	8	4
Andong Kim	8	4
Chuksan Pak	8	3
Kyŏngju Yi	8	2
P'yŏngyang Cho	7	6
Ch'ŏngju Han	7	4
Chŏnju Ch'oe	7	1
Hanyang Cho	6	4
Chinju Kang	6	3
Miryang Pak	6	2
Ch'ŏngju Yi	5	5
Kyŏngju Kim	5	3
Kwangsan Kim	5	3
Sunhŭng An	5	3
Paekch'ŏn Cho	5	3
Ŭiryŏng Nam	5	3
Ch'angnyŏng Sŏng	5	2
Tongnae Chŏng	5	1
Tanyang U	5	1
Sŏngju Yi	4	2
Kyŏngwŏn Yi	4	2
Namyang Hong	4	1
Yŏnan Kim	4	1
Haeju Ch'oe	4	1
Sŏngju Pae	4	1
Yŏngch'on Hwangbo	4	1
Andong Chang	3	3
Ch'ŏngju Kyŏng	3	2
Ch'ŏngju Kwak	3	2
Yŏngil Chŏng	3	2
Ponghwa Chŏng	3	2
Ch'ŏngju Chŏng	3	2
Ch'ŏngsong Sim	3	2
Kosŏng Yi	3	1
Total	216	107

TABLE 3.8
Status of Powerful Chosŏn Descent Groups in the Late Koryŏ

Descent Group	1139–1351	Kongmin	U-Ch'ang	Kongyang
Chŏnju Yi	1 (0)	4 (1)	5 (2)	6 (3)
Hwangnyŏ Min	7 (4)	4 (2)	3 (1)	2 (2)
Andong Kwŏn	8 (7)	8 (4)	6 (3)	8 (1)
P'ap'yŏng Yun	9 (5)	5 (0)	6 (5)	5 (4)
Munhwa Yu	5 (4)	2 (0)	2 (0)	2 (1)
Andong Kim	7 (7)	5 (3)	—	4 (1)
Chuksan Pak	4 (2)	3 (2)	3 (1)	2 (1)
Kyŏngju Yi	10 (3)	8 (3)	3 (1)	7 (0)
P'yŏngyang Cho	6 (5)	3 (1)	5 (2)	3 (2)
Chŏnju Ch'oe	6 (4)	5 (1)	4 (2)	2 (1)
Ch'ŏngju Han	5 (4)	8 (5)	—	4 (1)
Hanyang Cho	—	2 (0)	3 (2)	5 (2)
Chinju Kang	1 (1)	1 (1)	2 (1)	4 (3)
Miryang Pak	3 (2)	6 (3)	2 (0)	2 (1)
Kyŏngju Kim	5 (4)	1 (1)	1 (1)	3 (0)
Ch'ŏngju Yi	1 (1)	—	3 (0)	1 (1)
Kwangsan Kim	15 (9)	11 (3)	—	4 (1)
Sunhŭng An	4 (4)	4 (1)	4 (2)	5 (1)
Paekch'ŏn Cho	2 (0)	1 (0)	2 (1)	3 (1)
Ŭiryŏng Nam	—	—	3 (2)	2 (1)
Ch'angnyŏng Sŏng	1 (0)	3 (0)	4 (3)	2 (2)
Tongnae Chŏng	—	1 (0)	—	1 (1)
Tanyang U	3 (0)	3 (1)	5 (3)	6 (3)
Sŏngju Yi	8 (3)	7 (6)	6 (3)	2 (1)
Kyŏngwŏn Yi	2 (1)	1 (0)	2 (1)	5 (1)
Namyang Hong	9 (6)	15 (8)	5 (5)	4 (2)
Yŏnan Kim	—	1 (0)	2 (0)	1 (0)
Haeju Ch'oe	1 (1)	3 (1)	—	—
Sŏngju Pae	—	1 (0)	3 (1)	1 (1)
Yŏngch'on Hwangbo	—	1 (0)	1 (1)	1 (1)
Andong Chang	—	—	1 (0)	1 (1)
Ch'ŏngju Kyŏng	1 (0)	2 (1)	3 (2)	3 (1)
Ch'ŏngju Kwak	2 (1)	3 (1)	—	1 (0)
Yŏngil Chŏng	1 (0)	2 (1)	2 (1)	2 (1)
Ponghwa Chŏng	—	1 (1)	1 (0)	3 (1)
Ch'ŏngju Chŏng	3 (2)	2 (2)	1 (1)	1 (1)
Ch'ŏngsong Sim	—	—	1 (1)	2 (1)
Kosŏng Yi	1 (1)	4 (1)	4 (3)	3 (0)
Total	131 (81)	131 (54)	98 (51)	113 (46)

Note: Figures in parentheses are *chaech'u* officials.

and a substantial proportion maintained a presence in the central bureaucracy all the way back to pre–military coup Koryŏ.

The conventional interpretation contends, however, that the new social forces, defined as government service examination–oriented "new scholar-officials," that founded the Chosŏn dynasty first appeared in large numbers in the Koryŏ government only after the enthronement of King Kongmin in 1351.[13] This means that treating the late Koryŏ as a single period may lead us to overlook important new social elements that arose after 1351. Table 3.8 shows the status of our 38 most powerful early Chosŏn descent groups during various reigns of the late Koryŏ. We can see that nine of the most powerful early Chosŏn descent groups first appeared in the central bureaucracy after the ascension of Kongmin in 1351, and that seven others had only one known official in the years prior to Kongmin, before flourishing in the late Koryŏ and early Chosŏn. Are these 16 descent groups, then, the "new scholar-officials"? First we must eliminate the Haeju Ch'oe, which, although it had only one known member in the pre-1351 bureaucracy, was a well-known Koryŏ *yangban* descent group. That leaves 15 new groups. Seven of these, however, were predominantly or totally military: the Chŏnju Yi, Hanyang Cho, Yŏngch'on Hwangbo, Andong Chang, Ch'ŏngsong Sim, Ch'ŏngju Yi, and Ch'ŏngju Kyŏng. This eliminates them from consideration as "new scholar-officials." The remaining eight new groups—the Ŭiryŏng Nam, Tongnae Chŏng, Yŏnan Kim, Ponghwa Chŏng, Chinju Kang, Ch'angnyŏng Sŏng, and Yŏngil Chŏng—were predominately civil-branch descent groups who first appeared in the central government in significant numbers after 1351.

Let us assume, for the sake of argument, that the eight new civil-branch descent groups were all "new scholar-officials." They accounted for 21 percent of our 38 most powerful early Chosŏn groups, but only 15 percent of all officials from powerful descent groups (32 of 216) and only 14 percent of *chaech'u* from powerful descent groups (15 of 107). Thus they were somewhat underrepresented in the new dynasty's bureaucracy. In contrast, the seven new military branch descent groups provided 18 percent (39 of 216) of all officials from the most powerful descent groups and 30 percent (32 of 107) of *chaech'u.*

The putative "new scholar-official" descent groups compare equally poorly with the old *yangban* as well. The eight most powerful descent groups of the early Chosŏn (excluding the new royal family), all prominent Koryŏ *yangban,* produced 36 percent (78 of 216) of powerful descent-group officials and 27 percent (29 of 107) of *chaech'u.*

Even if the eight new civil-branch descent groups did not dominate the early

Chosŏn central bureaucracy numerically, is it not possible that their individual members played important roles far out of proportion to their descent groups' numbers? At first glance, this approach seems promising. Of 18 men who were made first-class merit subjects by King T'aejo in reward for their support in establishing the new dynasty, two were members of the royal family, five were military men (including Nam Ŭn of the Ŭiryŏng Nam), and 11 appear to have been civil officials.[14] Three of these 11 came from "new scholar-official" descent groups: Pae Kŭng-nyŏm of Sŏngju; Chŏng To-jŏn of Ponghwa, and Nam Chae of Ŭiryŏng. Six came from well-established late Koryŏ descent groups: Cho Chun and Cho Pak from P'yŏngyang; Kim Sa-hyŏng from Andong; Yi Che from Sŏngju; and Chŏng T'ak and Chŏng Ch'ong from Ch'ŏngju. One, Cho In-ok of Hanyang, was a civil-branch member of the northeastern military Hanyang Cho. The background of the final merit subject, Chŏng Hŭi-gye of Kyŏngju, is uncertain, but he was a relative of King U's favorite consort, which suggests that he was tied in with the old elites.[15] Thus only three of 18 (17 percent) of T'aejo's first-grade merit subjects came from potential "new scholar-official" descent groups, a proportion similar to their share of total powerful descent group officials and *chaech'u*. This makes it difficult to argue that "new scholar-officials" were the main force behind the 1392 change of dynasties.

Is it possible that focus on top descent groups distorts our understanding of the bureaucracy of the new dynasty? Did new elements, scholar-officials or others gain a place in the central bureaucracy too late in the Koryŏ to place significant numbers of second-generation members in office during the 1392–1405 period? Given the urgency of the military situation in the late Koryŏ and the large number of supernumerary appointments granted by King U, the question seems worth investigating. Table 3.9 shows descent groups new to the central bureaucracy for each reign after 1351, along with the total number of officials and *chaech'u* they produced. The data suggests, at first glance, significant social mobility in the Koryŏ-Chosŏn transition. Between 14 and 20 percent of identified descent groups in each reign period were new to the central bureaucracy and nearly one-third of the early Chosŏn groups made their first known appearance in the bureaucracy after King Kongmin took the throne in 1351. When we look, however, at the proportion of known officials and *chaech'u* accounted for by these new descent groups, they appear to have had very little effect on the bureaucracy's overall social composition or power configuration. The range of known officials from new groups runs below 6 percent, and the range of known *chaech'u* from the new groups never exceeds 4 percent. Furthermore, the new groups appear to have had little staying power. Only 25 percent (5 of 20) of those in King Kongmin's reign, for example, were

TABLE 3.9
Descent Groups New to the Central Bureaucracy, Late Koryŏ–Early Chosŏn

	Late Koryŏ			Early Chosŏn
	Kongmin *(1351–74)*	*U–Ch'ang* *(1374–89)*	*Kongyang* *(1389–92)*	*(1392–1405)*
New descent groups	20 (16%)	20 (20%)	13 (14%)	28 (18%)
Officials from new groups	25 (4%)	27 (6%)	13 (5%)	32 (4%)
Chaech'u from new groups	9 (4%)	4 (3%)	0	1 (1%)

Representation of Above Descent Groups in the Early Chosŏn Bureaucracy

				Early Chosŏn totals
New descent groups	5 (3%)	5 (3%)	8 (5%)	46 (29%)
Officials from new groups	6 (1%)	·13 (2%)	11 (1%)	62 (8%)
Chaech'u from new groups	4 (2%)	5 (3%)	2 (1%)	12 (7%)

NOTE: Parentheses indicate new descent groups as a percentage of all descent groups represented in the central bureaucracy; new group officials as a percentage of all officials; and new group *chaech'u* as a percentage of all *chaech'u*. The lower half of the table shows how the new descent groups of each period fared in the early Chosŏn; the figures under "Early Chosŏn totals" include both new descent groups of the late Koryŏ who still had members in office after the founding of the Chosŏn and those descent groups that first appeared in the early Chosŏn.

still represented in the early Chosŏn bureaucracy. The low proportion of both total known officials (8 percent) and *chaech'u* (7 percent) of the early Chosŏn who came from descent groups that made their first known appearance in the central bureaucracy after 1351 indicates that new descent groups as a whole played a minimal role in the central government during the years immediately after the founding of the new dynasty.

If the rise of new social elements was not behind the change of dynasties, what of the other half of the conventional interpretation: the destruction of the late Koryŏ ruling class? Although five of the 15 descent groups on King Ch'ungsŏn's list of great ministerial families appear among the great descent groups of the early Chosŏn, what of the other 10? Were they and other prominent late Koryŏ descent groups wiped out in the dynastic change? Table 3.10 depicts the fortunes of great official descent groups from the late Koryŏ who were not included in the 38 most powerful descent groups of the 1392–1405 period.

The groups are of two types: the first four are from the 22 great *yangban*

TABLE 3.10

Status of Fallen Late Koryŏ Great Descent Groups

Descent Groups	Pre-Kongmin	Kongmin	U-Ch'ang	Kongyang	Chosŏn
Ŏnyang Kim	4 (3)	5 (2)	1 (0)	2 (2)	1 (0)
Kyŏngju Ch'oe	5 (1)	4 (1)	3 (1)	—	2 (1)
Wŏnju Wŏn	6 (5)	3 (2)	—	—	3 (0)
P'yŏnggang Ch'ae	7 (6)	1 (1)	—	—	—
Haengju Ki	3 (1)	5 (1)	—	—	—
Kyoha No	2 (1)	4 (4)	1 (1)	—	3 (0)
P'yŏngt'aek Im	—	2 (1)	5 (3)	—	—
Hansan Yi	2 (1)	1 (1)	3 (2)	4 (1)	3 (1)
Pongsŏng Yŏm	2 (2)	2 (1)	3 (2)	—	—
Ch'angwŏn Ch'oe	5 (3)	3 (1)	1 (1)	—	—

( ) *Chaech'u* officials

descent groups of the late Koryŏ dealt with in chapter 2; the final six are from numerically small but historically important late Koryŏ groups. Three of the four descent groups of the first type seem to have maintained a continuing, if diminished, presence in the central bureaucracy after the founding of the Chosŏn. The P'yŏnggang Ch'ae, however, seem to have disappeared totally from the ranks of the central bureaucracy.[16] While never as strong numerically as other great descent groups of the late Koryŏ, the P'yŏnggang Ch'ae had some very powerful members during the early and mid-fourteenth century, including Ch'ae Hong-ch'ŏl, Lord of Sunch'ŏn in 1340,[17] and his reputedly illegitimate son Ch'ae Ha-jung, senior first-grade right chancellor (*u chŏngsŭng*) in 1354.[18] Ch'ae Ha-jung died in disgrace, committing suicide in jail; after his death no members of the P'yŏnggang Ch'ae are known to have held office in the late Koryŏ or the early Chosŏn. The Ch'aes' fall from power seems to have resulted from having few members, suffering political misfortune, and, perhaps, the social stigma of Ch'ae Ha-jung's illegitimacy.

Two of the six descent groups of the second type maintained a presence in the bureaucracy after 1392: the Kyoha No and Hansan Yi each placed three men in office. The other four—who seem to have been totally eliminated after the founding of the new dynasty, or more precisely, after Yi Sŏng-gye's group seized power in 1388—were the Haengju Ki, Pongsŏng Yŏm, P'yŏngt'aek Im, and Ch'angwŏn Ch'oe. The Ki, one of whose daughters became a Yüan empress, are the descent group most commonly cited as typical *kwŏnmun sejok*. The Ki appear to have been well-established members of the Koryŏ bureaucracy, with members in office before the 1170 military coup.[19] They lost power as a consequence of a purge of Mongol-connected elements during the reign of King Kongmin. The Pongsŏng Yŏm, of which Yŏm Che-sin and Yŏm Hŭng-bang were members, is also often noted as a powerful late Koryŏ descent group. Yŏm Che-sin was a top-ranking official of the mid-fourteenth century.[20] His son, Yŏm Hŭng-bang, who had passed the examinations under King Kongmin and attained high office under King U, was executed along with Im Kyŏn-mi after Yi Sŏng-gye took power in 1388.[21] No members of the group are known to have held office in the early Chosŏn. There also can be no doubt about the exalted status of the Ch'angwŏn Ch'oe, which was one of the 15 great min-isterial families designated by King Ch'ungsŏn. Important members of the descent group in office in the late Koryŏ included Ch'oe On, senior second-grade associate chancellor in 1268, and the famous military official Ch'oe Yŏng, who played an important role in the final years of the Koryŏ dynasty.[22] Yŏng, of course, was removed from power along with Yŏm Hŭng-bang by Yi Sŏng-gye in 1388, but the Ch'oes' demise was not attributable solely to political misfortunes. Regarding their decline, Yi Su-gŏn says, "After the fall of Ch'oe Yŏng at the end of the Koryŏ, the family's fortunes fell rapidly; however, the cause of this, in addition to political reasons, lay in the childlessness of sev-eral high-ranking members."[23]

The Ki, Yŏm, and Ch'oe all fit the aristocratic mold, but what about the P'yŏngt'aek Im? Far from being well-established members of the late Koryŏ elite, the Im appears to have been a new group that rose in the late Koryŏ through the military exploits of its members. The *Koryŏsa* biography of Im Kyŏn-mi, the most prominent member of the group, states, "Im Kyŏn-mi was a P'yŏngt'aek man. His father, Im Ŏn-su, became suddenly noble because of Im Kyŏn-mi's achievements and was given the title Lord of P'yŏngsŏng."[24] Im On-su is shown in the clan genealogy as the founder, indicating that the P'yŏngt'aek Im had no previous background in the bureaucracy and may not have even had roots in the *hyangni* class.

Thus we have five powerful late Koryŏ descent groups who seem to have been eliminated from the central bureaucracy after the founding of the Chosŏn. Two, the Haengju Ki and P'yŏnggang Ch'ae, actually fell during the reign of Kongmin, while the other three lost power after Yi Sŏng-gye's group took control of the central government in 1388. That only three powerful descent groups were eliminated as a consequence of the rise of Yi Sŏng-gye to power is further evidence that the change of dynasties from Koryŏ to Chosŏn did not entail a social revolution.

It is interesting to note that two of these five groups eventually recovered a

place for themselves at the center. Members of the P'yŏnggang Ch'ae reap-
peared in the central bureaucracy in the mid-Chosŏn,[25] and even the Haengju
Ki regained some measure of prominence by the early sixteenth century.[26]

Branch Affiliations

Although the men who founded the Chosŏn belonged to descent groups that
were, for the most part, powerful Koryŏ *yangban,* we cannot automatically
rule out the possibility that they had somehow evolved during the late fourteenth century into "scholar-officials" qualitatively different from late Koryŏ
elites. This line of reasoning is implicit, for example, in Chŏng Tu-hŭi's treatment of Cho Chun discussed earlier in this chapter. In order for the Chosŏn
founders to be considered "scholar-officials," they must meet two basic criteria: they must have been members of the civil branch of government and
graduates of the government service examinations.

Although the civil branch continued to dominate the regular bureaucracy
in the early Chosŏn, there was a significant military element among the 207
chaech'u (165 from 1392–1400, and 42 new *chaech'u* from 1401–1405) of
the 1392–1405 period. At least 20 percent (42) of the official elite were men
whose careers originated in the military branch. Some were from the northeastern military coalition, but a surprisingly large number came from prominent central *yangban* descent groups, including the Munhwa Yu, Chuksan Pak,
Haeju Ch'oe, Ch'ŏngju Kwak, and Hwangnyŏ Min.

One of the most prominent fourteenth-century descent groups, the Munhwa
Yu, produced a number of officials whose careers indicate that they were scholars, including Yu Kwan, an examination graduate who was a senior third-
grade remonstrance official in 1397,[27] and Yu Sa-nul, a graduate who was a
fifth-grade censor in 1400.[28] Yet one of the most important early Chosŏn members of the group, Yu Man-su, was a member of the military branch. His biographical note in the *Veritable Records* says:

> Yu Man-su's ancestral seat is Munhwa and he is the son of the right assis-
> tant transmitter [*u pu taeŏn,* senior third grade] Ch'ŏng. He became a "jewel
> horse" attendant during Kongmin's reign and in 1363 was appointed gen-
> eral. He changed posts several times and rose to assistant royal secretary
> [*milchik pusa,* junior second grade]. In 1377 he went with the king [Yi Sŏng-
> gye] to attack the Wako in P'unghae Province. In 1388 he followed the king
> [Yi Sŏng-gye] to Wihwa Island, where he joined in the discussion to with-
> draw the army. Upon return, he was appointed chancellery supervisor [*chi*

munha, senior second grade] and given the title of merit subject. In 1390 he became state councillor and in 1391 he assumed the concurrent post of supreme general. When the king took the throne, he was given the title of original follower merit subject and appointed to the consulting chancellor position.[29]

Although Yu Man-su ultimately gained appointment to first- and second-grade posts in the civil branch, it is clear that he was originally a member of the military branch whose rise to high position was at least partly a result of his military activities.

The Chuksan Pak also featured both scholarly and military elements. Pak Hyŏng, an examination graduate, was one of the leading scholars of the early Chosŏn, retiring as "grand scholar" before his death in 1398. His son, Pak Chung-yong, also passed the examinations.[30] Pak Hyŏng's cousin, Pak P'o, first appears in the histories as a grand general and merit subject when the Chosŏn dynasty was founded in 1392.[31] Pak P'o later held a variety of posts, including a command position in the Consolidated Army Command in 1398,[32] and was executed for his part in Yi Pang-gan's revolt.[33]

The Haeju Ch'oe, one of the great ministerial families designated by King Ch'ungsŏn, placed several members in the central bureaucracy between 1392 and 1400, including such civil officials as Censorate inspector Ch'oe Ho.[34] Chief among them was Ch'oe Yŏng-ji, who held a junior first-grade assistant chancellor post in 1392.[35] The biographical sketch of Ch'oe Yŏng-ji in the *Veritable Records* says that although his family was poor and he was uneducated, he rose to fame as a soldier and became a capable administrator because when he had someone read a document to him, he could grasp it at one hearing and take the necessary steps.[36] The Ch'ŏngju Kwak also included both scholarly and military elements. Kwak Ch'u was an examination passer[37] who rose to the senior second-grade Chancellery scholar post before being banished in 1399.[38] On the military side, there was the infamous Kwak Ch'ung-bo and his son Sŭng-u. The *Veritable Records* relate that

the former consulting royal secretary Kwak Ch'ung-bo was exiled to Ch'ŏngju. Ch'ung-bo and Sŭng-u had a grievance and captured the former assistant director Hwang Mun and his wife, along with the student Kim Hwan, tied them up, nearly beat them to death, and smeared human excrement on their lips and cheeks. The Ministry of Punishment memorialized: "Kwak Ch'ung-bo is of an originally inferior nature and has become a *chaesang* only due to his military skill. Instead of being truly sincere and striving to repay the king's kindness, he has, along with his unworthy son, indulged in personal vengeance. We request that you confiscate the office certificates of Kwak Ch'ung-bo and his son and punish them severely according to law." Because Kwak Ch'ung-bo had shown military merit, the king merely banished him to Ch'ŏngju and dismissed his son Kwak Sŭng-u from his special commander post.[39]

The Chinju Ha, of which Ha Yun was a member, included the general Ha Sŭng-hae.[40] The Hwangnyŏ Min, of which Min Chi and Min Yŏ-ik were members, included the grand general Min Mu-gu.[41] Even the Ŭiryŏng Nam, which we earlier included among the possible "new scholar-official" descent groups, had a strong military orientation, with both Nam Un[42] and Nam Chi[43] having military-branch affiliations.

It is evident from these examples that the central *yangban* descent groups, both old and new, of the early Chosŏn dynasty included civil and military officials. Even though the civil branch retained its structural superiority and the vast majority of early Chosŏn *chaech'u* were of civil branch origins, it would be misleading to characterize the men who founded the Chosŏn simply as "scholar-officials."

Recruitment

The examination system was the primary means of recruitment of officials in the Chosŏn dynasty, even more so than in the Koryŏ. Its importance is illustrated by one study showing that over 90 percent of those who held first-grade offices in the State Council during the entire dynasty were examination graduates.[44] It does not necessarily follow, however, that 90 percent of the Chosŏn founders were examination graduates.

There is not sufficient biographical data on the middle- and low-ranking majority of the bureaucracy to permit us to make confident statements about the importance of examination system graduates in the bureaucracy as a whole. There is, however, a comparative wealth of information about high-ranking officials, particularly those of *chaech'u* rank. Since the *chaech'u* constituted the new dynasty's power elite, determining the proportion of examination graduates among these men is more meaningful for assessing the political importance of examination products than is determining the proportion of examination graduates among all officials.

Using the biographical information given in the *Veritable Records* and late Koryŏ examination rosters, I have ascertained the means of entry into the bureaucracy for 91 of the 207 known *chaech'u* of the 1392–1405 period. Of those, nine were known beneficiaries of the *ŭm* privilege and 82 were known examination passers. Thus 90 percent of the early Chosŏn *chaech'u* whose means of entry into the bureaucracy can be ascertained were graduates of the examination system.

Taken by themselves, however, these figures are misleading. We can get a better picture of the early Chosŏn *chaech'u* from the examination rosters for the final 30 years of the Koryŏ dynasty, which—unlike earlier rosters—appear to be complete. Assuming 25 to be a typical age for passing the examinations, any official age 55 or younger at the time of the founding of the Chosŏn dynasty would have passed the examinations in 1362 or later and should be on the examination rosters. Given this situation, the fact that only 40 percent (82 of the 207) of early Chosŏn *chaech'u* are known to have passed the examinations indicates that examination graduates accounted for fewer than half of the early Chosŏn *chaech'u*. This percentage is far lower than that noted for the Chosŏn dynasty as a whole, but close to that noted for the Koryŏ bureaucracy, where we found that roughly 60 percent of *chaech'u* were examination graduates and that 44 percent of the officials who belonged to the most powerful descent groups were products of the examination system.

A number of the early Chosŏn officials who were examination graduates are known to have been already in office at the time they sat for the examinations. Han Sang-gyŏng of Ch'ŏngju, for example, was a seventh-grade official of the Royal Provisions Office when he took the examinations in 1382, and Hŏ Hae of Kongam was a seventh-grade granary official when he sat for the examinations in the same year.[45] A number of men held military positions when they passed the examinations. Examples include Hŏ Si of Kongam, who was a senior seventh-grade special commander (*pyŏlchang*) when he passed the examinations in 1362,[46] as was Chŏng Chun of Ch'ogye in 1382.[47] Both Cho Pak of P'yŏngyang and Yi Tang of Kyŏngju were identified as former special commanders in 1382, while Yi Chong-sŏn of Hansan was a senior sixth-grade assistant commander (*nangjang*) and Hong Sang-bin of Namyang was a senior eighth-grade captain (*sanwŏn*).[48] It is unlikely that all these men from illustrious descent groups first gained office through military merit, especially since it was common practice to give the children of established official descent groups their first *ŭm* posts at very young ages. Pak Yong-un's study on the *ŭm* privilege in the Koryŏ shows not only that the *ŭm* privilege was used often and widely in the late Koryŏ, but that over time a change occurred in the posts granted as initial *ŭm* appointments. Whereas in the first half of the Koryŏ most *ŭm* appointments were limited to clerical posts, in the second half many were entry-level military posts.[49] It is virtually certain, therefore, that although we can identify only nine *ŭm* recipients among the early Chosŏn *chaech'u,* many of the first-and second-grade officials of the early Chosŏn first gained official posts via the *ŭm* privilege. This apparently heavy reliance on the *ŭm* privilege is yet another example of significant continuity between the Koryŏ and the early Chosŏn.

To summarize, we have seen that the Koryŏ dynasty's civil-dominated government structure continued basically unchanged after the founding of the Chosŏn and that, despite the military origins of the new ruling family, civil-branch institutions continued to play significant political roles. The social composition of the early Chosŏn bureaucracy was similar to that of the Koryŏ except that the top descent groups seem to have significantly strengthened their hold on the upper levels of government after 1392. The bulk of the most powerful descent groups of the early Chosŏn were of old Koryŏ *yangban* descent-group origins, and such prominent Koryŏ descent groups as the Andong Kwŏn, Hwangnyŏ Min, P'ap'yŏng Yun, and Munhwa Yu were the most powerful of the new dynasty. Some newer descent groups that might fit the "new scholar-official" mold appeared among the top descent groups of the early Chosŏn, but they enjoyed much less power than the old official descent groups; descent groups that first appeared in the central bureaucracy after the mid-fourteenth century accounted for less than 10 percent of all officials and all *chaech'u* during the 1392–1405 period. Only a small number of powerful late Koryŏ descent groups were eliminated from the central bureaucracy after the founding of the Chosŏn in 1392. Although the overwhelming majority of early Chosŏn *chaech'u* were of civil-branch origins, military officials played an important role. The means by which officials of the early Chosŏn entered the bureaucracy were largely identical to those of the Koryŏ period.

This investigation of the early Chosŏn central official class clearly indicates that there was no social revolution behind the change of dynasties from Koryŏ to Chosŏn. To the contrary, it appears that the most remarkable social aspect of the change of dynasties was continuity, both in structure and composition, of the central bureaucracy.

THE INTERNAL STRUCTURE OF *YANGBAN* DESCENT GROUPS

The foregoing analysis of the early Chosŏn bureaucracy was based primarily on *pon'gwan* descent-group affiliations. The later Chosŏn descent group was a complex entity with many branches, each embracing numerous lines of descent, some of illustrious social and political backgrounds and others obscure and undistinguished. Although the descent groups of the late Koryŏ–early Chosŏn era were organized differently from later ones and were not as fully articulated, the distinct possibility exists that many of the men identified as belonging to our top descent groups were only remotely related to each other and that some, if not most, came from descent-group segments that had only recently appeared in the central bureaucracy.[50]

The overwhelming majority of genealogies for Korean descent groups show them first beginning to branch out in the fifteenth and sixteenth centuries, but a few, such as that of the Munhwa Yu, indicate branching in the late Koryŏ period.[51] We have seen that it was not uncommon for Koryŏ kinship groups to separate into capital-based central official lines of descent and locally based *hyangni* segments, as seen in such politically prominent groups as the Andong Kwŏn, Kyŏngju Kim, and Kyŏngju Ch'oe. A finding that many men from the top descent groups of the early Chosŏn dynasty were of recent *hyangni* backgrounds would cast serious doubt on the degree of continuity indicated by analysis of descent groups alone.

Ancestry of Powerful Descent Groups of the Early Chosŏn

A review of the ancestry of each of the 38 most powerful descent groups would be long, tedious, and perhaps unnecessary. The first 10 groups, excluding the royal family, listed in table 3.7 are shown in table 3.8 as having had members in central offices throughout the late Koryŏ, from the pre-Kongmin era to the fall of the dynasty in 1392. The crucial question is whether the early Chosŏn officials from these ten top groups were direct descendants of prominent late Koryŏ officials or whether they came from other segments within the broadly defined surname/ancestral seat kinship group. These ten groups are the Hwangnyŏ Min, Andong Kwŏn, P'ap'yŏng Yun, Munhwa Yu, Andong Kim, Chŏnju Ch'oe, Chuksan Pak, Kyŏngju Yi, P'yŏngyang Cho, and Ch'ŏngju Han.

The Hwangnyŏ Min. The Hwangnyŏ Min were the single most powerful *yangban* descent group of the Koryŏ–Chosŏn transition. Table 3.7 shows that they had 12 members in the early Chosŏn central bureaucracy, with seven holding *chaech'u* rank. The Hwangnyŏ Min genealogical chart shows ancestry of early Chosŏn members of the Min. We can see that the early Chosŏn members belonged to two major segments, both of which trace back to the early Koryŏ senior second-grade associate chancellor Min Yŏng-mo (1112–93).[52] Min Chi (1248–1326), who made frequent trips to China and even received appointment to a post in the Yüan Hanlin Academy, rose to the top ranks of the Koryŏ government, holding a senior first-grade chancellor (*chŏngsŭng*) post.[53] Min Sang-jŏng held the senior second-grade associate chancellor post before his death in 1352.[54] Min Chong-yu (1245–1324) also achieved the associate chancellor post, and his son Min Chŏk (1269–1335) held a junior second-grade post in the Security Council (Milchiksa), while Min Sa-p'yŏng (1295–1359) rose to assistant chancellor under King Kongmin.[55]

Hwangnyŏ Min Genealogy

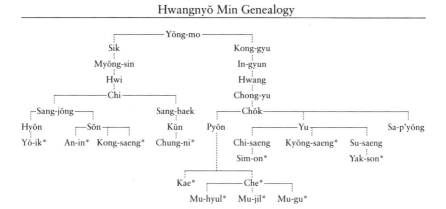

* Chosŏn officeholders

SOURCE: *Yŏhŭng Min-ssi sebo*, verified by other sources, including *KS* biographies, tombstone inscriptions and genealogies of other descent groups.

Late Koryŏ Min descendents continued to hold high offices in the early Chosŏn. Min Yŏ-ik, who was the head of the Censorate in 1397,[56] was a dynastic foundation merit subject.[57] Min Che was the senior first-grade State Council superintendent (*p'an* Ŭijŏngbu *sa*) in 1400,[58] and both Min Mu-gu and Min Mu-jil were merit subjects of T'aejong's enthronement.[59] The Hwangnyŏ Min form a prime example of an old Koryŏ *yangban* descent group at the top of the government after 1392.

The Andong Kwŏn.   One of the greatest descent groups of the late Koryŏ–early Chosŏn era, the Andong Kwŏn had 12 known officials recorded in the *Veritable Records* between the founding of the Chosŏn dynasty and the twelfth month of 1405, including five men who held *chaech'u* posts. The Andong Kwŏn genealogical chart shows that early Chosŏn members belonged to two segments: segment A, derived from Kwŏn Chung-si, a ninth-generation *hyangni* of the late twelfth–early thirteenth century; and segment B, from Kwŏn Yang-jun, a *hyangni* contemporaneous with Kwŏn Chung-si's grandchildren. Eleven of the 12 early Chosŏn members came out of Kwŏn Chung-si's line and counted among their direct ancestors such illustrious late Koryŏ

Andong Kwŏn Genealogy

SEGMENT A	SEGMENT B

```
                        ┌──────── Chung-si ────────────────────────┐          ?
            Su-p'yŏng                               Su-hong                    ?
                Wi                                   Cha-yŏ      Yang-jun
                Tan                                   Chŏk        Chŏng
Chae (Wang Hu) ──────┬── Pu ──────────────────┬── Kyŏm   Han-gong   Hyŏk
                     Ho                      Chun       Chung-hwa*   Yong-il
            ┌─── Hŭi*──────┬────────┐     ┌─Yŏm─┬────────┐          Hŭi-jŏng
          Kŭn*  Hwa*   Ch'ung*   U*    Yong  Kyun   Ho   ┌─Su─┐     Chin*
                                      Chŏng-ju  Hong* Tam* Po* Hun*
                                       Hŭi-dal*
```

* Chosŏn officeholders
SOURCE: Derived from *Andong Kwŏn-ssi songhwa po.*

officials as Kwŏn Tan (d. 1311, senior second-grade associate chancellor) and Kwŏn Pu (1262–1346, senior first-grade chancellor [*yŏng to* Ch'ŏmŭisa *sa*]).[60] Some might argue that Kwŏn Chung-si's descendants offer a good example of the "new scholar-officials" on the grounds that the segment first appeared in the central bureaucracy after the military coup. But by the Mongol era Kwŏn Chung-si's descendants were well established in the central bureaucracy. Members who typified the Andong Kwŏn's exalted status included Kwŏn Pu's sons Wang Hu (1296–1349, original name Kwŏn Chae), who was such a favorite of King Ch'ung-sŏn that he was adopted by the king and given the royal surname Wang, and Kwŏn Kyŏm, who married a daughter to the Yüan emperor and allied himself with Ki Ch'ŏl against King Kongmin's anti-Yüan reforms.[61] There seems no reason to doubt that the 11 early Chosŏn officials who belonged to this segment were descendants of a major late Koryŏ central *yangban* descent group.

What then of the one early Chosŏn member of the other segment, Kwŏn Chin? None of his antecedents appear in the *Koryŏsa,* suggesting a less than illustrious ancestral history. This is borne out by the entries in the genealogy: Kwŏn Chin's father, Kwŏn Hŭi-jŏng, is shown as a junior sixth-grade censor; no post or status is indicated for Kwŏn Yong-il; Kwŏn Hyŏk is shown as an examination graduate; and both Kwŏn Chŏng and Kwŏn Yang-jun are recorded as *hyangni.* This suggests that Kwŏn Chin may meet the "new scholar-official" criterion of recent *hyangni* origins.

Did Kwŏn Chin play a more significant role than his kinsmen in the founding and early consolidation of the Chosŏn? He did not hold *chaech'u* status during the first three Chosŏn reigns, nor was he on any of the lists of merit subjects promulgated during that time. In contrast, five members of Kwŏn Chung-si's segment held *chaech'u* posts: Kwŏn Chung-hwa, senior first-grade Finance Commission director (*yŏng* Samsa *sa*) in 1394;[62] Kwŏn Hwa, junior second-grade official of the Finance Commission in 1396;[63] Kwŏn Kŭn, important scholar and senior second-grade Chancellery scholar (*chŏngdang munhak*) in 1399;[64] Kwŏn Hong, a second-grade Security Council official in 1404;[65] and Kwŏn Hŭi, retired as junior first-grade Finance Commission superintendent (*p'an* Samsa *sa*) in 1400.[66] The central-official segment greatly outweighed Kwŏn Yang-jun's line in both numbers and importance.

P'ap'yŏng Yun Genealogy

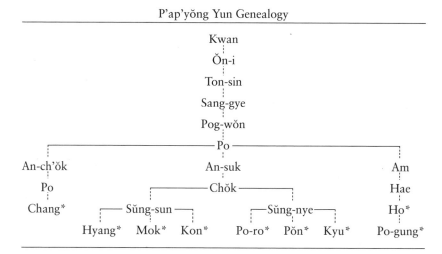

* Chosŏn officeholders

SOURCE: Derived from *P'ap'yŏng Yun-ssi sebo*, verified and supplemented by *KS* biographies and tombstone inscriptions.

The P'ap'yŏng Yun.   In the early Chosŏn bureaucracy the P'ap'yŏng Yun had nine members, including two first-grade officials. Their genealogical chart shows that all the known members of the P'ap'yŏng Yun in the early Chosŏn bureaucracy were descendants of Yun Po (d. 1329), a retired chancellor who was the direct descendent of the prominent early Koryŏ official Yun Kwan. All of his ancestors after Yun Kwan can be found in the *Koryŏsa* except his father, Yun Pog-wŏn, who nevertheless is mentioned in Yi Saek's *Mogŭn chip* as having held a senior ninth-grade recorder post.[67] Other prominent late Koryŏ members include Yun An-suk, an associate chancellor in 1349,[68] and Yun Hae, a senior third-grade official in 1363.[69]

This prominent Koryŏ *yangban* descent group played a major role in founding the Chosŏn. Yun Sŭng-sŏn, who died in 1392, was an important actor in the dethronement of King Ch'ang in favor of King Kongyang in 1389,[70] while Finance Commission superintendent Yun Ho was a dynastic foundation merit subject.[71] Most of the early Chosŏn Yun were civil officials, but there was also a significant military element in the junior third-grade grand general Yun Kon[72] and senior fourth-grade general Yun Po-ro.[73] The P'ap'yŏng Yun provide yet another example of a prominent early Chosŏn descent group that had been in the central bureaucracy since the early Koryŏ.

Munhwa Yu Genealogy

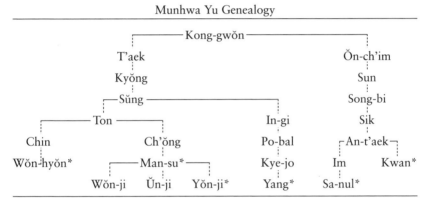

* Chosŏn officeholders

SOURCE: Based on Kawashima, "Clan Structure and Political Power in Yi Dynasty Korea," 23–27.

The Munhwa Yu. The Munhwa Yu, another illustrious late Koryŏ descent group, had eight members in the early Chosŏn government, including four *chaech'u*. Their genealogical chart shows that the members of the Munhwa Yu in the early Chosŏn bureaucracy belonged to two major segments. As with the Hwangnyŏ Min, however, heads of both segments were direct descendents of a single early twelfth-century official, in this case the famed scholar and calligrapher Yu Kong-gwŏn. Yu Kyŏng was a major official of the mid-thirteenth century and one of the prime movers behind the overthrow of the Ch'oe house. Yu Sŭng and Yu Ton also held *chaech'u* posts in the early fourteenth century.[74] Although the genealogy states that Yu Sun and his immediate descendants all held posts in the central government, no member of the segment is found in the dynastic histories until Yu Kwan appears in the *Veritable Records* under Yi T'aejo.[75] This may indicate that Yu Sun's segment was less illustrious than Yu Kyŏng's, but it does not mean that Yu Kwan and Yu Sa-nul were "new scholar-officials." Their forebears were not *hyangni*, but members of a less prominent line of a major central *yangban* descent group.

The Munhwa Yu had four early Chosŏn *chaech'u*: Yu Man-su, junior first-grade assistant chancellor in 1393;[76] Yu Wŏn-ji, junior second-grade official of the Security Council in 1393;[77] Yu Yang, junior second-grade consulting member of the Security Council in 1397;[78] and Yu Kwan, junior second-grade official in 1398.[79] Yu Yang was also a T'aejong enthronement merit subject.[80]

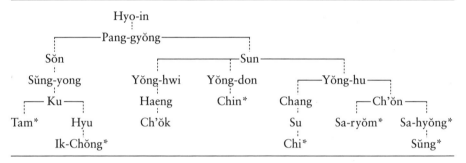

Andong Kim Genealogy

* Chosŏn officeholders
SOURCE: Based on Pak Yong-un's reconstruction of this segment in *Koryŏ sidae ŭmsŏje wa kwagŏje yŏn'gu*, 80–81, supplemented by the *Andong Kim-ssi taedongbo*, KS biographies, and tombstone inscriptions.

The Andong Kim.   The Andong Kim, who went on to become one of the most famous *yangban* descent groups of the mid- and late Chosŏn, had eight members in the early Chosŏn central government, including four men of *chaech'u* status. The segment that produced all eight began with the mid-Koryŏ chief of the Board of War (Pyŏngbu *sangsŏ*) Kim Hyo-in. Their genealogical chart shows that all early Chosŏn members of the Andong Kim were descended from Kim Sŏn or Kim Sun, sons of the famous official and military commander Kim Pang-gyŏng. Kim Sŭng-yong held a *chaech'u* post in the Security Council in 1328,[81] while all three of Kim Sun's sons—Yŏng-hu, Yŏng-don, and Yŏng-hwi—rose to become chancellors in the 1340s.[82] This segment of the Andong Kim was among the most powerful *yangban* descent groups of the late Koryŏ.

The Andong Kim were just as prominent in the early Chosŏn. The aged Kim Chin was honored as Lord of Sangnak (Sangnak *kun*) in 1393,[83] Associate Chancellor Kim Sa-ryŏm was a dynastic foundation merit subject,[84] Kim Sŭng attained *chaech'u* status in 1398,[85] and Kim Sa-hyŏng was appointed chancellor in 1401.[86] The Andong Kim suffered no loss in stature through the change of dynasties.

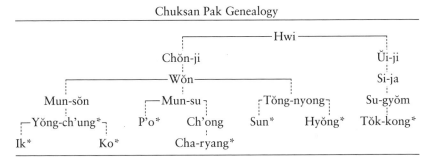

Chuksan Pak Genealogy

* Chosŏn officeholders
SOURCE: *Chuksan Pak-ssi Ch'unghŏn'gong p'abo,* verified and supplemented by tombstone inscriptions, literary collections, and *KS* biographies.

The Chuksan Pak.   The Chuksan Pak had two major *yangban* segments in the late Koryŏ. One, which first appeared in the early twelfth century and flourished during the military period, began with Pak Yŏng-hu and included such notables as Pak In-sŏk, Pak Mun-sŏng, Pak So, and Pak Hong, before fading in the early fourteenth century.[87] The other segment, descending through Pak Hwi, appeared in the central bureaucracy at about the same time and went on to produce eight officials and three *chaech'u* in the early Chosŏn. Although the Chukson Pak genealogical chart of this segment shows that Hwi was a direct descendent of Pak Yŏng-hu, I have been unable to confirm this. Pak Hwi appears in the *Koryŏsa* as a third-grade official in 1274.[88] His son Pak Chŏn-ji retired as a senior-second grade associate chancellor in 1321,[89] while his grandson Wŏn was a *chaech'u* and merit subject in 1327,[90] and his great grandson Tŏng-nyong was a mid-ranking censorate official under King Kongmin.[91] Whatever the early origins of this segment of the Chuksan Pak, by the late thirteenth century its members had clearly established themselves among the great central *yangban* descent groups of the late Koryŏ.

Chuksan Pak members were also prominent in the late fourteenth and early fifteenth centuries. The senior third-grade Pak Ch'ong, Wŏn's grandson, was made a merit subject for his support of Yi Sŏng-gye's seizure of power in 1388;

Ch'ong does not appear in the early Chosŏn bureaucracy because he died in 1390.[92] Eight members of Pak Hwi's segment did, however, hold office in the early Chosŏn, including Pak Yŏng-ch'ung, who held a second-grade post in the Security Council in 1393;[93] Pak Hyŏng, who held a junior second-grade post when he retired in 1398;[94] and Pak P'o, who also reached *chaech'u* status in 1398.[95] Pak Ch'ong's role in helping Yi Sŏng-gye indicates that the Chuksan Pak were active supporters of the new regime.

Kyŏngju Yi Genealogy

SEGMENT A			SEGMENT B			
Suk-chin	┌────────	Haek ────			────┐	
Ye	Chin				Se-gi	
Son-bo	┌Che-hyŏn┐		┌─────	Ch'ŏn──		───┐
Kil-sang	Ch'ang-no	Tal-chon	┌──Tal-ch'ung──┐			Kyŏng-jung
Chon-o	Pon*	Hang-nim	Song	Chon*	Su*	┌──Yuk── ┐
Nae*		Tam*	Sŭng-sang*			Chong-gyŏn* Chong-bo*

*Chosŏn officeholders
SOURCE: *Kyŏngju Yi-ssi sebo*, confirmed and supplemented by *KS* biographies, tombstone inscriptions, and literary collections.

The Kyŏngju Yi.   The Kyŏngju Yi, another prominent late Koryŏ *yangban* descent group, also placed eight officeholders in the early Chosŏn government, including one *chaech'u*. Early Chosŏn members came from two segments, both appearing in the dynastic histories during the late thirteenth century. The first member of segment A to appear in the Koryŏsa was Yi Suk-chin, a junior fourth-grade Chancellery official in 1270.[96] His son, Yi Ye, who served in the Yüan Chancellery during King Ch'unghye's reign (1330–32 and 1339–44), was, along with Cho Ik-ch'ŏng and Ki Ch'ŏl, an advocate of making Korea a Yüan province.[97] Yi Son-bo was a mid-ranking censorate official during the early fourteenth century,[98] and Yi Chon-o served as a mid-ranking official under King Kongmin.[99] Although the progenitor of segment B, Yi Haek, does not appear in the dynastic histories, Yi Saek[100] noted that he held a second grade post.[101] The first member of the segment to appear in the histories, Yi Chin (1244–1321), held a variety of top-level posts, including senior second-grade assistant chancellor under King Ch'ungsuk (r. 1313–30 and 1332–39),[102] and his son was the renowned scholar and official Yi Che-hyŏn, who was a close associate of King Ch'ungsŏn and spent many years in Yüan China. Yi Ch'ŏng held a state councillor (*ch'amni*) appointment in 1345,[103] and Yi Tal-ch'ung (d. 1385) was a mid-level official under King Kongmin.[104]

At the beginning of the Chosŏn, the Kyŏngju Yi had only one *chaech'u* member, the junior second-grade academician Yi Nae,[105] who was also a T'aejong enthronement merit subject.[106] On the other hand, however, the Yi placed several members in important mid-level surveillance and censorate posts, including Yi Su in 1393,[107] Yi Chong-gyŏn in 1396,[108] and Yi Sŭng-sang in 1399.[109]

Some historians have argued that Yi Che-hyŏn was a typical "new scholar-official." It is difficult, however, to see how this descent group, with its close ties to the Yüan court and the Koryŏ royal family and its large number of late Koryŏ officials, can be seen as anything other than part of the late Koryŏ *yangban* establishment. The Kyŏngju Yi appear to be a prime example of the transformation of men of *hyangni* origins into new central *yangban* descent groups that occurred throughout the Koryŏ period. Its members continued to enjoy considerable power and prestige after the founding of the Chosŏn dynasty.

P'yŏngyang Cho Genealogy

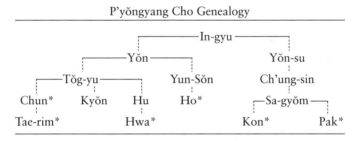

*Chosŏn officeholders
SOURCE: Based on *P'yŏngyang Cho-ssi sebo,* verified and supplemented by *KS* biographies and tombstone inscriptions.

P'yŏngyang Cho. The P'yŏngyang Cho had seven members in the early Chosŏn central bureaucracy, including five *chaech'u.* All P'yŏngyang Cho officeholders in the early Chosŏn were descendants of Cho In-gyu, who—as is well known—rose to fame and power under Mongol patronage in the late thirteenth century. Although the history of this descent group prior to Cho In-gyu is murky and at least one scholar believes that the Cho were of commoner origins, there is no question that by the first half of the fourteenth century they were well-established members of the Koryŏ central *yangban* class.[110] Cho Yŏn held a senior third-grade post in 1344,[111] Cho Yŏn-su held the senior second-grade assistant chancellor post before being exiled in the early fourteenth century,[112] Cho Ch'ung-sin was granted the noble title Lord of Sangwŏn County in 1354,[113] Cho Sa-gyŏm held a senior third-grade superintendent post in 1376,[114] and Cho Tŏg-yu also rose to a senior third-grade office.[115] The P'yŏngyang Cho were a prominent Koryŏ *yangban* descent group from Cho In-gyu's time until the very end of the dynasty.

There can be no doubt of the important role the P'yŏngyang Cho played in the early Chosŏn. Cho Chun is famed as the architect of the Rank Land Law (Kwajŏn Pŏp) reform and he, Cho Pak, and Cho Kyŏn were dynastic foundation merit subjects.[116] Cho Chun was a chancellor from 1392 to 1400, Cho Pak became a senior second-grade state councillor in 1398,[117] and Cho Hwa was a second-grade academician of the Secretariat in 1398.[118] Like the P'ap'yŏng Yun, the Cho had a military element in the senior fourth-grade general Cho Kon.[119] The P'yŏngyang Chos' influence was even greater than would be suggested by their not inconsiderable numbers in the early Chosŏn.

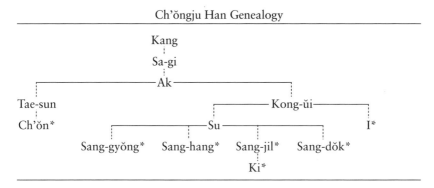

Ch'ŏngju Han Genealogy

*Chosŏn officeholders

SOURCE: Derived from the *Ch'ŏngju Han-ssi sebo*, verified and supplemented by *KS* biographies and tombstone inscriptions.

The Ch'ŏngju Han.   The Ch'ŏngju Han, who developed into one of the most important *yangban* descent groups of fifteenth-century Korea, had seven members in the bureaucracy during the 1392–1400 era, including four first- and second-grade officials. The Ch'ŏngju Han first appear in the histories with Han Kang (d. 1303), who rose to the position of senior second-grade associate chancellor before retiring.[120] Other prominent members in the late Koryŏ include Han Ak, who became chancellor in 1330;[121] Han Tae-sun, an associate chancellor in the mid-fourteenth century;[122] and Han Su, who was named Lord of Ch'ŏngsŏng[123] near the end of a career that included service as chief of rites.¹²⁴ This segment of the Ch'ŏngju Han was clearly a full-fledged part of the late Koryŏ *yangban* class. Important members in the early Chosŏn include Han Sang-gyŏng, a dynastic foundation merit subject¹²⁵ and director of the Security Council in 1395;¹²⁶ Han Sang-jil, senior second-grade Chancellery academician in 1396;¹²⁷ Han I, junior second-grade academician of the Security Council in 1393;¹²⁸ and Han Ch'ŏn, who retired as junior first-grade Finance Commission superintendent in 1400.¹²⁹ With merit subjects and *chaech'u* among their ranks, the Ch'ŏngju Han were one of the most prominent early Chosŏn *yangban* descent groups.

Chŏnju Ch'oe Genealogy

SEGMENT A	SEGMENT B
Kyun	Sun-jak
Po-sun	Sung
Yun-ch'ing	Nam-bu
Sŏ	Chŏn
Pi-il	Chŏng-sin
Sŏng-ji	Tŭk-p'yŏng
Mun-do	Chae
Sa-gyŏm	Yu-gyŏng*
Ŭr-ŭi	Sa-ŭi* Sa-gang* Sa-wi* Sa-gyu*
Sŏn* Koeng*	

* Chosŏn officeholders
SOURCE: Compiled from information in *KS* biographies, literary collections, and tombstone inscriptions.

The Chŏnju Ch'oe.   The Chŏnju Ch'oe placed seven members in the early Chosŏn bureaucracy, including one *chaech'u.* These men came from two segments, as detailed in the Chŏnju Ch'oe genealogical chart. The Chŏnju Ch'oe present an interesting example of a late Koryŏ *yangban* descent group that includes both military and civil segments. Segment A descended from Ch'oe Kyun, an examination graduate under King Injong who rose to a mid-ranking position and played an important role in suppressing Cho Wi-ch'ong's revolt during the early years after the military coup of 1170. His son Po-sun also passed the examinations and held a senior second-grade associate chancellor post in the mid-thirteenth century, while his grandson Yun-ch'ing held a low-ranking post.[130] The *Koryŏsa* does not tell us anything about Yun-ch'ing's offspring. The *Koryŏsa* biography of Ch'oe Sŏng-ji, a prominent *chaech'u* of the early fourteenth century, mentions only that he was a fourth-generation descendent of Po-sun and that his father was Pi-il.[131] Pak Yong-un, using examination-graduate rosters and literary collections, was able to establish that Pi-il's father was a mid-ranking civil official named Sŏ. A tombstone inscription written by Yi Che-hyŏn and contained in Yi's *Ikchae nan'go* confirms that Sŏ was Yun-ch'ing's son.[132] Later notable Koryŏ members of this segment include Sŏng-ji's son Mun-do, state councillor in 1345;[133] and Mun-do's grandson Ŭr-ŭi, a second-grade official in the Security Council in 1385.[134] Ch'oe Ŭr-ŭi's sons, Sŏn and Koeng, held mid-ranking posts in the early Chosŏn.[135]

Segment B of the Chŏnju Ch'oe appears as a line of military officials in the *Mansŏng taedongbo,* but none of the men in the Chŏnju Ch'oe genealogical chart can be found in the histories until Tŭk-p'yŏng appears as a mid-ranking civil official in 1314.[136] All, including Tŭk-p'yŏng, however, are listed in a tombstone inscription contained in Yi Saek's *Mogŭn chip.* This inscription shows that all of the men from Sun-jak to Chŏng-sin held mid- and high-ranking military posts, and that Tŭk-p'yŏng was a grand general who concurrently held a post as revenue minister.[137] Tŭk-p'yŏng's son Chae passed the government service examination during Ch'ungsuk's reign and held a variety of mid-ranking civil posts before being made Lord of Wansan (Wansan *kun*) by King U in the late fourteenth century.[138] Chae's son Yu-gyŏng held a variety of *chaech'u* posts and played an important role in helping T'aejong consolidate control over the military.[139] Perhaps as a consequence of their father's merit, all four of Yu-gyŏng's sons held civil posts in the early Chosŏn.

The Chŏnju Ch'oe not only provide us an example of an unbroken line of central officeholders from the early Koryŏ down to the early Chosŏn in segment A, but they also give us an example in segment B of a military line converting to a civil one in the late Koryŏ.

This examination of the ancestry of the 10 most powerful descent groups of the early Chosŏn reveals that all but one of the 86 members of these groups holding office in the new dynasty were direct descendants of important late Koryŏ *yangban.* Early Chosŏn members of these groups typically descended from a single important official of the Koryŏ period: only the Andong Kwŏn, Kyŏngju Yi, and Chŏnju Ch'oe had two segments that were apparently not closely related. All were well established in the central bureaucracy long before

King Kongmin took the throne in 1351, and at least four—the Hwangnyŏ Min, P'ap'yŏng Yun, Chŏnju Ch'oe, and Munhwa Yu—featured ancestors who had been continuously in office since before the military coup of 1170. It is abundantly clear that the most powerful descent groups at the beginning of the Chosŏn came from the great *yangban* descent groups of the Koryŏ.

Marriage Relations of the Great Descent Groups

The exclusive nature of these hereditary lines of central officeholders is further evidenced by their marriage patterns. Throughout the Koryŏ dynasty, marriage with the royal family was a virtual guarantee of power and prestige, as seen in such descent groups as the Ansan Kim, Kyŏngwŏn Yi, and Chŏngan Im. Six of the 10 top early Chosŏn descent groups had marriage ties with the Koryŏ royal family during the late thirteenth and fourteenth centuries. The Kyŏngju Yi and the P'yŏngyang Cho each married with the Wang royal family three times, the P'ap'yŏng Yun and Andong Kwŏn twice, and the Chuksan Pak and Chŏnju Ch'oe once. Furthermore, the Andong Kwŏn, in the person of Kwŏn Kyŏm, even married a daughter to the Yüan Mongol imperial family,[140] and the P'yŏngyang Cho married a daughter to a high-ranking Yüan official.[141]

We have seen how the great central official descent groups of the early Koryŏ used marriages to forge alliances that would secure their position at the top of society and politics. What kind of marriage relations, then, did the top 10 early Chosŏn descent groups have with each other and with other major descent groups of the late Koryŏ central bureaucracy? Table 3.11 shows the number of times these 10 groups married with each other during the late thirteenth and fourteenth centuries. We can see that these *yangban* descent groups were closely intermarried, sometimes as often as five times. This is similar to the pattern of intermarriage displayed by the Kyŏngwŏn Yi and other great descent groups of the early Koryŏ and, together with marriage ties to the royal family, suggests that the social stratum to which these descent groups belonged remained largely closed.

This likelihood is strengthened when we examine the marriage relations these 10 descent groups had with other prominent fourteenth- and early fifteenth-century elites. The P'ap'yŏng Yun, for example, entered into three marriages each with the Sŏngju Yi and the Namyang Hong, and two each with the Kwangsan Kim, Ch'angnyŏng Sŏng, Sunhŭng An, and Ŏnyang Kim. The P'yŏngyang Cho married three times with the Kwangsan Kim and twice each with the Kyoha No, Andong Kim, Hansan Yi, and Namyang Hong.

What then of the marriage relations of descent groups generally considered

TABLE 3.11
Intermarriage among the Top Ten Descent Groups,
Late Thirteenth and Fourteenth Centuries

	MH Yu	PP Yun	PY Cho	AD Kwŏn	KJ Yi	HN Min	CJ Han	CJ Ch'oe	AD Kim	CS Pak
Munhwa Yu	—	2	2	4	4	5	1	0	2	2
P'ap'yŏng Yun	1	—	3	1	3	5	5	1	0	1
P'yŏngyang Cho	2	3	—	1	3	1	2	1	2	3
Andong Kwŏn	4	1	1	1	5	2	1	1	3	1
Kyŏngju Yi	4	3	3	5	—	2	4	2	3	2
Hwangnyŏ Min	5	5	1	2	2	—	2	3	3	2
Ch'ŏngju Han	1	5	2	1	4	2	—	2	2	1
Chŏnju Ch'oe	0	1	1	1	2	3	2	—	2	1
Andong Kim	2	0	2	3	3	3	2	2	—	2
Chuksan Pak	2	1	3	1	2	2	1	1	2	—
Totals	21	21	18	20	28	25	20	13	19	15

SOURCE: Genealogies and tombstone inscriptions.

to be "new scholar-officials"? If they indeed constituted a new, distinct social class, we can reasonably expect that they would have married largely with descent groups of the same background. The known marriages of the Hansan Yi and the Ch'angnyŏng Sŏng, two of the most prominent "new scholar-official" descent groups, suggest otherwise. Late fourteenth- and early fifteenth-century marriage partners of the Hansan Yi included such illustrious old *yangban* as the Andong Kwŏn (three times),[142] Kwangsan Kim, Kyŏngju Kim, Kyŏngju Yi, and Wŏnju Wŏn. The Ch'angnyŏng Sŏng married with the P'ap'yŏng Yun, Sŏngju Yi, and Andong Kwŏn twice each, as well as with the Kwangsan Kim, Sunhŭng An, and Munhwa Yu. This pattern of extensive intermarriage between these two newer descent groups and established central official descent groups suggests that the Hansan Yi and the Ch'angnyŏng Sŏng were doing what successful groups of provincial origins had always done: become part of the capital establishment through intermarriage with other central descent groups.

What kind of marriage relations did Yi Sŏng-gye's northeastern military group have? Did they, too, seek to join the great descent groups, or did they maintain themselves as a largely separate social entity? There is no evidence of marriage between the northeastern military and the great central descent groups until the second half of the fourteenth century, when Yi Pang-gan married his daughter to Cho Pak of P'yŏngyang,[143] and Cho On of the Hanyang Cho married his daughter to Yun Kon of P'ap'yŏng.[144] That the two groups did not intermarry earlier reflects the northeastern military's status as newcomers to capital politics and society in the late Koryŏ.

This situation is well illustrated by the marriage history of the Chŏnju Yi, as recorded on the tombstone of Yi Sŏng-gye's father in 1393.[145] The three generations prior to Yi Sŏng-gye married women from northeastern backgrounds: Yi Sŏng-gye's great-grandfather Yi Hŭng-ni married a woman named Ch'oe from Anbyŏn; his grandfather Yi Ch'un married a woman named Pak from Munch'ŏn; and his father, Yi Cha-ch'un, married a woman named Ch'oe from Yŏnghŭng. Yi Sŏng-gye's first marriage was to a woman named Han from Anbyŏn, and his brother-in-law was Cho In-byŏk of the northeastern-based Hanyang Cho. It was not until Yi Sŏng-gye's children's generation that the Chŏnju Yi began to marry into established *yangban* descent groups. Yi Sŏng-gye's daughter married Yi Che of the Sŏngju Yi, and his sons married women from the Kyŏngju Kim, Hwangnyŏ Min (two), and Ch'angwŏn Ch'oe, as well as from the Koryŏ royal family. Chŏngjong obtained daughters-in-law from such well-established descent groups as the Namyang Hong (two) and the Chŏnju Ch'oe, while marrying his own daughters to sons of the Kyŏngju Kim, Kyŏngju Yi, and P'yŏngyang Cho. T'aejong followed the same pattern, marrying his offspring with descent groups such as the Kwangsan Kim, Andong Kwŏn, and P'yŏngyang Cho.[146] Such broad intermarriage with established *yangban* descent groups indicates that, like the Hansan Yi and the Ch'angnyŏng Sŏng, Yi Sŏng-gye and his northeastern military allies were joining, rather than overthrowing, the *yangban* descent groups of the Koryŏ.

The 10 most powerful early Chosŏn descent groups of Koryŏ central *yangban* origins seem to be representative of the early Chosŏn as a whole. Other prominent descent groups with pre-1351 roots—such as the Haeju Ch'oe, Kwangsan Kim, and Sŏngju Yi—also feature ancestry that can be traced back to mid- or early Koryŏ, and were closely intermarried with other top descent groups. The old Koryŏ central-official establishment survived largely intact into the fifteenth century and formed the nucleus of the central bureaucracy at the beginning of the Chosŏn dynasty.

THE GREAT *YANGBAN* DESCENT GROUPS AT MID-CENTURY

Even though the great official descent groups lasted through the change of dynasties and the political upheavals of the new dynasty's first decade, they could have been weakened or even destroyed soon after the Chosŏn had consolidated its power and T'aejong had reshaped the government through institutional reform. To investigate this possibility, I have compiled and analyzed data on the bureaucracy for two three-year periods at intervals of 25 and 50 years after T'aejong's institutional reforms were completed in 1405.

The Mid-Fifteenth-Century Bureaucracy

The first three-year period, 1430–32, falls near the middle of King Sejong's reign (1419–50), a time of confidence and vigor when the new dynasty was pushing forward in many areas, while the second three-year period, 1455–57, was a time of political turmoil when Sejo (r. 1455–68) seized the throne from his nephew Tanjong (r. 1452–55).

By the time Sejong took the throne, the new institutional structure had been in place for nearly 15 years and the number of chaech'u posts had been greatly reduced. The only officials participating in policy deliberations in the State Council were three senior first-grade state councillors, two junior first-grade associate councillors (ch'ansŏng), and two senior second-grade assistant councillors (ch'amch'an). A second set of elite officials in the early Chosŏn was made up of the men who filled the top posts of the Six Boards; these posts had been raised to the senior second-grade, and their incumbents had been authorized to bring matters directly to the throne instead of going through the State Council, giving them much greater authority than their Koryŏ predecessors, who were under the direct supervision of concurrently appointed members of the Todang. There was a scattering of other first- and senior second-grade posts, including the first minister of the Security Council, three directors of the Royal House Administration (Tollyŏngbu), and the chief magistrate of Seoul (Hansŏngbu p'anyun), for a grand total of 18 first- and senior second-grade chaech'u posts, a figure similar to the number of chaech'u posts in the early Koryŏ.

Tables 3.12 and 3.13 are based on the reduced number of chaech'u and depict the descent-group structure of the bureaucracy in sample years under Kings Sejong and Sejo, respectively. They show that the descent-group structure of the central bureaucracy appears to have been essentially a continuation of what we have seen in the late Koryŏ and the beginning of the Chosŏn. There was fairly broad representation in the bureaucracy as a whole, with around 100 different descent groups placing members in central offices, but a relatively small number of groups producing a disproportionately large number of top-

TABLE 3.12

Descent Structure of the Central Bureaucracy, 1430–32

Total known officials	293
Officials of known descent	182 (62%)
Total known *chaech'u*	48
Chaech'u of known descent	40 (83%)
Total descent groups	90
Descent groups with only one known official	50 (56%)
Most powerful descent groups*	30
Officials from most powerful descent groups	114 (39%)
Chaech'u from most powerful descent groups	33 (69%)

* Groups with three or more officials or two officials including one *chaech'u* or noble titleholder.

ranking officials. The major differences between tables 3.12 and 3.13 and their counterparts for the Koryŏ (tables 2.1 and 2.5) and the beginning of the Chosŏn (table 3.3) are a greater proportion of officials of known descent origins (62 and 65 percent, vs. 49 percent in 1392–1400) and a higher representation of the most powerful descent groups in the bureaucracy as a whole (35 and 37 percent as opposed to 23 percent in 1392–1400). The differences are probably due to the greater availability of information on descent backgrounds as we move into the fifteenth century and do not appear to reflect any major shift in the overall structure of the bureaucracy.

Who, then, made up the bureaucracy of the mid-fifteenth century? Did old Koryŏ *yangban* descent groups continue to flourish, or did they give way to new groups? Table 3.14 arrays the most powerful descent groups of the 1430–32 and 1455–57 periods. Seventeen of the 22 powerful late Koryŏ central *yangban* descent groups appear among the 43 groups in table 3.14. Their members included such famous political giants as Han Myŏng-hoe of Ch'ŏngju, Kwŏn Nam of Andong, and Yu Sŏng-wŏn of Munhwa. On the whole, these old descent groups, led by the Andong Kwŏn and P'ap'yŏng Yun, still dominated the central government a half-century after the establishment of the Chosŏn. The five missing groups are the old Koryŏ royal family and the Kongam Hŏ, Ŏnyang Kim, Kyŏngju Ch'oe, and P'yŏnggang Ch'ae. The demise of the Kaesŏng Wang is no surprise, and we have already seen that the Ŏnyang Kim

TABLE 3.13
Descent Structure of the Central Bureaucracy, 1455–57

Total known officials	377
Officials of known descent	246 (65%)
Total known *chaech'u*	46
Chaech'u of known descent	44 (96%)
Total descent groups	108
Descent groups with only one known official	62 (57%)
Most powerful descent groups*	32
Officials from most powerful descent groups	141 (37%)
Chaech'u from most powerful descent groups	39 (85%)

* Groups with three or more officials or two officials including one *chaech'u* or noble titleholder.

and P'yŏnggang Ch'ae were already in decline well before the fall of the Koryŏ dynasty. Although clearly diminished in strength, neither the Kyŏngju Ch'oe nor the Kongam Hŏ vanished totally from the bureaucracy in the early Chosŏn; each had one known official during the 1430–32 and 1455–57 periods.

If 17 of the 43 descent groups in table 14 are prominent old Koryŏ *yang-ban,* what of the other 26? Eleven of these can be identified as lesser, but still established, members of the late Koryŏ bureaucracy.[147] That leaves 15 descent groups that do not appear to have been members of the old Koryŏ central *yang-ban* class. This suggests that sometime around the founding of the Chosŏn, members of new descent groups began to rise in the central bureaucracy.

In order to give this possibility the fairest possible review, I count as descent groups new to the mid-fifteenth century the nine from table 14 that actually first appeared in the central bureaucracy during the last 40 years of the Koryŏ,[148] in addition to the six new groups that can be confirmed in central offices only after 1392.[149] Together these 15 new groups (36 percent of all powerful descent groups) accounted for 17 officials (12 percent of all powerful descent-group officials) and eight *chaech'u* (21 percent of all powerful descent group *chaech'u*) during the 1430–32 period and 31 officials (28 percent of all powerful descent-group officials) and 11 *chaech'u* (28 percent of all powerful descent-group *chaech'u*) during the 1455–57 period. The six truly new descent groups (14 percent of all most powerful descent groups) accounted for 12 offi-

TABLE 3.14
Most Powerful Descent Groups, 1430–32 and 1455–57

1430–32		1455–57	
Descent Group	*Officials*-Chaech'u	*Descent Group*	*Officials*-Chaech'u
Andong Kwŏn*	8-3	Andong Kwŏn*	13-3
P'ap'yŏng Yun*	7-2	P'ap'yŏng Yun*	11-3
Chŏnju Yi	7-2	Hansan Yi	8-4
Munhwa Yu*	7-1	Ch'angnyŏng Sŏng	8-3
Ch'angnyŏng Sŏng	5-1	Namyang Hong*	8-1
Chinju Kang	5-1	Ch'ŏngju Han*	6-3
Chŏnŭi Yi	5-0	Sŏngju Yi*	6-1
Sŏngju Yi*	4-1	Kwangju Yi	6-1
Hansan Yi	4-1	Chinju Kang	5-1
Chŏnju Ch'oe*	4-1	Munhwa Yu*	5-0
Hwangnyŏ Min*	4-1	Hwangnyŏ Min*	4-1
Sunhŭng An*	4-1	Sunch'ŏn Pak	4-1
Yangju Cho	4-1	Kwangsan Kim*	4-0
Miryang Pak	4-0	Sunhŭng An*	4-0
Chinju Ha	3-3	Yangsŏng Yi	4-0
Yŏngil Chŏng	3-2	Hadong Chŏng	3-2
Hadong Chŏng	3-1	Tongnae Chŏng	3-2
Ch'ŏngju Han*	3-1	Kyŏngju Yi*	3-1
Hayang Hŏ	3-1	Yŏnan Kim	3-1
P'yŏngsan Sin	3-1	Yŏngil Chŏng	3-1
P'yŏngyang Cho*	3-1	Kimhae Kim	3-1
Chinju Chŏng	3-0	Andong Kim*	3-0
Tanyang U*	3-0	Kyŏngju Kim	3-0
Hanyang Cho	3-0	Ch'angnyŏng Cho	3-0
Hoedŏk Hwang	2-2	Nŭngsŏng Ku	3-0
Hwangnyŏ Yi	2-1	Yŏnan Yi	3-0
Tongnae Chŏng	2-1	Chŏnju Yi	2-2
Yŏnan Kim	2-1	Chinju Ha	2-2
Wŏnju Wŏn*	2-1	Kaesŏng Yi	2-2
Yŏnan Yi	2-1	Changsu Hwang	2-1
		Wŏnju Wŏn*	2-1
		Yangju Cho	2-1
Total: 30	114-33	32	141-39

* Powerful *yangban* descent group of the late Koryŏ

cials (11 percent of total powerful descent-group new officials) and four *chaech'u* (12 percent of all powerful descent-group officials) during the 1430–32 period, and six officials (4 percent of all powerful descent-group officials) and four *chaech'u* (10 percent of all powerful descent group *chaech'u*) during the 1455–57 period. In both 1430–32 and 1455–57 new descent groups were underrepresented in the bureaucracy as a whole and at the top levels, as was the case in earlier periods.

One can argue, of course, that the focus on the numerical representation of descent groups obscures the rise of important individuals of numerically under-represented groups who came up through the examination system and made their way to the top not through hereditary privilege or family connections but rather through talent and hard work. The presence of significant numbers of such men in the early Chosŏn bureaucracy would suggest that underneath the strongly aristocratic facade presented by the great *yangban* descent groups the way was now open for "scholar-officials" to rise on the basis of merit. Indeed, there are a number of men who passed the government service examinations in the closing years of the Koryŏ and went on to play important polit-ical and intellectual roles in the first half of the fifteenth century who seem to fall into this category: Hŏ Cho of the Hayang Hŏ, Maeng Sa-sŏng of the Sinch'ang Maeng, Pyŏn Kye-ryang of the Miryang Pyŏn, Ha Yun of the Chinju Ha, and Hwang Hŭi of the Changsu Hwang.[150]

The tombstone inscription for Hŏ Cho, however, indicates that all of his immediate patrilateral forebears had held offices in the late Koryŏ. His father, Kwi-ryong, was a mid-ranking censorial official, his grandfather Yun-ch'ang a surveillance official, his great-grandfather a mid-ranking civil official, and his great-great-grandfather a grand general. His matrilateral forebears included members of prominent late Koryŏ descent groups, including Yi Chik of the Sŏngju Yi and An Hyang of the Sunhŭng An. Furthermore, Hŏ Cho first entered official service, prior to taking the examinations, via the *ŭm* privilege.[151] This suggests that Hŏ Cho belonged to a line of less prominent but nonetheless well-established late Koryŏ *yangban*.

We have less information about the background of Maeng Sa-sŏng, but we know that his father Hŭi-do held a low-ranking civil office in the late Koryŏ and his mother was the granddaughter of the great Ch'oe Yŏng of the Ch'angwŏn Ch'oe.[152] We also have only limited information on Pyŏn Kye-ryang's origins. None of his immediate forebears appears actually to have held office in the dynastic government, although all were honored, probably because of Pyŏn Kye-ryang's achievements, with posthumous appointments. Nonetheless, Pyŏn, too, seems to have been connected with prominent late

Koryŏ *yangban;* his mother was a daughter of Cho Sŏk of the Ch'angnyŏng Cho.[153]

According to Ha Yun's tombstone inscription, his father, grandfather, and great-grandfather all held low and mid-ranking posts in the Koryŏ bureaucracy, and his mother was the daughter of an honorary officeholder of the Chinju Kang.[154] Furthermore, his eulogy in the *Veritable Records* tells us that his wife was the daughter of Yi In-mi of the Sŏngju Yi.[155] Ha Yun's background suggests that he, too, was not a newcomer to the ranks of central *yangban*.

The father of the great scholar and official Hwang Hŭi held a mid-ranking post in the late Koryŏ, but neither his grandfather nor great-grandfather seems to have held an actual office. Also, Hwang Hŭi's mother was from a comparatively obscure descent group, the Yonggung Kim. Hwang Hŭi's career and what is known about his family background suggests that he may have been a relative newcomer who rose primarily on the basis of his merit. Even here, however, caution is in order. His tombstone inscription states that he was born in the Koryŏ capital and that he first entered government service via the *ŭm* privilege as a palace recorder.[156]

The backgrounds of these five men indicate that they either had close connections with the old Koryŏ *yangban* establishment or, as in the case of Hwang Hŭi, benefited from ascriptive privilege in *ŭm* appointments. This does not totally preclude the possibility that genuinely "new" men may have been able to use the examination system to achieve a place in the central bureaucracy during the Koryŏ-Chosŏn transition, but it suggests that it was probably difficult to rise to any position of prestige and authority without ties to established *yangban* descent groups.

Some descent groups that were very powerful at the beginning of the Chosŏn—such as the Hwangnyŏ Min and P'yŏngyang Cho—appear to have lost much of their power by the time of Sejong. It is not clear what factors lay behind the decline of the P'yŏngyang Cho, but the downturn in the Hwangnyŏ Min's fortunes date to the purge of Min Mu-gu and Min Mu-hyul by T'aejong. The Min were not only the most powerful *yangban* descent group at the beginning of the dynasty, but they were also royal in-laws. T'aejong's purge of the Min seems to have been motivated by a determination to prevent the rebirth of the kind of royal in-law government that had plagued the Koryŏ. It is significant that the Min were not totally destroyed by T'aejong's purges; they were already making a comeback by Sejo's reign and would later reclaim their place at the top of the central *yangban* establishment. Another descent group worthy of note here, one that had suffered a significant setback during the Koryŏ-Chosŏn transition but was now reemerging as a major political force, is the Hansan Yi, of which Yi Saek was a member. The Yis' resurgence is not as dramatic as it may seem, however. Yi Saek himself had been allowed to return to the capital and reclaim his noble title as Lord of Hansan in 1395.[157] His children and grandchildren were already back in office by the time T'aejong took the throne in 1400.[158]

The ability of the great *yangban* descent groups to restore themselves, as seen in the Hwangnyŏ Min, Hansan Yi, and others, is an intriguing feature of the traditional elite. No doubt the close marriage ties the *yangban* maintained with each other was a factor, but it suggests that in the eyes of the *yangban* inherited social status ultimately outweighed whatever political sins members of a prominent descent group might have committed.

The Examination System in the Mid-Fifteenth Century

Conventional wisdom holds that the major difference between the Koryŏ and the Chosŏn was the new dynasty's emphasis on recruitment through the examination system. Certainly by the mid-Chosŏn virtually all high officials were examination graduates, but Kim Yŏng-mo's data on the means of entry of top officials in the early Chosŏn, which shows that only 66 percent of the senior first-grade officials of the State Council were civil service examination passers, casts doubt on how radically the new dynasty revised its recruitment policies.[159]

This suspicion gains strength from investigation of the examination system as a means of entry for mid-fifteenth century *chaech'u*. We have almost complete lists of successful examination candidates from the 1360s on. Thus, unlike for earlier periods, we should with near-total accuracy be able to ascertain whether mid-fifteenth-century officials were examination graduates. Of the 33 *chaech'u* in office from 1430 to 1432, 19 (58 percent) were examination graduates; of the 39 *chaech'u* of the 1455–1457 period, 20 (51 percent) were graduates. These are far short of the 90-plus percentages Kim Yŏng-mo reports for later in the Chosŏn, and much closer to the 40 percent proportion we found at the beginning of the Chosŏn. These figures suggest that rather than looking at the founding of the Chosŏn as a turning point in the development of the examination system, we would do better to consider it as one moment in a period of gradual transition.

How important was the examination system to the top descent groups of Sejong's and Sejo's reigns? The answer is mixed. Some of the old official descent groups made heavy use of the examination system in the mid-fifteenth century. In the case of the Andong Kwŏn, 12 of the 14 men in office in 1430–32 and 1455–57 were examination graduates, as were five of eight Sunhŭng An

TABLE 3.15

Descent Groups with the Most Examination Graduates, 1392–1592

Descent Group	Graduates
Andong Kim	112
Chŏnju Yi	103
Kwangsan Kim	78
P'ap'yŏng Yun	70
Chinju Kang	69
Andong Kwŏn	65
Namyang Hong	63
Hwangnyŏ Min	55
Kyŏngju Yi	54
Chŏnŭi Yi	54

SOURCE: Edward Wagner, cited in Clark, "Chosŏn's Founding Fathers," 39.

and five of eight Hwangnyŏ Min. On the other hand, some of the old *yang-ban* descent groups seem to have relied almost totally on other means, such as the *ŭm* privilege. The Namyang Hong had only two examination passers among nine officials of the 1430–32 and 1455–57 periods, and the Sŏngju Yi and Ch'ŏngju Han had only one each. Even such relatively new descent groups as the Hansan Yi and Ch'angnyŏng Sŏng made light use of the examination system. Just three of 11 Hansan Yi officials were products of the examinations, as were only three of the 12 Ch'angnyŏng Sŏng. Clearly many of the descent groups relied on traditional privileges to maintain themselves at the top of the mid-fifteenth-century Chosŏn sociopolitical order.

Perhaps, however, a small number of the descent groups new to the bureaucracy in the mid-fifteenth century represented the advent of a more meritocratic element that was to lead the way to a new sociopolitical structure centered around the examination system. Here, again, the evidence is mixed. Some of the new groups seem to have relied almost totally on the examination system. Examples include the Chinju Ha (of which Ha Yun was a member), with three examination graduates out of four officials; the Yangju Cho and Kwangju Yi, with five out of six; the Sunch'ŏn Pak, with four out of four; and the Nŭngsŏng Ku, with three out of three. On the other hand, none of the four Hanyang Cho officials of the 1430–1432 and 1455–1457 periods, the Hoedŏk Hwang *chaech'u*, or the Changsu Hwang officials of the 1455–57 period passed the examinations, and only one of the six Yŏngil Chŏng officials passed.[160] This makes it difficult to say that the descent groups new to the bureaucracy in the mid-fifteenth century were precursors of a more meritocratic system. Edward Wagner's compilation of the descent groups with the most higher civil-service examination passers for the first two hundred years of the Chosŏn may be instructive here. The data in table 3.15 strongly suggests, pending detailed review of the direct ancestry of the examination graduates, that descendants of old Koryŏ *yangban* descent groups continued to dominate the examination system. This indicates two things. First, the groups that rose through the examinations after the founding of the Chosŏn, such as the Chinju Ha and Kwangju Yi, were not precursors of a new sociopolitical order, although they may have served as catalysts in the development of the examination system. Second, the rise of the examination system as the necessary prerequisite to official success in the sixteenth century did not subvert the highly ascriptive sociopolitical order that the Chosŏn dynasty inherited from the Koryŏ.

The Powerful Descent Groups as Central Yangban

One of the most important points of the conventional interpretation is that the old aristocrats of the Koryŏ were capital-based and the "new scholar-officials" of the Chosŏn were locally based.[161] As Song June-ho has pointed out, in the later Chosŏn *yangban* were found widely dispersed throughout the country in locales where they had lived for generations (*segŏ*).[162] There is also evidence that some of the most powerful *yangban* of the Koryŏ–Chosŏn transition maintained their permanent homes in, or at least maintained close ties with, the countryside.

We have a number of examples of late Koryŏ–early Chosŏn officials returning to the countryside after leaving office. One such example is Yun Hwan, who was prime minister in 1380.[163] According to his biography in the *Koryŏsa*, Yun, a wealthy man who had served five kings and had been a *chaech'u* under three, requested permission to return to Ch'irwŏn, his ancestral seat. Arriving there, he found that the area was in the grip of a terrible famine. In order to succor the people, he burned all of the notes of debt he was holding.[164] This not only shows that Yun Hwan returned to his descent group's provincial home, but that he had substantial economic interests there. Another example of a late Koryŏ *yangban* descent group with close ties to its ancestral seat is the Sŏngju Yi, whose members continued to be buried in Sŏngju even after several generations of service as dynastic officials.[165]

There are also instances of central officials returning to local bases that were not their ancestral seats. For example, in 1404 Yi Kŏ-i and his son Yi Chŏ, royal in-laws and members of the Ch'ŏngju Yi, were banished to their native place (*kohyang*) in Chinch'ŏn.[166] How long their forebears had been in Chinch'ŏn is unknown. Another example was Yi Sŏng-gye, who in 1391 requested permission to retire to P'yŏngsan in Hwanghae Province, saying that he had decided "to return to the fields and villages to spend what was left of his life."[167] Although the term "fields and villages" (*chŏlli*) is often taken by historians to mean native home districts, Yi Sŏng-gye's home district, as is well known, was in modern day Hamgyŏng Province, not Hwanghae. It seems, likely that Yi Sŏng-gye had acquired, through royal grants or other means, an estate in P'yŏngsan to which he felt he could retire, or at least claim to retire.

These examples show a variety of provincial bases with which central officials had ties and to which they could return after leaving office: ancestral seats, home districts other than ancestral seats, and estates or other lands acquired through government service or other means. This evidence would seem to bolster the argument that the men who founded the Chosŏn were locally based elements.

One possible indicator of permanent residence is the location of tombs. There is a natural tendency for people to be buried in the area they consider home; furthermore, in a Confucian society such as fourteenth- and fifteenth-century Korea, the demands of ancestor worship ritual required that burial sites be reasonably close to where the deceased's descendants were expected to live. Kim Yong-sŏn's recent study on Koryŏ ruling-class tombsites, which uses data from tombstone inscriptions to analyze burial sites as indicators of residence, finds a gradually increasing tendency for high officials, typified by members of the Sŏngju Yi, to be buried outside the capital region throughout the Koryŏ, especially in the final years of the dynasty, and concludes that this provides further evidence of the rise of locally based new elements in the late Koryŏ.[168]

It should be noted, however, that even Kim Yong-sŏn's study shows that the vast majority of late Koryŏ officials were still being buried in the environs of the capital city. There is other substantial evidence to indicate that the powerful *yangban* descent groups of the Koryŏ-Chosŏn transition maintained their permanent homes in the capital. In 1393, when Yi T'aejo was on a trip to check sites for a new capital, an official of the Security Council brought him a message from the Todang that a royal consort was ill and that bandits had appeared in P'yŏngju (P'yŏngsan) and Pongju. Sensing an effort to lure him back to the capital, T'aejo said, "All the great families dislike relocating the capital and are using these excuses to stop me. The *chaech'u* have long lived in Songgyŏng [Kaegyŏng] and don't want to move elsewhere; how could it be their intention to relocate the capital?"[169] This entry, anecdotal though it may be, indicates that the great descent groups who still dominated the Todang in the years right after the founding of the new dynasty were capital-based elements.

In hopes of providing a more definitive answer to the question of where the great *yangban* descent groups of the Koryŏ-Chosŏn transition maintained their permanent homes, I compiled and analyzed data on burial sites from the genealogies of the 10 most powerful descent groups of the 1392–1405 period. I was able to identify tombsites for 58 officials of the late Koryŏ and 39 of the early Chosŏn. Forty-five of the 58 late Koryŏ officials were buried in the environs of the capital, with favored locales being Ubong, Changdan, and P'ungdŏk; of the 13 men not buried in the capital district, eight were buried in their ancestral seats (Andong, Munhwa, P'aju, and Yŏju), three in the environs of Hanyang, and two in Ch'ŏngju. Of the 39 officials of the early Chosŏn, 29 were buried in the Hanyang region, with favored locales being Kyoha, Koyang, Kwangju, and Yongin. Four were buried near Kaegyŏng, which suggests some residual ties with the old Koryŏ capital, and the other six were buried in a variety of locations extending from Namwŏn in the south to P'yŏngsan in the north. It would appear, therefore, that most of the powerful *yangban* of the late Koryŏ and early Chosŏn maintained their permanent homes in the capital region.

How, then, did *yangban* come to be dispersed throughout the country in later years? Substantial evidence in the case of one descent group, the Munhwa Yu, is offered by Fujiya Kawashima, who analyzed the distribution of burial places for the Munhwa Yu throughout the Koryŏ and Chosŏn dynasties. Kawashima found that during the late Koryŏ–early Chosŏn era Munhwa Yu members were all entombed in the environs of the capital, and that they were first buried in the provinces in significant numbers late in the fifteenth century, probably having moved from the capital to the areas where their Rank Land prebends were located.[170] Similar patterns in the distribution of burial sites can be found in other late Koryŏ–early Chosŏn *yangban* descent groups such as the Ch'ŏngju Han and Wŏnju Wŏn.[171]

It is doubtful that the majority of *yangban* who occupied high office at any time in the Chosŏn maintained primary residences out in the countryside. Nonetheless, the evidence indicates that if the central bureaucracy of Chosŏn was ever made up primarily of locally based elements, it would have been a phenomenon of mid- and late Chosŏn, not of the Koryŏ-Chosŏn change of dynasties.

What, then, about central officials who, for whatever reason, left the capital and established permanent homes in the countryside? Did these men lose their status once they left office and departed the capital? That seems unlikely in a society as conscious of hereditary rights and privileges as traditional Korea. Han Yŏng-u's study on the late Koryŏ–early Chosŏn *hallyang* (locally based former central officials and provincially domiciled children of central officials) shows that they were considered to be members of the ruling stratum because their official ranks were recognized whether they lived in the capital or in the provinces.[172] Han's findings, taken in conjunction with remarks in the *Veritable Records* about local *yangban,* suggests that former officials retained their status as *yangban* even after returning to the provinces. These men should not, however, be confused with the *hyangni* local elites of the early and mid-Koryŏ period. Whereas the Koryŏ *hyangni* derived power and prestige from their status as semiautonomous local rulers, the locally based former officials of the late Koryŏ–early Chosŏn period derived power and prestige from their backgrounds as former holders or descendants of holders of offices in the central government—in short, from their status as *yangban.*

ECONOMIC RESOURCES OF THE EARLY CHOSŎN *YANGBAN*

Nowhere in the sources for the early Chosŏn period is there a systematic treatment, or even a basic description, of land tenure arrangements. This leaves us with no choice but to rely on whatever bits of information we can glean from the *Veritable Records* and literary collections. The pickings are sparse. What can be found, however, contradicts the conventional assumption that the founding of the new dynasty entailed the destruction of the great *nongjang* estates of the late Koryŏ aristocracy. On the contrary, it indicates that continued ownership of large landed estates was a prominent feature of the early Chosŏn.[173]

Several sources mention the ownership of estates by central officials in the early Chosŏn. In 1398 Nam Chae of the Uiryŏng Nam, who had been involved in Yi Pang-gan's revolt, was arrested after fleeing his family's *nongjang* in Kwaju, where he had been visiting his mother.[174] Nam Chae was a dynastic foundation merit subject who had received from Yi Sŏng-gye a land grant—perhaps this estate in Kwaju. But why was it located in Kyŏnggi Province, which supposedly had been set aside in its entirety for Rank Land prebends? And why was it referred to as a *nongjang,* the term used for the great estates of the Koryŏ period?

The *Veritable Records* also tell us that in 1399 Kwak Ch'u of the Ch'ŏngju Kwak was banished to his estate (*nongjang*) in P'yŏngju.[175] This was only seven years after the new dynasty was founded. Another piece of evidence for the continued existence of the great *nongjang* estates of *yangban* comes from a *Veritable Records* entry for the fifth month of 1393 describing how Pak Yŏngch'ung took revenge against a magistrate for drafting into military service four commoners who were hiding on Pak's Chuksan estate.[176] Pak was made a merit subject in the seventh month of 1393, but whatever lands he received then could not have formed this estate, since the incident had already occurred. Pak had an estate, at his ancestral seat, only two years after implementation of the the Rank Land reform.

Yet another example of the survival of an estate from the late Koryŏ into the early Chosŏn is the case of the lands of the Sunhŭng An in the P'ap'yŏng area of Kyŏnggi Province. Sŏng Hyŏn wrote in the second half of the fifteenth century that An Mok, a high-ranking official of the mid-fourteenth century, had "reclaimed wastelands west of P'aju, where he cultivated broad fields and built a large residence. His descendants have flourished, owning many thousand *kyŏl* of fields, over 100 households of slaves, and woodlands that shade 10 *li* (one *li* equals approximately one-third mile). Now over 100 of his descendants live on those lands."[177]

Here we see an estate, located in the capital district, that continued to flourish and provide economic sustenance for the early Chosŏn descendants of a high official of the late Koryŏ. Evidence of this sort, fragmentary though it may be, suggests that the change of dynasties did not significantly alter the pattern of landed estate holding that had developed in the Koryŏ.

The early Chosŏn *yangban* had two sources of labor to work their estates: slaves and tenant farmers. Some scholars argue that officials used both tenants and slaves to till their fields,[178] while others, such as Sudo Yoshiyuki and Yi Sŏng-mu, argue that early Chosŏn officials primarily used slaves.[179]

There is considerable evidence of the importance of slaves to central *yangban*. Grants of slaves invariably accompanied land grants to merit subjects, as in the ninth month of 1392, when the king gave Pae Kŭng-nyŏm and Cho Chun 220 *kyŏl* of land and 30 slaves each; Kim Sa-hyŏng, Chŏng To-jŏn, and Nam Ŭn 200 *kyŏl* of land and 25 slaves each; Yi Che, Yi Hwa, Chŏng Hŭigye, Yi Chi-ran, Chang Sa-gil, Cho In-ok, Nam Chae, Chŏng T'ak, and Cho Pak 170 *kyŏl* of land and 20 slaves each; Chŏng Ch'ŏng, O Mong-ŭl, and Kim In-ch'an 150 *kyŏl* of land and 15 slaves each; and various second-grade merit subjects 100 *kyŏl* of land and 10 slaves each.[180] Again in 1398, first-grade merit subjects were given 200 *kyŏl* of land and 25 slaves, second-grade merit subjects were given 150 *kyŏl* of land and 15 slaves, and the rest were given 100 *kyŏl* of land and 10 slaves.[181] The throne provided both land and the labor power to work it, perhaps hoping to prevent the growth of tenancy and thereby maximize its access to human resources.

The concurrent giving of land and slaves indicates that officials were dependent to some degree on slaves to work the land. There is other evidence, qualitative in nature, of the importance of slaves to the *yangban*. Ha Yun stated in 1402 that "our people love their slaves as they do their hands and feet," while Yang Sŏng-ji wrote in 1452 that "our country's slave law is old and the officials rely on it for their livelihood. If land is a person's lifeline, then slaves are his hands and feet."[182]

The closest thing to quantitative evidence presents itself in royal attempts to limit slave ownership. In 1414 King T'aejong tried to limit the number of slaves to 130 for first-grade officials, 100 for second-grade, 90 for third-grade, 80 for fourth-grade, 60 for fifth and sixth-grade, and 30 for seventh-grade and lower. When this encountered resistance, he raised the limits in the next year, allowing 130 slaves for first- and second-grade officials, 100 for third- through sixth-grade, and 80 for seventh-grade and lower. Even this attempt floundered in the face of official opposition and was never enacted.[183] Whether this meant that many officials owned, or hoped to own, more slaves than T'aejong's limits is not certain, but even at the proposed limits officials would have owned huge numbers of slaves. These slaves would, of course, have included domestics as well as agricultural production laborers, but 100 slaves was more than would have been found on most plantations in the antebellum American South.[184]

Yangban living in the provinces seem to have enjoyed an economic base similar to that of central officials. Yi Su-gŏn's study on rusticated literati of Kyŏngsang Province shows that those locally based *yangban* not only had substantial landed property, but also large numbers of slaves.[185]

Does this dependence on slaves by the ruling stratum mean that the early Chosŏn was a slave society? James Palais, in his review article on slavery in the Koryŏ, notes two widely used criteria for identifying slave societies.[186] One is whether a certain proportion—usually 30 percent—of the society's total population were slaves. In the case of the early Chosŏn, we have no reliable figures for either the number of slaves or the total population. The other criterion is whether political and economic elites were dependent on slave labor. The importance of the slavery issue in the late Koryŏ–early Chosŏn period, the concurrent granting of slaves with land, and the apparently common ownership of more than 100 slaves by central officials, not to mention the statements by early Chosŏn figures that slaves were the "hands and feet" of officials, all suggest that the early Chosŏn ruling stratum was highly dependent on slave labor for its livelihood.

It is not certain, however, that slaves provided sufficient labor to work all the lands that *yangban* owned. Although the actual area of a *kyŏl* varied according to the fertility of the land, according to the conservative estimate of Ch'ŏn Kwan-u, one *kyŏl* of first-grade land equaled approximately 1,844 *p'yŏng*.[187] Since one *p'yŏng* equals approximately 36 square feet, one *kyŏl* of first-grade land would have equaled about 66,384 square feet, or slightly more than 1.5 acres.[188] If these figures are correct, Cho Chun's merit subject grant, for example, would have amounted to about 330 acres of first-grade land and 30 slaves to work it. Until we know much more about the kinds of land involved and the crops and methods of cultivation used in the fourteenth and fifteenth centuries, we can do little more than speculate, but it seems unlikely that one slave per 10 acres would have been sufficient to cultivate the merit subjects' land grants. Thus it is possible that, despite the state's efforts to keep the peasantry out of *yangban* control (see chap. 5), there was inherent in early Chosŏn land arrangements some potential for growth in both slavery and tenancy, at least to the extent that *yangban* landlords needed additional labor to work their lands.

Was there any other source of wealth for the central official kinship groups beyond the estates they owned and the merit subject lands and prebends they received from the dynasty? We have already seen that certain members of tribute missions to China carried on private trading activities at the Ming court in the final years of the Koryŏ. In 1395, after the founding of the Chosŏn, Yi Kŏ-in and Chŏng Nam-jin were censured for trading while in China as emissaries. Yi, who was accused of secretly dealing in silk, was dismissed from his post.[189] Although some officials may have engaged in such trade, opportunities were infrequent, limited to only a few men, and likely to result in punishment if detected. Smuggling could hardly have been a source of major economic support for the bureaucracy. With regard to other forms of commerce, Yi Sŏng-gye's group took strong measures to limit commercial activities, as seen in 1391, when An No-saeng was appointed special superintendent for the northeastern border region, with orders to stop commerce with China. He put an end to the trade by beheading 10 or so merchant leaders.[190] Given such a hostile political environment for commerce and Korea's overall lack of commercial development, it is unlikely that commercial activities were an important source of funds for the central bureaucracy of the new dynasty. Land was the major source of wealth in the early Chosŏn.

It is dangerous, however, to assume that all members of the early Chosŏn central bureaucracy were wealthy. An incident that occurred in 1397 reveals that even members of some very prominent kinship groups had limited assets. The Censorate, at Chŏng To-jŏn's instigation, denounced Kwŏn Kŭn of the Andong Kwŏn for telling lies to the Ming emperor while on a mission to China and argued that the gold Kwŏn had in his possession while in China (which had, in fact, been given to him secretly by King T'aejo) was proof of his perfidy. T'aejo asked, "How do you know that Kwŏn Kŭn was rewarded with gold by the emperor?" Chŏng To-jŏn replied, "I heard that Kwŏn spent gold. How would such a poor scholar get gold if not from the emperor?" T'aejo laughed and said, "Is their no way for even a poor scholar to get gold?"[191] This anecdote is interesting, of course, for what it tells us about court rivalries in the early years of the Chosŏn, but it also reveals that Kwŏn Kŭn, scion of the great Andong Kwŏn and a high-ranking official, was a man of very modest circumstances. Kwŏn was surely not alone in his penury, and the compensation he and men like him received from the state must have been very important to their livelihood.

The mix of wealthy landed and less affluent elements in the early Chosŏn is similar to the situation that prevailed in the late Koryŏ. It seems clear that there was no substantial change in the economic base of *yangban* power as a result of the change of dynasties and that the ownership of large landed estates cultivated by slaves and tenant farmers continued to be a central feature of the economic base of the *yangban* class as a whole.

SUMMATION

This examination of the composition, social origins, and economic bases of the early Chosŏn ruling stratum has shown substantial continuity between the Koryŏ and Chosŏn periods. The overwhelming majority of the most powerful descent groups of the early Chosŏn were descended from prominent members of the Koryŏ central bureaucracy, and they continued to hold great landed estates farmed by slaves and tenants. The only identifiable new social group of any significance involved in the founding of the Chosŏn was the northeastern military coalition led by Yi Sŏng-gye. But even Yi's group did not seek to establish a new sociopolitical order; instead its members integrated themselves with the *yangban* through political alliances and marriage ties, while amassing their own large landed estates.

The great *yangban* descent groups displayed a remarkable continuity from eleventh-century Koryŏ to fifteenth century Chosŏn Korea. There were accretions to and deletions from the central *yangban* establishment's membership over the centuries, but a core of descent groups persisted from beginning to end, including the P'ap'yŏng Yun, Munhwa Yu, and Hwangnyŏ Min. These great descent groups endured and even prospered despite the military coup of 1170, the Mongol invasions, and the change of dynasties. The way in which the mid-Koryŏ military dictators and the new rulers of the Chosŏn courted these groups—heaping rewards on their members, promoting them to high positions, and even seeking them out as marriage partners—reveals an irreducible truth about premodern Korean society: one could hold overwhelming military might and even dethrone a king but still not govern the country without the cooperation and support of the great *yangban.*

The enduring importance of the *yangban* descent groups marks a major difference between the Korean and the Chinese historical experience. Historians have long held the view, first articulated by Naito Konan, that the aristocratic ruling class of interregnum and T'ang China gave way to a new gentry-based ruling class in the Sung dynasty.[192] This view has, in its essentials, not been significantly revised by more recent studies. For example, Patricia Ebrey, in her study of the Po-ling Ts'ui, provides a case study of the demise of a great aristocratic clan in the tenth century.[193] David Johnson argues, based primarily on an examination of the family backgrounds of the top-ranking officials of the Northern Sung, for substantial discontinuity in the social makeup of central political and social elites.[194] Peter Bol modifies this view, contending that although aristocratic bases of great T'ang clans were destroyed in the chaos of the late T'ang and Five Dynasties, the *shih,* many of whom came from families that had produced T'ang officials, reemerged in the Northern Sung as a class of nonaristocratic civil bureaucrats.[195] Although these scholars may vary somewhat in their understanding of the nature of the great clans of the T'ang or in their interpretation of the origins and composition of the Sung scholar-officials, they all agree that the great clans, as a distinct social entity, did not survive the fall of the T'ang. It appears, therefore, that in China the great clans lost much of their power and their sense of themselves as a discrete status group during the chaotic years of the late T'ang and the Five Dynasties, and that the new class of civil bureaucrat *shih* that emerged in the Northern Sung was qualitatively different from its predecessors. Korean elites, however, never underwent such a profound transformation. They were preserved, both as individual descent groups and as a collective social entity with a strong sense of their illustrious ancestry, throughout the years of military rule, Mongol domination, and the change of dynasties from Koryŏ to Chosŏn.

In Korea it was especially appropriate for those in the ruling stratum of the late Koryŏ and early Chosŏn dynasties to refer to themselves as *yangban,* a term that (1) identifies officials of the two branches of the central government and (2) reflects central officials' awareness of themselves both as members of the bureaucracy and, more significantly, as a social group whose defining characteristic was an ancestral tradition of office holding in the central government. Indeed, we can see a distinct awareness of the importance of *yangban* descent groups in Korean society in such fifteenth-century men as Sŏng Hyŏn, who compiled a listing of Korea's great descent groups (*kŏjok*).[196] Perhaps the clearest expression of this awarness comes, however, in the comments of Yang Sŏng-ji, a high-ranking official of the mid-fifteenth century:

> In China there have been 26 dynasties from the time of T'ang and Yao to the Great Ming, but in Korea there have been only seven dynasties from the time of Tan'gun to now. This is not simply because of differences in customs between the Chinese and us. In Korea the great hereditary descent groups [*taega sejok*] have been spread out in the capital and the provinces so that even when treacherous elements arise, they are not able to get through the great hereditary descent groups.[197]

One can, of course, find similar sentiments among Chinese thinkers of the Sung period, such as Ch'eng I-ch'üan, who "recognized the *shih* as a distinct, self-perpetuating social group, and at times . . . spoke nostalgically of the clan system of the T'ang as being in accord with Heaven's pattern and of the prospect of once more having a court with hereditary ministers."[198] The difference is that whereas Ch'eng mused about what had once been in China, Sŏng Hyŏn and Yang Sŏng-ji talked about concrete realities in Korea.

4 / Institutional Crisis in the Late Koryŏ

Was the change of Korean dynasties in 1392 a mere "palace coup" devoid of long-reaching historical significance after all? The lack of evidence of fundamental change in social composition of the ruling stratum between the late Koryŏ and early Chosŏn might seem to suggest this, but when we look for other ways to explain the Koryŏ-Chosŏn transition, we see that the reformers were trying to achieve a restoration (*chunghŭng*).[1] Underlying the rhetoric about restoration, the question of institutional reform—particularly that involving political renovation, fiscal rehabilitation, and status system maintenance—formed a major ground of controversy. This concern is reflected in the prefaces, written in the early Chosŏn, to the *Koryŏsa* monographs on officials, recruitment, and food and money (Sikhwa chi), all of which deplore the institutional decay of the late Koryŏ.[2] Although these laments indicate a sense of dynastic decline, it seems to me that these institutional difficulties were less the result of deterioration in a formerly well-functioning system than of more fundamental problems rooted in the early Koryŏ sociopolitical settlement, specifically the limitations on the centralized polity imposed by the low level of differentiation in early Koryŏ society. We have already seen how this was reflected in the practice of leaving prefecture and county administration in the hands of local strongmen, which limited the dynasty's access to resources, and in the prevalence of hereditary privilege, which both ensured local strongman access to central office and facilitated the rise of a new central bureaucratic aristocracy. The consequence was prolonged struggle among the throne, the central aristocracy, and local elites. Conflict erupted in three areas in the thirteenth and fourteenth centuries: political power, control over resources, and the status system.

Politically, the tradition of ascriptive privilege undermined the early Koryŏ kings' attempt to adopt the Chinese model of centralized bureaucratic rule and ultimately led, as we have seen, to the creation of a central bureaucratic aristocracy that was able by the twelfth century to contest royal control over the organs of political struggle. This struggle resumed in intensified form after the overthrow of the Ch'oe military house in 1258 and left the dynasty politically paralyzed.

Fiscally, the kings were eventually unable to keep free-floating human resources, their control over which was never too strong, from falling under aristocratic control. Although a major direct cause of this was growth of *nong-jang* estates owned by central *yangban* descent groups, an important underlying condition was the compromise the dynasty had made between the Chinese ideal of a centralized, hierarchical system of regional administration and the Korean tradition of local autonomy, which left the state largely dependent on the hereditary *hyangni* elite to represent its interests and collect taxes in the countryside. While this system may have once provided the state with some access to resources, it proved unworkable after foreign invasions and the penetration of central economic interests destroyed the local social order throughout large areas of the country in the thirteenth and fourteenth centuries.

Socially, the concessions the kings had made to avoid alienating their local strongman constituency in the tenth century meant that the strongmen's *hyangni* descendants continued to be recognized as a hereditary elite who enjoyed institutionalized access to offices in the dynastic government. This engendered conflict between central *yangban* and local *hyangni*, intensifying in the late Koryŏ when large numbers of *hyangni*, uprooted by widespread disruption of the local social order, flowed into the capital in search of opportunity and security.

Unable to maintain significant amounts of generalized political power and to keep control over much of the country's resources, the late Koryŏ kings could not implement the kind of root-and-branch reforms needed to deal with problems stemming from the tradition of ascriptive privilege. Instead, they resorted to a variety of expedients that only further undermined the dynasty's institutional foundations. The collapse of Mongol hegemony and the rise of the Wako pirates in the second half of the fourteenth century brought the dynasty's problems to crisis stage.

THE STRUGGLE FOR POWER

At first glance, it appears as though the beleaguered dynasty experienced something of a restoration after peace was made with the Mongols in the mid-thirteenth century. Externally, Yüan domination of Northeast Asia protected Korea from the threat of invasion. Internally, the Ch'oe house of military dictators was overthrown and the Koryŏ royal family intermarried with the Mongol imperial family and ruled with the backing of the Yüan empire.

Mongol overlordship, however, did not guarantee complete political tranquility. Although the royal family's special relationship with the imperial family may have protected the kings from deposal at the hands of their own subjects, they had no protection from Mongol interference; Koryŏ kings were frequently called back to the Mongol capital at Tatu and on several occasions were even removed from the throne.³ Furthermore, the Mongol princesses married to Koryŏ kings often interfered in politics and used their position to amass great wealth. Periodic attempts at reform, such as those attempted under kings Ch'ungsŏn and Ch'ungmok (r. 1344–48), achieved little beyond provoking fierce political infighting.

The sudden collapse of the Yüan empire in the 1360s set the stage for great political instability in Korea. Externally, the decline of Mongol hegemony in Northeast Asia opened the way for invasions by the Yellow Turbans between 1359 and 1362 and severe raiding by the Japanese Wako pirates throughout the second half of the century. Internally, the Koryŏ kings, now bereft of outside support, were left on their own to face an increasingly fractious bureaucracy. Isolated and commanding neither power nor respect, the last four kings were unable to exert sustained leadership. The dynasty finally came to an ignominious end with the deposal of Kongyang (r. 1389–1392) by his own officials.

The Structure of Political Institutions in the Late Koryŏ

The beginning of the end of era of military rule came in the third month of 1258 when Ch'oe Ŭi, the last of the Ch'oe line, was ousted by a group of officials dismayed at the costs of the Ch'oes' stubborn resistance to the Mongol invaders. The two decades after the ouster of the Ch'oe house were a transitional period for dynastic political institutions, marked by struggle between new would-be military dictators and the civil branch of government.

Immediately after Ch'oe Ŭi's execution the *chaech'u* resumed a leading role in political affairs. In the seventh month of 1258, for example, ostensibly concerned that harm might fall to the crown prince on a visit to the Mongols, they dispatched an emissary to the Mongols with the message that the crown prince was ill and unable to travel.⁴ The *chaech'u* can be seen flexing their political muscle again after the death of King Kojong in the sixth month of 1259, when they were able to prevent Grand General Kim Chun (Kim Injun) from placing his favorite on the throne,⁵ and once more in the seventh month of 1260, when they gathered to discuss the issue of detaining a Mongol emissary.⁶

Despite the apparent resurgence of *chaech'u* authority, however, Kim Chun began to exert dominance over the government. By 1264 he had himself appointed supervisor of the Directorate General for Policy Formulation, and he appeared to be in a position to restore military control over the government. The limits of this revival of military rule were revealed, however, in the next year when Kim took the unprecedented step, for a military strongman, of having himself appointed chancellor. While this indicates that he was in charge of the bureaucracy, it also suggests that in the post-Ch'oe era he found the trappings of the civil branch necessary for the exercise of political power. At any rate, Kim Chun's time in the limelight was brief. In the ninth month of 1267 he was ordered to take a provincial military post; when he refused, he was banished and subsequently executed.[7] His place as chancellor was taken by the civil official Yi Chang-yong of the Kyŏngwŏn Yi.

Within seven months of the execution of Kim Chun, another military man, Im Yŏn, made a grab for power. In the sixth month of 1269 Im called the *chaech'u* together to remove chancellor Yi Chang-yong on grounds of incompetence. When Im failed to gain the backing of the *chaech'u,* he decided to take action on his own, summoning the officials to Prince Ch'ang's residence, where he dethroned Kojong's successor, Wŏnjong, and enthroned Ch'ang. The next month Im had himself appointed supervisor of the Directorate General for Policy Formulation. These activities aroused the suspicions of the Mongols, who in the eleventh month sent an edict calling for the restoration of Wŏnjong. In desperation, Im Yŏn summoned the *chaech'u* to his residence, where he sought their advice on how to respond to the Mongol edict. What the *chaech'u* told him is not recorded, but Im then had a meeting with the Mongol emissary, after which "he had no choice but to meet with the *chaech'u* to discuss the removal of Ch'ang and the restoration of Wŏnjong."[8] Shortly thereafter Im Yŏn was banished and executed. Although Im Yŏn's son Im Yu-mu was appointed to succeed his father as supervisor of the Directorate General of Policy Formulation in the third month of 1270, he too was executed just two months later, bringing to an end the Koryŏ's century of military rule.

This sequence of events shows us the shifting balance of power between military men and civil officials of the regular bureaucracy during the years immediately after the fall of the Ch'oe house. It is quite clear that the revived *chaech'u* presented an insurmountable obstacle to the ambitions of would-be military dictators. The significance of this is revealed in the *Koryŏsa* entry for the fifth month of 1270 describing the abolition of the extrainstitutional agencies of military rule, "to the great joy of the court and the rest of the country."[9]

Although the Koryŏ court submitted to Mongol control in 1259, the Mongols were too occupied with their conquest of the Sung court in China to set up formal institutional means of overseeing Korea. It wasn't until 1280 that they finally established the Eastern Expedition Field Headquarters (Chŏngdong Haengsŏng) to prepare for their invasion of Japan. Although in 1294 the Mongols abandoned their attempt to conquer Japan, the Field Headquarters remained in place to represent their interests in Korea. Although there is no evidence of direct Field Headquarters involvement in day-to-day government, it did interfere at times in Koryŏ's domestic affairs, particularly in the years right after its establishment. Nonetheless, for the most part the Field Headquarters, which was headed by the Koryŏ king and largely staffed— particularly in later years—by Koryŏ officials, seems to have been generally content to let the dynasty run its own affairs. Its greatest significance seems to have been the role it played in receiving and sending off Mongol emissaries, which made it an institutional symbol of Koryŏ submission to the Mongols.[10]

The other major institution the Mongols established in Koryŏ was a system of local military administration under myriarchs and chiliarchs ("leaders of 1,000," *ch'ŏnho*) posted at strategic locations throughout the country. In the early years of Mongol domination, all or most of the myriarchs and chiliarchs may have been Mongols, but as the focus of the myriarchies shifted from enforcing submission to the Mongols to protecting Korea against foreign aggressors such as the Wako, it became routine practice for Koreans to be appointed to these posts.

The Mongols also forced the Koryŏ court to reorganize its political institutions to reflect subordination to the Yüan. This reorganization involved eliminating certain posts and organs at the very top of government and renaming agencies. The Mongols no longer allowed the Koryŏ king to appoint honorary senior first-grade preceptors (*samsa samgong*), since those were the exclusive preserve of the Emperor. Also, the Mongols abolished the Executive Department (Sangsŏsŏng) and formally transferred its functions to the Secretariat/ Chancellery. At the same time, the Secretariat/Chancellery was retitled the Grand Chancellery (Ch'ŏmŭibu), and all other agencies headed by officials of the third grade or higher ranks—including the Security Council, the Six Boards, the Royal Confucian Academy, and the Office of the Inspector-General—were also renamed to reflect Koryŏ's inferior status.

This reorganization was not as radical as it may seem. Abolition of the honorary senior first-grade preceptors would have had little effect on government operation. Although the loss of the Executive Department seems more significant, by the late tenth century it had already come under the de facto control of the Secretariat/Chancellery, whose *chaesin* held concurrent posts as Six Board superintendents. In effect, the abolition of the Executive Department and the allocation of its functions to the Grand Chancellery represented nothing more than the formalization of a situation that had obtained for centuries. A diagram of the structure of political power in the late Koryŏ would show the king at the top, directing the activities of the bureaucracy and exercising final authority in all matters. He was to be assisted by the Todang, a *chaech'u* deliberative council established in 1279. Its members had two roles: as councillors they were to deliberate on major issues and make recommendations to the king, and as chief ministers of the bureaucracy they were to oversee the execution of the king's decisions. The role of the Todang in formulating policy made it the supreme organ of political struggle in the late Koryŏ. Whereas the *chaech'u* of the early Koryŏ had been a de facto deliberative council usually convened by the king, the late Koryŏ Todang was a formally constituted body with specific functions and a specified membership made up of first- and second-grade officials.

Proper distance between the throne and the bureaucracy was to be maintained by the document transmitters of the Security Council. Channeling all official communications between the throne and the bureaucracy through these officials, whose importance was reflected in their relatively high third-grade ranks, was intended to ensure the free flow of communication and to prevent individuals or cliques from exercising undue influence on the king.

Two other important entities in the bureaucracy are worthy of mention here: the Hallim Academy, whose officials served as advisors and private secretaries to the king; and the mid-level censorial officials of the Secretariat/Chancellery and the surveillance officials of the Office of the Inspector General, collectively known as the *taegan*, who jointly ratified personnel actions and policy decisions and frequently remonstrated against kings and top ministers. Finally, actual implementation of policy was to be carried out in the administrative agencies of the bureaucracy, including the Six Boards and various offices, directorates, and bureaus charged with specific areas of responsibility.

This describes the way that the late Koryŏ *yangban* thought the system should work. In reality, political power often flowed around, rather than through, the formal institutional structure as kings and inner palace elements sought to circumvent the *yangban*-dominated bureaucracy.

Political Power in the Mongol Era

The late Koryŏ kings were not, despite their position at the apex of the formal power structure, in a position to exercise effective authority over the bureaucracy. The kingship had lost much prestige during the military years and, although kings now reigned with the backing of the Yüan empire, the frequency with which the Mongols recalled them certainly did nothing to boost their stature. Furthermore, kings did not have significant state military forces with which to enforce their will. The Two Armies and Six Divisions of early Koryŏ times now existed in name only, their officer posts given out as sinecures, so that throughout the late Koryŏ period the dynasty had to form armies on an ad hoc basis to deal with such emergencies as the Red Turban invasions and the Wako raids.[11] Underlying the dynasty's impotence was its loss of control over much of the kingdom's human and material resources.

Two other factors contributed to the weakness of the late Koryŏ kingship. One was the youthfulness of many late Koryŏ rulers: six of the last nine monarchs came to the throne in their teens or younger, with two (Ch'ungmok and Ch'ang [1388–89]) being enthroned at the tender age of eight and two others (Ch'unghye and U) at ten. The other factor was the well-documented tendency of several of the kings to neglect affairs of state. Some, such as Ch'ungnyŏl, Ch'ungsŏn, and Ch'ungsuk, spent much of their time at the Mongol capital, leaving supervision of their kingdom in the hands of people left behind in Kaegyŏng, while others, such as Ch'unghye and U, preferred the pleasures of hunting, drinking, and womanizing to the tedium of court sessions. Even Kongmin, the most vigorous of the late Koryŏ kings, spent much of the last half of his reign planning and building a massive Buddhist temple in memory of his deceased consort. The occupants of the late Koryŏ throne lacked the prestige, resources, and, in many cases, the personal commitment needed to wield effective power.

The prevailing view is that it was the central aristocratic descent groups who, in collusion with the Mongols, exercised real political power in the late Koryŏ. Certainly the central *yangban* had a number of advantages. They enjoyed great social prestige and had traditions of hereditary access to political office. They also had, in many cases, great wealth in their landed estates and slave holdings. Furthermore, some *yangban* elements developed their own private military forces, as seen in a 1365 entry in the *Koryŏsa chŏryo* describing how two high-ranking officials engaged in a show of force by mobilizing their private forces (*sabyŏng*) to hunt in the suburbs of the capital.[12] Although sources tell us nothing about the origins and size of these private forces, we can guess that they must have greatly enhanced *yangban* power vis-à-vis the throne. *Yangban*, it would appear, were in a good position to dominate the dynasty's political life.

The supreme institutional manifestation of aristocratic power, according to the conventional interpretation, was the Todang, where the powerful descent groups deliberated virtually all important matters and, after reading decisions by consensus, passed them up to the king for rubber-stamp approval.

The sources make it abundantly clear that the Todang was composed of high-ranking officials. Initially membership was limited to the *chaech'u* (first- and second-grade officials of the Secretariat-Chancellery and the Security Council), although by the end of the thirteenth century it expanded to include other second-grade officials, such as those who headed the Finance Commission.[13] There seems to be no reason to doubt that the Todang operated on the consensus principle. Yi Che-hyŏn, writing in 1342, gave a concise summary of the council's procedures: "When the chief registrar announces the items on the agenda before them, everyone expresses a yes or no based on his opinion on the issues. The registrar moves back and forth among them and tries to bring the discussion to a consensus, and after consensus is reached, it is then implemented. This is called *ŭihap* [deliberating for consensus]."[14]

It is apparent that the Todang dealt with a wide range of issues, including such policy concerns as finances and taxation as well as penal affairs, personnel matters, military issues, and foreign relations. The Todang was also an administrative center, frequently communicating directly with subordinate agencies of the central government as well as with prefects and magistrates out in the countryside. Evidence for this comes from a number of sources, including descriptions of the Todang and examples of the Todang in action found in the annals of the *Koryŏsa* and *Koryŏsa chŏryo*.[15]

Although the Todang appears to have been the political powerhouse of the late Koryŏ, nearly all examples of the Todang in action come in the final 20 years of the dynasty. This discovery prompted me to go back to the sources and trace actual records of Todang activity throughout the entire late Koryŏ period. The data in table 4.1 show a count of entries mentioning the Todang (both by that name and the alias Top'yŏngŭisasa) in the *Koryŏsa* (including annals, monographs, and biographies) from the establishment of the Todang in 1279 to the enthronement of King Kongmin in 1351. This array of data reveals that there was very little Todang activity during this period, when Mongol influence was at its peak. Four of the 11 times the Todang appeared in the sources came within four years of its establishment. During those years it appears to have functioned as a major policy-making and administrative organ, as seen in a 1279 entry showing the Todang discussing the establishment of way stations for envoys to the Yüan court,[16] and a 1283 entry depicting the Todang issuing instructions to halt the impressment of students into military duty.[17] The two 1298 entries, which come during the first brief reign of Ch'ungsŏn, after 15 years of silence, do not show the Todang in action, but

TABLE 4.1
Levels of Todang Activity, 1279–1351

Period	1279–83	1298	1299–1343	1344–47	1348–51
Koryŏsa entries	4	2	2	3	0

suggest activity by the council through the entry telling of the king's relieving an aged councillor from daily participation in Todang deliberations on major affairs of state.[18] There are only two entries for the years from 1299 through 1343, both showing the Todang memorializing against the proposal to make Korea a province of Yüan China.[19] This suggests that although the Todang became active at a time of extraordinary crisis for the state during this period, it was not involved in the day-to-day affairs of government. The remaining three entries come from the reign of Ch'ungmok, a period of reform when the interests of certain Mongol favorites were under attack. In short, the Todang was, except for brief spates of activity under unusual circumstances, almost totally quiescent between 1283 and 1351. It is unlikely that the council was the vehicle through which the central aristocratic descent groups (or anybody else) could have dominated dynastic politics.

Did the Todang, then, not convene at all during these periods of absence from the sources? Such does not appear to have been the case. Evidence that the Todang continued to meet can be found in Yi Che-hyŏn's comments of 1342, which describe the conduct of Todang members during one period when the council does not appear in the histories: "Nowadays the state councillors of both the Secretariat/Chancellery and Security Council have needlessly increased in number. . . . They come and go as a group, frequently making loud conversation and laughing. They show no restraint in talking about the personal matters of others and even about profiting from their gains and losses in rice and salt market prices."[20]

Yi Che-hyŏn is, of course, complaining about expansion in Todang membership and particularly about the unseemly behavior of its members. The growth in Todang membership is usually seen as evidence of its importance as an aristocratic power center. But, if the Todang was in fact the locus of political power, how do we explain the frivolity of its members? From a perspective that takes into consideration the Todang's inactivity, the growth in its membership and its members' inattention to the business of government can be seen as evidence not of its power but rather of its impotence. Holding a seat in the Todang may have been seen as an honor, but it was an honor that was for the most part devoid of any real power.

Why did the Todang not wield effective authority? One possible answer lies in the nature of Todang procedures. The consensus principle on which the Todang operated seems to have hampered its effectiveness and could have provided motivation to find a more efficient way of conducting the dynasty's business. Early evidence for this can be found in a *Koryŏsa* entry for 1278, which states: "According to the old system, all state affairs were discussed by the *chaech'u*. They ordered the document transmitters to report their decisions to the throne and receive the king's orders, which were then carried out. Kim Chu-jŏng said, 'Now the *chaech'u* are many and are not appropriate for discussing policy.'"[21] Further evidence can be found in a proclamation issued by King Ch'ungsŏn in 1298: "The number of chief ministers is now double that of old. Their views on state affairs differ from each other and issues are not getting resolved. We must reduce their numbers."[22] Although Ch'ungsŏn appears to have tried to revitalize the Todang, his efforts were for naught. He was removed from the throne a few months later. Todang membership was soon back up to 28 and it once again disappeared from center stage.[23] It is possible that the unwieldy nature of Todang operations was one reason why it was relegated to the sidelines.

We cannot rule out the possibility that compilers of the histories simply substituted the term *chaech'u* for Todang or that *chaech'u* were making policy outside the Todang. Such does not, however, seem to have been the case. After the creation of the Todang in 1279, *chaech'u* rarely appear in the histories except on ceremonial occasions.

If *chaech'u,* either in the Todang or in another venue, were not the center of political power, we must consider the possibility that actual authority resided elsewhere, such as in the Hallim Academy or in the *taegan* policy critics or surveillance officials. There is little evidence, however, to indicate that this was the case. Ch'ungsŏn made an abortive attempt to develop the Hallim Academy into a major power center in 1298, but there is no other evidence to suggest that the Academy ever wielded significant political power. Pak Yong-un has argued that the *taegan* became more active during the Mongol period, but again there is nothing to suggest that they, or any other agency of the regular bureaucracy, were routinely involved in high-level decision making.[24]

One possible political power center during the years of Mongol overlordship was the Eastern Expedition Field Headquarters. But Ko Pyŏng-ik has shown that the Field Headquarters was headed by the Koryŏ king, staffed almost entirely by Koryŏ officials, and, except for the first few years after its founding, rarely interfered in Koryŏ domestic affairs. The main responsibilities of the Field Headquarters, according to Ko, were conducting liaison activities between the Yüan and Koryŏ courts and standing as a symbol of Korea's subservience to the Mongols.[25] Indeed there is little to indicate that the Field Headquarters was involved in routine political decision making. The evidence shows that, except for extraordinary situations, political power in the late Koryŏ resided neither in the *yangban*-dominated bureaucracy nor in the Field Headquarters. This leads us to look elsewhere for the location of power.

Eisenstadt notes that rulers of historical bureaucratic societies frequently attempted to overcome the power of entrenched aristocratic or bureaucratic groups by using palace retainers or court officials who were drawn from a variety of other social groups.[26] The kings of the late Koryŏ, faced with a *yangban*-dominated bureaucracy, appear to have followed just such a practice.

A close examination of the histories reveals that throughout the Mongol era the inner palace enjoyed substantial political clout. The inner-palace elements were centered around the kings' Mongol consorts, who invested great power in their personal retainers, eunuchs, and other men of non-*yangban* origins, promoting them to key offices in the palace and bureaucracy. The consequence was subversion of the dynasty's civil branch–centered political institutions and undermining of the kingdom's status system.

The pattern for control of politics by the inner palace and palace favorites was set during the reign of King Ch'ungnyŏl. Ch'ungnyŏl himself seems to have actively promoted the exercise of power by his consort and palace favorites, although it is not clear whether that was because he was under the sway of his consort or whether he was deliberately trying to take advantage of his Mongol backing to undermine *yangban* power. At any rate, it was during his years on the throne that the Mongol consorts, who were princesses of the Yüan imperial family, became main players in politics and a variety of special groups rose to power, including the non-Korean retainers of the princesses, eunuchs, men of servile backgrounds, and even some *yangban* who had special ties with the Mongols.

Princess Cheguk, Ch'ungnyŏl's consort and the daughter of Kublai Khan, exerted tremendous influence at the Koryŏ court, frequently coming into conflict with and overruling the *chaech'u* on a variety of issues, including palace and temple construction and the establishment of falconries to supply the Mongols with hunting birds.[27] Ch'ungsŏn's consort, Princess Kyeguk, upset with her husband's behavior and policies, played the central role in having Ch'ungsŏn recalled to the Yüan Court in 1298.[28] Ch'unghye's Mongol consort, Princess Tŏngnyŏng, was able to stymie reform efforts in the mid-1340s and emerged as the kingdom's power broker upon the death of her son King Ch'ungmok in 1348.[29] The Mongol era kings and their consorts relied on a number of elements to run the government for them. One such element was foreigners. Mongols and Central Asians, such as In Tang and Chang Sun-nyong, came to Korea as retainers of Mongol consorts and subsequently rose through palace favoritism to the highest levels of government, where they frequently came into conflict with Korean *yangban* officials.[30]

Another important inner-palace element was eunuchs. Although eunuchs had been significant actors in Chinese politics from the Later Han on, before the Mongol era they had seldom been seen on the center stage of Korean history.[31]

The *Koryŏsa* tells us that Kim Cha-jŏng became the first eunuch to be appointed to regular office when he was made attending general (*chongch'in changgun*) in 1277.[32] Other eunuchs soon followed suit to gain official appointments, including Ch'oe Se-yŏn, who was made a general in 1288,[33] and Yi Suk, a favorite of the Mongol imperial family who was granted a noble title and made a merit subject in 1297 after his return to Korea.[34] The *Koryŏsa* biography of Ch'oe Se-yŏn provides us with some sense of the role eunuch favorites played in Ch'ungnyŏl's reign:

> Ch'oe Se-yŏn, angry at his wife's jealousy, castrated himself and became a eunuch. The eunuch To Sŏng-gi had won favor with the king and the princess. Ch'oe attached himself to To and gained entry into the palace, where he soon enjoyed even greater favor than To. Ch'oe and To were appointed as generals and exercised vast power. . . . Ch'oe wielded complete control over affairs and received many bribes. He decided promotion and demotion of officials by word of mouth. Even royal relatives and chief ministers did not dare to cross him.[35]

The *Koryŏsa* also makes special mention of a number of other men of non-*yangban* origins who rose to power through palace connections, including Son Ki, a merchant who enjoyed the particular favor of Ch'unghye,[36] and Pae Chŏn and Kang Yun-ch'ung, men of servile origins who were protégés of Princess Tŏngnyŏng.[37]

One final element that must be mentioned are those *yangban* who had special ties with the Mongols, including Kwŏn Kyŏm of the Andong Kwŏn, Ki Cha-o of the Haengju Ki, and No Ch'aek of the Kyoha No. Representative of these were the Haengju Ki, one of whose daughters became the consort of

Emperor Shun-ti (r. 1333–67). The Ki, several of whose members were given honorary titles as kings (*wang*) by the Mongol emperor, were able to parlay their connections with the imperial house into wealth and prestige that rivaled those of the Koryŏ kings.[38] The Ki can perhaps be seen, along with the immediate relatives of Kwŏn Kyŏm and No Ch'aek, as typical *kwŏnmun sejok*. It should be noted, however, that these families were a distinct minority among the *yangban*. Like other Mongol favorites, their power was derived primarily from close connections with the inner palace, as seen when Princess Tŏngnyŏng gave control over the bureaucracy to Ki Ch'ŏl and Kwŏn Kyŏm upon the death of King Ch'ungmok in 1348.[39]

Reliance on foreigner retainers, eunuchs, men of nonelite backgrounds, and imperial protégés was not the inner palace's only means of getting around the *yangban*-dominated bureaucracy in the late Koryŏ. The politics of the period also featured a number of institutional innovations designed to concentrate power in the hands of palace favorites.

One such feature involved personnel administration. The Personnel Authority of the military era was converted during Wŏnjong's reign into a palace-based agency that subsequent kings and their consorts used to appoint favorites to posts in both the palace and the regular bureaucracy.[40] This was, of course, a serious infringement on the principle that all personnel actions were to be handled through the boards of Personnel and War, subject to ratification by the *taegan*. The Personnel Authority, despite occasional attempts to abolish it, persisted throughout the Mongol period.[41]

One area where the rulers created new institutions was policy formulation. The *Koryŏsa chŏryo* tells us that in the tenth month of 1278 King Ch'ungnyŏl established a new entity called the P'iltoji (a Mongol term meaning "literary officials"), which was to take the place of the *chaech'u* in deliberating on state affairs. The P'iltoji, which was nicknamed the "special office" *chaech'u* (*pyŏlch'ŏng chaech'u*) and met in the palace, was staffed by such palace favorites as Kim Chu-jŏng (d. 1291), a scion of the Kwangsan Kim whom Ch'ungnyŏl favored greatly;[42] Sŏl Kong-gŏm, who had accompanied Ch'ungnyŏl when he went to the Yüan court as crown prince during Wŏnjong's reign;[43] palace attendant Yi Chi-jŏ, who had long been one of Ch'ungnyŏl's pets;[44] and Yŏm Sŭng-ik, who gained Ch'ungnyŏl's favor through Yi Chi-jŏ. Kim Chu-jŏng's biography states that he and his fellow members of the "special office" *chaech'u* met regularly in the palace.[45] At the same time, Ch'ungnyŏl also established an entity known as the Sinmunsaek, staffed by palace attendants, which was charged with the document transmission function that had been the prerogative of the third-grade officials of the Security Council.[46]

Although the P'iltoji appears to have been superseded by the Todang in 1279, the *Koryŏsa chŏryo* tells us that in 1304 Ch'ungnyŏl again brought five men into the palace to deliberate on affairs; this group, too, was known as the "special office."[47] Regardless of the duration of the P'iltoji and the Sinmunsaek, important precedents had been set for inner-palace control over policy deliberations and document transmission.

There is no mention of the "special office" *chaech'u* after 1304. A close reading of the sources, however, reveals that kings continued to invest political authority in small numbers of favored men. The *Koryŏsa chŏryo* tells us, for example, that when King Ch'ungsŏn was ruling from the Mongol capital at Tatu, he entrusted all affairs, including state policy and fiscal matters, to officials personally close (*kŭnch'in*) to him.[48] The *Koryŏsa chŏryo* also states that Ch'ungsuk did not personally oversee political affairs for several years, and that in his stead a small group of favored officials monopolized the state's authority.[49] It is not clear whether these men operated informally or within an institutional format, as did the "special office" *chaech'u,* but it is evident that the practice of circumventing the bureaucracy by investing power in a small number of favored officials persisted throughout the Mongol era, when kings attempted to overcome the limitations presented by *yangban* domination of the Todang by creating separate organs of political struggle vested in smaller groups of personal favorites.

The appointment of foreigners, eunuchs, and men of mean origins to high office and the existence of irregular agencies such as the Personnel Authority and "special office" *chaech'u* is usually cited as proof of the corruption of the late Koryŏ aristocracy. The evidence we have reviewed here, however, indicates that the formation of these agencies and the rise of new social elements during the Mongol era came not through the collusion of corrupt *yangban* bent on dominating the throne, but rather as a result of palace efforts to overcome the power of the *yangban.* Indeed it is hard to understand how the *yangban* would have colluded with eunuchs and men of servile origins, since the rise of such elements would have undermined the ascriptive basis of *yangban* prestige.

Political Power in the Post-Mongol Era

The decline of Mongol power after the mid-fourteenth century offered the Koryŏ dynasty an opportunity to cast off the influence of Mongol consorts and their favorites. Although King Kongmin made an attempt to free Korea from Mongol influence and carry out basic political reforms, the throne's institutional base was too weak, and the precedent of inner-palace involvement in politics was too well established. The Mongol princess Tŏngnyŏng remained influential in the early years of Kongmin's reign, but by the mid 1350s the king's Korean in-laws emerged to take the place of the Mongol consorts. Kongmin's mother was a Koryŏ woman, a daughter of the Namyang Hong who wielded some power from the very beginning of Kongmin's reign. She was able, for example, to overrule the Todang regarding the conduct of ancestor worship services in 1352.[50] But it was only after the purge of pro-Yüan elements in the mid-1350s that she and her relatives really began to flourish. Led by Hong Ŏn-bak, the queen mother's nephew who became prime minister in 1357, the Namyang Hong were the most powerful descent group during the years Kongmin was on the throne, producing 15 officials and no fewer than eight chaech'u.[51] Some sense of the nature and extent of Namyang Hong influence can be gleaned from the Koryŏsa biography of Hong Ŏn-bak:

The king, wanting to move the capital to Kanghwa Island, ordered that portents be divined at the hall containing the portrait of the dynastic founder at Kaet'ae Temple. The people were concerned. Queen Mother Hong, who was Hong Ŏn-bak's aunt, summoned him and said: "You are a royal in-law from a great family and the highest official. All the kingdom looks up to you. Now the king wants to move the capital against the wishes of the entire kingdom. You must remonstrate and stop him." Hong Ŏn-bak then spoke to the king, who said, "I have not decided to move the capital. I merely wanted to know what the signs said. The signs were repeatedly bad."[52]

Here we see not only the expectation that a royal in-law from a great yangban descent group would be able to influence the king, but also the king's apparent temporizing in the face of the Namyang Hongs' overt opposition to his plans. Although the Namyang Hong lost power during the middle years of Kongmin's reign, the queen mother and her supporters reemerged to play an important role in later years. Thus Kongmin's reign can perhaps be characterized as a period when political power shifted from Mongol-related inner-palace elements to Korean consorts and their relatives. While the rise of the Namyang Hong may appear to be a reassertion of yangban power, to the extent that they, too, constituted an inner-palace-based clique, it could not have been a welcome development to the yangban class as a whole.

Kongmin's successor, U, came to the throne at the age of 10 through the sponsorship of Yi In-im, who prevailed against Queen Mother Hong's support for another candidate. U was enthroned amid suspicion that he was not of royal birth. That, plus his tender age, made him particularly vulnerable to domination by outside forces. The generally accepted view is that Yi In-im and his supporters dominated the kingdom throughout nearly all of U's reign. It seems to me, however, that this interpretation overly stresses Yi In-im's control. Yi In-im won a victory over Queen Mother Hong with the enthrone-ment of U in 1374, but that did not mean that her power was broken. On the contrary, she retained supporters in the government during the early years of U's tenure. These included her affinal relative Kim Song-myŏng, who handled affairs in the palace and wielded considerable political influence until he was banished by the Yi In-im group in 1377, at which time the queen mother was said to have lost her right hand.[53] Although the influence of the Namyang Hong may have been sharply curtailed, Yi In-im still had to share power with other *yangban,* mostly notably Ch'oe Yŏng and his supporters, whose ranks included a number of military leaders such as Pyŏn An-nyŏl and Yi Sŏng-gye, who had gained influence as a result of their leadership of campaigns against the Red Turbans and the Wako. It was in fact Ch'oe Yŏng who eventually eliminated the Yi In-im group in the first month of 1388, before he himself was removed by Yi Sŏng-gye six months later.[54] The picture of U's years that emerges here, therefore, is not one of total domination by Yi In-im but rather of a sharing of power, however unwillingly, between Yi In-im and other groups, first with the Namyang Hong, with their base in the inner palace, and later with Ch'oe Yŏng, whose support came mostly from military men. Whereas Kongmin's reign marked a shift from Mongol-related to Korean inner-palace control, U's reign presents itself as a transition from domination of the throne by the inner palace to a period of struggle among various *yangban* factions.

In the midst of these shifting power relations, the post-Mongol era kings continued to try to counterbalance *yangban* power by using eunuchs and other men of low social status. The *Koryŏsa* states that the power of the eunuchs during Kongmin's reign was so great that they were able to avoid punishment even when caught doing wrong.[55] One particular favorite of Kongmin was Kim Sa-haeng, whose power and greed made him the enemy of many *yang-ban.* Kim was expelled from the capital and made a slave shortly after Kongmin died.[56] Men of servile origins such as Pae Chŏn and Kang Yun-ch'ung were still in prominent positions early in Kongmin's reign, and, of course, Kongmin's notorious regent, Sin Ton, was born to a slave mother. Although men such as Pae Chŏn and Kang Yun-ch'ung probably represent the contin-uing influence of Princess Tŏngnyŏng in the early years of Kongmin's reign, there is no evidence of close connections between Kim Sa-haeng or Sin Ton and the Namyang Hong. This suggests that Kongmin was trying to use these non-*yangban* elements to offset the power of the *yangban,* including the Namyang Hong.

U, once he grew old enough to assert himself, also appears to have tried to use eunuchs to counter *yangban* power. For example, in the eighth month of 1382 he put command over capital defense forces in the hands of two eunuchs.[57] Furthermore, in the ninth month of 1384 U, who disliked Im Kyŏn-mi, forced him to retire and, unhappy with the resistance of Yi In-im and other officials, appointed a eunuch to a senior second-grade post and put him in charge of the Todang.[58] Of course, no discussion of U's reign would be complete without mention of his notorious profligate and constant companion Yi Kwang-bo, described as a "ruffian of the streets," who became a high-ranking official and U's closest advisor after the demise of Yi In-im early in 1388.[59]

It becomes apparent, therefore, that the Mongol-era practice of using eunuchs and men of humble origins to thwart the *yangban* bureaucracy continued into the post-Mongol years, although it was now the kings, rather than their consorts, who employed them. The use of eunuchs and non-*yangban* social elements was not the only Mongol era practice to persist, however. Institutional innovations linked to the palace politics of the Mongol era also continued as central political features.

The Personnel Authority was a prime target for reform-minded elements in the 1350s, but remained an important center of power in Kongmin's early years. Abolished in 1356, it was reinstituted by Kongmin's de facto regent, Sin Ton, almost immediately after he came to power in 1365, apparently in order to stack the bureaucracy with his supporters. The Personnel Authority continued to operate throughout U's reign. A memorial calling for its abolition was submitted in 1374, the year U took the throne, but the *Koryŏsa* tells us that someone prevented implementation of the proposal.[60] Exactly who that was is not clear, but at any rate the Personnel Authority was available for Yi In-im and his group to use as a means to appoint and promote their supporters. That Yi strove to do so is borne out by statements in the dynastic histories. The *Koryŏsa Chŏryo* tells us, for example, that in 1379

> Hong Chung-sŏn was banished from the capital. Yi In-im and Im Kyŏn-mi had been sitting together in the Personnel Authority with Hong Chung-sŏn, but they didn't like sharing the power with Hong. They had Hong appointed as emissary to the Ming, but Hong did not depart right away. The remonstrance official Sŏ Kyun-hyŏng, who had a grudge against Hong and hoped to curry favor with Yi In-im, denounced Hong, whereupon Hong was banished.[61]

Hong Chung-sŏn was a nephew of Hong Ŏn-bak and a relative of Queen
Mother Hong. His expulsion from the Personnel Authority represented further weakening of Namyang Hong power and meant a greater consolidation
of authority, especially over personnel issues, under Yi In-im. An entry from
the third month of 1383 tells us that

> Prime Minister Hong Yŏng-t'ong retired and was replaced by Cho Min-su.
> Im Kyŏn-mi was in charge of the Personnel Authority along with To Kil-
> bu, U Hyŏn-bo, and Yi Chon-sŏng. The precedent was for the prime min-
> ister to handle personnel affairs, but when Hong and Cho were prime
> ministers they were unable to do so. That was because Im Kyŏn-mi had total
> authority.[62]

This entry indicates that even though the Yi In-im cabal might have had to
tolerate high officials—even prime ministers—from outside their own inner
circle, they were able to restrict the outsiders' exercise of power, at least with
regard to personnel decisions. It appears, therefore, that the Personnel
Authority, which Mongol-era kings used to place their favorites in positions
of power, was now being used to further the interests of special cliques.

The practice of establishing separate organs of political struggle in the palace
continued during the post-Mongol era. The *Koryŏsa Chŏryo* tells us that in
the fifth month of 1365, right after Kongmin invested the monk Sin Ton with
political authority, Yu T'ak and Yi In-im were ordered to handle politics in
the Todang, and Kim Nan, Im Kun-bo, and Mok In-gil were to handle affairs
in the palace. Prime minister Kyŏng Pok-hŭng was not able to participate in
political affairs.[63]

Here once again we see palace-based interests—this time Kongmin and Sin
Ton—convening a select group of officials to circumvent the regular bureaucracy and the Todang, of which Kyŏng Pok-hŭng was the titular head. This
practice, under the name "palace *chaech'u*" (*nae chaech'u*), became a regular
feature during Sin Ton's tenure as regent.

Although there is no mention of palace *chaech'u* during the first several years
of U's reign, by the late 1370s Yi In-im's group appears to have reactivated
that institution. Specific mention of palace *chaech'u* comes in 1379, when two
high-ranking officials went to the palace to see U's wet nurse, one madam
Chang, and prevailed on her to ask U to dismiss the palace *chaech'u* Im Kyŏn-
mi and To Kil-bu. U then confined Im and To to their homes. They appealed
to Yi In-im and Ch'oe Yŏng, who intervened to restore them to their duties
and banish madam Chang.[64]

More concrete discussion of the palace *chaech'u* under U is included in the *Koryŏsa* biography of Im Kyŏn-mi: "U selected officials as palace *chaech'u* to handle the transmittal of edicts; Im Kyŏn-mi, Hong Yŏng-t'ong, and Cho Min-su were appointed. They stayed in the palace and all affairs, large and small, had to go through them before implementation."[65]

This terse statement reveals a number of things. First, although the *Koryŏsa* does not give a date, the inclusion of Hong Yŏng-t'ong and Cho Min-su suggests that the event must have occurred in the early 1380s. Second, although this entry does not describe the palace *chaech'u* as deliberating on affairs, the emphasis on their control over transmittal of royal documents again gives voice to *yangban* concerns about limitation of political participation and circumvention of regular bureaucratic channels by a palace-based entity. Third, we find men in the palace *chaech'u* who, as we saw earlier, were not part of Yi In-im's inner circle.

If we take the *Koryŏsa* entry literally, Cho Min-su and Hong Yŏng-t'ong were appointed by U. U had been only 15 when Yi In-im and Ch'oe Yŏng made him back down over the dismissal of Im Kyŏn-mi and To Kil-bu in 1379, but he was now 19 and apparently trying to assert himself, as noted earlier with regard to the use of eunuchs. Of course, in this case he was vesting power not in inner-palace elements but in certain *yangban*. Perhaps his selection of *yangban* from outside Yi In-im's clique represented an effort to play different *yangban* groups against each other.

Despite U's apparent desire to assert the royal prerogative, however, he spent much of his time during his final few years on the throne hunting, drinking, and womanizing, neglecting his kingly duties and leaving the affairs of government in the hands of a few favored officials.[66] This situation is typified by the following statement in Yŏm Hŭng-bang's biography in the *Koryŏsa:* "U was not personally conducting the affairs of government. Yŏm Hŭng-bang, his younger brother Yŏm Chŏng-su, and U Hyŏn-bo monopolized power. State affairs were all decided by word of mouth and carried out without informing the king."[67]

Although the *Koryŏsa* does not give a date for this entry, the prominence of the Yŏm brothers indicates that it was in the final years of U's reign.[68] The Yŏm brothers and U Hyŏn-bo were close associates of Yi In-im, which suggests that Yi In-im's clique had managed to oust Cho Min-su and Hong Yŏng-t'ong and reestablish firm control over the palace *chaech'u*. This situation obtained until Ch'oe Yŏng split with and purged Yi In-im early in 1388.[69]

It seems evident, therefore, that such palace-based institutions as the Personnel Authority and the "special office" or palace *chaech'u* were still used in the post-Mongol years both by palace-based elements such as Sin Ton and *yangban* factions such as the Yi In-im group as tools for circumventing the *yangban*-dominated bureaucracy. The struggle in the Mongol era was primarily between palace-based elements and *yangban* bureaucrats; although the struggle between palace and bureaucracy remained an important theme in the post-Mongol era, the situation became more complex and unstable as a consequence of the rise of factions, such as the Hong or Yi In-im, who sought to dominate the government through the same extraordinary institutions the palace had used in earlier years. Despite the apparent resurgence of *yangban* power, the regular bureaucracy was still excluded from meaningful political participation.

Attempts at Reform

Any attempt to curtail bureaucratic power was sure to have engendered opposition from the *yangban,* but the means employed by the palace and its supporters were particularly noxious. First, reliance on extraordinary institutions, such as the Personnel Authority, threatened the political clout of the country's *yangban* elites at a time when they had come to redefine themselves in terms of hereditary traditions of service in the dynastic government. Second, the use of men of traditionally unacceptable social origins—such as slaves, merchants, and eunuchs—threatened to undermine the ascriptive social hierarchy at whose apex stood the great *yangban* descent groups.

Yangban unhappiness with domination of politics by the inner palace, and later by the Yi In-im clique, manifested itself in several ways. The histories contain frequent complaints about the impropriety of men of unacceptable social origins holding dynastic offices and about the amalgamation of lands and slaves by consorts and such powerful court-connected descent groups as the Haengju Ki. The histories also record *yangban* discontent with the institutional structure of palace politics. But perhaps the clearest statement of *yangban* dismay was given by Yi Che-hyŏn, who wrote: "Yu Kyŏng and Kim In-jun executed Ch'oe Ŭi and returned the government to the king, but the Personnel Authority was not abolished. Thus a major duty of the throne was perpetuated in the private hands of powerful subjects. This is lamentable."[70]

Yi Che-hyŏn's description of personnel actions as a "major duty of the throne" should not be taken as an expression on Yi's part of a desire to have the king exercise absolute authority over personnel actions; rather, Yi was referring to the ideal system whereby personnel decisions were made by the regular bureaucracy and then presented to the king for his approval. Yi Che-hyŏn's attitude seems to have been widely shared; several major attempts to curb the circumvention of bureaucratic authority by the inner palace and palace favorites were made in both the Mongol and post-Mongol periods.

The first attempt to address some of the basic institutional problems, particularly irregularities in recruitment and abuses by palace favorites, was made by King Ch'ungsŏn during his brief initial stay on the throne in 1298. Ch'ungsŏn launched a direct attack on palace favorites. Upon his return from the Yüan court in the fifth month of 1297, Ch'ungsŏn, then the crown prince, arrested and executed the eunuch Ch'oe Se-yŏn, who was a particular favorite of King Ch'ungnyŏl and his Mongol consort Princess Cheguk. Once Ch'ungsŏn took the throne, he immediately implemented a reform program based largely on an 18-point memorial submitted two years earlier by Hong Cha-bŏn of the Namyang Hong, which had called for changes designed to alleviate the dynasty's financial distress.[71] Ch'ungsŏn's reform program went beyond fiscal renovation, however, and also made major changes in the conduct of political affairs. He abolished the Personnel Authority and reassigned its recruitment functions to the Hallim Academy, which was then renamed the Sarim-wŏn and staffed by men from central *yangban* descent groups such as Yi Chin of Kyŏngju and Pak Chŏn-ji of Chuksan.[72] The removal of recruitment authority from the palace to an agency of the civil branch and the key roles played by Hong Cha-bŏn, Yi Chin, and Pak Chŏn-ji suggest that one goal of Ch'ungsŏn's reform of political institutions was to return political authority to regular bureaucratic institutions. It is important to note that Todang activity, as shown in table 4.1, seems to have resumed at this time.

Ch'ungsŏn's first reign was short-lived, however. His Mongol consort, possibly concerned that the resurgence of *yangban* power might curtail her own prerogatives, provoked a dispute with a Korean consort of the P'yŏngyang Cho. The ensuing controversy led to Ch'ungsŏn's recall back to the Yüan capital after only eight months on the throne.[73] His departure meant the end of this reform effort. Although Ch'ungsŏn later resumed the kingship from 1308 to 1313, he seems to have lost heart for reform and spent almost his entire reign in the Yüan capital. There were no serious attempts at reform during the reigns of his successors Ch'ungsuk and Ch'unghye, during which time the Todang once again lapsed into inactivity.

The next serious attempt to deal with the issue of recruitment irregularities and palace favoritism came with the enthronement of the eight-year-old boy-king Ch'ungmok in 1344. Again, as in the case of Ch'ungsŏn's reforms, the way was prepared by a major memorial, this time by Yi Che-hyŏn of the Kyŏngju Yi, calling for a number of political reforms, including abolition of the Personnel Authority. Within two months after Ch'ungmok took the throne, Yi Che-hyŏn and his reformers did in fact shut down the palace-based personnel organ. This reform was soon stymied with the restoration of the Personnel Authority, apparently because of pressure applied by the queen mother, Princess Tŏngnyŏng.[74] The *yangban* reformers regathered their forces and struck again. Early in 1347 they established a special Directorate for Ordering Politics (Chŏngch'i Togam), whose top officials were men from well-established *yangban* descent groups, including Kim Yŏng-don of the Andong Kim, Kim Kwang-ch'ŏl of the Kwangsan Kim, Kwŏn Wi of the Andong Kwŏn, and An Ch'uk of the Sunhŭng An. The directorate was charged with a wide range of duties focusing mostly on restoring order in the countryside, but it also functioned as a vehicle for purging enemies of the *yangban*. The prime targets of the reformers seem to have been men of unacceptable social origins who rose through palace patronage such as the slave eunuch Chŏn Yŏng-bo, but when the reformers began to focus on imperial favorites such as Ki Sam-man, brother of the imperial consort, the Mongols intervened and put a stop to the activities of the directorate, barely two months after it was established.[75]

We should take note that the Todang, after being all but invisible for several decades, resurfaced during these years. The sources show it involved in a number of areas: in 1344 an official submitted a memorial to the Todang on penal affairs;[76] in 1345 circuit intendants were ordered to report on the activities of *hyangni* to the Todang;[77] and again in 1345 Yi Che-hyŏn submitted a memorial to the Todang on the important issue of the crown prince's lectures.[78] The nature of these reforms and the revitalization of the Todang indicate that a main purpose of this movement was to restore political power to the *yangban*-dominated bureaucracy. Once the reforms were reversed, however, the Todang again fell silent and power went back into the hands of palace-based elements and imperial favorites.

The reign of King Kongmin was one of the most turbulent in Korean history. From the outside, the dynasty was beset by incessant foreign incursions from the Wako, the Red Turbans, the Mongol rebel Nahach'u, and even the Yüan dynasty itself, which in 1364 invaded northwestern Korea with a force of 10,000 men in an unsuccessful attempt to put a pretender on the Koryŏ throne. Furthermore, in 1368 the Yüan dynasty was driven from China by the Ming, presenting the Koryŏ with the delicate diplomatic problem of switching loyalties and convincing the Ming of its sincerity. On the inside Kongmin faced a number of revolts (such as that of Cho Il-sin in 1352) and assassination attempts (such as that of Kim Yong in 1363) before finally meeting his end in 1374 at the hands of palace courtiers acting in concert with a eunuch.

Despite all the distractions, however, Kongmin's reign is also noted for its attempts at reform. A significant attempt to curb the abuses of palace politics and restore power to the bureaucracy came right after Kongmin took the throne in late in 1351. As in the case of Ch'ungmok's reforms, the leading role was again played by Yi Che-hyŏn, who took office as acting prime minister (sŏp chŏngsŭng) immediately after Kongmin was enthroned. One of the first things Yi Che-hyŏn did was to jail or banish a number of palace favorites, including Princess Tŏngnyŏng's protégés Pae Chŏn and No Yŏng-sŏ of the Kyoha No.[79] A few months later the Personnel Authority was abolished, its duties reverting to the Board of Personnel and the Board of War, where they had originally resided.[80] Despite this promising beginning, however, the Personnel Authority was soon restored and Pae Chŏn was pardoned.[81] Once again the Mongol-backed inner palace was able to frustrate yangban reformers.

Another, more comprehensive, reform was initiated in 1356. Kongmin, encouraged perhaps by the visible decline of Mongol power and supported by Yi Che-hyŏn, launched this round of reforms by executing powerful imperial in-laws, including members of the Haengju Ki, Kwŏn Kyŏm, and No Ch'aek. He then abolished that most tangible symbol of Mongol domination, the Eastern Expedition Field Headquarters, ordered his subjects to stop following Mongol fashions, and reorganized the bureaucracy along the lines of the old pre-Mongol system. He also abolished the Personnel Authority. It seems apparent that Kongmin, with the support—or, perhaps more accurately, at the urging—of prominent yangban such as Yi Che-hyŏn, was striving to regularize political procedures and restore power to the bureaucracy.

Kongmin's 1356 reforms were limited, however, by a number of factors. One problem, of course, was Mongol unhappiness with the reforms. Displeased with Kongmin's show of independence, the Mongols threatened to invade. Kongmin had to back down, restoring the Field Headquarters in 1361 and revising the nomenclature of the bureaucracy once again to reflect subordination to the Yüan in 1362. A more important reason for the limits of his reforms, however, was the weakness of the kingship's institutional foundations. The Koryŏ royal house still suffered from its loss of prestige—in fact, Kongmin's anti-Yüan stance may have been a calculated effort to recover prestige for the throne. Kongmin still had no standing army, no better control over the country's resources than did his predecessors, and was still under the influence of powerful, albeit now Korean, royal in-laws. To complicate matters even further, his chief supporter in the reform effort, Yi Che-hyŏn, was growing old, retiring in 1357 at the age of 74.

By the 1360s, however, a feel of change was in the air. The Namyang Hong's grip on power was weakened by the death of Hong Ŏn-bak in 1362. In addition, by mid-decade the decline of the Yüan dynasty was apparent to all. It seemed that an opportunity for real reform might finally be at hand. Rather than lead the fight for reform himself, however, Kongmin, grief struck by the death of his favorite consort, the Mongol princess Noguk, in the second month of 1365, decided to turn the reigns of government over to the monk Sin Ton, whom he appointed state preceptor (*Kuksa*) and ordered to participate in court deliberations in the fifth month of 1365.[82] Within six months Sin Ton was appointed chancellor plentipotentiary (*yŏng to* Ch'ŏmŭisa*sa*) and became in effect regent for Kongmin, who withdrew from active participation in politics to devote his time to designing and building a Buddhist temple in memory of his deceased consort.

Kongmin's motives for entrusting the government to Sin Ton are described in Sin's *Koryŏsa* biography:

> The king had been on the throne for some time but the *chaech'u* did not support his desires. The private factions of the great hereditary official families were all interlinked and concealed things [from the king]; new elements from the outside were behaving hypocritically in hopes of gaining names for themselves and, being ashamed of their obscure origins, they were trying to elevate their status by marrying with great families; the Confucians, on the other hand, were weak and not forthright and formed factions based on master-disciple relations from the examination system. None of these was reliable. The king therefore, in order to root out old abuses, thought to find and use someone who was independent and not compromised by worldly considerations.[83]

Thus it appears that, unlike Kongmin's earlier attempts at reform, which under the influence of Yi Che-hyŏn tried to restore authority to the bureaucracy, his 1365 reform represented an effort to get around the *yangban*-dominated bureaucracy and arrogate power to the palace. The first thing Sin Ton did after taking supreme power was to initiate a series of purges. Targets included members of the Namyang Hong, who seem to have been effectively eliminated from power during Sin Ton's tenure: only one of their members held office during those years.[84] Having curbed the royal in-laws, Sin Ton next embarked on an ambitious reform program. In 1366 he established a directorate for determining the status of lands and people, with himself as head, in an effort to reassert the dynasty's control over resources. He also presided over a revitalization of the state educational system, in what appears to have been an effort to break the power of the *yangban*-dominated private schools. Finally, and perhaps most tellingly, Sin Ton floated a proposal to relocate the capital from Kaegyŏng to P'yŏngyang, a move designed to get the court away from powerful *yangban* descent groups.[85]

Sin Ton's proposal to move the capital reflected his awareness of the biggest problem facing him and his king: they were isolated elements without a strong institutional base. It was this weakness that led Sin Ton to revive the Personnel Authority and the palace *chaech'u*. This, along with the excesses of his purges, provoked strong *yangban* opposition. A number of *yangban* risked life and fortune to memorialize against Sin Ton. Sin was eventually driven from power and executed in 1371.

Once Sin Ton was out, the *yangban* began to reassert their authority. First on their list of reforms was the palace *chaech'u*, as seen in a memorial calling for the abolition of the palace *chaech'u* that was submitted shortly after Sin Ton's demise:

The *chaesang* meet in the Todang to regulate the *ŭmyang* [Ch. *yin-yang*], dispose of affairs, and handle personnel issues. When they have deliberated on an issue, they report it to the palace; when they receive the king's edict, they implement it. Now individuals enter the palace for audiences with the king at improper times and emerge monopolizing glory and fortune. Their peers in the Todang do not know the course of affairs, and officials of the court and outside gather at their doors. How can they wish to exceed the bounds of propriety like this? According to our country's system, there is one administrator of memorials [*chisinsa*] and four royal transmitters (*sŭngsŏn*); all are third-grade posts. They take turns on night duty at the court, handle ritual, report memorials, and transmit royal edits. They dare not say even the smallest thing on their own. This is called the "dragon's throat" [*yonghu*, a term for the transmittal of royal documents]. Also, with regard to the palace ministers [*naesang*], it is said that no one who has followed the laws of former kings has exceeded the bounds of propriety. The key to security for both lord and minister lies in abolishing the palace *chaech'u* at once.[86]

In this memorial we see expressed once again *yangban* concerns about palace favorites bypassing regular institutional channels, especially with regard to the monopolization of power by a small number of men and the usurpation of the document transmission officials' role in the "dragon's throat."

This effort to restore political power to the bureaucracy was, however, lim-

TABLE 4.2

Levels of Todang Activity, 1351–88

Period	1351–55	1356–58	1359–65	1366–70	1371–77	1378–82	1383–85	1386–88
Entries	1	5	2	0	21	2	7	2

ited after the enthronement of U by the failure to abolish the Personnel Authority and by the late 1370s revival of the palace *chaech'u* by Yi In-im. Subsequently, there were no concentrated efforts at institutional reform during U's tenure on the throne. Whether the Yi In-im group was simply not interested in reform or whether they did not feel they had a strong enough grip on power to push reforms through is not clear, but at any rate the dynasty's deeply rooted political problems continued to fester throughout U's 14 years as king.

One final significant feature of post-Mongol era politics was the gradual revitalization of the Todang. Table 4.2 tallies recorded instances of Todang activity during the years 1351–88, showing that activity was very sporadic and irregular during the post-Mongol era. The entry for 1351 was the aforementioned involvement of the Todang in the ancestor worship issue at the time of Kongmin's first attempt to remove palace favorites and abolish the Personnel Authority. After that attempt failed, the Todang fell silent again until Kongmin's second round of reforms between 1356 and 1358, when it reemerged as an active center of political power, as seen in a 1356 edict calling for it to supervise the activities of circuit intendants,[87] and a 1357 Todang memorial on military affairs in the northern border regions.[88] After this round of reforms was reversed, the Todang again disappeared from the sources except for a 1362 session dealing with the threat of Red Turban invasions and the previously noted mention of the Todang under Sin Ton in 1365.[89]

The Todang was silent during Sin Ton's tenure; once Sin was removed, however, it once again emerged as an important power center. An edict of the twelfth month of 1371 stated, "The duties of all officials are decided in the Todang. In recent years various agencies have handled state affairs on their own and passed orders down to the provinces. . . . This has caused much grief for the people. Henceforth all affairs must be carried out only at the orders of the Todang."[90]

For the next several years, a period when the palace *chaech'u* are absent from the sources, the Todang was involved in a wide range of issues including the conduct of ritual,[91] establishing garrison lands to support field armies,[92] personnel issues,[93] rebuilding the country's system of postal stations,[94] determination of Kongmin's successor,[95] punishments,[96] and military affairs.[97] The high level of Todang activity between 1371 and 1377 may be a reflection of the balance of power that obtained between Yi In-im and the Namyang Hong, of the inability of either side to enforce its will unilaterally. Further evidence for this is the sharp drop in Todang activity after the queen mother lost her main supporter, Kim Song-myŏng, in 1377 and the Yi In-im group reinstituted the palace *chaech'u*.

The next burst of Todang activity came in the mid-1380s when U was attempting to assert himself against Yi In-im and was using eunuchs to supervise the Todang. Indeed, four of the seven entries for 1383–85 have to do with eunuchs reporting to or instructing the Todang, the last one in 1385 showing a eunuch urging U to oversee political affairs because the Todang was unable to act and issues were piling up.[98] Once U resumed his hunting and drinking pastimes and the Yi In-im group reestablished control over the palace *chaech'u*, however, the Todang once more lapsed into obscurity.

There appears, therefore, to be a pattern in these alternating periods of Todang inactivity and activity. The Todang seems to have been most active when no one group was able to establish domination or when the kings, whether of their own volition or at the behest of reform-minded *yangban* elements, attempted to push through programs of reform and least active when the throne was under the domination of special interests, such as the inner palace or the Yi In-im clique.

Further illustration of the problems in the Todang comes from a 1389 observer, who stated:

> Unfortunately, since 1374 [the year U took the throne] villainous subjects have dominated politics. When men bribed them with fields and houses, they promoted the bribers to ministerial posts without examining their worth. There were many offering bribes, but few offices to give them. Eventually they established consulting posts so that the number of men in the Todang has reached 70 or 80. Even though this is supposed to be the deliberative body of the chief ministers of the Secretariat-Chancellery and the Security Council, the members play as they come and play as they go, and many do not even participate in the governing of the state.[99]

This was written 57 years after Yi Che-hyŏn's complaints about the Todang, yet the author sounds the same themes: excessive membership and frivolous behavior. But the situation in 1389 was worse than in 1342. Many of the men sitting in the Todang had gained their seats by bribery, and membership had swollen to nearly 80. In such a situation, it is highly unlikely that the Todang could have functioned effectively. Illustrative in this regard is an instance in 1384 when Ch'oe Yŏng, under orders from U to oversee affairs, went to the Todang and argued strongly for the council members to agree to prohibitions against land amalgamation, but was unable to achieve a consensus.[100] Decades of inner-palace and special interest group circumvention of the dynasty's regular political institutions had left them corrupt and incapable of effective governance.

In summary, it seems safe to say that the *yangban* sought, in the years following the overthrow of the Ch'oe house military dictatorship, to restore political power to the civil branch of the bureaucracy. They were struggling, of course, against the kings' practice of vesting power in non-*yangban* elements such as foreign retainers, eunuchs, and slaves. Their concern was expressed primarily in attempts at institutional reform, such as their efforts to abolish the palace-based Personnel Authority, to maintain the integrity of the political process by keeping the crucial function of document transmission in proper hands, and to restore power to the Todang. The *yangban* were, however, repeatedly frustrated, by Mongol-connected palace elements in the Mongol era and by powerful cliques during U's reign. As a consequence, the political history of the late Koryŏ was essentially the story of conflict between the palace, which sought to circumvent *yangban* domination of the bureaucracy and the organs of political struggle, and *yangban,* who tried to wrest political power away from palace-based groups or special factions and restore it to the agencies of their bureaucracy. Preoccupation with this struggle and the failure of either side to achieve a decisive victory meant continuing erosion of the dynasty's political institutions and delay of critical reforms in other areas.

THE STRUGGLE FOR CONTROL OVER RESOURCES

During its final two centuries the Koryŏ state suffered serious erosion of its access to free-floating resources. The most immediate and obvious reason for this was the devastation wreaked by foreign invasions, by Mongols in the mid-thirteenth century and by Red Turbans and the Wako in the second half of the fourteenth century. Less obvious, but of equal importance, was penetration of the countryside by capital-based elements seeking to enhance their economic status. This took two forms: amalgamation of large landed estates and conversion of *kongjŏn* general revenue lands into *sajŏn* prebends.

An important underlying cause of the dynasty's loss of access to resources was the decline of the traditional *hyangni*-centered local order. Although *hyangni* local domination may have limited the amounts of resources available to rulers, *hyangni* did collect taxes and mobilize manpower from lands and people not under aristocratic control. Their continuing existence was important to the fiscal well-being of the state, but foreign military incursions and economic penetration of the countryside by central *yangban* descent groups disrupted the local social order and uprooted *hyangni.* Lacking a strong central presence in the countryside, the state had no other systematic means of reasserting its control over resources.

Foreign Invasions

Foreign military incursions came in two waves. The first was the Mongol invasions of the mid-thirteenth century. The second came after the collapse of Mongol hegemony a century later, in the invasion of the Red Turbans and the raiding of the Wako.

The Mongols invaded Korea seven times between 1231 and 1259, with some campaigns lasting as long as four years. Many Korean peasants abandoned their villages and retreated to islands and mountain fortresses. The invaders' response was to lay waste to the land. In 1254, for example, the Mongols burned fields and villages wherever they passed and took 206,800 prisoners of war back to the mainland.[101] The long years of war wreaked havoc on local society, particularly in northern and western Korea, where Mongol ravages were most severe.

Some sense of the dynasty's financial situation in the immediate post-Mongol invasion years can be gleaned from a *Koryŏsa* entry of 1271 discussing the establishment of the Salary Rank Land (Nokkwajŏn) system. "Due to the recent military difficulties, our granaries are empty; because of this we cannot pay salaries and have no way to encourage our officials. We request that lands in the eight counties of the capital region be allocated as Salary Rank Land fields in accordance with the recipients' ranks."[102] This entry serves as an illustration of the extent to which the state suffered from a lack of operational funds in the immediate post-invasion years. It also tells us that the dynasty placed a high priority on providing for the welfare of its officials, most probably to ensure their loyalty. The new system was not designed as a replacement for the Field and Woodland Rank system, which appears to have still been in effect, if only as a means for distributing *sajŏn* prebends in areas of the country outside the capital region.[103] Rather, as the name suggests, the new system was conceived as a way for the state to make up for the salaries it could no longer pay. Much of the land in the capital region was already under the control of powerful *yangban,* either as private estates or as *sajŏn* prebends; therefore, the lands that were actually allocated under the new system were limited to "reclaimable lands" *(kanji),* primarily fields that had been abandoned during the preceding decades of war.[104]

Nonetheless, the dynasty was not totally without resources. The agriculturally rich three southern provinces suffered less damage during the Mongol invasions than the northern and central reaches of the peninsula and had been able to provide the wartime Koryŏ capital on Kanghwa Island with tax grain shipments by sea throughout the war years.[105] At the end of the war, therefore, the dynasty still had one significant source of tax revenue. Furthermore, it appears that post-war recovery brought some degree of expansion in the tax base. By 1280 the state was able to restore salaries,[106] and in 1321 salaries were even increased for certain groups of officials.[107]

Korea enjoyed a 90-year respite from foreign troubles after peace was made with the Mongols. Nonetheless, the Koryŏ dynasty's financial troubles continued. In the first half of the fourteenth century revenues had once again declined and the state experienced serious fiscal shortages. The first evidence of this came in 1331, when land grants in the capital region, which had earlier been given to royal favorites, were rescinded and used for Salary Rank prebends.[108] By 1343 the worsening situation prompted two additional seizures of land grants, one to provide for palace granaries and the other to fill granaries for military expenditures.[109]

The situation was made worse by new invasions in the second half of the fourteenth century. Large stretches of northern and central Korea were laid waste by the Red Turbans, who ravaged the country between 1359 and 1362. Even more damaging were the Japanese Wako pirates. The Wako had been making occasional forays in Korea since early in the thirteenth century, but they began to raid in earnest after 1350. Vast areas of coastal Korea were devastated, particularly in the southern provinces, as villagers abandoned their homes and fled inland to escape the plundering.

By 1358 the dynasty did not have sufficient funds to pay salaries to all its officials. *Koryŏsa* states, "When salaries were paid in the ninth month of 1358, nothing was given to officials of the ninth grade."[110] Salary shortages were noted again in 1359, 1379, and 1381 amidst general commentary about a lack of operating funds greatly hampering the state's ability to field defensive forces against the Wako raiders. The fiscal situation reached its nadir in 1391 when the dynasty could pay salaries only to officials of the first three ranks, and even those officials received only one measure (sŏk) of rice each,[111] only a tiny fraction of the 330 measures top-ranking officials had received during King Injong's reign in the twelfth century.[112] Some sense of the degree of destruction wreaked on local society in the late fourteenth century can be gained from contemporaneous accounts in the dynastic histories. A 1377 entry in the Koryŏsa tells that an emissary sent to the three southern provinces to compile a register of the sons of inactive officials living there found conditions so bad that people were even selling their children.[113] Another memorial from 1392 noted that people of mean status were wandering, stealing, and slaughtering animals that belonged to others, and recommended that local authorities register the vagrants, settle them, and make them farm.[114]

While these two instances suggest serious problems in late fourteenth-century local society, an even bleaker picture is painted by a 1391 memorial on current affairs: "Since the Wako began coming in 1350, our districts and prefectures have been devastated, and some now have no population left."[115] By the second half of the fourteenth century, local society was in a state of disorder, even in the agriculturally rich southern provinces that had supported the Kanghwa capital during the Mongol invasions. To make matters worse, the pirates also frequently intercepted the seaborne shipments of what tax grains the dynasty was able to collect. Many of the salary shortages noted in the histories were attributed to Wako capture of tax transport ships.[116] This situation not only deprived the state of needed income, but also created widespread unhappiness among officials, particularly those who relied on compensation from the state for their livelihood.

Penetration of the Countryside by Central Interests

Foreign depredations help to explain the immediate fiscal shortages the dynasty faced in the 1260s and 1270s and in the final decades of the dynasty. They do not, however, provide the key to understanding the state's inability to recover from wartime destruction, nor do they shed any light on the causes of the dynasty's worsening financial situation during periods free of foreign depredation. For that we must turn to an internal factor: penetration of the countryside by the economic interests of capital-based elements. The most obvious form of this expansion was the nongjang estate. Nongjang owners amassed their estates either by appropriating lands belonging to other persons (usually peasants), or by taking over some of the so, pugok, and hyang that had been set aside for the support of specific state activities.[117]

The spread of *nongjang* is usually attributed to *yangban* greed, and perhaps rightly so, but we must not overlook the fact that the inner palace and its favorites were among the worst abusers. Princess Cheguk, for example, was a leading figure among those who appropriated others' lands and slaves to create privately held estates, and the *Koryŏsa* tells us that in Ch'ungnyŏl's reign "the princess's foreign retainers and palace attendants have widely taken over good lands, using mountains and rivers as the boundaries [of their estates]. Many of them have obtained these lands as royal grants and do not pay taxes."[118]

There is no doubt that the rise and spread of *nongjang* estates resulted in a direct reduction of tax receipts and other exactions. In the Koryŏ peasants were subject to three kinds of exactions: land tax (*cho*), paid either directly to the state in the case of *kongjŏn* or to the prebend holder in the case of *sajŏn*; corvée labor (*yong*); and local tribute (*cho*), special local products levied against the household. Although the estates were not legally exempt from taxes, their owners frequently found ways to evade taxation and even to arrogate to themselves the corvée services and local tribute of their tenants. Evidence of this can be found not only in the previous entry regarding palace favorites, but also in a 1278 *Koryŏsa* entry discussing abuses related to powerful persons forcing peasants into tenancy: "The *ch'ŏgan* cultivates others' lands. He pays rent to the landlord and provides corvée labor and local tribute to the state. In short, the *ch'ŏgan* is a tenant farmer. Lately, however, the powerful and noble have seized large numbers of peasants, called them *ch'ŏgan*, and have evaded all three exactions. These abuses are very severe."[119]

Further evidence of the estate owners' ability to evade land taxes and other exactions is found in a 1318 *Koryŏsa* entry lamenting that they "have widely occupied *kongjŏn* and hidden large numbers of peasant households."[120] The peasant households were being "hidden" from tax collectors and corvée organizers. It is clear that estate owners' ability to evade taxes made the spread of *nongjang* an important factor in the fiscal debility of the late Koryŏ.

Amalgamation of landed estates was not, however, the only way in which the central *yangban* sought to enhance their economic position. There was also tremendous growth in the amount of land set aside for *sajŏn* prebends in the late Koryŏ, to the extent that by the fourteenth century prebends were widespread even in the two northern border regions whose lands had originally been set aside as garrison fields for support of the border defense forces stationed there.[121] One suspects that a major reason this growth was the kings' need to buy the loyalty of their officials. At any rate, this expansion in prebends in the late Koryŏ meant a reduction in the amount of free-floating resources available to the state for operational expenses.

But expansion in prebends meant more than simple diminishment of tax receipts from *kongjŏn*. In the late Koryŏ it was common practice for two or more *yangban* officials to claim prebendal rights to the same piece of land. The enormous burden of having to support all these officials caused many peasants to abandon their lands and flee, leading to further disruption of the local social order.

The deteriorating rural situation was remarked on by a number of travelers in the early and mid-fourteenth century. An Ch'uk, on a trip to east central Korea in 1330, noted that the streets of the town of Towŏn were overgrown with weeds and half the residents were gone.[122] Yi Kok, also writing in the first half of the fourteenth century, encountered a large number of homes gone to ruin at Kŭmju, a subordinate county of Kyŏngsan, and reported that they had been abandoned by runaway peasants.[123] The linkage between the central officials' economic penetration and devastation in the countryside is best seen in the remarks of Wŏn Ch'ŏn-sŏk, who commented on conditions at Yanggu County in central Korea in his record of a 1351 trip:

On the fifteenth day [of the eighth month] I left Pangsan and arrived at Yanggu Prefecture, where I found the houses of both the *hyangni* and the peasants falling down and their cooking hearths cold. When I asked passersby what had happened, they said, "This county has been administered by the officials at Yangch'ŏn. It has always had limited land and the soil is poor, so there have been few people and products. Recently powerful families have seized the fields and caused distress for the peasants. Rents and taxes are great, but there is no room to work even an additional button's worth of land. Every winter the rent collectors come in large numbers. If the peasants cannot pay, they are hung up by their hands and feet and caned to the bone. The residents, unable to endure this, have fled."[124]

It is significant that these documented instances of local disarray were in subordinate counties where the central government had not established magistrates. This suggests that prefects and magistrates of control prefectures, laboring under the dual handicaps of limited staffing and large territorial responsibilities, were unable to cope with the forces eroding local society in outlying subordinate prefectures and counties and that the *hyangni* responsible for those areas were either absent or unable to prevent powerful central elements from forcing themselves on the peasantry.

The destructive effects of foreign invasions and central penetration on the local sociopolitical order were intensified by poor weather in the second half of the fourteenth century. Severe droughts occurred in 1365, 1368, 1372, 1374, 1376, and 1377.[125] The effects of these on the populace were aggravated because the financially strapped state had few, if any, resources to succor the victims. With the rural population suffering from a combination of foreign invasions, penetration of central economic interests, and natural disasters, it is no wonder that whole districts were depopulated by the closing years of the dynasty.

Attempts to Resolve the Financial Problem

One way in which the dynasty attempted to restore order in the countryside and regain a measure of access to resources was through the establishment of General Directorates for Determining the Status of Lands and People (Chŏnmin Pyŏnjŏng Togam), which were set up seven times during the last 130 years of Koryŏ rule. The directorates were instituted by the state in order to return to tax-paying status lands and people that had been seized by powerful elements.[126]

At times the directorates appear to have had some success, as in the case of Sin Ton's directorate during Kongmin's reign. Sin Ton was even praised as a saint by those unjustly enslaved persons whom he freed.[127] Nonetheless, resistance and evasion by wealthy *yangban* seem to have significantly limited the effectiveness of these efforts to reestablish state control over resources.

Another limiting factor may have been the narrow scope of directorate reforms. Recent studies have noted that the establishment of directorates frequently coincided with the fall of prominent officials. The 1269 directorate, for example, was charged with disposing of the lands and peoples that had belonged to Kim In-jun,[128] while the 1381 directorate seems to have been used to purge supporters of Sin Ton.[129] The *Koryŏsa* "Monograph on Officials" states baldly that the 1388 directorate disposed of the lands and peoples that had been seized by Im Kyŏn-mi.[130]

The actual provisions of the directorates are not always spelled out, but on at least four occasions the histories tell us that one purpose of the directorates was to return lands and people to their original owners *(ponju)*. One instance was in 1301, when the directorate was charged with returning slaves emancipated by the Mongols to their original owners.[131] The next came in 1352 when King Kongmin issued a proclamation that called, among other things, for the return of lands and people to their original owners.[132] Again in 1366, the directorate had as one of its goals the restoration of stolen lands and people to their owners.[133] Finally, the 1388 directorate for disposing of the lands and people seized by Im Kyŏn-mi also returned them to their original owners.[134]

Perhaps the "original owners" were *hyangni* and peasants out in the countryside, and the return of these lands and slaves did represent restoration of
resources to the tax rolls. But the history of prolonged and bitter litigation
over ownership of land and slaves among central officials throughout the late
Koryŏ and early Chosŏn strongly suggests that the "original owners" were
often central *yangban* whose lands and slaves were taken from them by strongmen such as Kim In-jun and Im Kyŏn-mi.[135] In short, the directorates appear
to have functioned as much to maintain *yangban* socioeconomic foundations
as to restore the local social order and carry out fiscal reform.

The dynasty also made periodic attempts to restore certain land grants to
the tax rolls and to marginally refine its collection and transport of taxes. Several
times in the mid- and late fourteenth century, for example, the state sought
to enhance its tax receipts by taking over lands previously granted to temples
and monasteries that were now abandoned or by seizing lands that had belonged
to formerly powerful but now weak or deceased descent groups. In 1343, for
example, the state appropriated lands that had belonged to now defunct temples and to the merit subjects of previous reigns to fill palace storehouses.[136]
In 1356 the state used land rents from abandoned temple lands to supplement
military expenditures,[137] and in 1388 lands that previous kings had donated
to temples were restored to state control.[138] Beyond these attempts to revoke
land grant patents and restore their fields to the tax rolls, the only other attempts
to improve the dynasty's fiscal situation were such limited measures as a 1384
dispatch of supplementary collectors (*ch'ujing saek*) to collect local tribute
not received from the prefectures and counties,[139] and a 1372 proposal to transport tax revenues overland in order to avoid Wako raiders.[140]

One factor behind the dynasty's failure to take radical action to resolve the
fiscal problem was the inability of the throne to exert itself effectively against
entrenched *yangban*. This is illustrated in a 1387 passage in the *Koryŏsa:* "U
instructed the Todang to prepare a list of all those who have plundered the
lands and people of the granaries and palace offices, but the Todang members, worried about their own selves, did not comply."[141]

Another reason was the irregular system of dynastic finances that developed
during the post-1170 era. The dynasty had used privately held *chang* and *ch'ŏ*
estates, rather than general tax receipts, to provide for the royal family and
its consorts from early on; but, as Sudo Yoshiyuki has shown, late Koryŏ kings
and their consorts aggressively expanded the royal family's private landholdings by establishing direct palace control over rural villages and by seizing lands
and peoples that belonged to others.[142] State agencies in the late Koryŏ appear
to have followed the palace's lead to form their own private estates to pro-

vide for both operating expenditures and salaries.[143] This tendency for the royal household and major governmental agencies to establish independent sources of income may have insulated them from many of the negative effects of the deepening fiscal predicament, but in effect it represented a retreat from the effort to create and maintain free-floating resources. The palace's reliance on privately held resources must have weakened impetus toward major fiscal reform.

In the final analysis, however, the most important underlying reason for the state's inability to cope with the forces that were undermining its fiscal foundations was the tradition of weak central control over local administration. Despite the serious deterioration in rural conditions, no attempt was made in the late Koryŏ to bring the countryside under more effective central control. The *Koryŏsa* "Monograph on Geography" shows the establishment of only twelve new prefects, magistrates, and lesser magistrates from 1177 to 1388. These postings occurred singly or in pairs at irregular intervals between 1232 and 1384, and included one prefect, five magistrates, and six lesser magistrates. The low numbers and lack of any pattern suggest that these new postings came about in response to specific local conditions rather than as part of any effort to increase central control over prefectures and counties.

The sources are silent regarding the dynasty's reasons for ceasing to expand its official presence in the countryside after 1176. Perhaps the chaotic conditions that prevailed in the countryside as a result of the various revolts of the military period, the prolonged Mongol invasions, and the raids of the Wako Japanese pirates are to blame. Earlier kings such as Yejong and Injong, however, had taken advantage of locally unsettled conditions to dispatch centrally appointed officials to new locales, so once things settled down after the surrender to the Mongols in 1270, the Koryŏ kings of the late thirteenth and early fourteenth centuries should have been able to do likewise, at least until the Wako raids began to intensify in the second half of the fourteenth century. Another possible reason for the lack of new magistrates was the rapid spread of large private estates in the post-1170 era. It seems plausible that powerful figures would have resisted the establishment of magistracies in areas where they had their estates.

One additional factor behind the dynasty's failure to establish new prefectureships and magistracies during the post-military period may have been the implementation of the provincial military administration modeled after the Mongol myriarchy system. Myriarchs and chiliarchs were established under the aegis of the Sun'gun Manhobu (Patrolling Myriarchy) in the late thirteenth century at various locations throughout the country, where they were charged with a wide variety of administrative duties, including law enforcement and hearing disputes over land and slaves. By 1310, however, their authority seems to have been restricted to police functions.[144] It is not clear why the myriarchs lost their civil powers. Perhaps it was because some modicum of order had been restored during the preceding half-century of peace. There may have also been some concern that the combination of broad civil and military powers might have enabled the myriarchs to develop into locally based entities capable of challenging the central regime. What is certain, however, is that after curtailing the civil powers of the myriarchs, the dynasty made no new efforts to revamp its administrative control over the countryside.

The 1298 reforms of King Ch'ungsŏn and the 1344 reforms of King Ch'ungmok did attempt to address the rural problem by targeting corrupt local elements and putting great emphasis on efficient conduct of government by the existing prefects and magistrates.[145] Neither of these reform movements lasted more than a few months, however, and neither proposed any expansion in the number of prefectures and counties under the direct supervision of centrally appointed officials.

The real thrust of the dynasty's program to restore order in the countryside centered on reestablishing *hyangni* in their ancestral seats. These local elites were, of course, the linchpins of the local sociopolitical order and the group on whom the dynasty relied to maintain order and collect taxes, corvée, and local tribute. Yi Kok's comments on the situation at Kŭmju, a subordinate county of Kyŏngsan, are instructive in this regard. Yi reported that when he asked the magistrate in Kyŏngsan why there were so many run-down houses in Kŭmju, the magistrate told him, "Those are the hearths of people who have run away and not returned. Recently when I went on inspection I was met by a *hyangni* who was able to answer my questions about what had happened. His surname is Chin and his given name is Sil-lo. He is capable of restoring the situation."[146]

The dynasty's concern with keeping the *hyangni* at home is expressed repeatedly in the sources. In 1298, for example, all former *hyangni* holding military ranks below the sixth grade were ordered to return to their ancestral seats and resume their duties as local officials.[147] In 1312 the sons of *hyangni* were prohibited from taking entry-level posts in the military branch.[148] In 1325 the king noted that many *hyangni* had deserted their duties in the countryside and ordered that all lower ranking men of *hyangni* origins who had not passed the government service examinations be returned to their original duties.[149] Another attempt to stabilize the *hyangni* came in 1375, when the government prohibited men who had taken the local preliminary examinations (*hyangsi*) in locales other than their own ancestral seats from sitting for the metropolitan examination (*hoesi*).[150]

In conjunction with evidence such as Yi Kok's comment on how centrally appointed magistrates looked to *hyangni* to resuscitate local society, these entries from the histories leave little doubt that the centerpiece of the dynasty's policy to deal with disruption of local society, and thereby restore its fiscal health, was to tie *hyangni* to their ancestral seats and lean on them to restore the traditional local order.

The frequency with which kings found it necessary to issue proclamations returning *hyangni* to the countryside underscores the state's lack of success in binding local elites to their ancestral seats. Some *hyangni*, no doubt, were attracted to life in the capital because of its cultural sophistication and opportunities for advancement. Equally if not more important, however, was the situation the *hyangni* faced at home. The populace over which they had once ruled was scattered, and the fields whose largess they had once enjoyed were abandoned and overgrown with weeds.

In short, in many areas the local social hierarchy, whose ascriptive tradition had guaranteed a privileged place to the *hyangni*, no longer existed. The collapse of the *hyangni*-centered local order made it difficult, if not impossible, for the state to maintain order and collect taxes throughout large areas of the country.

THE STRUGGLE TO MAINTAIN THE STATUS SYSTEM

A prominent feature of late Koryŏ sociopolitical history was, as Yi Sŏng-mu has shown, expansion of the central official class.[151] We have already noted how proliferation of capital-based descent groups and the continuing recruitment of men of *hyangni* backgrounds swelled the central official class and created intense competitive pressures in the pre-1170 era. This trend, which was aggravated by the palace preference for using foreigners and men from nonelite strata to counterbalance the *yangban*, accelerated in the late Koryŏ.

The dramatic growth in the number of men who could claim membership in the central official class had deleterious effects in several areas. Increasing numbers of official status holders meant greater demand for salaries and *sajŏn* prebends, further aggravating the dynasty's financial ills. At the same time, it also led to intense competition for offices and political power, contributing to the political instability that plagued the dynasty in its final years. But perhaps the greatest problem presented by the growth of the central official class was the threat it presented to the social hierarchy and particularly to the dominant position of established *yangban* descent groups. The greatest single factor in the growth of the central official class in the late Koryŏ was the influx of *hyangni* into the capital.

Origins of the Problem

A number of factors contributed to the bloating of the central official class in the late Koryŏ, such as the ability of established central descent groups to reproduce themselves, the continuing recruitment of new blood through the examination system, and the opportunities for advancement presented by military campaigns. But underlying all of these was the Koryŏ tradition of ascriptive privilege, especially that deriving from the territorial status system, which guaranteed the social qualifications of *hyangni* to hold office in the dynastic government.

Let us begin with the question of natural increase in the size of central *yangban* descent groups. We have already seen how capital-based descent groups were able to use *ŭm* appointments, educational privileges, and marriage ties to maintain themselves in office generation after generation. The central descent groups' success in reproducing themselves appears to have been enhanced in the late Koryŏ by a marked decrease in infant mortality. Yi Tae-jin, based on an examination of tombstone inscriptions, notes a sharp decline in infant mortality in the second half of the dynasty, which he attributes to better and wider use of medicine. Yi argues from these findings that there was a general population increase in the late Koryŏ.[152] I am not convinced that this was so. One reason is the lack of any statistical basis for comparison of population figures. Another is that all of Yi's subjects were members of the central elite and may have been the only members of society who had access to new medicines. Nonetheless, it is plausible that better survival rates among the offspring of *yangban* families could have resulted in a numerically larger central elite class. Another possible factor was the increasing tendency of officials to enter into plural marriages and thus produce more sons. It is difficult, with the limited data now available, to gauge the practical effect of increase in family size on the *yangban* class, but it seems almost certain that growth occurred.

Another significant factor in the bloating of the central-official class was the continuing recruitment of men of *hyangni* origins through the government service examinations. Hŏ Hŭng-sik has shown that *hyangni* continued to rise through the literary and classics licentiate examinations during both the mil-

itary and post-military periods.[153] At least some of these late Koryŏ examination graduates, such as Yi Cho-nyŏn of Sŏngju and Yi Kok of Hansan,
founded new capital-based descent groups, as was discussed in chapter 2.
Technical examinations formed another route for social mobility.[154] Because
under the Koryŏ system such technical posts as legal specialist, mathemati-
cian, and physician were considered part of the civil branch of the bureaucracy, it was not uncommon for men of clerk or lower level *hyangni*
backgrounds to enter the bureaucracy as technicians and rise to hold powerful political posts. A case in point was An Hyang's father, An Pu, who came
to the capital as a physician but then rose in the regular bureaucracy, retiring
as a senior third-grade official of the Security Council.[155] It is impossible, with
the sources available to us, to determine how many examination graduates,
either regular or technical, of *hyangni* backgrounds there were in the late Koryŏ,
but it is clear that local elites continued to move up to the capital through the
examination system, at least until the final few decades of the dynasty, when
there was a noticeable decrease in the numbers of men of *hyangni* backgrounds
passing the regular civil service examinations.[156]

Examination graduates were not the only *hyangni* making their way to the
capital, however. Many other local elites, fleeing the disruption of rural society, were coming to Kaegyŏng in search of opportunity. The histories record
several complaints about *hyangni* in the capital during the late thirteenth and
early fourteenth centuries, such as the 1278 entry alleging that *hyangni* from
various locales concealed their origins and attached themselves to powerful
persons in the capital.[157] In 1325 King Ch'ungsuk stated, "In our country
hyangni who have not passed the government service examinations cannot be
exempted from their duties in order to become dynastic officials. Recently many
hyangni have fled their posts, gained the sponsorship of powerful persons, and
improperly gained capital offices."[158] It is clear that these uprooted *hyangni*
were seen as a disruptive element in the capital.

Another important means for *hyangni* to rise politically was the dynasty's
tradition of giving honorary posts to men of extraordinary merit and to certain social elites who did not hold regular government offices. As Yi Sŏng-mu
has pointed out, this system—which provided *kŏmgyo* (Ch. *chien-chiao*) with
posts at higher ranks (fourth grade and above) and *tongjŏng* (Ch. *t'ung-cheng*)
with posts at lower ranks—appears to have been similar to T'ang Chinese practice.[159] In the Koryŏ, however, the origins of this practice can be found in the
late tenth century, when King Sŏngjong gave out large numbers of honorary
posts to local strongmen in order to diminish resistance to his reorganization
of local offices and to incorporate local elites into the new political system.[160]

Subsequently these honorary posts were given out to both *hyangni* and unemployed sons of central official descent groups, often as initial *ŭm* appointments. Such posts entailed no actual duties, but conferred official ranks and entitled appointees to salaries and/or prebends depending on rank.[161] Also, appointees could, after waiting a fixed number of years,[162] advance on to regular dynastic offices.[163] In short, these honorary appointments both constituted symbolic and concrete recognition of the appointees' status as members of the central official class and formed a route by which men of *hyangni* backgrounds could attain office in the central bureaucracy without passing the government service examinations.

The rights and privileges associated with such honorary appointments began to be curtailed in the mid-Koryŏ, apparently because the growth in the numbers of appointees led to a drain on state finances and because honorary appointees contributed to competitive pressures for regular offices. In the late eleventh century honorary appointees were excluded from the revised prebend system and in the late twelfth century new requirements made it more difficult for honorary appointees to make the transition to the regular bureaucracy.[164]

With the advent of serious military emergencies in the late Koryŏ, however, honorary posts once again became a major route to the center as kings chose this method to reward *hyangni* for meritorious service. A good example of this was Han Hŭi-yu, a *hyangni* who first gained notice for his fighting skill and bravery while serving in Kim Pang-gyŏng's campaigns to pacify anti-Mongol rebels on Chin Island and Cheju Island in the 1260s. Han eventually rose to high civil office before dying while on a mission to the Yüan capital in 1306.[165]

This route became particularly important as a consequence of the Red Turban and Wako invasions of the second half of the fourteenth century. In its desperation to field military forces, the dynasty adopted a policy of rewarding men for their military service with appointments to the so-called supernumerary posts (*ch'ŏmsŏl chik*) at or below the third grade in the central bureaucracy. These late Koryŏ honorary posts do not appear to have come with prebends or stipends, but supernumerary appointees did get official ranks, which meant that they, too, could claim membership in the central official class. This policy was begun by King Kongmin, who gave out over 450 supernumerary posts in the military branch in 1355.[166] Subsequently such posts were granted on several occasions throughout the reigns of Kongmin and U, including the 1364 granting of civil branch supernumerary posts as high as the third grade and U's 1376 rewarding of "countless numbers of soldiers [*kunsa*] with supernumerary posts ranging in rank from the junior second grade down to the seventh and eighth grades." When the Wako attacked Kanghwa Island in the fifth month of 1377, King U mobilized all his forces to protect the capital and granted supernumerary offices to "brave soldiers" [*yongsa*].[167] The recipients of these appointments were mostly men of *hyangni* backgrounds or the yet-unemployed sons of central *yangban*, although some men of traditionally unacceptable social origins, such as merchants, artisans, and slaves, also received supernumerary appointments in the final years of U's reign.[168] These late fourteenth-century honorary appointments were particularly worrisome because of the ability of the appointees to circumvent the traditional restrictions and gain regular dynastic offices, as evidenced by a 1379 remonstrance official memorial complaining that men who had been supernumerary officials for a long time were taking regular offices and that some supernumerary officials were taking advantage of similarities between their names and those of genuine officials to gain appointments to regular offices.[169]

Yi T'ae-jin has shown that a substantial proportion of the men who received supernumerary appointments under Kongmin and U were of *hyangni* backgrounds.[170] Yi T'ae-jin's research, however, was primarily concerned with the status and activities of supernumerary appointees who returned to the country-side and not with those who remained in the capital to become part of the central bureaucracy. Concrete evidence that men of *hyangni* backgrounds were parlaying their honorary appointments into regular central offices can be found in the *Kukpo hojŏk* (National treasure household registers), a collection of several late fourteenth-century household registers from the capital area. The registers have been analyzed by Hŏ Hŭng-sik, who found that they described 25 households, 12 of which were headed by men of recent *hyangni* origins. The fathers and grandfathers of eight of these household heads had held *kŏm-gyo* or *tongjŏng* honorary posts in the military branch, indicating that honorary appointments, probably supernumerary posts given by kings Kongmin or U, had provided the means for these *hyangni* households to advance to the center. Two-thirds of the household heads of *hyangni* origins were identified as *haksaeng* (lit., "student"), a designator that Hŏ believes to be analogous to the *yuhak* ("young student") of the Chosŏn dynasty, a semiofficial status that entitled its holders to many of the privileges (such as exemption from corvée and military service) enjoyed by regular officials. Of the remaining four, one held an honorary (*tongjŏng*) seventh-grade civil post, one was a former military official, and two were active-duty regular military officials.[171]

The remaining 13 households in the *Kukpo hojŏk* present something of a mixed bag. Four household heads were descended from three generations of honorary officeholders, without any mention of *hyangni* connections; these may represent lines of central-official descent groups that were not successful in attaining posts in the regular bureaucracy but were able to maintain their *yangban* status as honorary appointees. The other eight had immediate fore-bears of mixed backgrounds, including active and honorary officials, *haksaeng,* and six instances where the household head had one or more ancestors with no official status (*sŏ,* Ch. *shu*). The presence of men identified as *sŏ* presents an interesting issue of interpretation. Hŏ Hŭng-sik believes them to have been commoners (*ilban yangin*). This would support the contentions of scholars such as Yŏng-ho Ch'oe and Han Yŏng-u, who believe that the early Chosŏn was a comparatively open society in which there were no legal or formal distinctions between *yangban* and commoners and in which commoners were able to rise on the basis of ability and merit.[172] These commoners would have been able to rise through supernumerary appointments (as might be expected given the indiscriminate granting of honorary offices late in U's reign) and thus there would have been substantial upward social mobility for common-ers in the late Koryŏ. It does not appear, however, that supernumerary appointments were important to these *sŏ* elements; there was only one hon-orary officeholder among the 30 men in the six *sŏ* lines. Furthermore, as Song June-ho has noted, the term *sŏ* is not an indicator of social class, but rather is simply a term distinguishing official status holders from nonholders that was applied to commoners and to members of official descent groups who held no office.[173] This raises the possibility that men indicated as *sŏ* in the reg-isters were actually marginal members of the central-official class.

There are no complaints about peasant commoners holding office. The lack of objections to peasants in office can perhaps be seen as indirect evidence that in the late Koryŏ there were no legal or even de facto social restrictions against peasant commoners joining the bureaucracy. I have not, however, been able to find any evidence to support the idea that peasant commoners were finding their way into dynastic offices. Nowhere are there entries describing officials' origins in terms—such as *nong* (farmer), *min* (people), *nongmin* (peas-ant), or *paeksŏng* (commoners)—that would suggest upward peasant mobil-ity, either in the dynastic histories or in such primary source materials as tombstone inscriptions, literary collections, and *komunsŏ.* Given the limita-tions of our source materials and the present state of research in the field, we cannot rule out the possibility of upward peasant mobility during the Koryŏ-Chosŏn transition. It seems more likely, however, that keeping peasants tied to the land for taxation and corvée purposes was a larger issue.

The frequency and animosity of complaints about *hyangni* suggests that the established central *yangban* of the late Koryŏ saw their biggest threat in upwardly mobile local elites. Typical of complaints about *hyangni* in the final years of the dynasty is a 1389 memorial decrying the presence of men of *hyangni* backgrounds in the capital: "In recent years discipline has grown lax. Countless *hyangni* have improperly gained office by claiming military merit, have schemed to avoid their duties by relying on the technical examinations, or have improperly risen in rank by attaching themselves to powerful individuals."[174]

The fundamental reason for hostility towards the *hyangni* was the competitive threat they posed to the great central *yangban* descent groups. Not only was there a long tradition of *hyangni* upward mobility through the examination system, but widespread granting of honorary posts in the final years of the dynasty provided unprecedented opportunities for men of local backgrounds to move to the capital. Many of these new arrivals were able to attain regular government posts and thus gain for themselves and their offspring the same rights and privileges enjoyed by the established *yangban,* including prebends and salaries, exemption from corvée and military service and, if their ranks were high enough, the *ŭm* privilege for their sons and grandsons. It should be noted, however, that these *hyangni* were of a different nature than the "new scholar-officials" posited by advocates of the internal development theory: they did not come to the capital through the government service examination system, but rather through military service or by attaching themselves to powerful personages in the capital.

Other threats to the established central *yangban's* domination of capital society and politics in the late Koryŏ included men of artisan, merchant, and servile backgrounds who gained office through royal patronage.[175] These elements, however, were small in number and ultimately had no sanctioned claim to membership in the official class. *Hyangni,* on the other hand, not only came to the capital in huge numbers, but their basic social qualification for membership in the ruling stratum was guaranteed by the dynasty's traditional territorial status system. Thus it was men of *hyangni* backgrounds who presented the greatest danger to the established *yangban* descent groups.

Efforts to Maintain the Status System

Despite the deep institutional roots of the social dilemma in the late Koryŏ, the dynasty did not attempt to deal with the problem through a major reorganization. Instead it sought to maintain the old system via piecemeal reforms.

The problem posed by the *hyangni* was addressed in three ways. One was the enactment of legislation tying them to their ancestral seats, which was seen as crucial to restoration of order in the countryside. At the same time, however, the frequency of complaints by late Koryŏ officials regarding the presence of *hyangni* in the capital suggests that the dynasty was finding it difficult to keep *hyangni* down in the villages. One can postulate that the capital at Kaegyŏng had, for some reason, become much more attractive than ever before. Certainly, in a situation where the dynasty found it difficult even to pay stipends to its officials, we cannot argue that service in the central government was now more lucrative. Kaegyŏng's status as the point of contact with the Yüan empire and its cosmopolitan culture may have drawn in some men, but Kaegyŏng had always been the gateway to China and the outside world. It seems to me that the main reason *hyangni* poured into the capital in the late Koryŏ was the deterioration of conditions in the countryside. Because of the expansion of *nongjang* estates and the ravages of foreign invaders, the traditional infrastructure that had supported local elites was no longer there in many parts of the peninsula. *Hyangni* who returned home found that the villages they had ruled were depopulated and the fields whose harvests they had once reaped were overgrown with weeds.

A second way in which the Koryŏ attempted to limit *hyangni* relocation to the capital was in the recruitment system. By the late thirteenth century legislation had been enacted limiting the number of sons of any one *hyangni* who could hold central office to one of three.[176] How effective this restriction was is not known, but the same one-of-three limitation was advocated for the classic licentiate and technical examinations during the reign of U, and again in the reign of the final Koryŏ king, Kongyang.[177] Whether it was due to these restrictions or to the widespread disruption of local society, the number of examination graduates of *hyangni* backgrounds did decline in the second half of the fourteenth century. Efforts to tie *hyangni* to their ancestral seats and to restrict their flow to the capital represented an attack on the symptoms and not on the root cause: the principle that the *hyangni* were part of the dynasty's ruling stratum.

Finally, the late Koryŏ appears to have pursued a policy of maintaining the great *yangban* descent groups. Initially no attempts were made to curtail the advantages the central *yangban* enjoyed in the recruitment system. On the contrary, the late Koryŏ practice of giving juvenile offices (*yakkwan*) to the offspring of central officials further entrenched the established *yangban*. Also, King Ch'ungsŏn's promulgation of the list of great ministerial families socially qualified to marry with the royal family may have come about because of Yüan pressure to abandon the age-old practice of endogamous marriage for daughters of the royal house, but it was also a clear statement of the exalted position of the great *yangban* descent groups. Other efforts to bolster the established official class included steps designed to ensure the perpetuation of descendants of merit subjects. In 1310, for example, King Ch'ungsŏn ordered that descendants of merit subjects be restored to their "merit subject lands" (*kongsinjŏn*) and be given posts as regular officials of the dynastic government.[178] In 1352 King Kongmin ordered the registration of descendants of merit subjects and the giving of generous rewards to those still living.[179] Maintenance of the great hereditary central *yangban* was, even in the midst of great growth in the size of the official class, a consistent concern of the late Koryŏ.

The main factor behind the threat the *hyangni* posed to the central *yangban* was the structure of the dynasty's social and political institutions, especially its territorial status system. These institutions, which were laid down in the tenth century, when central authority was weak and most of the country was under the control of semiautonomous local strongmen, created and maintained a two-tiered sociopolitical elite composed of a central *yangban* elite, whose prestige derived from holding office in the dynastic bureaucracy, and a local *hyangni* elite, whose prestige was rooted in ancestral histories as autonomous local rulers. The concessions that the tenth-century kings made to the local elites, such as guaranteeing access to government service examinations and granting honorary central offices in effect incorporated the *hyangni* into the dynasty's ruling class and ensured continuing upward mobility for large numbers of local elites, even as the kings simultaneously pursued a policy of elevating the status of the officials of the dynastic government. The result was chronic competition between established central *yangban* descent groups and new arrivals for political power, which occasionally erupted into open political strife, as seen, for example, in the events swirling around the Han An-in group in the early twelfth century. In the late Koryŏ, however, the deterioration of conditions in the countryside and the Red Turban and Wako incursions of the second half of the fourteenth century led to an even greater influx of *hyangni* into the capital. These developments not only further limited the dynasty's access to resources, but also threatened the position of the great *yangban* descent groups—already under challenge from palace favorites of nonelite social backgrounds—at the apex of the Korean sociopolitical order.

SUMMATION

The late Koryŏ faced two major problems. One was the debility of the kingship, which had lost effective control over much of the country's resources and had suffered a loss of prestige because of its domination by Ch'oe house

dictators and the Mongols. The other was the rise of a self-aware central bureaucratic aristocracy within a system whose basic institutional structure was still
oriented toward the local strongmen of the Silla-Koryŏ transition.

Although the *Koryŏsa* tells us that political authority was restored to the
king upon the overthrow of the Ch'oe military dictatorship in 1258, the reality was that the institutional bases of the throne's power, never too solid, had
been badly weakened during the twelfth and thirteenth centuries. Although
conventional interpretations have explained the weakness of the Koryŏ kingship in terms of the rise of the central aristocracy and the military coup of
1170, it seems to me that the basic underlying cause was the low level of differentiation in Koryŏ society.

Even though the early Koryŏ kings had attempted to create a bureaucratic
administration independent of the major social groups, the men they recruited
to fill the ranks of their bureaucracy were drawn primarily from a strongly
ascriptive local strongman stratum. The result was the creation of a new central bureaucratic aristocracy—the *yangban*—which managed to arrogate to
itself substantial political power, including control over the organs of political struggle. Thus any resolution of the problems plaguing the late Koryŏ
depended on the kings' ability to curtail the power of the *yangban* and recover
authority for themselves. At times the kings appear to have attempted to do
just that, primarily by vesting power in inner-palace officials and personal
favorites and by creating extraordinary institutional mechanisms, such as the
palace *chaech'u,* to bypass the *yangban*-dominated institutions of the regular
bureaucracy.

Despite their attempts to circumvent the *yangban*, the late Koryŏ kings were
unable to effect meaningful reforms. They were hampered by a number of
factors, including loss of prestige as a result of domination by military dictators and Mongol overlords. But a more fundamental reason for royal weakness was the kings' lack of access to the country's resources. This, too, can
be attributed to the low level of social differentiation. The Koryŏ economy
was relatively undeveloped and did not have sizable urban artisan and merchant sectors that might generate significant amounts of free-floating resources.
This meant that the bulk of the country's resources was in land and people.
From the very beginning, the kings' ability to tap into those resources was
curtailed by the privileges afforded to the local strongmen who were the de
facto rulers of most of the countryside. The kings' access to resources was
even further limited from the twelfth century on by the rise of great *nongjang*
estates among capital-based descent groups. The situation changed from
chronic fiscal debility to crisis in the final decades of the dynasty by contin-

uing *yangban* expropriation of resources and particularly by the devastation of the countryside by foreign invaders, who not only destroyed resources but also forced the state to use the free-floating resources that remained for military campaigns.

But the kings were not the only ones facing serious problems in the late Koryŏ. Although the central *yangban* had carved out a position for themselves at the apex of the status system, their privileged position was threatened by two new developments. One was the kings' vesting of power in men of non-*yangban* backgrounds, such as foreign retainers, eunuchs, and slaves, a turn of events that promised to undermine the ascriptive principles on which the status system was organized. The other was the bloating of the central official class with the inrush of displaced *hyangni* into the capital.

Both of these developments were colored by the relatively low degree of social differentiation in Koryŏ society. The absence of significant merchant or other urban elements meant that there were no other powerful social groups that kings might use to counterbalance *yangban* power, leaving them little choice but to turn to foreign retainers, slaves, and eunuchs—men who had no social power base. While this policy may have been workable as long as the kings ruled with the backing of the Mongols, the collapse of Yüan hegemony in the mid-fourteenth century left the kings without any external backing. Although Kongmin and U continued to rely on eunuchs and other persons of non-*yangban* backgrounds, such as the monk Sin Ton, the kings and their trusted retainers were isolated entities, lacking any cohesive social base that would enable them to offset *yangban* power.

The *hyangni* problem was rooted in the early Koryŏ dynastic settlement. In order to avoid alienating their local strongman constituents, the early Koryŏ kings extended to them a number of privileges that in effect guaranteed them and their *hyangni* descendants membership in the dynasty's sociopolitical elite, including access to government service examinations and receipt of honorary offices and titles. Thus when large numbers of uprooted *hyangni* poured into the capital in the thirteenth and fourteenth centuries, they were able to assert a hereditary claim to membership in the central-official class. Kings Kongmin and U pursued policies that, in rewarding *hyangni* with supernumerary posts for their service in campaigns against the Red Turbans and the Wako, further encouraged the influx of *hyangni* into the capital. One might ask, at this point, if the *hyangni* did not constitute an alternative social group to which the kings could have turned for support against the *yangban*. But by this time the foundations of *hyangni* power in the countryside had been badly eroded throughout the country. Thus even though the dynasty's institutions still guaranteed a privileged place for the *hyangni,* they, too, had become an uprooted element without any significant socioeconomic power base.

Given the extent of disorder in rural areas and the weakness of the dynasty's institutional means of control over the countryside, one wonders why the late Koryŏ did not experience an outbreak of regionally based rebellions. Whereas in China the declining years of the T'ang saw the rise of powerful provincial governors, widespread popular revolts such as that of Huang Ch'ao, and the eventual dissolution of the polity into several competing regional states before the empire was reunified by the Sung, the Koryŏ-Chosŏn transition was marked by an absence of breakaway movements. The rise of powerful provincial regimes was in all likelihood forestalled by the low rank, small staffs, and limited author-ity of the Koryŏ governors. The institutional weakness of the governorship appears to have been the consequence of deliberate policy; the Koryŏ rulers were almost certainly aware of the problems the T'ang had experienced with powerful governors and, given the limits of their control over the country-side, may very well have chosen to keep their governorship weak as a means to prevent the development of powerful regional entities. Disaffected central elements, many holding extensive estates out in the provinces, could have taken advantage of the chaos to form regionally based rival regimes. But in most cases, their estates were made up of a number of widely scattered parcels and would not have provided consolidated, easily defended power bases. There were a few peasant revolts in the late Koryŏ, such as those on Cheju Island in 1375 and in Yŏnghae in 1382, but these were small and easily suppressed. We can only speculate as to the reasons for the lack of widespread peasant revolts. Perhaps peasants were kept from organizing in coastal areas because of the frequency and severity of Wako raids; in inland areas, it seems likely that *yangban* control over the peasants, either as tenants or slaves, may have restrained the populace. Finally, the *hyangni,* whose traditional position at the apex of rural society would have made them the natural leaders of local revolts, had already lost the practical socioeconomic base of their local power and were widely dispersed, either to other locales or to the capital, where they sought to secure their fortunes in the central bureaucracy.

The threat the mobile *hyangni* posed to the *yangban* highlights a fundamental contradiction in the Koryŏ sociopolitical system: the rise of a powerful cen-tral bureaucratic aristocracy within an institutional framework that was designed in many ways to accommodate the interests of the local strongmen who had been the dominant social group in the tenth century. What was needed was a radical reshaping of the dynasty's institutions to reflect the reality of the central *yangban*'s emergence as the dominant social group.

Throughout the late Koryŏ, reform-minded *yangban* such as Yi Che-hyŏn strove, when they could gain the ear of sympathetic kings, to restore political power to the regular institutions of the civil bureaucracy, to curb the worst economic abuses of palace favorites, and to maintain the status system by returning *hyangni* to the countryside. These attempts at reform came to naught for several reasons. One obvious reason was the resistance of Mongol-related groups and the Yi In-im clique. Another was that the kings, having lost prestige and control over much of the country's resources, were simply not in a position to force through basic reforms. But we should also note that the reforms advocated by men such as Yi Che-hyŏn were essentially marginal adjustments designed to perpetuate the Koryŏ system. It was not until near the end of the fourteenth century that reformers began to think about a radical reshaping of institutions that would reflect the rise of a central bureaucratic aristocracy as the dominant social group in Korea.

5 / Reform and Dynastic Change

Historians generally recognize that the establishment of the Chosŏn dynasty in 1392 was accompanied by a major reordering of institutions. Many scholars, including mainstream historians in Korea, describe this as the realization of the economic, social, and political interests of a new social group thought to have seized power with the founding of the new dynasty. We have already seen, however, that a major feature of the Koryŏ-Chosŏn transition was the continued domination of the central bureaucracy by the great *yangban* descent groups of the Koryŏ, making it very unlikely that revamped institutions represented the concerns of a new social class. Other scholars attribute the reform movement to the influence of Ch'eng-Chu Learning (Chŏngjuhak). There is no doubt that Confucian ideas informed much of the debate in the late fourteenth and early fifteenth centuries, but the reforms that ultimately carried the day were designed to address the concrete institutional problems that had plagued the Koryŏ dynasty in ways that reflected the interests of both the new royal family and established central *yangban*.

The immediate goals of the reform party that established the new dynasty were to put the state on a solid fiscal foundation, reduce the size of the bloated central-official class, and free up the paralyzed political system. The way in which these reforms were implemented, however, amounted to a major restructuring of Korean sociopolitical institutions by which the old Koryŏ system, which had been based on a semiautonomous local aristocracy, was replaced by a new system that revolved around the central *yangban*.

The key to successful reform during the Koryŏ-Chosŏn transition was the overwhelming military might of Yi Sŏng-gye's party. As soon as Yi and his allies gained a dominant position in the central government in 1388, they began to agitate for reform. They encountered heavy resistance from a group of conservative officials with substantial military backing, however, and it wasn't until they had eliminated the military component of the opposition—men such as Ch'oe Yŏng and Cho Min-su, who had sizable private military forces—that they were able to push through their reform program.

Although Chŏng To-jŏn is widely acclaimed as the "architect" of the early Chosŏn system,[1] the blueprint for reform was actually laid out by Cho Chun, who submitted two major memorials in the summer of 1388.[2] The first, presented in the seventh month, was a lengthy document discussing the abuses leading to the current fiscal difficulties and calling for reform of the prebend system. The second, set forth in the eighth month, laid out the main outlines of the early Chosŏn restructuring of social and political institutions. This memorial included a number of minor technical recommendations such as improving horse administration and way station operations, as well as a number of purely political proposals to honor certain deceased officials and demote others, but the heart of the memorial was its many significant policy initiatives. One major area of concern was rural society, where Cho Chun recommended that better qualified men be appointed as prefects and magistrates and that their grades be raised; that areas devastated by the Wako be repopulated and rebuilt by settling vagrants, who in return for a 20-year exemption from taxes and corvée would provide support for naval forces; that registers of commoner and slave households be compiled to facilitate the conscription of men for corvée and military service; and that "nonproductive" (*muhangsan*) elements such as entertainers and butchers be settled on the land and encouraged to farm like the common peasants. In sum, these proposals were intended to enhance the state's control over human and material resources.

Cho Chun also made several recommendations designed to reduce the size of the central-official class, including a direct proposal to reduce the overall number of official posts, a recommendation to restrict the number of junior second-grade appointees, and a proposal to limit the *ŭm* appointments of officials' sons to ninth-grade military posts.

Reform of central political institutions was also on Cho Chun's mind. He strove to restore prestige and authority to the throne by recommending that decisions on the misdeeds of powerful officials be left for the king. He also urged a reduction in the number of men in the Todang, called for the restoration of the Six Boards to their position at the functional center of government, argued that special directorates should be abolished once the specific tasks with which they were charged were finished, proposed better procedures for transmitting and safeguarding the veracity of royal documents, and suggested that qualifications and grade levels be raised for lower-ranking censorial and surveillance officials.[3]

The first major change actually implemented by the men who founded the Chosŏn dynasty was a restructuring of state finances; the Rank Land Law was carried out in 1391, the year before Yi Sŏng-gye assumed the Korean throne.

This reform, which strengthened the state by giving it much greater access to resources, made it possible to implement a host of major reform initiatives that fell into three major categories similar to those of Cho Chun's 27-point memorial: establishment of greater control over the countryside through a restructuring of local administration; reduction of competition for official posts through the exclusion of certain social groups; and redressing the imbalance of political power through reorganization of the central government. Taken together, these interrelated reforms constituted a major restructuring of Korea's social and political institutions which, on the one hand, generated greater amounts of generalized power and gave kings greater access to free-floating resources while, on the other hand, recognizing the paramount position of the great central *yangban* descent groups who had come to dominate Korean society and politics during the Koryŏ period.

FISCAL REFORM

Restoring the fiscal health of the state was the first task undertaken by Yi Sŏng-gye and his supporters. This was, of course, a prerequisite for their program of renewal, since without the resources to field military forces and fund regular government operations there could have been no way to carry out other basic reforms. It was this commitment to strengthening the state that distinguished Yi Sŏng-gye's party from other groups that had periodically dominated the polity, such as the military rulers of the mid-Koryŏ and the Yi In-im/Im Kyŏn-mi cabal of the 1370s and 1380s, who had operated essentially as private interest groups. The founders of the new dynasty addressed the issue of state access to free-floating resources in two ways: promulgation of the Rank Land Law reform in 1391 and implementation of a series of policy initiatives during the early decades of the new dynasty. It is important to note that although these particular efforts were primarily fiscal in nature, they were closely related to other reforms, particularly in the local administrative and social spheres.

The Rank Land Law

Cho Chun's memorial of the seventh month of 1388 opened up a prolonged debate over the issue of fiscal reform. While Yi Saek and his group of conservatives remained opposed to any substantial change, members of the reform party presented a wide variety of proposals. The most radical was Chŏng To-jŏn's plan. Chŏng, basing himself on the well-field system of Chinese antiquity, argued for state ownership of all land and rejected such later models as the Han limited field and the T'ang equal field systems because they contained provisions for private ownership. The state, according to Chŏng's plan, would distribute land to household heads, who would cultivate their grants as long as they lived, but upon the death of the recipient the land would return to the state for redistribution. By doing away with private ownership, Chŏng hoped to eliminate the problems of tax evasion and private control (through tenancy arrangements) of the peasant population, thus increasing tax revenues and freeing up peasants for corvée and military duty. But Chŏng's plan received little backing, apparently because it called for the abolition of private property and contained no separate provisions for support of the official class.

Chŏng's was the only plan that harked back to Chinese antiquity. The other memorialists looked elsewhere, mostly calling for a restoration of the system of the early Koryŏ, which they also believed was based on the principle of state ownership. One memorialist, like Chŏng, urged the abolition of privately held property and the distribution of lands to individuals by the state, but, unlike Chŏng, he made special provisions for the support of officials and soldiers. Another memorialist argued for the implementation of an equal field system in order to provide funds for state operations and military activities and make lands available for distribution to all officials. Other reformers took a less radical approach, arguing for restoration of the early Koryŏ system, but not addressing the issue of privately held property beyond calling for curbing the abuses of amalgamation and excessive exploitation of sharecroppers by landlords.

It was Cho Chun's proposal that eventually formed the basic framework for the Rank Land Law reform. Cho presented a plan that seems to have been designed to provide the state with greater access to resources without alienating the *yangban* descent groups whose backing was necessary for successful reform. He began by reviewing the successes and failures of the land systems of various Chinese dynasties—including the Chou (1134–250 B.C.E.), Ch'in (249–207 B.C.E.), Han, and T'ang—before turning to a revival of what he saw as the equal field system of the early Koryŏ. His proposal called for abrogation of all existing prebends and their conversion to general revenue *kongjŏn*. This was to be followed by a new distribution of prebends to all men who performed services for the state, including officials (both incumbent and former), soldiers, and even slaves such as those public menials who toiled at post stations. These prebends were to be given only for the lifetime of the recipient and returned to the state upon the beneficiary's death. The proposal, however, contained special provisions for officials who lived in the capital. They were to receive new *sajŏn* prebends in the capital district (Kyŏnggi), a portion of which could be passed on to their heirs as hereditary stipend fields (*serok-chŏn*). Another feature of importance for enlisting the support of the central official descent groups was the absence of any provisions for the abolition or limitation of private land holdings, as well as any mention of distribution of land to peasants. Cho was concerned, however, about maintaining a free peasantry, whose harvests and labor represented the single most important free-floating resource, and attempted to alleviate their burden by setting the land tax at 10 per cent of harvests and prohibiting additional exactions.[4]

It seems safe at this point to draw some tentative conclusions about the nature of the fiscal reform debate of the late fourteenth century. First, the proposals were based on the reformers' understandings of historical Chinese and Korean systems and, particularly in the case of the ultimately successful plan of Cho Chun, were significantly conditioned by the economic interests of the established *yangban* descent groups, whose private landholdings they left untouched and whom they proposed to provide with new prebends. Second, the proposals sought to increase state revenues by sharply reducing the amount of land that had been set aside for prebends, restoring the bulk of the country's cultivated lands to general revenue *kongjŏn* status, and keeping the peasants free.

Proponents of the "new scholar-official" thesis argue that the establishment of the Rank Land Law represented "the destruction of the old economic order and the establishment of a new one by the new scholar-officials."[5] According to this view, "new scholar-officials" of the "medium and small landlord" class seized the great estates of the central aristocracy, burned their land documents, set aside Kyŏnggi Province to be granted as *sajŏn* prebends to people with official rank, and converted the land of the rest of the country to *kongjŏn* general revenue lands. This is thought to have marked the destruction of the Koryŏ central aristocracy as an economic entity and thus to have represented victory for "new scholar-officials" as the leaders of a new economic order.

This interpretation has recently been challenged by Yi Kyŏng-sik, who argues that there were two forms of land control in the late Koryŏ period—prebendal collection of rents and ownership—and that the Rank Land Law dealt only with the former and not the latter.[6] Yi's argument supports our findings of the persistence of *nongjang* estates into the early Chosŏn.

Indeed, a dispassionate consideration of the provisions of the Rank Land Law bears out the contention that the 1391 reform was not the embodiment of a new economic order. Earlier historians, perhaps under the influence of the king's land theory, believed the term *sajŏn* to connote land owned by individuals and *kongjŏn* lands owned by the state, and therefore assumed that conversion of the whole country outside Kyŏnggi to *kongjŏn* status meant confiscation by the state of private *nongjang* estates of the late Koryŏ aristocracy. There now exists, however, virtually unanimous agreement among historians that the terms *sajŏn* and *kongjŏn* do not refer to ownership status but rather to the assignment of tax revenues from the land, with *sajŏn* receipts going to individuals as prebends and *kongjŏn* receipts going to the state treasury. This means that the famous 1390 burning of *sajŏn* and *kongjŏn* registers did not entail the abrogation of private ownership rights and leaves the Rank Land Law with no provisions regarding private ownership.

The Rank Land Law had two major objectives: putting the central government (and especially its military operations) on firm financial ground and providing for the livelihood of the officials who served in the state bureaucracy. The Rank Land reform, based on the results of a nationwide land survey conducted in 1390, beefed up the government's finances by restoring all of the land outside the capital region to general revenue *kongjŏn* status. This not only furnished the state with greater operational funds, but also allowed for increased military expenditures to be used in the struggle against the Wako, to prepare for whatever might occur along the northern border, and, perhaps most important of all, to give the state the military might it needed to back up other reforms.[7] As the name indicates, however, the Rank Land Law was also very much concerned with the livelihood of the bureaucracy and in that regard may perhaps be seen as a continuation of late Koryŏ efforts, such as the Salary Rank Land Law, to provide for the central official class. The Rank Land Law was, however, more than a system to compensate active officials for services rendered. Its prebends were granted to all holders of official rank living in the capital, whether active or retired; it also provided that all or a portion (depending on family circumstances) of prebends be retained by the recipient's wife and children after his death and that if the official's wife had also died, the prebends be given to his "young and weak children and grandchildren." Thus, the Rank Land Law did not simply compense officials for services rendered, but rather supported and ensured the perpetuation of a category of people who (1) lived in the capital and (2) themselves had held office in the central government or whose forebears had done so. In short the system enhanced the state's access to resources and supported the *yangban* descent groups who made up the central bureaucracy.

What, then, of former officials and other status holders living outside the capital? Officials who left the capital after their term of office had to relinquish their Rank Lands, which were then redistributed to other officials residing in the capital.[8] The category of locally based, former central officials and honorary rank holders known as *hallyang* did not get regular prebends under the Rank Land Law, receiving instead small grants of Soldiers' Land (Kunjŏn).[9] In return for these lands, they were required to serve in the capital armies a minimum of 100 days each year.[10] The *hyangni,* who had once received prebends under the old Field and Woodland Rank system, also suffered unfavorable treatment under the new system. The Rank Land Law initially provided limited Provincial Service Fields (Oeyŏk-chŏn) for this group, but those grants were put in a separate category from regular prebends and were much smaller than they had been under the Koryŏ system; even those were eliminated by 1445. Thus it is evident that the prebendal provisions of the Rank Land Law were designed primarily to support the capital-based members of the official class—that is, the central *yangban* descent groups—and discriminated sharply against other social entities outside the capital.

One final feature of the Rank Land Law that reveals the social considerations behind this reform is its provision forbidding allocation of prebends to the descendants of artisans, merchants, fortune tellers, professional entertainers, and monks.[11] Although the sources do not go into the reasoning behind this provision, it seems clear that it was designed to weaken the position of men of such origins already in the bureaucracy and to inhibit the rise of such elements in the future. In short, while the Rank Land Law was designed to put the state on a sound financial foundation and to provide for the sustenance of its officials, it was also intended to bolster the social position of the central-official descent groups and eliminate competition from *hyangni* and various other social groups who had threatened the *yangban* monopoly on political power in the late Koryŏ period.

The Rank Land Law itself was not long-lived. Because of the persistence of large landed estates within the capital district, creation of large merit-subject land grants, and inevitable growth in the numbers of inheritable prebends, the state was soon unable to provide prebends in the capital district to new officials. By T'aejong's reign, the state found it necessary to begin granting Rank Lands outside the capital district in the three southern provinces. Even this soon proved insufficient, leading to the abolishment of the Rank Land system in favor of the Office Land (Chikchŏn) system in 1457. The new system provided prebends only to incumbent officials and eliminated the hereditary portions of the old Rank Land system. This of course greatly reduced the amount of land allocated to prebends and seems to have given the state some breathing room, but even this system eventually proved insufficient, so that by 1555 it too was abolished and the state henceforth provided its officials only with salaries.[12]

The ultimate demise of the prebendal system should not, however, blind us to the significance of the Rank Land Law for the founding of the new dynasty and for subsequent reforms in other areas. The Rank Land Law restored large areas of land to the tax rolls at a time when the state was bankrupt, thus providing a fresh influx of funds for both civil administrative and military operational purposes. It also played a key role in enlisting the support of the central *yangban* for Yi Sŏng-gye. It provided for their sustenance, which was undoubtedly attractive even to those men who owned landed estates and was absolutely essential to less affluent members of the central *yangban* class who were dependent on compensation from the state. Equally as important as economic sustenance was the way the Rank Land Law defined the membership of the official class by bestowing special benefits on members of the established central-official descent groups and discriminating against men from outside the capital and those of nonelite backgrounds. Thus the Rank Land Law, as it was drawn up by Cho Chun—a relative (by marriage) of Yi Sŏng-gye and a member of one of the greatest central *yangban* descent groups—contained elements that appealed to the interests of both the new royal family and the *yangban*.

The State's Attempts to Create and Control Resources

Although the Rank Land Law did not call for abolition of private property rights, it did contain some provisions designed to curb the worst abuses of the great estate system. Those provisions included prohibiting prebend recipients from dispossessing the tillers of their prebendal lands and punishing individuals who tried to expand their landholdings through appropriation of prebendal *sajŏn* and general revenue *kongjŏn*.[13]

These provisions do not appear to have been effective, however, since by 1406, barely 15 years after promulgation of the Rank Land Law, memorials complained that shortages in tax receipts and the corvée labor force had arisen because of certain elements who were amassing large estates and exacting excessive rents from their tenants.[14] This threatened the state's access to free-floating resources and prompted a proposal, approved by the king, that sharecropping be forbidden except in special cases, such as when the landowners were widows living alone or people without children or slaves.[15] This measure, however, does not appear to have been any more successful than the original provisions of the Rank Land Law in resolving the problems of land amalgamation and exploitation of tenants. In 1415 yet another memorial appeared decrying the actions of wealthy and powerful persons who amalgamated lands and rented them out to impoverished peasants.[16] This, too, was unsuccessful and appears to have been the last attempt to prohibit sharecropping, although later proposals, which were not enacted into law, called for the implementation of a limited field (*hanjŏn*) system in an effort to control the spread of large estates.[17]

Early Chosŏn efforts to enhance the state's access to resources were not limited to legislation regarding tenancy. Several concrete measures attempted to tie the peasant and slave population to the land so they could be taxed and mobilized for corvée labor and military service. There were two main elements of the new program to bring the population under strong state supervision. One was revitalization of the household register (*hojŏk*) system. Implemented during T'aejong's and Sejong's reigns, this reform featured the destruction of old registers and compilation of new ones that recorded the numbers of adult commoner males who were eligible for corvée and military service. The result was a tremendous increase in the number of adult males under state control, especially during Sejong's reign, when a census showed the number of adult males to have doubled over T'aejong's time.[18]

The other main means of establishing control over the population was the identification tag (*hop'ae*) law, first enacted by T'aejong in 1413. This law, which appears to have been modeled after a Yüan dynasty system, required each subject to carry an identification tag on which was recorded the bearer's name, place of birth, status, and residence. T'aejong's motives are revealed in the edict promulgating this law, in which he stated that he wanted to eliminate commoners' inclination to wander and alleviate the problem of local increases and decreases in population.[19] His implementation of the identification tag law seems to have been a temporary expedient designed to facilitate compilation of new household registers, since it was abolished as soon as the new registers were completed in 1416, although commoner opposition is often cited as a main cause of the abolition.[20] The registration tag law was revived, however, in 1458 by King Sejo, who was concerned about the support given to the rebel Yi Ching-ok by wandering peasants in Hamgil Province (the former Eastern Border Region of Koryŏ) in 1453.[21] This time the identification tag law remained in effect for twelve years. The control this gave the kings over the population was reflected in Sejo's 1460 relocation of 4,500 "prosperous households" (*pusil ho*) from the three southern provinces to the northern provinces of P'yŏngan, Hwanghae, and Kangwŏn.[22]

These steps gave the new dynasty much greater control over human resources than had been exercised by the Koryŏ kings. We noted earlier that the limited amounts of free-floating resources available to the Koryŏ kings led them to rely on special collectivities, such as the *so*, *hyang*, and *pugok* to provide for specific administrative needs. Of nearly 200 special collectivities in the Koryŏ period,[23] only 13 remained in the whole country by King Sŏngjong's reign (1469–94).[24]

We must keep in mind that although the change of dynasties freed up greater amounts of free-floating resources for the use of the state, the *yangban* managed to maintain control over significant amounts of land and human resources. There is little doubt that the new dynasty's need to enlist the support of the great *yangban* descent groups was the root cause of the perpetuation of the pattern of great estate holding in the Chosŏn dynasty. Thus even though the first few Chosŏn kings succeeded in achieving much greater control over resources than had been exercised by the late Koryŏ kings, they, too, were ultimately unable to break the old tradition of aristocratic control of land and people. The result was a perennial struggle between the Chosŏn state and its *yangban* officials for access to the country's resources.[25]

REDEFINING THE STATUS SYSTEM

The issues of access to bureaucratic posts and membership in the central official class were outlined in the preceding chapter. This section focuses on the two aspects of the late fourteenth- and early fifteenth-century reforms that impinged most directly on those issues: establishment of strong central control over local society (which entailed a major loss of status and privilege for the *hyangni* class) and the effort to reduce competition for posts in the central government.

The Restructuring of Local Government

A foremost concern of the reformers was local society. Unless some semblance of order could be established in the countryside, they could hardly hope for effective implementation of their program of fiscal reform, nor could they expect to resettle uprooted *hyangni* and reduce the threat that *hyangni* posed to *yangban*.

One of the first actions the reformers undertook after coming to power in 1388 was resurrection of the early Koryŏ drive for greater central control over the countryside. Changes were made in two areas: strengthening of intermediary provincial offices and posting of centrally appointed prefects and magistrates to the prefectures and counties that had been without a permanent central official presence.

The basic features of the early Koryŏ circuit-commissioner system reemerged intact after peace was made with the Mongols. Commissioners were still chosen from relatively low-ranking sixth- or fifth-grade officials, served terms of only six months, and had no standing staffs of their own. The commissioners still had very little authority, and prefectures and counties still usually reported directly to the center (the Todang). Although the dynasty experimented with a few minor changes in the early fourteenth century, including extending the term of service to one year, the early Koryŏ system still obtained when Yi Sŏng-gye and his supporters ousted King U in the summer of 1388.

Over the next two years Cho Chun presented a series of memorials calling for reform in the system of intermediary provincial offices, including recommendations that the circuit commissioners be replaced by provincial governors, that the governors be selected from first- and second-grade officials, and that governorships be established in all areas of the country, including the capital district and the two northern border regions. All of Cho Chun's proposals were enacted, and in 1390 each provincial governor was provided with his own permanent staff (*kyŏngnyŏksa*) and given authority over the prefectures and counties in his province.[26] Korea now had, for the first time in its history, a genuine system of civilian provincial governorship.

At the same time the reform party worked to bring more prefectures and counties under centrally appointed officials. Five new lesser county magistracies were established in 1389, 25 more in 1390, and an additional seven in 1391. These were the first significant postings of centrally appointed officials to new counties since 1176. They reduced the total number of subordinate prefectures and counties to 161 and presaged even more vigorous reform efforts to come. Centrally appointed officials continued to be dispatched to new areas throughout the early Chosŏn, so that by the end of Sejong's reign (1450) prefectures and magistracies had been established in 330 prefectures and counties, leaving only 107 subordinate prefectures and counties.[27]

The importance of the renewed dispatch of centrally appointed prefects and magistrates for the plans of the Yi Sŏng-gye group is suggested by the timing and location of the new postings. Three of the five counties to receive new lesser county magistrates in 1389 were located in the capital region; at the same time, one additional lesser county magistrate post, which had been abolished in earlier years, was reestablished in a capital region county. That this initial effort came shortly before implementation of the Rank Land reform in the region set aside for prebends indicates that the reformers thought that the presence of centrally appointed officials in prebendal areas was necessary to the success of their plan for fiscal revitalization. Also of interest is the fact that 23 of the 25 magistracies established in the second wave of new postings in 1390 were in Kyŏngsang Province. Perhaps this reflects the devastation wrought on southeastern Korea by the Wako, but it also may be worth our while to recall that the opposition to Yi Sŏng-gye was led by men with close ties to the Kyŏngsang area, including Yi Sung-in, Chŏng Mong-ju, Kil Chae, and Yi Saek.[28] At the same time, a new myriarchy, presumably staffed with military forces loyal to Yi Sŏng-gye, was established at Yŏngil in Kyŏngsang.[29] From this perspective, it is not difficult to imagine that the 1390 posting of centrally appointed officials may have been designed to forestall a Kyŏngsang-based revolt against Yi Sŏng-gye.

The dispatch of centrally appointed officials was, however, only the first step in regularizing local government. The new dynasty inherited an irrational patch-work of units whose territories were not always contiguous and whose designation as district, prefecture, or county had less to do with their actual size or population than with the ancestral status of their *hyangni* descent groups. This irregular system not only created logistical and administrative headaches— it also represented, albeit in vestigial form, the old territorial status system.

The new dynasty's first full-scale attempt to create a more rational hierarchy of local administrative units came in 1413, under the third Chosŏn king, T'aejong (1400–18), and featured three important measures. First, it sought to make the designations of local units correspond to their actual size and importance. In China, the term for "district," *chou* (K. *chu*), was reserved for major administrative centers; in Koryŏ Korea, however, it was given—usually to denote the favored status of native son notables—to local units of all sizes, including prefectures and counties. The 1413 reform changed all districts to regular place names (e.g., Chukchu became Chuksan and Kŭmju became Kŭmsan), except for those places where major administrative or military centers were located. This affected no fewer than 59 place names and was a major step toward the creation of a regular administrative hierarchy.[30]

Second, the reformers sought to elevate the quality and status of lesser county magistrates. Concern about the stature of prefects, magistrates, and lesser county magistrates had been voiced during the late Koryŏ, as in a 1359 memorial:

We request that only civil officials be appointed to magistrate and lesser magistrate posts. Under the old system, only examination graduates were used for magistrate and lesser magistrate posts. Recently only the clerks of the various agencies have been used; they are greedy and rapacious and have plundered the people. Also their ranks are all seventh and eighth grades, so that people look down on them and the strong take them lightly, violating the law and creating abuses in their areas.[31]

Similar themes were sounded by Cho Chun's 27-point memorial, which decried the low caliber of the men appointed to magistrate and lesser magistrate posts, urged that only worthy and experienced men be given those posts, and proposed that their rank be upgraded to the sixth grade. Cho Chun's proposal was accepted and the lesser county magistrate post was upgraded to a sixth-grade slot.[32] Efforts to enhance the status of the lesser county magistrate continued after the founding of the Chosŏn: in 1413 the title was changed to county superintendent (*hyŏn'gam*) to reflect the higher grade of the appointees.

The third, and most difficult, measure was the actual restructuring of the patchwork of local units. This involved changing the status—up or down—of some, abolishing others, and combining units on the basis of area and population. This effort got underway in 1409, with the abolition and combining of subordinate prefectures and counties in Chŏlla Province, where 51 subordinate counties still existed at the end of the Koryŏ.[33] When the policy proved to be a success there, it was extended to the rest of the country.[34]

These three measures constituted a major step forward in the struggle to establish central control over the countryside. They were not all, however, unqualified successes. Although the first and second measures were implemented with little difficulty, local opposition forced the government to rescind its orders abolishing or combining units in many areas. The limited success of the third measure is revealed in a statement made by an high-ranking official in 1450, 37 years after implementation:

> The prefectures and counties of the various provinces, whether large or small, do not have proper territories. Their lands penetrate into each other, causing the people to suffer abuses for years. Our country's prefectures and provinces originally had no set system. When they were first set up, the local strongmen and men with official ranks fought among themselves. The strong got many and the weak got few of the rich and fertile lands. As a result, the lands of one county can extend alternatively into several bordering counties, or they can exist totally cut off from the county in several other counties. Whenever it is time to transport taxes in kind, exact levies, or hear litigation, one official has to traverse several counties, having to rush about without rest.[35]

This indicates that despite the successes of the early Chosŏn, the struggle to establish direct central control over the whole country would not be easily resolved. By the late 1450s another strong-willed monarch, King Sejo, resumed the effort to regularize the local administrative hierarchy. The instructions the king issued to the provincial governors at the time stated:

> Although our country is small, we have many prefectures and counties, so that the people have long suffered. Recently I combined several counties in Kyŏnggi Province. Examining the situation of the people there, I found that although the local clerks [*hyangni*] were unhappy with the change, the people were very pleased. Thus, in accordance with the wishes of the people, I have decided to combine small counties and post two magistrates at each of the newly consolidated locales. You are to understand my intentions and, relying on the Provisions for combining prefectures and counties, which I am issuing, examine and report in detail on counties that should be combined and areas that should be separated in your respective provinces.[36]

Sejo's reform was based on extensive surveys and studies of local conditions and was much more systematic than earlier attempts, as indicated in the instructions contained in *Kunhyŏn pyŏnghap samok* (Provisions for combining prefectures and counties), which was issued along with the edict in the twelfth month of 1457. These instructions called for, among other things, a preliminary survey of the locales to be combined to determine the number of residents, collection of land taxes, litigation, and distances officials would have to travel; consideration of the possibility of combining not just two, but three or even four counties where merited by circumstances; and a report of the numbers of local clerks, government slaves, commoner households, territory, and geographic features of the newly combined units.[37] Sejo's efforts led to a further diminishment in the numbers of subordinate counties; by the early sixteenth century only 72 remained and those, too, were eventually eliminated.[38]

King Sejo's achievements marked the climax of the early Chosŏn effort to restructure local government. Centrally appointed officials were established in local administrative units throughout the country, subordinate counties no longer existed in any significance, and local administration had been organized into a regular hierarchy based primarily on land area and population size. These achievements were important in bringing the commoner population under strong state control, but expansion of the central government's presence in the countryside meant a corresponding loss of status and authority for the old *hyangni* descent groups who had enjoyed a high degree of autonomy during the Koryŏ period.

The reform in local administration benefited both the throne and the *yangban* officials of the central bureaucracy. Better control over the countryside meant

greater power for the throne and its agents, the officials of the dynastic government. It also meant more efficient collection of tax revenues and thus regular payment of stipends. Finally, bringing the countryside under firmer control
was the key to reducing the threat mobile local elites posed to established central *yangban* descent groups. The ability of the reformers to perceive that their
interests as capital-based officials lay in enhancing the power of the dynastic
government over the countryside was what made this reform possible.

Reducing the Size of the Ruling Class

In his lengthy 1389 memorial on current affairs Cho Chun argued for reducing the number of officials, noting that "Emperor Kuang-wu of the Han had
the largest and wealthiest country in the world, and he achieved his revival
by reducing the number of officials to one for every 10. We should eliminate
all unnecessary officials and clerks and restore the law of officials set up by
the ancestors on behalf of heaven in order to show that our dynasty is flourishing and has been restored."[39] Cho Chun was giving voice to a long-standing
concern, but now that his group had seized power, effective action was finally
being taken. The effort to reduce the size of the central-official class focused
on supernumerary officials, especially those of *hyangni* backgrounds.

Cho Chun launched the effort to reduce the number of former *hyangni* in
the central bureaucracy in the twelfth month of 1389, when he memorialized:

> In recent years discipline has grown lax. Countless are the *hyangni* who have
> gained office by claiming military merit, have tried to avoid their duties by
> pretending to be graduates of the technical examinations, and who have
> improperly risen to high rank by attaching themselves to powerful fami-
> lies. . . . I request that henceforth men of *hyangni* origins be forcibly returned
> to their original duties, including even those who have been exempt from
> the local duties for three or four generations according to the provisions that
> allow one of every three sons of a *hyangni* to sit for the government service
> examination but do not have proper documentation; those *hyangni* who have
> been exempted from their local duties due to military merit but have not
> received special badges; those *hyangni* who are technical examination grad-
> uates but did not study at the legal and medical schools of the Royal
> Confucian Academy (Sŏnggyun'gwan *yusaeng*); and those *hyangni* who have
> received supernumerary offices below the third grade. . . . Henceforth do not
> allow *hyangni* who pass the classics examinations or the technical exami-
> nations to be exempted from their original duties.[40]

The only response Cho Chun received in 1389 was rescission of some appointments to supernumerary offices. The attack was renewed in the first month of 1390, when the Office of the Inspector General again called for elimination of all supernumerary offices awarded by King U. At this time, the *Koryŏsa* tells us, King Kongyang followed the advice of Chŏng To-jŏn, who recommended that the king adhere to the old law, dismissing all but those men who had passed the civil or military examinations, who had come up through the clerical ranks, or who had the *ŭm* privilege. When the king asked about how to deal with supernumerary officials who held high rank, Chŏng To-jŏn advised him to incorporate them into a specially created Office of the Palace Guard (Kungsŏng Sugwibu).[39] Whether this measure was effectively implemented is not clear, but there was little further controversy about supernumerary officials in the remaining few years of the Koryŏ.

The attack on supernumerary appointees of *hyangni* origins resumed shortly after the founding of the new dynasty in the ninth month of 1392. As Yi Sŏngmu has discussed, all men of *hyangni* origins holding central ranks below the third grade (second grade for supernumerary officials) were returned to their original status, except for those who had passed the government service examinations or had achieved special merit. Further restrictions were promulgated in 1395, when measures were taken to prevent men from using their supernumerary appointments to elevate themselves, and in 1405, when the last supernumerary posts were eliminated by King T'aejong.[42] Although we have no way of knowing exactly how many men were removed from the capital and restored to their original *hyangni* status as a result of this measure, the subsequent lack of controversy regarding the presence of *hyangni* in the capital suggests that the measure was effective.

The founders of the new dynasty were not content with simply removing *hyangni* from the capital. They also commonly moved *hyangni* from one prefecture or county to another, thus severing them from their traditional power bases in their ancestral seats.[43] Next, the new rulers promulgated a law, the Bad Local Official Punishment Law (Wŏnak Hyangni Ch'ŏbŏl Pŏp), penalizing *hyangni* for such offenses as taking advantage of centrally appointed officials to dominate their localities and establishing estates and forcing people to work them. The purpose of this new law appears to have been to prevent *hyangni* from entrenching themselves in their localities in the manner of their Koryŏ forebears. Finally, a series of legal and social restrictions were added that made it all but impossible for men of *hyangni* backgrounds to sit for the government service examinations.[44] The local aristocrats of the Koryŏ were well on their way to becoming the local clerks of the Chosŏn, and the established central *yangban* descent groups had eliminated a powerful threat to their privileged position at the top of government and society.

The narrowing of the ruling class did not stop with the exclusion of supernumerary officials and *hyangni*. Measures were also taken that greatly reduced the numbers of central clerks who rose to hold offices in the regular bureaucracy, including revocation of the prebend and stipend rights central clerks had once enjoyed under the Koryŏ and severe restrictions on the numbers of clerks who could be promoted to regular official posts.[45] Thus the central-clerical ranks, which had served as an avenue of entry into the central-official class for various groups—including *hyangni*—in the Koryŏ period, were placed outside the regular career path of the Chosŏn central bureaucracy.

Technical officials—such as physicians, astronomers, and interpreters—also suffered new restrictions after the change of dynasties. In the Koryŏ period men who initially entered the bureaucracy through the technical examinations were able to rise to the highest ranks. After the founding of the Chosŏn, however, technical officials formed a hereditary status group, known as *chungin,* whose members were eligible only for the technical examinations and not regular civil service examinations. Those *chungin* who passed the technical examinations held low-ranking posts allocated to agencies that handled technical functions, such as the Translation Office (Sayŏgwŏn), but were prohibited from rising to first- and second-grade posts.[46]

One additional area of particular concern for reformers of the Koryŏ-Chosŏn transition was the rise, almost always through palace patronage, to high office of men of unacceptable social origins. We have already seen how this concern was reflected in the Rank Land Law provision that prevented merchants, artisans, and men of servile origins (and their descendants) from receiving Rank Land prebends. A number of memorials in the late fourteenth and early fifteenth centuries decried the rise of men of unacceptable backgrounds in the late Koryŏ and called for the prevention of such a phenomenon in the new dynasty. In the twelfth month of 1392 Cho Chun condemned the social chaos of the late Koryŏ: "Unnecessary officials were consuming state stipends; favorites were defiling state offices; artisans, merchants, and mean persons were impudently holding office; persons enjoying the prerogatives of monks were holding much land; and young children and men without merit who had been titled lords were neglecting their duties."[47] A remonstrance official memorial in the eleventh month of 1398 noted that in the late Koryŏ artisans, merchants, and slaves were appointed to high posts and requested that henceforth they not be given offices but rather rewarded for their merit with goods.[48] In the seventh month of 1400 a Chancellery memorial said,

The capital is the place of the court officials, the place of culture and civilization, and the model for the whole kingdom. Discipline was lax in the late Koryŏ and the system of etiquette was the first to fall. Wealthy merchants and public and private slaves rode fat horses and wore fine clothes, mixing on the road with officials so that the court officials' dignity suffered and one could not distinguish between noble and base. Such abuses still continue; this is truly lamentable. . . . Merchants, slaves, and such persons should not be allowed to ride horses and oxen in the capital.[49]

The success of the reformers' efforts to exclude men of such unacceptable origins is borne out by the almost total lack of men with slave, merchant, or other undesirable backgrounds in office during the Chosŏn.[50]

One final element in the early Chosŏn policy to reduce the size of the central officialdom addressed the problem of the natural increase within the *yangban* class itself. This was the prohibition of office holding by sons of secondary wives and concubines. An earlier interpretation holds that discrimination against secondary sons arose out of power struggles between Yi Pang-wŏn, son of Yi Sŏng-gye's first wife, and Yi Pang-sŏk, a secondary son.[51] More recent scholarship, however, argues that the primary motive for limitations on secondary sons was the need to reduce the bloated central-official class.[52] Also, we should recall that it was common practice in the late Koryŏ for high-ranking officials to take concubines from the lower ranks of society; from this perspective, as Martina Deuchler has pointed out, discrimination against secondary sons can also be understood as a means to maintain social class boundaries.[53]

Thus *hyangni*, central clerks, technical officials, and secondary sons of *yangban*, all of whom had been able to advance into central office during the Koryŏ period, now found themselves excluded from holding office in the regular bureaucracy. This left current and former officeholders as the only full-fledged members of the ruling stratum. Seen in the broader context, this was the long-term consequence of the early Koryŏ policy of elevating officials of the central bureaucracy above local members of the ruling class. More immediately, however, it was also a victory for the established *yangban* descent groups because it elevated them above—and protected them against competition from—the rest of society.

Here again, as in the case of local government, it is evident that there was a substantial community of interest between the throne and central-government officials. Both had something to gain from a reduction in the numbers of men eligible to hold office in the dynastic government. The throne benefited from the removal of large numbers of men from the prebendal and stipend rolls and from having a less wieldy bureaucracy, while the established official-descent groups eliminated a variety of threats to their domination of society and government.

RESTRUCTURING THE CENTRAL GOVERNMENT

It was one thing to carry out reforms in areas where the throne and *yangban* had an obvious community of interest. It was quite another to reorganize the central government itself, the arena where royal prerogative and *yangban* power came into direct conflict. Nonetheless, the founders of the Chosŏn dynasty were able to restructure the dynastic government, establish a better balance of power between the throne and the bureaucracy, and resolve some of the thorny institutional issues of the late Koryŏ through a series of compromises over key issues during the first 15 years of the new dynasty.

Once again, the call for reform came from—who else?—Cho Chun. His 27-point memorial of the eighth month of 1388 sounded the main themes when he decried the excessive growth of the Todang, lamented the deterioration of bureaucratic administration, and called for a restoration of authority to the Six Boards and the lesser agencies.[54] Although Cho's proposals were not immediately put into effect, they set much of the agenda for reform of the central government in the years following establishment of the new dynasty.

The reform of political institutions in the early Chosŏn was not dictated from above, as might be expected from the military founder of a new dynasty, but rather came about through a process of struggle and compromise between the new dynasty and its officials. The process developed in two distinct phases: the first was a transitional period lasting from Yi Sŏng-gye's enthronement in 1392 to 1400, when the new rulers continued to use some of the extraordinary institutions through which the late Koryŏ kings had striven to enhance their power while the throne and the bureaucracy hashed out certain procedural issues and grappled with the problem of eunuch and monk involvement in politics; the second, which began after T'aejong took the throne late in 1400, entailed a major restructuring of central political institutions.

Political Reform: The First Phase, 1392–1400

The authority of the bureaucracy to ratify official appointments (*sŏgyŏng*) was one of the first major issues in the struggle between royal prerogative and official power after the establishment of the new dynasty. Throughout the Koryŏ period all appointments to official positions made by the king had been subject to ratification by the surveillance officials of the Office of the Inspector General and the remonstrance officials of the Secretariat-Chancellery. There is no need to emphasize that this was a powerful weapon for the officials in their efforts to resist and contain royal power.

In the twelfth month of 1392, only five months after the founding of the new dynasty, the remonstrance officials requested continuation of the Koryŏ ratification system. King T'aejo (Yi Sŏng-gye) replied, "Because there are inconveniences in the Koryŏ system of ratifying appointments, I hereby change the system. From now on, officials of the fourth grade and higher will be appointed by royal order and officials of the fifth grade and lower will be given letters of appointment by the Chancellery. If an appointee is not suited for his duties, you should immediately impeach him." [55] With this proclamation King T'aejo eliminated, at least for the time being, ratification for all appointments to offices of the fourth grade or higher, offering the sop of impeachment to remonstrance officials. Since it would be much more difficult to remove an official already in office than to block his appointment, this proclamation in effect eliminated the bureaucracy's say in appointments to higher posts.

The matter did not end there, however. In the ninth month of 1398 the remonstrance officials requested a reduction in officials appointed without ratification from all fourth-grade and higher posts to just the first- and second-grade posts of the Chancellery and the Security Council. [56] King T'aejo refused, but a year and a half later the officials renewed their effort to recover their full rights of ratification, this time with greater success. In the first month of 1400 the Chancellery requested that all appointments be ratified; this time the throne compromised a bit, allowing ratification for fourth-grade officials. Four days later, the Office of the Inspector General requested ratification for all appointments. The king referred the issue to the Todang, who agreed; the king subsequently concurred with the request. [57] Thus, although King T'aejo had achieved what appeared to be a substantial reduction of the bureaucracy's power in 1392, by 1400 the *yangban* officials, through steady concentrated effort, were able to recover all they had lost.

The proper role of eunuchs was another key issue in the struggle between the throne and *yangban* in early the Chosŏn. Such eunuchs as Cho Sun and Kim Sa-haeng (who had been a favorite of Kongmin) became important political actors through royal sponsorship, much as in the late Koryŏ. Kim Sa-haeng, for example, held an appointment to the post of superintendent of the Todang (*p'an* Top'yŏngŭisasa *sa*) in 1394, and in 1397 was put in charge of palace construction. [58] Cho Sun was entrusted with the even more crucial duty of handling treasury receipts and disbursements in 1398. [59] T'aejo appears to have followed the lead of some late Koryŏ kings in using eunuchs to bolster his power vis-à-vis the bureaucracy.

The bureaucracy's attack against eunuchs began immediately after the founding of the dynasty. In the seventh month of 1392 the Office of the Inspector General presented a 10-point memorial urging the new king to, among other things, use rewards and punishments clearly, listen to remonstrance, guard against sloth and desire, remove eunuchs, purge monks, and build impressive palaces. T'aejo concurred with the recommendations except for the removal of eunuchs and monks, who, he said, could not be suddenly purged at the crucial time of dynastic foundation.[60] Two months later the inspector general tried again, arguing for reducing the number of eunuchs and limiting their role to cleaning and guarding doors because their flattery and scheming was dangerous.[61] This time also the officials failed to eliminate the eunuchs.

The officials renewed their attack in 1398, when they succeeded in having Cho Sun relieved of his responsibilities.[62] Another round took place in 1399. In the second month of that year, the Chancellery requested that eunuchs not be allowed to hold titles, noting that although King Chŏngjong had previously prohibited eunuchs from holding posts higher than the third grade and from holding court offices, many eunuchs were in second-grade and higher ranks.[63] This indicates that at some time after he took the throne, King Chŏngjong had acceded to some of the officials' demands for limitations on eunuch power, but that officials were unable to make it stick. Further evidence of this is found in an Office of the Inspector General memorial of the twelfth month of 1398. The memorial lamented that although Chŏngjong banished all but 10 eunuchs to the countryside when he took the throne, all of them returned to the capital within two or three months, and the inspector general requested that they be dismissed. The inspector general's plea notwithstanding, the king refused to comply.[64] Despite T'aejo's and Chŏngjong's adamancy regarding the role of eunuchs, however, after the deaths of Kim Sa-haeng and Cho Sun eunuchs never again played an important political role.[65]

Despite the strong anti-Buddhist agitation of the reform party in the final years of the Koryŏ, royal patronage of Buddhism continued to be an issue at the beginning of the Chosŏn dynasty. Officials' concern about Buddhist influence was expressed in a variety of ways, including provisions of the Rank Land Law that prohibited granting lands to monks and an Office of the Inspector General memorial submitted right after the founding of the new dynasty that called for the purge of eunuchs and monks. As mentioned above, Yi Sŏng-gye demurred on the removal of monks from the palace on the grounds that Buddhism was an established tradition that could not be suddenly eliminated at the time of dynastic foundation. In fact, as is well known, Yi Sŏng-gye was a devout Buddhist, as is evident in his reliance on the monk Chach'o (also known as Muhak). As soon as Yi Sŏng-gye took the throne in the seventh month of 1392, he called Chach'o in and appointed him royal preceptor. Yi relied heavily on Chach'o for advice and even put him in charge of the task force charged with selecting a new site for the national capital. This was a source of considerable friction between Yi Sŏng-gye and the officials,[66] but they dared not challenge the founder of the new dynasty directly. It wasn't until Yi Sŏng-gye had stepped down from the throne in the eighth month of 1398 and Chach'o had submitted his resignation as royal preceptor and retired to Yongmun that the officials reopened their attack. This came in the form of a memorial from the remonstrance officials that argued, "A preceptor is one who models the Way. The Koryŏ dynasty believed in Buddhism and used monks as preceptors, completely losing the ancient system. We implore you to henceforth select as your preceptors high-ranking officials of great learning and lofty virtue and thereby do away with the old abuses."[67] The new king, Chŏngjong, concurred, bringing to a close the old tradition of appointing monks as preceptors and effectively marking the end of Buddhist political influence.[68]

These issues reveal much about the nature of the struggle for political power between the throne and the *yangban* in the early years of the Chosŏn dynasty. First, although Yi Sŏng-gye had come to power with the active assistance of a significant portion of the established *yangban* official class and with at least the acquiescence of most of the rest, there were still significant differences of opinion between the king and the bureaucracy about the exercise of political power. Second, the new kings experienced significant difficulties in imposing their will on the bureaucracy and often found it necessary to give in to officials' demands. Third, because the Chosŏn had yet to carry out significant reform of the central political system, much of the tension between throne and bureaucracy derived from unresolved issues leftover from the old dynasty.

Political Reform: The Second Phase, 1400–1405

The real test of the Chosŏn's viability lay in its effort to carry out a meaningful reorganization of central-political institutions. This began in earnest in 1400. Although the restructuring was actually launched under King Chŏngjong, it began right after T'aejong was formally designated heir apparent, leaving little doubt that T'aejong was the real mastermind from the very beginning. Most scholars assess the significance of this revamping of the political system in terms of the enhancement of royal power. A stronger throne no doubt was one important result of T'aejong's reforms, but another aspect of this reform has recently been pointed out by Chŏng Tu-hŭi: dispersal of bureaucratic power away from one monolithic agency to several different organizations within the bureaucracy.[69]

The need for a major restructuring of political institutions was underlined by continuance of extrainstitutional agencies from the late Koryŏ. While these agencies may have been useful to the new kings during the transition from Koryŏ to Chosŏn, their persistence ultimately threatened to undermine the legitimacy of the new dynasty.

One important auxiliary entity that survived during the transition period was the Personnel Authority. After Yi Sŏng-gye's return from Wihwa Island in 1388, he had himself and his supporters Mun Tar-han and An Chong-wŏn appointed as superintendents of the Personnel Authority (now known as the Sangsŏsa). At that time, however, the reformers were still not in complete control of the government and had to share control over the Personnel Authority with Yi Saek.[70] Once Yi Saek had been purged in the twelfth month of 1389, however, his place was taken by Cho Chun, giving Yi Sŏng-gye's group a monopoly over the top posts in the Personnel Authority.[71] There is no doubt that the reform party then was able to use the Personnel Authority to place supporters in key bureaucratic posts as vacancies occurred, either by purge or eventualities such as resignation or death. The Personnel Authority appears to have continued to play an important role in personnel actions even after the founding of the new dynasty, as evidenced in a 1400 entry in the *Veritable Records* describing controversy within the Personnel Authority over superintendent Ha Yun's monopoly over recommendations.[72]

Another major extrainstitutional body that persisted into the new dynasty was the palace *chaech'u*. As for the late Koryŏ period, the sources tell us precious little about its activities, again probably because meetings took place within the palace and were not open to the historians who recorded affairs for the *Veritable Records*. It seems probable that the early Chosŏn palace *chaech'u* was made up of such key supporters of Yi Sŏng-gye as Cho Chun and Chŏng To-jŏn and almost certainly played a major role in shaping the policies of the infant dynasty. The palace *chaech'u* was abolished at the request of the Secretariat/Chancellery in the eighth month of 1400. It is interesting to note that this took place at a time when Cho Chun was temporarily jailed as the result of false charges lodged against him by other officials.[73]

Before T'aejong could address the potentially volatile issue of regularizing the flow of political power and restructuring the new dynasty's central bureaucracy, he first had to consolidate dynastic control over the military. This change

TABLE 5.1

Consolidated Army Command Officials, 1393–98

Date	Name	Ancestral Seat
1393.10	Yi Pang-gwa	Chŏnju*
1393.10	Yi Pang-bŏn	Chŏnju*
1393.10	Yi Che	Sŏngju
1394.01	Chŏng To-jŏn	Ponghwa
1395.04	Ch'oe Yu-gyŏng	Chŏnju
1397.12	Cho Chun	P'yŏngyang
1398.09	Cho Yŏng-mu	Hanyang*
1398.09	Yi Hwa	Chŏnju*
1398.09	Chang Sa-gil	Andong*
1398.09	Yi Chi-ran	Jurchen*
1398.09	Cho On	Hanyang*
1398.09	Kim No	Yŏnan
1398.09	Yi Pang-ŭi	Chŏnju*
1398.09	Yi Pang-gan	Chŏnju*
1398.09	Yi Pang-wŏn	Chŏnju*

* Northeastern military

was carried out through the Consolidated Army Command, which was organized in 1391 around a nucleus of forces under Yi Sŏng-gye's command and
which included members of the new royal family and their supporters. Table
5.1 lists the men known to have held Consolidated Army Command commissioner posts. Ten of the 15 known appointees to top level Consolidated
Army Command posts were members of the northeastern military group, and
six of those 10 were Chŏnju Yi members. Two of the other five, Yi Che and
Cho Chun, had married into Yi Sŏng-gye's family. This domination of the
Consolidated Army Command by the northeastern military group in general
and by Yi Sŏng-gye's family in particular indicates that the Command and the
troops under it formed the bulk of the new royal family's military muscle.

Although the Consolidated Army Command was an important power center for the new dynasty, it was at best a transitional institution, since outside
of the northeastern military coalition significant private military forces still
existed under the command of various individuals, many of whom had supported Yi Sŏng-gye's overthrow of the Koryŏ but who still guarded their pre-

rogatives jealously. Abolition of these private guards and incorporation of the Consolidated Army Command into the regular dynastic institutional structure came about in a series of measures taken after the notorious princes' revolts. In the eighth month of 1398 Yi Pang-wŏn (Yi Sŏng-gye's fifth son and the future T'aejong) mobilized the private forces of Yi Suk-pŏn and others to attack and kill the supporters of the Crown Prince Yi Pang-sŏk, men who had their own private forces. Nam Ŭn, one of the crown prince's supporters, was later reviled in a remonstrance official's memorial for his role: "The traitor Nam Ŭn abused his power, entrusting military control to his family and followers and placing them at various encampments."[74] The second revolt occurred in the second month of 1400, when Yi Sŏng-gye's fourth son, Yi Pang-gan, fearful of harm at the hands of Yi Pang-wŏn, mobilized his own private forces. Yi Pang-wŏn's response was to send forth his soldiers to capture and banish Yi Pang-gan.

The revolts led to measures designed to bring private military forces under greater control. An Office of the Inspector General memorial of the eleventh month of 1399, which urged the elimination of private forces on the grounds that the new dynasty had achieved stability and secured the borders,[75] resulted in replacement of commanders of provincial private military forces with trusted members of the royal family and select merit subjects. Immediately after the second revolt Yi Pang-wŏn was designated crown prince and given control over all military forces.[76] Two months later, in the fourth month of 1400, Kwŏn Kŭn and Kim Yak-ch'ae memorialized against having royal relatives and merit subjects control private military forces as provided for in the 1399 measure, and urged instead that command over all military forces should be concentrated in the Consolidated Army command. King Chŏngjong, who was controlled from behind the throne by his brother Yi Pang-wŏn (the future T'aejong), concurred.[77] This marked the end of private military forces in the Chosŏn.

There remained, however, the task of incorporating royally controlled military forces into the dynastic institutional framework. This began with the prohibition of officials of the Consolidated Army Command from concurrently holding positions in the civil branch of government. This move was presaged by a 1394 memorial by Pyŏn Chung-nyang that criticized Cho Chun, Chŏng To-jŏn, and Nam Ŭn for exercising both military command and political leadership on the grounds that military control belonged to the royal family and political power to officials of the bureaucracy. Although King T'aejo did not follow Pyŏn's suggestion, his reasoning—that those three individuals were like family and of the same mind as himself—suggests that he accepted the basic principle behind Pyŏn's argument.[78] Shortly thereafter, in the seventh month of 1401, the Consolidated Army Command was renamed the Security Council (Sŭngch'ubu), a new civil agency created to assume the military coordination functions of the old Security Council, which was then disbanded.[79] We have no way of knowing the grade structure of the new Security Council, but several of its posts had names almost identical to those of posts in the old Koryŏ Security Council, suggesting that the new Council may have been staffed along the same general lines. At any rate, the new Security Council itself was a transitional agency that was absorbed into the Board of War (Pyŏngjo) in 1405. This completed the incorporation of the Consolidated Army Command into the regular institutional structure.[80]

Consolidation of royal control over all military forces was almost immediately followed by restructuring of the civil branch of government, where political power resided. The Todang was abolished in 1400, and its deliberative functions were allocated to a new agency, the State Council. The *Kyŏngguk taejŏn* shows that the State Council was headed by a senior first-grade chief state councillor (*yŏngŭijŏng*) and staffed by two additional senior first-grade state councillors (*chwa/u ŭijŏng*), two junior first-grade associate state councillors (*chwa/u ch'ansŏng*), and two junior second-grade assistant state councillors (*chwa/u ch'amch'an*), along with several mid- and low-ranking officials. This radical reduction in numbers from the 40 plus Todang members noted by Kwŏn Kŭn in 1400 indicates that T'aejong was attempting to establish greater control of the organs of political struggle by curtailing the number of *yangban* who could sit in deliberation on policy issues.

The *Veritable Records* indicate that the Secretariat/Chancellery was abolished in 1401. The executive functions of the old Secretariat/Chancellery were assigned to the new State Council and its remonstrance officials transferred to the new Office of the Censor General (Saganwŏn).[81] The *Veritable Records*, however, continue to show appointments to top posts in the old Secretariat/Chancellery until early in 1404.[82] During this three-year period frequent selections were made for posts whose titles are amalgams of the old and new systems. For example, several appointments were made to the post of *ch'amji* Ŭijŏngbu *sa*, which appears to have been a modification of the old *ch'amji chŏngsa* (state councillor) post, and several more were made to the post of *chi* Ŭijŏngbu *sa*, which appears to have been a modification of the old *chi* Munhasŏng *sa* (Chancellery administrator, junior second-grade). These mixed titles suggest that the offices of the old Secretariat/Chancellery were maintained temporarily while the State Council gradually absorbed its functions. This could have been simply a matter of bureaucratic transition or a tactic by which

T'aejong sought to dampen official resistance to his reform. At any rate, it appears that the new governmental structure, which entailed a sharp reduction in the number of officials who deliberated on policy issues and the dispersion of the executive and other powers of the once monolithic Secretariat/Chancellery, was fully in place by 1404. This appears to have marked a substantial redress of the balance of power between the throne and the *yangban* bureaucracy in favor of the throne.

T'aejong's reform also addressed the issues presented by the persistence of extraordinary political organs. The Personnel Authority was downgraded to the status of a subordinate agency of the Board of Personnel and its functions were limited to handling the royal seals that were used to certify appointments.[83] The inner *chaech'u* was, of course, abolished right before T'aejong began his political restructuring. It can perhaps be argued that the new State Council represented a formalization of the old inner *chaech'u*, but there are some significant differences. One is that whereas the inner *chaech'u* was an extraordinary entity that convened behind closed doors in the palace, the State Council was a regular bureaucratic institution whose deliberations were recorded for inclusion in the *Veritable Records*. Another is that while the inner *chaech'u* usurped the transmission of royal documents, T'aejong restored that function to the proper officials and relocated it in a separate agency independent of the State Council. Thus it can be said that T'aejong's reform not only addressed the issue of the imbalance of power between the throne and officials, but did so in a manner that eliminated the tensions between throne and bureaucracy that had arisen out of the old Koryŏ kings' use of extrainstitutional entities.

Another important, but largely neglected, aspect of T'aejong's reordering of the central bureaucracy was his dispersal of bureaucratic authority. As we have seen, in the Koryŏ virtually all significant bureaucratic power was monopolized by the first- and second-grade *chaech'u* of the Secretariat/Chancellery and the Security Council. Not only did they deliberate and make decisions on major policy issues in the Todang, but they also controlled the actual implementation of policy through their concurrent appointments as superintendents of the Six Boards. Furthermore, they exercised direct administrative supervision over the mid-ranking officials of the Secretariat/Chancellery responsible for remonstrance and the third-grade officials of the Security Council charged with the important function of transmitting royal documents, and they dominated other key agencies, such as the Office of the Inspector General, through concurrent appointments to top posts there. This concentration of political power in the *chaech'u* enabled the bureaucracy to dominate the throne and caused a tremendous expansion in the number of first- and second-grade posts when growth in the size of the central-official class led to increasing competitive pressures. T'aejong's restructuring of the central bureaucracy addressed these problems by greatly curtailing the practice of giving top-ranking officials concurrent appointments at the top levels of outside agencies and by establishing a number of new independent centers of bureaucratic power, thereby both dispersing power and creating new opportunities for ambitious men.[84]

At the time of T'aejong's initial reorganization of the central bureaucracy in 1400, the Six Boards, although no longer headed by concurrently appointed superintendents, were placed directly under the State Council. Concerned, however, about the leverage this combination of deliberative and executive powers gave the State Council over the throne, T'aejong amended the system in 1414 to allow the Six Boards to bypass the State Council and present memorials directly to the king. The State Council was able to recover its control over the Six Boards briefly under Sejong, only to lose it again to King Sejo in 1455.[85]

This repeated withdrawal and restoration of State Council control over the Six Boards indicates that the struggle for power between the throne and the *yangban* continued to be a feature of Korean political life even after the founding of the Chosŏn. Nonetheless, the ability of strong-minded monarchs such as T'aejong and Sejo to wrest power away from the State Council is a sign that Chosŏn kings enjoyed substantially greater authority than did kings of the Koryŏ.

T'aejong's plan for making the Six Boards independent of the State Council also involved enhancement of the post of board chief. Whereas chiefs (*yukpu sangsŏ*) of the Koryŏ period were relatively lackluster senior third-grade posts, chiefs (*yukcho p'ansŏ*) of the Chosŏn were senior second-grade positions, and the men who held them—particularly the chief of Personnel—enjoyed prestige nearly as great as that of the state councillors.[86] Thus independence of the Six Boards represented not only a weakening of State Council authority, but also an expansion in the number of positions exercising real political power.

The new political system designed by T'aejong also weakened State Council authority by relocating the remonstrance function in the new, independent Office of the Censor-General, which was headed by a senior third-grade censor general (*taesagan*). This move greatly reduced the potential for State Councillor interference in the remonstrance function and, while it did not raise the grade levels of the remonstrance officials, it did represent the creation of a prestigious new power center in the bureaucracy. The old practice of giving concurrent appointments to top posts in the Office of the Inspector General (now called Sahŏnbu) was also halted, giving this office a greater degree of independence than it had enjoyed in the Koryŏ. At the same time, the top post was upgraded from senior third grade to junior second grade. Thus, like the Office of the Censor General, the Office of the Inspector General emerged as a significant center of bureaucratic power in the new dynasty.

Finally, we should note that the vexatious problem of the transmission of royal documents was also addressed by T'aejong. In the Koryŏ the *chaech'u* had exercised administrative authority over officials charged with transmit- ting memorials to and edicts from the king, but in later years the inner *chaech'u* had usurped that function. T'aejong relocated this responsibility to a new, inde- pendent agency called the Sŭngjŏngwŏn. Although this agency was staffed at the same senior third-grade level as the old transmitters of the Koryŏ, its estab- lishment apart from the State Council was intended to ensure that the State Councillors and other top-ranking officials would not be able to interfere with the free flow of information to and from the throne.

This dispersal of bureaucratic authority away from the State Council had obvious implications for the balance of power between the throne and the *yang- ban* in that it effectively broke up the combination of policy making and exec- utive functions enjoyed by the Koryŏ *chaech'u* and made it possible, at least in theory, for Chosŏn kings to play various agencies against each other in a way that was unthinkable for Koryŏ kings. Chŏng Tu-hŭi argues that this dis- persal of bureaucratic authority among several independent agencies was due to the influence of Confucian ideology, with its emphasis on open channels of communication (*ŏllo*).[87] Chŏng's point seems well taken, especially in con- sideration of the issue of the Six Boards' right to memorialize the throne directly, the importance attached to the roles of the Office of the Censor General and the Office of the Inspector General, and the establishment of an independent agency to safeguard the transmission of documents.

It seems to me, however, that an additional reason for dispersal of bureau- cratic authority in the early Chosŏn may lie in the need to respond to the demand for the sharing of power that arose from growth of the central-official class. A general upgrading of positions occurred during the Koryŏ-Chosŏn transition. The Koryŏ allotment of first- and second-grade posts was, of course, greatly increased, primarily by irregular means, during the final years of the dynasty, but the Koryŏ system originally called for no senior first-grade posts, three junior first-grade (only one of which was filled), six senior second-grade (two of which were honorary), and nine junior second-grade, for a total of sixteen regularly filled first- and second-grade posts. In contrast, the Chosŏn system, while cutting back sharply on the number of irregular first- and sec- ond-grade posts that had come into being in the late Koryŏ, still provided for substantially more top-ranking posts: four senior first-grade (not counting concurrent and honorary posts), four junior first-grade, 11 senior second-grade, and ten junior second-grade, for a total of 29 regularly filled first- and second-grade offices. This upgrading would seem to be a natural response to pressures for greater sharing of power and status. Furthermore, establishment of independent centers of bureaucratic authority outside the State Council can also be seen as a response to the demand for greater sharing of power, since men seeking to exercise real authority would now have alternatives to membership in the State Council.

While this stratagem may have worked fairly well initially, by the late fifteenth century, as Edward Wagner has shown, men holding offices in the new independent agencies—especially the Offices of the Inspector General and the Censor General—developed those agencies into organs of political struggle in competition with the State Council.[88] Although other issues, including ideological commitment and personal animosities, undoubtedly contributed to the political instability of the late fifteenth and early sixteenth centuries, I cannot help but believe that an important factor was the tradition of power sharing among Korean elites, whose claim to participation at the highest levels derived as much from birthright as from achievement.

SUMMATION

It seems evident that the reforms accompanying the founding of the Chosŏn dynasty reflected the actual economic, social, and political interests of the great central *yangban* descent groups. This was particularly true in the areas of fiscal and social reform, where *yangban* who maintained permanent residence in the capital received special benefits from the Rank Land Law and benefited from the elimination of other social groups from competition for power. Although the benefits accruing to the *yangban* are not so obvious in the area of political reform, more aware members of the official class, typified by men such as Cho Chun, were clearly cognizant that without some correction of the badly skewed balance of power between throne and *yangban,* the system that had served them and their descent groups so well simply could not continue to function. Additionally, dispersal of significant bureaucratic power among several different agencies served the interests of central *yangban* descent groups by providing greater opportunities for meaningful participation in government and lessening, at least temporarily, the fearsome competition for power.

The new institutional framework that emerged in the early fifteenth century was qualitatively different from the sociopolitical institutions of the Koryŏ.

Politically, the new dynasty abandoned the old monolithic *chaech'u*-centered system in favor of a new setup separating the policy-making State Council from other agencies. In short, a differentiation of political roles separated the organs of political struggle—the State Council and the Censorate—from administrative agencies. This indicates, according to Eisenstadt's analysis, that the Chosŏn system, with its greater differentiation of political functions, was more bureaucratic than that of the Koryŏ.

Fiscally, the new dynasty was able, through reform of the prebend system and a variety of steps establishing greater control over the commoner population, to create more free-floating resources than had existed in the Koryŏ period. This made possible other reforms that enhanced the rulers' power and put the central regime on a solid foundation. At the same time, however, we must not lose sight of the fact that the dominant social group, the *yangban,* still controlled extensive landed and human resources.

Socially the new dynasty redefined membership in the ruling class in ways that significantly reduced the number of men eligible to hold office in the dynastic government. It prohibited men of nonelite backgrounds—such as merchants, slaves, and eunuchs—from occupying positions of political power. It discarded the old territorial status system, which had protected the social and political privileges of the local strongmen and their *hyangni* descendants, in favor of a new system designed to protect the interests of central *yangban.* In the sense that *yangban* derived their power and prestige from their status as officials of the state, this change implies further bureaucratization of Korean society. But we must also keep in mind that *yangban* constituted a hereditary status group with command over substantial resources and that there were other hereditary status groups, such as *chungin,* who filled specific political roles. Thus, despite greater bureaucratization of political institutions, the early Chosŏn rulers were still unable to foster a significant degree of differentiation between political and social roles.

Institutions of the Chosŏn dynasty were also different from those of the Yüan and the Ming. Although the central bureaucracy of the Chosŏn may seem, at first glance, to bear a strong resemblance to the Grand Secretariat/Censorate system of the Yüan, the highly centralized Chosŏn system was actually radically different from the decentralized political Mongol system in which the Grand Secretariat and Censorate at the capital handled only the metropolitan area while "replicate" or branch Grand Secretariats and Censorates administered other areas of the empire.[89] Socially, of course, the differences were vast: the Yüan was a conquest dynasty in which Mongols presided over native

Han Chinese and other ethnic groups, whereas the Chosŏn dynasty came to power in a milieu of substantial continuity at the top levels of society.

Likewise, there were more differences than similarities between the Chosŏn and the Ming. Although T'aejong may have been inspired by Ming T'ai-tsu in making the Six Boards independent of the State Council, similarities in political structure end there. The Ming founder abolished the Secretariat and the office of prime minister in 1380 and took direct charge of government administration. Although later Ming emperors established special offices of advisors and scholars to advise them, those entities were a far cry from the old secretariats or the State Council of the Chosŏn, and the Ming emperors ruled in an autocratic fashion all but unimaginable in Korea. Also, in contrast to the Chosŏn purging of eunuchs from the government, in the Ming eunuchs not only handled the important role of transmitting imperial documents, but also held a wide variety of regular and extraordinary government posts.[90] Socially, both the Ming and the Chosŏn sought to establish and maintain hereditary occupational groups, but whereas slavery was abolished in Ming China, it was extremely important to the operation of the state and the livelihood of the official class in early Chosŏn Korea. But probably the biggest social difference between the Ming and the Chosŏn was that whereas Ming T'ai-tsu in effect created a new ruling class by seeking out supporters from a wide variety of social groups—including the Red Turbans and other rebels, militia leaders, and village chiefs, as well as the scholarly classes of South China—the early Chosŏn kings had to recruit support from a strongly aristocratic *yangban* class.[91]

The unique aspects of Chosŏn institutions can perhaps be attributed to such factors as the smaller size of Korea (which could explain why the Chosŏn did not develop a Yüan-style decentralized system) and Korea's position subordinate to China in the East Asian international order (which gave Korean officials a potent weapon to curb autocratic tendencies in Korean kings).[92] Ultimately, however, I think we have to focus in on the comparatively low level of social differentiation and the corollary importance of ascriptive privilege in Korea.

Unlike the early Koryŏ, when much of the country's resources were under the hereditary control of local strongmen descent groups and the dynasty's local administration was a highly stratified hierarchy made up of control prefectures and counties, subordinate prefectures and counties, and *hyang, so,* and *pugok,* the early Chosŏn featured much stronger state control over both land and human resources and a more regular system of local administration under direct central supervision. In comparison with the Koryŏ, therefore, the

Chosŏn represented a more differentiated society with greater free-floating resources.

In comparison with China, however, Chosŏn dynasty Korea remained poorly differentiated. Whereas by Sung and Ming times China had undergone a process of agricultural and commercial development that produced significant gentry and merchant groups, no such development had taken place in Korea as of the fifteenth century. The Korean economy remained agrarian and the level of social differentiation, while greater than in the early Koryŏ, remained comparatively low. There were few merchants or other urban elements. In the early Koryŏ Kwangjong at least had a vital local strongman class to turn to for support against the central warlord-aristocratic confederation, but by the end of the dynasty the local strongmen's *hyangni* descendants had suffered heavy erosion of their bases of power and had little to offer as potential allies. Thus the new rulers had virtually no alternative to the *yangban* in their search for a major social group to support the dynasty. Seen in this light, the institutional innovations that accompanied the 1392 change of dynasties emerge not as revolutionary changes to accommodate the needs of a new ruling class but rather as a reordering of institutions to protect the interests of the central *yangban* class of bureaucratic aristocrats that had been evolving over the preceding centuries.

6 / The Ideology of Reform

Amajor feature of the Koryŏ-Chosŏn change of dynasties was the rise of a new and vigorous Confucian discourse. Explanations of this have focused almost exclusively on the introduction and spread of Ch'eng-Chu Learning (Chŏngjuhak, Ch. Ch'eng-chu Hsüeh), often called Neo-Confucianism, seeing it either as the ideology of a new "scholar-official" class or as constituting, in itself, the driving force behind the founding of the Chosŏn dynasty in 1392. In either case, the primary emphasis has been on the displacement of a stagnant Buddho-Confucian, belletrist, T'ang-style literati learning by a dynamic new anti-Buddhist, anti-belletrist variety of Confucian learning that combined metaphysical speculation with a strong emphasis on study of the Confucian classics. This new Ch'eng-Chu Learning, named after its leading advocates, Ch'eng I (1033–1107) and Chu Hsi (1130–1200) of Sung dynasty China—and variously known as Sung Learning (Songhak, Ch. Sung Hsüeh), Nature and Principle Learning (Sŏngnihak, Ch. Hsing-li Hsüeh), Chu Hsi Learning (Chujahak, Ch. Chu-tzu Hsüeh), or the Learning of the Way (Tohak, Ch. Tao Hsüeh—was adopted as official state learning in Yüan dynasty China and introduced into Korea late in the thirteenth century.

The most widely accepted view of the intellectual history of the late Koryŏ–early Chosŏn period holds that Ch'eng-Chu Learning rose to dominance as the class ideology of a "new scholar-official" group of medium and small landlords who seized power with the founding of the Chosŏn dynasty. We have already seen, however, that "new scholar-officials"—if such a group existed at all—were not the main force behind the new dynasty's founding, so it is highly unlikely that Ch'eng-Chu Learning could have triumphed as their class ideology in 1392. The argument suffers from internal inconsistencies as well. Although the Chosŏn was supposedly established by Neo-Confucianist "new scholar-officials," some of the most prominent Ch'eng-Chu Learning scholars of the late fourteenth century, including Yi Saek and Chŏng Mong-ju, were adamantly opposed to overthrowing the Koryŏ. Furthermore, although proponents of the "new scholar-official" thesis argue that Ch'eng-Chu Learning represented the class interests of medium and small landlords against those of the aristocratic large landlords of the late Koryŏ, which presumably were reflected in Buddhism, they have yet to explain just how Ch'eng-Chu Learning or Buddhism were linked to economic issues. In fact, it is difficult to understand the basis on which this distinction is made, because the means of production (land) and the relations of production (slavery and tenancy) in which such ideological superstructures are presumably grounded would be basically the same for all landlords regardless of the size of their holdings.[1]

The other major interpretation of late Koryŏ–early Chosŏn intellectual history holds that the Chosŏn was founded as a direct consequence of the late-thirteenth-century importation of Ch'eng-Chu Learning. According to this view, the spread of Ch'eng-Chu Learning among the official class in the fourteenth century gave rise to a critique that attributed the problems of society to the decadence and corruption of Buddhism. The Koryŏ dynasty had a long and intimate relationship with Buddhism and was either unwilling or unable to carry out needed reforms, making it necessary—in the minds of the Confucian-inspired officials—to overthrow the Koryŏ in order to revitalize Korean society. A leading spokesperson for this interpretation is Kim Ch'ung-nyŏl, who emphasizes philosophical conflict between Buddhism and Ch'eng-Chu Learning as the key issue in the Koryŏ–Chosŏn change of dynasties. Kim argues that Ch'eng-Chu Learning was a sophisticated and comprehensive philosophical system that in the late Koryŏ "began to exercise the initiative in religion, politics, society, scholarship, culture, education, and even diplomacy; it manifested itself as a Confucianism concerned with protecting its Way and attacked without hesitation anything that impeded its exercise of that initiative as well as all heterogeneous systems."[2]

Martina Deuchler also emphasizes the role of Ch'eng-Chu Learning, contending that "the establishment of the Chosŏn dynasty was a moral and intellectual venture that set out to prove itself by articulating a sociopolitical program that would give the new dynasty a firm Confucian basis."[3] Deuchler, however, stresses the pragmatic aspects of the Confucian movement, arguing that a small vanguard of scholar-officials of the late fourteenth and fifteenth centuries saw in Ch'eng-Chu Learning a vehicle through which they could gain access to the Chinese past for a model of social and political reform to correct the ills of Koryŏ society.[4]

The kind of role that Ch'eng-Chu Learning played in the founding of the new dynasty in Korea seems to be without parallel elsewhere. In discussing the historical role of Neo-Confucianism in China, William Theodore de Bary has noted its limitations as a revolutionary force and argues that it was best suited to respond to the needs of an already established, centralized civil admin-istration. De Bary goes on to say, "The case of the Yi dynasty would seem to be a singular instance in which Neo-Confucians played a large role in the cre-ation of a new regime and in the formulating of its institutions."[5] This leaves us with the problem of explaining how Ch'eng-Chu Learning came to con-stitute a "revolutionary" ideology in late-fourteenth-century Korea.

There is no question that Confucian ideas played an important role in late-fourteenth-century politics and did much to inspire and shape the social and political reforms of the early Chosŏn. Nonetheless, the focus on Ch'eng-Chu Learning, which derives largely from an impulse to construct the origins of the Neo-Confucian orthodoxy of the mid-Chosŏn, has directed our attention away from other important aspects of late Koryŏ and early Chosŏn intellec-tual life, aspects that may help explain the singular activism of early Chosŏn Confucianism.

These interpretations of fundamental social and ideological change between the Koryŏ and Chosŏn periods seem to parallel historical scholarship on China. Conventional interpretations of the T'ang–Sung transition have stressed social change in the shift from an aristocratic sociopolitical order in the T'ang to a local gentry-centered society in the Sung, occurring in tandem with supplan-tation of a poetry-oriented, T'ang Buddho-Confucian intellectual tradition by a new Ch'eng-Chu Learning that was hostile to Buddhism and deprecated the poetic arts in favor of study of the classics and moral self-cultivation.[6] Although historians of Korea almost never make reference to the T'ang-Sung transition as a model, the parallels are too clear to be mere coincidence.

More recent interpretations of the T'ang–Sung social and intellectual tran-sition, however, present a more complicated picture. Hoyt Tillman, for exam-ple, questions the idea of a single line of development centering around Chu Hsi in Sung and later Chinese intellectual history and presents Ch'eng-Chu Learning as only one constituent of a widely defined Southern Sung Tao Hsüeh.[7] In an important study on the links between social and intellectual change, Peter Bol argues that the Chinese elites (*shih;* literati) underwent a transformation from aristocracy in the T'ang, to central scholar-officials in the Northern Sung, to local literati in the Southern Sung. This was paralleled by a shifting of intel-lectual orientations from the culture-oriented approach of the T'ang, which focused on the practice of belles lettres (*wen-chang,* K. *munjang*) as the key to maintaining culture and harmonizing the three teachings of Confucianism, Taoism, and Buddhism; to an activist movement of the Northern Sung that stressed the role of government in transforming society and sought to express the values of antiquity in Ancient Style Writing (Ku-wen, K., Komun); to a

Tao Hsüeh that placed primary emphasis on individual self-cultivation and morality. This "directed attention away from government and ideas for transforming society that could be effected through government" and downplayed the role of literary endeavor.[8] These studies question the assumption of the philosophical inevitability of the triumph of Ch'eng-Chu Learning and, in lieu of the linear approach that traces the origins of Neo-Confucianism from Han Yü through Chou Tun-i and Ch'eng I to Chu Hsi, offer a much more variegated and complex picture of Sung intellectual life.

There is evidence to suggest that the intellectual landscape of the Koryŏ–Chosŏn transition, too, was quite complex. The majority of early Chosŏn officials, as Deuchler has pointed out, were not committed to the Ch'eng-Chu Learning vision of society and politics.[9] Even the thinking of the reformist vanguard cannot be reduced to orthodox Ch'eng-Chu Learning, for many men who played important political roles in the early years of the Chosŏn dynasty espoused ideas, such as emphasis on the value of poetry as a vehicle for cultivating and manifesting morality, that seem to conflict with central tenets of Ch'eng-Chu Learning. Other historians have also noted the complexity of early Chosŏn literati learning. Han Young-woo, in his study on the social thought of the official class of the early Chosŏn, contends that although such prominent early Chosŏn officials as Chŏng To-jŏn and Yang Sŏng-ji were Ch'eng-Chu Learning scholars, they showed a higher degree of practicality and nationalistic autonomy than did the orthodox Neo-Confucianists of the mid-Chosŏn.[10] But whereas Han seems still to be committed to containing such intellectual diversity within the Ch'eng-Chu tradition, Yi T'ae-jin argues that early Chosŏn literati learning may best be understood as a broadly constituted "learning of encyclopedic works" (*yusŏhak*, Ch. *lei-shu hsüeh*) similar to that of the Northern Sung in its emphasis on the compilation of histories and geographies and its acceptance of a variety of literary styles.[11]

As this welter of interpretations suggests, literati learning in the Koryŏ and the early Chosŏn periods displayed much more complexity than is allowed for by conventional depictions of the supplanting of a moribund Buddho-Confucian, belletrist Koryŏ literati learning by a dynamic new Ch'eng-Chu Learning at the time of the change of dynasties. Far from being stagnant, Koryŏ literati learning was a vital tradition informed by a dynamic tension between competing belletrist and Ancient Style intellectual modes whose relative influence was closely linked to changes in the social and political spheres. The vitality of Koryŏ literati learning and the substantial sociopolitical continuity between the late Koryŏ and the early Chosŏn meant that old Koryŏ intellectual traditions continued to play important roles after the change of dynasties. This was particularly true in the case of Ancient Style learning, with its emphasis on a strong and activist central state.

THE COMPLEXITY OF LITERATI LEARNING

In recent years a number of scholars have begun to question the conventional depiction of Koryŏ intellectual history as stagnant and imitative T'ang Buddho-Confucianism. These scholars have noted the rise in the late eleventh and early twelfth centuries of a more practical Confucian learning oriented toward statecraft and study of the classics. Citing as evidence the names of the private schools that came into being at that time—such as Great Mean (Taejung, Ch. Ta-chung) and Illuminating Sincerity (Sŏngmyŏng, Ch. Ch'eng-ming), which appear to have been drawn from *The Doctrine of the Mean* (*Chungyong*, Ch. *Chung-yung*), one of the Four Books (Sasŏ, Ch. Ssu-shu) emphasized by Chu Hsi—they argue that this new trend represented a parallel and independent early development of Nature and Principle Learning in Korea. This new trend is believed to have been cut off, however, with the revival of belletrism after the 1170 coup.[12]

While we cannot dismiss out of hand the possibility of early Korean philosophical development along lines similar to those pursued by Ch'eng I and Chu Hsi, the empirical foundations of this argument are very tenuous. No texts survive from this time to give us any concrete sense of what kinds of ideas late-eleventh- and early-twelfth-century Korean thinkers were pursuing. The only evidence is the aforementioned names of private academies and occasional use of *The Doctrine of the Mean* for royal lectures.[13] A more serious problem with this interpretation is that it assumes the inevitable triumph of philosophical Neo-Confucianism, which in Korea was delayed only by the 1170 military coup, and reduces these new intellectual developments to forerunners of Chosŏn dynasty Nature and Principle Learning.

Once we step outside this teleological interpretive framework, however, and reexamine Koryŏ thought from a perspective that, like those offered by Tillman and Bol for China, looks for a plurality of intellectual styles, we can see Koryŏ intellectual history as a complex and rich tradition that included significant Ancient Style Learning tendencies.

Belles Lettres and Ancient Style in the Early and Mid-Koryŏ

Scholars almost universally agree that the dominant intellectual tradition among the central officials of the Koryŏ period was a belletrist T'ang style. Yi Pyŏng-do describes it as a coexistence of Confucianism with Buddhism wherein the former concerned itself with administrative techniques and belles lettres while the latter provided the philosophical foundations of society. Yi says, "The Confucian learning of this time had a strong tendency toward poetry and literary arts rather than toward study of the classics or of theory."[14] Although other scholars over the years may have modified this view somewhat, they have tended to stay within the same general framework. For example, Pak Sŏng-hwan characterizes Koryŏ Confucianism as Buddho-Confucian dualism in which Confucianism is typified as an official statecraft learning (*kwan-hakchŏk kyŏngsehak*) that lasted from Ch'oe Sŭng-no in the tenth century to Yi Saek in the fourteenth.[15]

A major problem in studying Koryŏ intellectual life is the lack of source materials. No literary collections survive from the early Koryŏ period. All we have are a few poetic compositions that have been preserved in later critical works and anthologies such as Ch'oe Cha's *Pohan chip* (Collected Works of Ch'oe Cha) and the *Tongmunsŏn* (Anthology of Korean literary works in Chinese). We therefore must turn to other types of evidence, including the observations of contemporary and later commentators and changes in the government service examinations and educational system, to assess early Koryŏ intellectual life.

Although precious few literary works survive from the tenth through the eleventh centuries, it is clear from those that do exist as well as from examination-system documents and the remarks of later commentators such as Ch'oe Cha, Yi Saek, and Sŏ Kŏ-jŏng[16] that the dominant genres were T'ang style poetry, rhyme-prose, and parallel prose. This was accompanied by a syncretic intellectual outlook that emphasized the coexistence of and complementary relationship between Buddhism (for cultivating the self) and Confucianism (for governing the state and ordering society).[17]

This intellectual style seems to have reached a climax during the early-twelfth-century reign of King Yejong, a noted poet in his own right and a man whose intellectual interests included Sŏn Buddhism and Taoism. Not only did he promote his program of syncretic learning through supportive officials such as the academician Pak Ho, but he is reputed to have eagerly sought out the company of similarly inclined men, including eremites such as Kwak Yŏ and Yi Cha-hyŏn.[18]

Even as the T'ang style flourished, however, a reaction set in among certain literati circles. This reaction manifested itself, as it had in late T'ang China, in Ancient Style Learning, the first known Korean practitioner of which was Kim Hwang-wŏn (1045–1117). Little is known of his career except that he was once forced out of his academician post by high-ranking officials who feared that his rejection of parallel prose would corrupt students.[19] Other Ancient Style advocates, however, stepped forth to criticize Yejong, including Ch'oe Yak of the powerful Haeju Ch'oe, who criticized the king's encouragement of Taoism and Buddhism and took him to task for his devotion to the "carving of insects" (a phrase frequently used by Ancient Style advocates and later by Ch'eng-Chu Learning adherents to deprecate the ornate literary composition of the T'ang style) and for keeping company with "frivolous poet-courtiers."[20] Although Ch'oe Yak and his comrades did not prevail during Yejong's time, the Ancient Style continued to gain strength in succeeding decades through the efforts of such champions as Kim Pu-sik (1075–1151), prime minister under King Injong and perhaps the most influential scholar of his time. By 1139 there was a proposal, inspired by Ancient Style advocate Fan Chung-yen's abortive 1044 reform of the Sung examination system, to revise the Koryŏ examinations. Whereas the existing system tested candidates first in their poetic skills, this proposal called for candidates to be tested on policy treatises and essays in the first two sessions; those who passed would then be tested in composition of poetry and rhyme-prose in the third session in order to determine their final rankings.[21] Whether this proposal was enacted at the time is not clear, but the *Koryŏsa* tells us that fifteen years later the examination system was revised to include essays and policy treatises in the first session, knowledge of the classics in the second, and poetry and rhyme-prose in the third.[22] The Ancient Style movement, which placed a premium on knowledge of the classics and practical policy issues, was clearly gaining momentum. From all outward appearances, it would seem that by the mid-twelfth century, Koryŏ intellectual culture was following the same general pattern as in late T'ang and Northern Sung China, in which the old T'ang style, with its philosophical syncretism and poetic floridity, was fading from the scene. It is important to note that Korean interest in the Ancient Style appeared after the great civil-official descent groups had established themselves at the capital and that it was advocated by prominent members of those groups. It seems natural that Ancient Style Learning, with its emphasis on a strong, activist state, would be attractive to men such as Ch'oe Yak and Kim Pu-sik.

The Ancient Style movement soon experienced a reversal. By the end of the twelfth century, apparently as a consequence of the purges after the 1170 military coup, adherents of the Ancient Style had virtually disappeared from the capital, and T'ang style belletrism had made a strong recovery. The literati, typified by members of the Noble Gathering of the Bamboo Grove (Chungnim Kohoe) such as Im Ch'un (fl. c. 1200) and Yi Il-lo (1152–1220), were once again actively proclaiming the ultimate unity of Buddhism and Confucianism, writing poetry in the old ornate and imitative style, and looking back to Yejong's reign as a period of past glory. This was accompanied, at an uncertain date, by a revision of the examination system that once again placed first priority on poetic composition.[23]

We should perhaps qualify this view of a resurgent T'ang style by noting that it was during the period of military rule that the Korean literati first came to admire and pattern their poetry after that of Su Shih (Su Tung-p'o), the great Ancient Style advocate of the Northern Sung. This may not be as contradictory as it seems, since it was Su's poetry, not his Ancient Style prose, that the military-era literati prized. We also should note that Su was unique among the Northern Sung Ancient Style literati for his commitment to an intellectual style that strove to find an underlying unity in Confucianism, Taoism, and Buddhism.[24]

Ancient Style Learning did not, however, completely vanish during the military era. It was kept alive by a handful of scholar officials such as Pak Insŏk (1143–1212), who went into hiding after the 1170 coup and subsisted on the margins of Koryŏ political and social life.[25] After surviving on the periphery for several decades, the Ancient Style eventually reemerged in the mid-thirteenth century among prominent members of the central bureaucracy. As a consequence of the Mongol invasions and the assumption of Ch'oe house leadership by Ch'oe Hang, who lacked the personal prestige and power of his predecessors, many members of the bureaucracy began to anticipate the end of military rule.[26] This change in the political situation seems to have translated into a change in intellectual attitudes as well, as seen in Ch'oe Cha (d. 1260) of the Haeju Ch'oe, a prominent scholar and official of the late military period.

Ch'oe Cha saw himself as successor to a great Korean Confucian tradition. In the preface to his *Pohan chip,* written in 1254, Ch'oe traces the Confucian tradition in Korea back to King Kwangjong's institution of the civil service examination in 958. He then lists men whom he considers famous Koryŏ Confucians from that time down to his own, noting that "Lord Munhŏn Ch'oe Ch'ung brought an upsurge in Confucianism so that our Way flourished in King Munjong's reign" and pointing out the contributions of, among others, the Ancient Style Learning advocate Ch'oe Yak.[27] Ch'oe Cha was, of course, a direct descendent of Ch'oe Ch'ung and Ch'oe Yak.

Ch'oe, who was a great admirer of such stalwarts of the Chinese Ancient Style movement as Han Yü, Liu Tsung-yüan, Ou-yang Hsiu, and Su Shih, looked back on the literary fashion of Yejong's reign with a negative eye.[28] He also displayed a critical attitude toward his contemporaries who devoted themselves to "stanza and verse" (*changgu*, Ch. *chang-chü*), a term used pejoratively for those concerned only with the form of literature.[29] Ch'oe manifested his basic Ancient Style attitude in the opening lines of his preface to the *Pohan chip*:

> "Literature [mun, Ch. *wen*] is the door to the Way; words that go against the Way should not be mixed in. . . . Literature moves the hearts of people and awakens them while manifesting subtle meaning and ultimately leading them back to what is proper. Thus, writing decoratively by imitating others and bragging about the beauty of one's work is something the Confucian steadfastly does not do.[30]

Here we see in Ch'oe Cha an attitude about the nature and role of literature that echoes the insistence of Han Yü and other Chinese Ancient Style advocates that literature should be a "vehicle transmitting the Way" for cultivating and manifesting moral values. This is not to say that Ch'oe Cha's attitudes were typical of those of his peers, or that Ancient Style Learning became dominant in the mid-thirteenth century. Many of Ch'oe Cha's peers, such as Kim Ku (1211–78) of Puryŏng, were renowned for their ornate poetry and parallel prose.[31]

Although Ch'oe Cha's emphasis is still on literary talent, in the main body of his collection he balances his interest in literature with discussions of the political and military achievements of earlier civil-branch officials, as in his depiction of Kang Kam-ch'an's early-twelfth-century victories against Khitan invaders[32] and the glorious political careers of members of the Kyŏngwŏn Yi family.[33] Ch'oe Cha even went so far as to argue that Confucian ministers should be given field command of military operations, citing, among other examples, the success of Kim Pu-sik against the twelfth-century rebels in P'yŏngyang.[34]

Ch'oe Cha also introduced a Confucian critique in his discussion of early Koryŏ objections to Buddhism:

> When T'aejo first founded the dynasty amid continuous fighting, he relied on Ŭmyang and Buddhism. The official Ch'oe Ŭng remonstrated, "In times of chaos, you must cultivate literary virtue [cultural virtue, *mundŏk*] to gain the hearts of the people. Even though a king is facing a time of military exigencies, he must cultivate literary virtue. I have never heard of gaining the hearts of the people by relying on Buddhism and Ŭmyang." The king responded, "How would I not know that? But the mountains and streams of our country are holy and mysterious, and our people live in remote vil-

lages. Thus our people like Buddhas and gods and seek from them good fortune. Now there is ceaseless fighting and there is no security, so people are constantly in fear and know not what to do. I can think only that they are hoping the mysterious aid of the Buddhas and gods and the spirits of the mountains and streams will be effective. How could I use this as the great way of governing the country and gaining the hearts of the people? Once the fighting has stopped and the people are secure, it will be possible to transform customs and realize the beauty of moral suasion."[35]

Although Ch'oe Cha does not appear to have been mounting a direct offensive against Buddhism, his resurrection of Ch'oe Ŭng's opposition to Buddhism and his depiction of T'aejo's lack of trust in the Indian religion as the way to rule the country suggests some degree of resistance to the Buddhist inclinations of the military rulers and presages later Confucian attacks on Buddhism.[36]

Thus Ch'oe Cha revealed himself to be not only a self-aware successor to a Koryŏ Ancient Style Confucian tradition, but also a harbinger of things to come. In apparent anticipation of the demise of military rule, he laid the groundwork for restoration of power to the civil branch of government while foreshadowing the late-fourteenth-century rise of an anti-Buddhist critique.

The trend toward Ancient Style literati learning seems to have continued after the fall of the military regime. In 1280 King Ch'ungnyŏl issued an edict that said, "Confucian scholars now practice only the literature of the examinations, and there is no one who is widely conversant in the classics and histories. Order those men who are conversant in one classic and one history to be teachers at the Royal Confucian Academy."[37] Although the Koryŏsa does not go into the reasoning behind this edict, it is significant that Ch'ungnyŏl's criticism of belles lettres and his call for emphasis on the Confucian classics came several years before the introduction of Ch'eng-Chu Learning to Korea.

It seems quite clear, based on the foregoing evidence, that the Koryŏ intellectual tradition prior to the introduction of Ch'eng-Chu Learning can no longer be seen as a monolithic T'ang belletrist tradition. From the twelfth century on there also existed a significant Ancient Style Learning strain, a strain whose strongest proponents came from powerful civil-official descent groups such as the Haeju Ch'oe and the Kyŏngju Kim.

Ancient Style and Ch'eng-Chu Learning in the Change of Dynasties

Conventional interpretations of the intellectual background to the change of dynasties focus almost exclusively on the late Koryŏ rise of Ch'eng-Chu Learning and on conflict between it and Buddhism. Chŏng To-jŏn tells us, however, that there were several prominent advocates of Ancient Style Learning in the fourteenth century, including Yi Che-hyŏn, Yi Kok, and Yi In-bok.[38] Chŏng's statement is somewhat puzzling, since these men are usually associated with the spread of Ch'eng-Chu Learning in the late Koryŏ.

Let us consider the case of Yi Che-hyŏn. This man, who held high offices throughout the first half of the fourteenth century, was one of the leading advocates of reform. Yi was also a historian and a proponent of Confucian statecraft learning (*kyŏngsehak*). These attributes, seen in the context of Yi's long stay in Yüan China and his association with leading Chinese Ch'eng-Chu Learning scholars, have led a number of historians to assign him a major role in the rise of Ch'eng-Chu Learning in Korea.[39]

Certain aspects of Yi Che-hyŏn's thought do seem to reflect strong Ch'eng-Chu influence. Despite his own considerable poetic achievements, he displayed some hostility to belles lettres. On one occasion Yi told King Ch'ungson that if the king instituted measures to encourage Confucian studies, no true Confucian would discard real learning (*sirhak*) to learn poetry from Buddhist monks.[40] Other evidence of Ch'eng-Chu Learning influences can be found in Yi Che-hyŏn's 1344 praise of the Korean king for cultivating royal virtue by listening to "lectures by wise Confucianists on *The Classic of Filial Piety, The Analects, Mencius, The Great Learning* and *The Doctrine of the Mean* and by learning the way of examining things, extending knowledge, attaining sincerity, and rectifying the heart."[41] Here we see distinct Ch'eng-Chu Learning elements in Yi's stress on the Four Books and the method of self-cultivation through examination of things and extension of knowledge. Yi also seems to have used Ch'eng-Chu ideas to criticize Buddhism. We have already seen his negative attitude toward students' learning poetry from Buddhist monks. Yi makes a more explicit anti-Buddhist argument in his *Ikchae nan'go* (Random Jottings of Yi Che-hyon), where he says that the Buddhist way (*sŏkto*) is not as well ordered as the *i* ("principle," Ch. *li*) of Confucianism.[42] Thus, even though Yi Che-hyŏn did not leave behind any expository writings on Ch'eng-Chu Learning, he does appear to have been an exponent of the school's ideas and values.

The issue, however, is not so clear cut. All of these positions, except for the Ch'eng-Chu method of self-cultivation, also fall within the parameters of Ancient Style Learning, especially Yi's emphasis on statecraft. Furthermore, despite Yi's apparent familiarity with the rudiments of Neo-Confucian metaphysics, as seen in his use of the Confucian concept of principle to criticize Buddhism, his biography in the *Koryŏsa* states that he did not like Nature and

Principle Learning.[43] It seems likely, especially in light of Yi's emphasis on the central government as the primary agent of reform and Chŏng To-jŏn's praise for Yi's contributions to the Korean Ancient Style tradition, that the kind of Confucian learning Yi represented was as closely related to the Ancient Style as it was to Ch'eng-Chu Learning.

All of those cited by Chŏng To-jŏn as leading exponents of Ancient Style Learning in Koryŏ were men whose careers peaked in the mid-fourteenth century. Yi Kok died in 1351, Yi Che-hyŏn retired from active service in 1357, and Yi In-bok, who was among those forced from office by Sin Ton in the late 1360s, died in 1374. It is possible, therefore, that these men, whose thinking combined elements of the old Koryŏ Ancient Style tradition and the new Ch'eng-Chu Learning brought in from Yüan China, represented a transitional phase that prepared the way for the rise of full-blown Ch'eng-Chu Learning in the final years of the fourteenth century.

There is, however, substantial evidence of the persistence of Ancient Style influences into the final decades of the Koryŏ and on into the Chosŏn. These are expressed in attitudes about literature. Yi Saek, for example, was cited by Kwŏn Kŭn as the founder of the School of Principle in Korea and praised for his rejection of belle lettres in favor of cultivation of the "mind and heart."[44] Despite his strong credentials as a scholar of Ch'eng-Chu Learning and his apparent repudiation of the literary arts, however, Yi Saek echoed Su Shih's argument that literature is basic to personal cultivation because Confucian principles are interpreted in the mind expressing itself through literature[45] when he wrote that "the Way of poetry is central to the moral transformation of kings. The human mind is revealed therein," and went on to say that "poetry shapes human nature and emotions."[46]

Yi Saek, of course, was a leader of those who opposed Yi Sŏng-gye's overthrow of the Koryŏ, and he held no office after the founding of the Chosŏn. It is possible, therefore, that his ideas were not typical of those who served the new dynasty. But important officials of the early Chosŏn, including men who were at least nominally Nature and Principle scholars, continued to express ideas about the literary arts that seem to reflect Ancient Style Learning influences. Ha Yun, a prominent scholar-official of the early Chosŏn who had studied, along with Kwŏn Kŭn and Chŏng Mong-ju, under Yi Saek, wrote in the early fifteenth century,

Poetry originates in the principle of heaven and human ethics and extends to governance, moral suasion, and customs. It reaches from the music and lyrics of the court on high to the songs of the streets and alleys below. Poetry makes it possible to manifest the good mind in one's emotions and to discipline the indolent spirit.[47]

Here we see a prominent political and intellectual figure of the early years of the new dynasty whose ideas were informed by an Ancient Style insistence on literature as the vehicle for the Way given an apparent Ch'eng-Chu Learning twist by reference to the principle of heaven. The impression one gets from these statements is that the thinking of the leading intellectual lights of the late fourteenth and early fifteenth centuries was not pure or orthodox Ch'eng-Chu Learning, but a combination of Ancient Style and Ch'eng-Chu elements.

This admixture of Ancient Style and Ch'eng-Chu Learning is indicated in comments from other early Chosŏn thinkers on both sides of the split between the meritorious elite and the rusticated literati in the second half of the fifteenth century, a split that is usually seen as a struggle between capital-based practitioners of belles lettres and locally based advocates of orthodox Ch'eng-Chu Learning. Consider the following lament by Kim Chong-jik (1431–92), a famed stalwart of the rusticated literati group:

People say that literati proficient in the study of the classics [*kyŏngsul,* Ch. *ching-shu*] are inferior in the practice of literature and literati proficient in the practice of literature are ignorant in the study of the classics, but I don't see it that way. The practice of literature derives from the study of the classics and the study of the classics forms the roots of the practice of literature. In the case of grass and trees, without roots how could their branches and leaves grow and flourish, and how could their flowers and fruit attain beauty? *The Book of Songs, The Book of History,* [and the other books in] the Six Classics are all classical learning, and the writing in the Six Classics is the practice of literature. If I can look for principle through literature, then I can observe it closely and achieve it without undue effort. If literature and principle are fused in my chest, then I can speak or write poetry and all is achieved without any effort on my part. Since antiquity, all who have lamented the state of the practice of literature and have passed it on to later generations have been thus.

Now, however, people see the study of classics as nothing more than the reciting of passages and textual exegesis and regard the practice of literature as nothing more than turning nice phrases in an ornate manner. How can reciting passages and textual exegesis be the way of governing heaven and earth, and how can turning nice phrases in an ornate manner be part of Nature and Principle Learning and morality? This will eventually lead to the separation of the study of classics and the practice of literature and the two will not be used together. This is truly a shallow view.[48]

Kim Chong-jik's deprecation of ornate literature and textual exegesis seems to be a clear attack on the old T'ang style.[49] Although Kim Chong-jik is generally considered a major figure in the development of orthodox Ch'eng-Chu Learning in Korea and does make reference to Nature and Principle Learning, his reasoning here seems to be informed less by a Ch'eng-Chu Learning distinction between study of the classics and literary endeavor than by an Ancient Style Learning view of literature's important role in governance and in forming public values. Our sense of Kim Chong-jik as an Ancient Style Learning thinker is strengthened by another statement he made in a 1464 memorial to King Sejo that the various learnings outside of poetry and history were not for Confucians.[50]

Cho Tong-il depicts the view of literature held by the meritorious elite opponents of Kim Chong-jik's rusticated literati group as emphasizing decorative aspects and as "rejecting the contention that literature had to be the learning of the Way, that only the literature of the classics had true value."[51] This would seem to suggest strong affinities between the learning of the meritorious elite and the old T'ang belletrist tradition.

The picture is not that simple, however. Let us consider the case of Yang Sŏng-ji (1412–82), a prominent member of the meritorious elite group and target of much rusticated literati criticism. In 1472 Yang presented a memorial that called for a revision in the higher civil-service examination to replace the first-stage test on the classics with a test on the writings of Han Yü, Liu Tsung-yüan, and Su Shih along with such histories as Ssu-ma Kuang's *Tzu-chih t'ung-chien* (Comprehensive mirror for aid in government), Kim Pu-sik's *Samguk sagi,* and the *Koryŏsa.*[52] Furthermore, Yang's writings in *Nuljae chip* (Collected works of Yang Sŏng-ji) reflect more than a passing familiarity with Ch'eng-Chu Learning; in fact, he was eulogized by Kim An-guk in the early sixteenth century as a great follower of Ch'eng-Chu Learning who "abided in reverence and fathomed principle" (*kŏgyŏng kungni,* Ch. *chü-ching ch'iung-li*).[53]

This of course raises fundamental questions about the extent of fundamental intellectual differences between the rusticated literati and meritorious elite groups,[54] but more relevant to our purposes here, it indicates that at least as late as the second half of the fifteenth century, prominent Korean Confucian thinkers on both sides of the meritorious elite–rusticated literati split continued to display an intellectual stance that combined aspects of Ch'eng-Chu Learning with Ancient Style attitudes about the importance of literature as the vehicle of the Way.

Vestiges of T'ang Style in the Early Chosŏn Period

We should not interpret the preeminence of the mixed Ancient Style–Ch'eng-Chu Learning to mean that the old T'ang belletrist style disappeared completely after the founding of the Chosŏn dynasty. There is ample evidence of the persistence of belletrist tendencies well into the fifteenth century. Survival of the ornate literary style was closely related to the persistence of Buddhist beliefs and practices not only among both the new royal family, as is widely known, but also among many of the *yangban* who staffed the new dynasty's bureaucracy.

Opposition to Buddhism was a feature of Chinese Confucian thought since the time of Han Yŭ and the rise of the Ancient Style movement, but it never reached the fevered pitch that it did in Korea. Anti-Buddhist activism was a main theme of late-fourteenth-century Korean politics. Scholar-officials such as Chŏng To-jŏn criticized Buddhism on both philosophical and ethical grounds, and the new dynasty pursued policies restricting Buddhists and Buddhist institutions. As a result, many historians describe early Chosŏn intellectual and cultural policy in such terms as "rejecting Buddhism and elevating Confucianism" (*ch'ŏkpul sungyu*).

Anti-Buddhist fervor notwithstanding, the change of dynasties did not bring the immediate demise of Buddhism. Several early Chosŏn kings, including T'aejo, Sejong, and Sejo, were devout believers in Buddhism, and many of the Buddhist controversies of the late fourteenth century persisted well into the fifteenth. Historians have long recognized this, but have generally viewed the controversy in terms of a struggle between Confucian *yangban* and the Buddhist royal family,[55] despite early studies by scholars such as Yi Sang-baek and Han Woo-keun demonstrating that the restrictive Buddhist policies of the early Chosŏn were more reflective of the state's financial concerns than of deeply felt philosophical opposition to Buddhism.[56] The Buddhist controversy of the early Chosŏn was complex and deeply rooted in social as well as ideological issues.

Before we can deal meaningfully with the question of the survival of Buddhism after 1392, we must establish an understanding of the position of

Buddhism in the late Koryŏ. Supporters of conventional views of the Koryŏ as a Buddhist society cite as evidence the importance of presumably Buddhist rituals such as the P'algwan festival[57] and the Yŏndŭng festival and the close ties between the Koryŏ royal family and Buddhism. Although this view has been widely accepted for several decades, it has not been backed up by detailed studies of the links between Buddhism and the sociopolitical elites of the late Koryŏ. Recently scholars such as Hŏ Hŭng-sik have provided concrete studies on how Buddhist values and family rituals informed and supported the organization of the Koryŏ family and society in general, but even these efforts do not deal specifically with the relationship between Buddhism and the great official descent groups of the late Koryŏ.[58]

A more recent study clarifies the institutional ties between Buddhism and late Koryŏ *yangban* and shows how Buddhism was fully integrated into Koryŏ *yangban* political, social, and religious life. Political life was closely linked to Buddhism through participation in Buddhist ceremonies such as the Yŏndŭng festival and through composition of memorial stelae for prominent Confucian members of the late Koryŏ bureaucracy such as Yi Saek and even Chŏng To-jŏn, for temple construction projects, and for deceased Buddhist monks. It was also common social practice for central *yangban,* including such prominent Confucians as Kwŏn Pu of the Andong Kwŏn, to dedicate one or more sons to the clergy and for their secularly oriented sons to study for the government service examinations under Buddhist monks, many of whom were famed for their skill in composing poetry. Religious belief in Buddhism also seems to have been widespread among the *yangban,* as can be seen in statements of belief contained in inscriptions on bells and other items donated to temples in hopes of gaining the blessings of the Buddha.[59] Buddhism was thus deeply rooted in everyday *yangban* life in the late Koryŏ.

Given the wholesale survival of the late Koryŏ *yangban* into the early Chosŏn, it should come as no surprise that Buddhism remained an important part of early Chosŏn elite life. Numerous historians have pointed out the private devotion to Buddhism of Kings T'aejo and Sejong, not to mention the openly pro-Buddhist policies of King Sejo. Edward Wagner's discussion of the political and intellectual tensions leading up to the literati purges of the early sixteenth century shows that the royal family's devotion to Buddhism remained an important issue at least until the end of the fifteenth century, fully one hundred years after the establishment of the Chosŏn.[60] But there is also evidence to show, as Han Woo-keun has argued,[61] that Buddhist beliefs and practices were still followed by members of the central *yangban* class.[62]

There is little doubt that Buddhism lost much of its potential to exert political influence in the new dynasty. Symbolic of this was the discontinuance of the Buddhist preceptorships that had been so prominent in the Koryŏ period. Although T'aejo appointed both a state preceptor, Chogu, and a royal preceptor, Chach'o, their deaths, in 1395 and 1405 respectively, are thought to have marked the end of Buddhist preceptorship in Korea.[63]

This did not mean, however, that Buddhism had lost all royal favor after T'aejo's departure from the scene. Despite the almost universally accepted view of T'aejong as a vigorously pro-Confucian, anti-Buddhist ruler, Yi Sang-baek has shown that T'aejong's motivation for pursuing an anti-Buddhist policy was as much financial as ideological and that T'aejong in fact turned to Buddhism for religious solace in his middle and later years.[64] Kings Sejong and Sejo were, as is well known, devout believers in Buddhism. But their faith, unlike T'aejong's, was given public political expression as Buddhist monks were brought into the palace and given high honors. The monk Sinmi, for example, was called into the palace to conduct Buddhist services when Sejong fell ill in 1449.[65] The next year Sinmi was give the extraordinary title "general commissioner of meditational and scholastic orders" (Sŏn Kyo chong to ch'ongsŏp) and "Hyegak *chonja.*"[66] The title *chonja,* or "venerable," had earlier been used in lieu of "state preceptor" to reflect Koryŏ subservience to the Mongols. Its reappearance at this time, when other offices and institutions had been renamed to reflect the inferior status of the Chosŏn dynasty vis-à-vis the Ming, suggests a resumption, however temporary, of the old practice of appointing Buddhist preceptors. Two months later Sinmi's title was changed from "Hyegak venerable" to "Hyegak religious preceptor" (*chongsa*).[67] We do not know how much political influence Sinmi wielded, but the histories tell that his brother Kim Su-on was given preferential treatment because of Sinmi's special relationship with the king.[68] In toto, the evidence indicates that Buddhism still enjoyed a surprising degree of royal favor and at least some potential for political influence more than a half century after the change of dynasties.

Composition by high-ranking officials of Buddhist memorial stelae also persisted into the new dynasty. Although early Chosŏn literary collections contain far fewer Buddhist memorial inscriptions than do those from the late Koryŏ, such writings do exist. Michael Kalton has noted that the famed Confucian Kwŏn Kŭn wrote many Buddhist-related commemorations and prayers in the years after 1392.[69] Another early Chosŏn official who wrote large numbers of Buddhist memorial inscriptions was Kim Su-on, who held high offices during the mid-fifteenth century. His *Sigu chip* (collected works of Kim Su-on) contains no fewer than fifteen Buddhist-related inscriptions, most of which describe royal support for construction or refurbishment of temples.

The Koryŏ *yangban* custom of sending sons to the clergy also seems to have continued into the early Chosŏn. Such sources as the *Andong Kwŏn-ssi songhwa po* (Andong Kwŏn genealogy), literary collections, and the *Veritable Records* identify a number of prominent monks as brothers of high-ranking officials. Kwŏn Kŭn, perhaps the most prominent Confucian scholar of the first decades of the Chosŏn, had an elder brother, Isa, who was a monk supervisor,[70] and Yun So-jong, a Confucian who played an important polit-ical role in the change of dynasties, also had a brother in the Buddhist clergy.[71] Both Kwŏn Kŭn's and Yun So-jong's brothers undoubtedly joined the clergy prior to the fall of the Koryŏ, but there are other examples of men who almost certainly committed themselves to monastic life after 1392. For instance, the monk Tokso, who came to the capital to conduct Buddhist services for a royal prince in 1450, was an elder brother of Inspector General (Taesahŏn) An Wan-gyŏng of Kwangju.[72] The age of neither Tokso nor An Wan-gyŏng is known, but An Wan-gyŏng passed the higher civil service examination in 1423, thirty-one years after the change of dynasties. Thus even if Tokso or An Wan-gyŏng were born before 1392, surely both came of age after the estab-lishment of Chosŏn. We do not know when Sinmi, the highly honored monk who served both Sejong and Sejo, was born, but his younger brother Kim Su-on was born in 1409, seventeen years after the establishment of the Chosŏn, making it very unlikely that Sinmi was born or had committed him-self to the clergy before 1392. Thus even though shifting philosophical loy-alties and curtailment of Buddhist institutional power under King T'aejong may have led some *yangban* families to abandon the custom of devoting sons to the clergy, other families appear to have continued the tradition well into the fifteenth century.

There is other evidence that religious belief in Buddhism was widespread among the early Chosŏn *yangban*. The *Veritable Records* tell us that in the seventh month of 1393, one year after the establishment of the Chosŏn, "the royal preceptor Chach'o was allowed to reside at Kwangmyŏngsa [temple]. Over one hundred men and women from within the walls [of the capital city] came each day to listen to Chach'o lecture."[73] Writing several decades later, Sŏng Hyŏn (1439–1504) told in his *Yongjae ch'onghwa* (Collected tales) of scholar-officials engaging in Buddhist rituals (*chae*) to gain earthly blessings.[74] Sŏng also noted somewhat bemusedly that the rusticated literati did not object to the con-secration of Buddhist bones by students of the Royal Confucian Academy.[75]

The survival of Buddhist belief and practice into the early Chosŏn was, of course, accompanied by continued anti-Buddhist agitation. The reigns of T'aejo, Chŏngjong, and T'aejong are well known for anti-Buddhist activities that climaxed in T'aejong's 1406 measures and continued throughout the early Chosŏn. In 1424, for example, students of the Royal Confucian Academy outlined Buddhist abuses and called for disestablishment of Buddhist temples and discontinuance of Buddhist rites.[76] Such anti-Buddhist agitation grew more frequent in the waning years of King Sejong's reign, as in 1446 when the State Council discussed the impropriety of holding Buddhist rites in the palace[77] and in 1448 when students at the Royal Confucian Academy went on strike in opposition to construction of a Buddhist shrine (*puldang*) in the palace.[78] These attacks, however, were focused not on *yangban* religious beliefs and practices, but on relations between Buddhism and the court. That these same themes had dominated the anti-Buddhist polemics of the late Koryŏ suggests that fear of Buddhist political influence was the primary issue.

We cannot assume, however, that even these attacks were launched by men who were consistently anti-Buddhist. Kwŏn Kŭn's attitude, for example, fluctuated between harsh anti-Buddhist criticism and positive confirmation of distinctively Buddhist values. Michael Kalton attributes Kwŏn's inconsistent attitude and apparent limited acceptance of Buddhism to both the cultural environment of the late fourteenth and early fifteenth centuries, when Buddhism was still widely accepted in Korea, and Kwŏn's own family situation, with his elder brother being a high-ranking monk.[79] Thus, what appears at first glance to be a clear disjunction between Confucianism and Buddhism turns out on closer inspection to be a very murky and complex situation where political and social considerations condition shifting ideological positions.

There is evidence linking survival of Buddhist practices and beliefs to persistence of the T'ang belletrist tradition. We know that the old Koryŏ *yangban* custom of having children study under Buddhist monks continued into the early Chosŏn. Kwŏn Kŭn, for example, had his sons educated by a monk,[80] and Yi Sŏngmu tells us that "King T'aejong intended to educate his eldest son, Prince Yangnyŏng, under the tutelage of a venerable monk at a remote mountain in accordance with the old Koryŏ tradition."[81] T'aejong, one of the most autocratically minded rulers in Korean history, may have been motivated less by religious commitment than by a desire to keep his heir out of the clutches of the central bureaucracy. Still, it is significant that it was a Buddhist monk to whom he wished to send the crown prince. Further evidence of the persistence of this custom comes over a quarter of a century later, in 1438, when the dynasty found it necessary to issue an edict ordering two temples, Hŭngch'ŏnsa and Hŭngdŏksa, to quit teaching children.[82] The edict does not say who studied there, but since both temples were located in the capital city, it almost certainly was the children of the central *yangban*.

The sources do not specify what those young men learned from the monks, but it seems probable that it was the poetic arts. Evidence of this dates from the fourth month of 1443, when Sejong ordered the Hall of Worthies (Chiphyŏnjŏn) to edit commentaries on the poetry of Tu Fu, the famed eighth-century T'ang master of *shih* poetry, for distribution throughout the capital and the provinces.[83] A few days later Manu, the abbot of Hoeamsa (near the old Koryŏ capital) was moved to Hŭngch'ŏnsa (in the new capital) and given a third-rank stipend. This was done so that Manu, who was well-versed in poetry, could be consulted regarding the commentaries on Tu Fu.[84]

The role of Buddhist monks as writers and teachers of poetry in the early Chosŏn was related to the survival of the old T'ang syncretic style, which sought to unify differing teachings through the composition of poetry. The aforementioned Kim Su-on provides the clearest example. Kim passed the higher government-service examination in 1441 and held a number of academic posts in the Royal Confucian Academy before ultimately rising to a senior first-grade post and receiving the noble title Lord of Yŏngsan (Yŏngsan Puwŏn Kun) under King Sŏngjong. Kim Su-on was educated in the Confucian classics and had more than a passing familiarity with Ch'eng-Chu notions of principle (*i*, Ch. *li*),[85] but he was also a devout believer in Buddhism. His syncretic intellectual attitude is revealed in the following statement:

> No one has ever achieved the beauty of the way of governance without upholding the benevolence [*in*, Ch. *jen*] and righteousness [*ŭi*, Ch. *i*] of Confucianism; but no one has ever clearly manifested the source of governance without basing himself in the clear mind [*ch'ŏngjŏng*] of Buddhism. . . .
> In striving for the learning of governance of the emperors and kings, one can see that Buddhism is the most honored of the Three Teachings and the master of all virtue.[86]

It is possible, of course, that Kim Su-on was an isolated example who did not represent the attitudes of a significant portion of early Chosŏn *yangban*. But taken within the context of evidence of widespread Buddhist religious beliefs among *yangban* and the continuing educational and political importance of Buddhist monks, the rise to prominence of a man such as Kim Su-on suggests that old T'ang style syncretism and belletrism remained a significant, if somewhat diminished, part of Chosŏn intellectual life at least until the second half of the fifteenth century.

STRUGGLES OVER THE EXAMINATION SYSTEM

We have already seen how the rise of Ancient Style Learning in the twelfth century was accompanied by efforts to revise the government-service examination system. Peter Bol argues that in Sung China the political fight for ideological supremacy among three groups—legalist Confucians (Wang An-shih, Ssu-ma Kuang), literary Confucians (Ou-yang Hsiu, Su Shih), and moralist Confucians (the Ch'eng-Chu school)—was waged primarily in struggles over the contents of civil-service examinations.[87] Such struggles also were a major feature of the late Koryŏ–early Chosŏn period. In Korea, however, the main battle was waged between an Ancient Style–Ch'eng-Chu Learning group and T'ang belletrists.

The Examinations in the Late Koryŏ

Strife over the examination system began in the early decades of the fourteenth century with a reaction against the dominance of the T'ang literary style. This was manifested in Yi Che-hyŏn's 1320 reform of the examination system, which, in the terse wording of the *Koryŏsa,* "abolished poetry and rhyme-prose and used policy treatises."[88] This change came about nearly thirty-five years after An Hyang's supposed introduction of Ch'eng-Chu Learning to Korea and just seven years after the establishment in Yüan China of an examination system based on Chu Hsi's commentaries on the Four Books. These circumstances would seem to suggest that Ch'eng-Chu Learning influences were at work, but the sources make no mention of Chu Hsi's commentaries or the Yüan system in connection with this reform. Furthermore, the key role played by Yi Che-hyŏn, the emphasis on policy treatises, and the absence of testing on the Four Books suggest that this was essentially an Ancient Style–inspired reform.

It seems certain, despite the lack of mention of controversy in the sources, that there was substantial belletrist resistance to this change. This was reflected in a modification, seven years later, that required candidates to recite one hundred poems of regulated verse (a new T'ang poetic form) and to be familiar with the tones and rhyming of *The Lesser Learning (Sohak,* Ch. *Hsiao-hsüeh)* before sitting for the examinations.[89] The addition of belletrist regulated poetry and *The Lesser Learning,* a text much stressed by the Ch'eng-Chu school, to the primary focus on policy treatises suggests a compromise between the old T'ang style and the Ch'eng-Chu Learning that was then spreading in certain *yangban* circles.

Such apparent gains notwithstanding, advocates of the T'ang style in Korea lost further ground with a 1344 revision of the examination system while Prime Minister Yi Che-hyŏn was actively pushing for reform. The new system, implemented by Yi Che-hyŏn's disciple Pak Ch'ung-jwa and his kinsman Yi Ch'ŏn, specified that candidates would be tested on the Six Classics and the Four Books in the first session, rhyme-prose composed in the Ancient Style in the second, and policy treatises in the third. We have no way of knowing whether this reform repealed the stipulation that prospective candidates first memorize regulated verse—although this seems likely—but the new requirements seem to reflect a combination of Ancient Style and Ch'eng-Chu Learning.

The Ancient Style–Ch'eng-Chu Learning advocates may have won the 1344 battle, but the war was not yet over. If anything, the struggle over the place and type of literature in the examination system was just beginning. The belletrists mounted a counterattack in 1362, when poetry and rhyme-prose were reinstated by Hong Ŏn-bak of the powerful Namyang Hong family.[90] In 1367 another memorial urged adoption of the Ch'eng-Chu Learning–based Yüan examination system. This proposal was enacted two years later when the dynasty implemented the Yüan system, with Yi In-bok (an Ancient Style practitioner) and Yi Saek (a noted Ch'eng-Chu Learning advocate with strong Ancient Style tendencies) serving as examiners. Just seven years later, in 1376, however, the dynasty reversed itself and once again reinstated poetry under examiner Hong Chung-sŏn, who was the nephew of Hong Ŏn-bak. In 1386 the emphasis shifted back to policy treatises under head examiner Yi Saek, before the final Koryŏ revision in 1388, when Yi Sŏng-gye's group restored the Yüan-style system of 1369.[91]

Some sense of the intensity of this struggle is conveyed by the comments of Yi Sung-in, a close associate of Yi Saek. Upon his return from several years in exile in 1386, the year Yi Saek changed the examination topics from poetry and rhyme-prose to policy treatises, Yi Sung-in lamented,

> When I was an instructor at the Royal Confucian Academy along with Chŏng Mong-ju, Ch'oe Ŏn-bu, and Pak Cha-hŏ we had so many students that the buildings overflowed. . . . Upon returning to the academy after spending three years in the countryside and becoming an instructor again along with Ch'oe Ŏn-bu and Pak Cha-hŏ. . . . I went to the academy but found there were no students. When I reported this to Pak Cha-hŏ, he laughed and told me that the students have all abandoned the study of the classics [kyŏnghak] for belles lettres.[92]

On this occasion at least, change in the examination system was accompanied by a radical shift in state support from one style of learning to another.

Examinations in the Early Chosŏn

The 1388 revision of the examinations in favor of a Yüan style system included elimination of poetry. This policy was reaffirmed in Yi Sŏng-gye's 1392 coronation edict, which formally abolished the literary licentiate examination (*chinsa kwa*), but the abolishment was neither immediate nor final. Despite the July 1392 pronouncement, the literary licentiate examination was held once more in late 1392 before being discontinued in 1393. It was reinstituted in 1435 and abolished again in 1437, only to be revived permanently in 1452.[93]

Early Chosŏn controversy over belles lettres was not limited to the literary licentiate examination. Whereas in the Koryŏ the literary licentiate and classic licentiate examinations were the highest tests, the Yüan style system favored by the founders of the Chosŏn relegated those tests to the status of qualifying examinations and added a final examination, the "higher civil-service examination" (*mun kwa*). Controversy over the contents of this examination focused on the issue of whether the first-stage test on the classics should be oral or written, with more orthodox Ch'eng-Chu Learning advocates arguing for oral examinations on the grounds that written ones measured only literary skill and could not plumb the depths of the candidates' moral character. Although King T'aejo's coronation edict called for the first-stage test to be oral, that given in 1393 was written. In 1395 the first stage was oral, but in 1407, at the urging of Kwŏn Kŭn, the written test was reinstituted. This oral-versus-written–test issue continued to be an item of controversy throughout the first half of the fifteenth century. The oral test was implemented in 1417, written in 1425, oral in 1442, and written again in 1450 before the oral test was finally made permanent in 1453.[94]

Evidence such as the 1340 remarks of Hŏ Cho (1369–1439)—a student of Kwŏn Kŭn and a strong proponent of Ch'eng-Chu Learning who opposed the use of a written test in the first stage of the higher civil-service examination on the grounds that it would result in neglect of the classics and "lead to the composition of belles lettres by Confucians"[95]—suggests that the early Chosŏn controversies over the examination system were indeed reflections of a struggle between Ancient Learning–Ch'eng-Chu Learning Confucians and T'ang belletrists. That the great T'ang stylist Kim Su-on passed the higher government-service examination in 1341, a year when candidates took the written test in the first stage, indicates that Hŏ Cho's concerns were not without foundation. The permanent abolition of the first-stage written test in 1453 appears to have been a major turning point in favor of the Ancient Style–Ch'eng-Chu Learning group.

If proponents of a mixed Ancient Style–Ch'eng-Chu Learning won a signal victory in 1453, why did rusticated literati make belles lettres a major issue in their early sixteenth-century struggle against the meritorious elite? We have already seen that the rusticated literati and meritorious elite of the mid-fifteenth century shared similar ideas about the role of literature. I suspect that by the beginning of the sixteenth century, Kim Chong-jik's disciples, who sought to do away with any form of written examination and implement instead a "recommendation examination" (*hyŏllyang kwa*), which placed primary emphasis on assessments of the candidates' moral qualities and behavior, had moved away from Kim's eclectic approach to one based more purely on Ch'eng-Chu Learning that relegated poetry to the status of a frivolous pastime. That would have made them contemptuous of the Ancient Style approach to literary endeavor favored by the meritorious elite and perhaps led them to try to paint the meritorious elite with the same brush used to discredit T'ang belletrists. This, however, was a sixteenth-century development; in the fifteenth century, a combined Ancient Style–Ch'eng-Chu Learning approach seems to have found favor with a majority of the politically active *yangban*.[96]

CONFUCIANISM AND REFORM

Why did a mixed Ancient Style–Ch'eng-Chu Learning approach became the prevalent intellectual trend during the fourteenth and fifteenth centuries? Some scholars, focusing on metaphysics, argue that the apparent inconsistencies in late Koryŏ and early Chosŏn Ch'eng–Chu Learning reflected immaturity in Korean understanding of the philosophical dimension of Ch'eng-Chu Learning.[97] According to this interpretation, Koreans did not really master Ch'eng-Chu Learning until the mid-sixteenth century, when men such as Ki Tae-sŭng, Yi Hwang, and Yi I began to develop a discourse on Nature and Principle metaphysics. But it seems improbable, especially in light of Kwŏn Kŭn's late fourteenth-century exposition of Neo-Confucian metaphysics in the *Iphak tosŏl* (Illustrated treatises for the beginner), that it took Koreans over 250 years to achieve an understanding of Ch'eng-Chu Learning sufficient to engage in debates on Nature and Principle metaphysics.

Along the same lines, one could argue that the presence of Ancient Style attitudes toward the nature and role of literature simply represent a vestigial

survival, in the transition to Ch'eng-Chu Learning, of earlier intellectual traditions. The problem with this argument is that Ancient Learning influences
among Korean *yangban* were not limited to ideas about literature. The *yangban* reformers of the fourteenth and fifteenth centuries also displayed a political attitude closer to that of Ancient Style Learning than to that of Ch'eng-Chu
Learning.

The Ancient Style scholar-officials of the Northern Sung were, as Peter Bol
has noted, committed to reforming society through a powerful and activist
central government.[98] In contrast, the Southern Sung Tao Hsüeh thinkers were
not interested in "increasing the power of government to transform society
from above," but rather in how society on the local level could be transformed
through such institutions of self-governance as the community compact.[99]

The reformers of the Koryŏ-Chosŏn transition showed virtually no interest in these local institutions. *Yangban* concern with typical Ch'eng-Chu
Learning local programs did not develop until the sixteenth century, over a
century after the establishment of the Chosŏn dynasty. On the contrary, the
founders of the Chosŏn were primarily interested in creating a more efficient
central government and in expanding its control over the countryside.

The blueprint for political revitalization used by the early Chosŏn reformers was, as has been detailed by Chai-sik Chung,[100] *The Rites of Chou* (Chou-
li), a text that is often cited as part of the Neo-Confucian canon. In reality,
however, Ch'eng-Chu Confucians had a decidedly ambiguous attitude toward
The Rites of Chou. While *The Rites of Chou* was accepted, along with *The
Book of Rites* (Li-Chi) and *The Ceremonial Rites* (I-li), as one of the three ritual classics (*san-li*), *The Rites of Chou* was more than a handbook of ritual;
it also purported to be a description of the political institutions of the Chou
dynasty (1134–250 B.C.E.). The model it presented of a comparatively powerful and intrusive central state was used by a variety of Sung reformers, including Ou-yang Hsiu and Wang An-shih of the Northern Sung and Ch'en Liang
of the Southern Sung, to justify their program for a more activist and regulatory state.[101] Although Chu Hsi ruled in favor of *The Rites of Chou* in the
controversy over the authenticity of the text and used *The Rites of Chou* in
his objections to the growing trend toward autocracy, arguing that greater
authority be given to the high ministers,[102] the main thrust of Chu Hsi's teachings emphasized that the creation of a harmonious society depended on moral-
istic self-cultivation and not on the kind of regulatory political institutions
prescribed by *The Rites of Chou* and favored by Northern Sung Ancient Style
activists. Neo-Confucian discomfort with *The Rites of Chou* has also been
noted by Frederic Wakeman, who states that although the statist ideal of *The*

Rites of Chou inspired Han and Sung reformers to enhance the regulatory powers of the state, it was usually disliked by Confucians, who "preferred a more relaxed laissez-faire policy of government noninterference in the natural workings of society."[103]

In his study of Chŏng To-jŏn's political thought, Chai-sik Chung relates that Chŏng favored the expansion of the powers of various bureaucratic figures and agencies—including the prime minister, the censorate, the central military command, the inspectors, and the local magistrates—and concludes that Chŏng showed a preference for the outer realm of political institutions over the moral transformation of the human mind in achieving a harmonious society. Chung suggests that this aspect of Chŏng's thinking may be due to the influences of Legalist thought or the statecraft thinkers of the Eastern Chekiang school of the Southern Sung.[104] It does not seem very useful to attribute Chŏng To-jŏn's statism to Legalist influences, since much Legalist thinking had been incorporated into Confucian discourse on the state since Han times. Although Chung's reference to the Eastern Chekiang school of the Southern Sung—by which I assume he means the utilitarian, or merit-and-profit, school of Ch'en Liang—is intriguing, I have been unable to find any evidence of interest in, or even mention of, the merit-and-profit school among late Koryŏ–early Chosŏn literati. On the other hand, as Chai-sik Chung himself notes, Chŏng was very much aware of and drew inspiration from such Northern Sung reformers as Wang An-shih. Based on this, and on what we have seen about the pervasiveness of Ancient Style attitudes in the early Chosŏn, it is difficult to avoid the conclusion that the centralizing political reforms of the early Chosŏn were very much informed by an Ancient Style emphasis on a strong activist state as the means for attaining social harmony. A prime example of this is found in Martina Deuchler's study of how the reformers relied on the central government's legislative authority, rather than on individual self-cultivation or autonomous local associations, in their effort to remake Korean society along Confucian lines.[105]

SUMMATION

How, then, do we assess the role of a revitalized Confucian discourse in the Koryŏ-Chosŏn change of dynasties? Did the spread of Ch'eng-Chu Learning among late Koryŏ *yangban* create a revolutionary mindset, a felt need to overthrow the Koryŏ dynasty in order to enact a program to reorganize politics and society according to Confucian principles? Or was the Confucian learning of the Koryŏ-Chosŏn transition nothing more than the ideological expression of *yangban* social interests? The best answer, it seems to me, is that it was a bit of both.

In his analysis of the roles of cultural and religious systems in the political processes of historical bureaucratic societies, S. N. Eisenstadt emphasizes the autonomy of cultural and religious elites and argues that their values and orientations usually transcended any one group or regime and that their support for a ruler was not automatic but conditional on the ruler's acceptance and support of their values and behaviors. He further argues that the development among such elites of universalistic value orientations and activist principles could result in a tendency to try to remake society in the "proper" way.[106]

With regard to the Koryŏ-Chosŏn change of dynasties, therefore, it would appear—as Martina Deuchler argues—that the spread of Ch'eng-Chu Learning produced a universalistic and activist orientation among certain *yangban* who sought to remake society according to the Ch'eng-Chu vision.[107] These activists were alienated by the late Koryŏ kings' patronage of Buddhism and gave their support to Yi Sŏng-gye in order to gain a platform from which they could pursue their program of radical reform.

This approach, with its emphasis on the autonomy of cultural and religious systems, seems particularly appropriate for the Korean case, since the system in question, Ch'eng-Chu Learning, orginated outside Korea and came to the peninsula with added prestige as Yüan-sanctioned imperial orthodoxy. The Yüan adoption of Ch'eng-Chu Learning not only provided it with elevated status over other varieties of literati learning, but it may have even contributed to the activist nature of Ch'eng-Chu Learning, because the Mongols, as William Theodore de Bary has noted, were primarily interested in the universalistic aspects of Neo-Confucian values.[108]

However much Ch'eng-Chu Learning aspirations to universality may have inspired the fourteenth-century *yangban* to social and political activism, it is clear that the kind of Confucian learning favored by the founders of the Chosŏn dynasty had little to do with the Ch'eng-Chu program of social reconstruction through individual self-cultivation and locally autonomous institutions. How, then, if it was a commitment to the universalistic aspects of Ch'eng-Chu Learning that led the *yangban* to turn away from the Koryŏ, are we to explain this deviance from fundamental Ch'eng-Chu Learning values?

The problem with applying the kind of Weberian approach advocated by Eisenstadt to this problem is that Eisenstadt, who emphasizes a high degree of interdependence among social, economic, and political systems, treats cultural and religious systems as independent variables. That is, he provides no analysis of how values and orientations are formed or how their acceptance is conditioned by the interests of social groups. Indeed, he sees religious and cultural elites as professionals and intelligentsia who are not embedded in any particular ascriptive social collectivity.[109] In Korea, however, Confucian learning was dominated by a hereditary social group, the *yangban*. As James Palais has pointed out, the Korean *yangban* found strong support for their aristocratic traditions in Confucianism's emphasis on bloodlines and genealogies.[110] It would seem, therefore, that while the values of the Confucian reformers of 1392 may have transcended the interests of the old regime, they did not transcend those of the *yangban* social group to which the reformers belonged. Socially, those interests included preservation of *yangban* hereditary privilege, and politically, strengthening of the central bureaucratic regime with which the *yangban* identified themselves.

Of course, the fourteenth- and fifteenth-century *yangban* emphasis on the central government can perhaps be seen less as the consequence of Ancient Style influences than as a reflection of the urgent need for political and social reform that directed the attention of Ch'eng-Chu Learning–inspired reformers away from issues of Nature and Principle metaphysics and local institutions of self-governance. This does not, however, explain the other main Ancient Style aspect of their thinking, their emphasis on literature as the vehicle of the Way, nor does it explain their great admiration for Su Shih, the archenemy of the Ch'eng-Chu school.[111]

In the final analysis, we must not lose sight of the long historical association between the great *yangban* descent groups and Ancient Style learning, which went all the way back to the early twelfth century and was revitalized by the return of political authority to the *yangban*-dominated civil branch of government in the second half of the thirteenth century. As we have seen in the preceding chapters, nearly all of the men who spearheaded the charge for reform and who dominated the early Chosŏn government were members of the great central *yangban* descent groups. It comes as no surprise, therefore, that these men, whose primary source of status and prestige was the offices they and their forebears held in the dynastic government, found attractive the Ancient Style emphasis on a strong, activist central regime.

Does this mean, then, that the fourteenth- and fifteenth-century reformers' frequent reference to Ch'eng-Chu Learning was nothing more than window dressing designed to provide them with some sort of intellectual legitimacy while they pursued venal purposes of self-aggrandizement? Certainly the fact that Ch'eng Chu Learning had been elevated to the status of state-sponsored orthodoxy during the Yüan dynasty must have given it greater prestige in the eyes the Koreans and lent it a certain credibility as a model for reform. Indeed,

Martina Deuchler has shown that the ideas of Ch'eng-Chu Learning did provide real stimulus toward reform. But, at least in the area of political reform, the application of Ch'eng-Chu Learning was significantly conditioned by a well-established Korean Ancient Style tradition that not only responded to the need to reshape political institutions but also reflected the concrete social and political interests of the *yangban*. It was the emphasis of Ancient Style learning on reforming society through the institutions of the state that provided the impetus and rationale for an activist central government.

7 / Some Final Considerations

Interpretive schemes that have been applied to Korean history, and particularly to the Koryŏ-Chosŏn change of dynasties, have not been well grounded in the source materials. To address the need for documentation, I have presented here an empirically founded depiction of Korean history from the early Koryŏ through the early Chosŏn. This treatment has focused almost exclusively on social and political elites, not as a matter of choice but because of the almost total lack of information on the other social strata that made up the vast majority of the Korean populace.

Although I have borrowed from Eisenstadt's work on historical bureaucratic empires, my purpose has not been to force the Korean experience into yet another alien mold, but rather to use Eisenstadt's study, which is based primarily on non-European, non-"modern" societies, as an alternative to Western European–derived modernizing models of historical interpretation and as a means to compare Korea with other historical political systems. I can only hope that the resulting perspective contributes to my readers' understanding of the Korean experience and provides a point of departure for further studies that will improve and deepen our appreciation of Korea's rich historical heritage.

The following summary considers how my findings are related to interpretive and comparative issues and draws out some of their implications for our understanding of Korean history.

SUMMARY OF FINDINGS

A central theme of Korean history throughout the Koryŏ and early Chosŏn dynasties was the effort to create a centralized bureaucratic polity. This began long before the rise of the Koryŏ. Monarchical states had developed in the Three Kingdoms of Koguryŏ, Paekche, and Silla several centuries earlier. The kings of Silla, in particular, took advantage of wartime stimulus for unity in the sixth and seventh centuries to curtail the authority of the Hwabaek aristocratic council, establish a standing state military, and create administrative organs under royal control. The centralizing impetus continued after Silla defeated Paekche and Koguryŏ, enabling the Silla kings to implement additional bureaucratizing reforms and bring the countryside throughout the peninsula under direct central control. The ability of the Silla kings to create a more truly bureaucratic system was limited, however, by the Bone Rank system, which gave True Bone aristocrats a monopoly over high political office and prevented kings from making active use of other social groups to offset aristocratic power. True Bone resistance to bureaucratizing reforms surfaced in the mid-eighth century, leading to the assassination of King Hyegong in 780 and ushering in a prolonged period of political instability that witnessed the rebirth of aristocratic council politics. By the late ninth century the Silla state no longer exercised effective jurisdiction over the territory within its borders. Much of countryside had fallen under the control of local elites who had their own private military forces and developed small-scale, independent systems of governance which, in their structure and nomenclature, asserted equivalence with the Silla state. In effect, the Silla polity had devolved into a decentralized, particularistic system dominated by local strongmen.

The period of disunion did not last long, however, and by 936 the new Koryŏ dynasty once again established unified rule over the Korean Peninsula. We can only speculate as to the impetus for unity in early tenth-century Korea. Perhaps the two-plus centuries of Silla rule had laid down the institutional and cultural foundations for lasting unity, although resurgence of local autonomy and the rise of regional political entities presenting themselves as successors to Paekche and Koguryŏ in the declining years of Silla would seem to confound such an interpretation. Nonetheless, Silla represented a precedent for unified rule, a precedent whose attractiveness may have been enhanced by the existence of an external model of a centralized polity in China. Certainly unification was facilitated by the relatively small size and compact shape of the peninsula. But the most important stimulus to unity may have come from the rise on Korea's northern frontier of a powerful and potentially hostile expansionist empire in the Khitan Liao, which overthrew the Tungusic Kingdom of Parhae (Ch. Pohai, 699–925) in 925.

Despite the Koryŏ's successes against the kingdoms of Silla and Later Paekche, its hold on the peninsula was tenuous. The regime over which Wang Kŏn presided was a confederation of warlords in which the king was essentially first among equals. The bulk of the countryside remained under the control of local strongmen who, though perhaps allied with or subordinated to the central warlords, still controlled private military forces and retained the trappings of independent local governance. Thus the Koryŏ faced two major internal obstacles to attaining lasting and effective rule: the central confederation, many of whose members enjoyed power and prestige rivaling that of the royal family itself; and the persistence of a high degree of local autonomy throughout the peninsula.

The most immediate challenge for the new dynasty lay in curbing the power of the central confederates and enhancing the authority and prestige of the kingship. Although his task may have been made easier by the bloodletting that took place during the reigns of the second and third Koryŏ kings, Hyejong and Chŏngjong, it was the fourth king, Kwangjong, who put the kingship on a firm foundation. Kwangjong carried out a number of institutional reforms, including promulgation of the Slave Investiture Act and implementation of a government service examination system—which was designed to undercut the military and political position of the confederates and elevate the authority of the crown—before he finally broke the back of confederation power in a series of bloody purges near the end of his reign. Kwangjong's measures, harsh though they may have been, cleared the way for the bureaucratizing reforms of his successors. The fifth Koryŏ king, Kyŏngjong, put the dynasty on firmer financial footing with the implementation of the Field and Woodland Rank Act. The sixth ruler, Sŏngjong, made a major stride toward the creation of a bureaucratic polity with his adoption of the Chinese Three Department–Six Board model, in which the organs of political struggle, the Secretariat and the Chancellery, were constituted within the regular bureaucracy and were thus structurally situated under the direct control of the throne.

The early Koryŏ monarchs also grappled with the challenge presented by local strongmen. Although Kwangjong's implementation of the examination system provided the means to recruit new blood as a counterbalance to the central confederation, it also constituted an institutionalized means by which members of local strongman descent groups could gain access to posts in the dynastic government. As such, it represented an effort by the throne to buy the loyalty of local strongmen by guaranteeing them the opportunity to participate in central political life. In the reign of Sŏngjong, however, the dynasty's policy of cultivating their allegiance shifted to one of curtailing their privilege and bringing them under a centrally sanctioned system of local administration. Measures taken during Sŏngjong's reign included abolition of privately controlled local military forces, incorporation of the apparatus of local governance into a country-wide *hyangni* system, and the initial establishment in the countryside of a permanent civil administrative presence in the "shepherds" posted to 12 strategically important regional centers. This was followed in the early eleventh century by King Hyŏnjong's posting of a small number of centrally appointed prefects and magistrates, which marked the first time that the Koryŏ dynasty had exercised direct supervision over the prefectures and counties that had been for 150 years under the largely autonomous control of local strongman descent groups. Over the next century and a half the central regime gradually expanded its presence in the countryside so that, by the second half of the twelfth century, nearly half of the country's prefectures and counties were under direct central supervision.

Despite apparent progress toward creation of a bureaucratic, centralized system of government, the kings were ultimately unable to overcome limitations imposed by the relative lack of differentiation in Koryŏ society. Following the destruction of maritime trading interests by landed interests in the midtenth century, Koryŏ kings had no alternative social stratum outside of landowning groups to turn to for support. Although Kwangjong sought to use local strongmen to offset the central confederation, the strongmen, too, were hereditary landed elites. As a consequence, the scions of strongman families recruited through the examination system were able to use their ascriptive privilege to establish themselves and their descendants as a new central aristocracy. By the beginning of the twelfth century, these capital-based descent groups came to dominate the upper echelons of the bureaucracy and to contest the throne for control of the organs of political struggle and for access to freefloating resources in land and the peasantry.

Although political power passed from civil aristocrats to military officials after the military coup of 1170, the coup did not alter the basic dynamics of the Koryŏ polity. The military dictators dominated the throne to a greater extent than had civil aristocrats, but soldiers created their own landed estates in *nongjang* and sought to bolster their own social prestige by marrying with civil aristocratic families. As a consequence, much of the old civil aristocracy was able to survive, and even prosper, during the military era. After the overthrow of the last of the Ch'oe house dictators in 1258, the civil branch of government, which was still largely dominated by aristocratic descent groups, reemerged as the center of bureaucratic power. Thus the late Koryŏ kings found themselves facing a situation essentially the same as that which had plagued their twelfth-century predecessors. If anything, the late Koryŏ kings were in a worse position because growth of privately held estates during the military period had reduced the amount of available free-floating resources. In the absence of any other significant social group, such as merchants, with whom they could ally themselves against the landed aristocracy, the late Koryŏ kings and their Mongol consorts tried to control the political process by relying on foreign retainers, eunuchs, and slaves. Although this policy was somewhat effective as long as the Koryŏ kings enjoyed the protection of the Yüan emperors, the kings and their palace favorites were isolated elements without any broad base of social support and were unable to prevent increasing amounts of material and human resources from falling under aristocratic control. After the collapse of Mongol hegemony in the mid-fourteenth century deprived the kings of external backing, they found themselves at the mercy of powerful *yangban* aristocrats, with the result that all of the last four Koryŏ kings were deposed by their own subjects.

It seems clear, therefore, that the rise of a landed central aristocracy in a society lacking other significant social strata (such as urban or merchant groups) to which the kings could turn for support was a major determining factor in the weakness of the Koryŏ kingship. The one other social group to which the kings might have turned was the *hyangni*, the descendants of the local strongmen of the Silla-Koryŏ transition. Indeed, when we consider that it took the dynasty two and a half centuries to establish a standing central presence in half of the country's prefectures and counties—and that it was able to do so only in unusual circumstances such as the threat of Khitan invasions during Sŏngjong's and Hyŏnjong's reigns, the time of heightened tensions with the Jurchen Chin in the early twelfth century, and the aftermath of Myoch'ŏng's rebellion in the mid-twelfth century—it becomes evident that the early Koryŏ *hyangni* were a powerful, entrenched group. Furthermore, the rulers pursued policies designed to enlist *hyangni* support by granting them prebendal privileges and guaranteeing them access to central office. Although Kwangjong and other tenth-century kings appear to have tried to use local elites to offset central confederation power, there were some very real limits to the *hyangni* as an alternative social group. Because *hyangni* were themselves hereditary landed elites, they belonged to the same general social stratum as many of the central confederates of the tenth century and the civil aristocrats of the eleventh and twelfth centuries. In fact, many of the aristocrats, such as the Kyŏngwŏn Yi and the Haeju Ch'oe, who dominated the central bureaucracy in the eleventh and twelfth centuries were of *hyangni* origins. The relative ease with which new *hyangni* recruits to the dynastic bureaucracy were able to transform themselves into central aristocratic descent groups throughout most of the dynasty is undoubtedly a reflection of the essential congruence of socioeconomic interests between them and the established central aristocracy. By the late thirteenth century, however, the material and social bases of *hyangni* power had been badly eroded throughout much of the country because of the devastation of foreign invasions and penetration of the countryside by the economic interests of central aristocrat descent groups. Thus even though the dynasty's institutions still guaranteed a place for *hyangni* among the ruling elite, the practical basis of *hyangni* power and prestige was gone and *hyangni* as a whole no longer constituted a viable, internally coherent social group to which kings could turn as a counterbalance to the central *yangban*.

Given the debility of the Koryŏ kingship and the power of the *yangban*, many of whom had extensive estates in the countryside, one wonders why some of the late Koryŏ *yangban* did not use their rural bases to form breakaway regimes. Certainly some who were alienated by the kings' policy of entrusting power in foreign retainers and servile palace retainers and who found themselves disadvantaged by the power of those few *yangban* descent groups who enjoyed the special favor of the Mongols would have had sufficient motivation to do so. One could argue that any such development was forestalled by the presence of the Mongols in the late thirteenth and early fourteenth centuries, but that does not explain the absence of any breakaway movements in the second half of the fourteenth century. One could also argue that the relatively small size and compactness of the kingdom mitigated breakaway movements, but those factors did not prevent the rise of regional regimes in the late Silla period. It seems to me that there were two factors at work here. One was the way in which *yangban* had come to identify themselves with service in the central bureaucracy. Another, perhaps more basic, factor was the nature of the late Koryŏ *yangban nongjang* estate. Although a few *nongjang* were reportedly so large as to encompass entire counties, the vast majority were composed of a number of parcels widely scattered in various locales. The diffuse nature of *yangban* landholdings made them unsuitable as bases for regional insurrections. As a consequence, the focus of competition for power remained at the capital.

Struggle for power at the center in the late thirteenth and fourteenth centuries revolved around three major issues. One was the question of access to material and human resources. Much of the country's arable land had been incorporated into *nongjang*, whose *yangban* owners were often able to evade taxation, and much of the population had been incorporated into *nongjang*, either as tenant farmers or slaves. Although kings made periodic attempts to reassert control over resources through special directorates established to determine the status of lands and people, they were not able to reverse the trend of increasing *yangban* domination of resources. Their failure resulted partly from the tendency for kings, their consorts, and palace favorites to form their own private estates, but a more basic reason was the entrenched power of *yangban*. This is illustrated by the way in which the special directorates often functioned not to return lands and people to the tax rolls but rather to redistribute them among *yangban*. An even more pressing problem was the diminishing amount of land designated as general revenue *kongjŏn*. The late Koryŏ kings routinely attempted to buy the loyalty of the officials by granting them land grants or giving them prebendal rights over lands that had previously been designated *kongjŏn*. The consequence was a severe shrinkage in tax revenues, made even worse by the raiding of the Wako, which left the state strapped for funds to field military forces and unable even to pay salaries to its officials.

A second issue was the question of control over the political process. Hampered by a lack of prestige and limited access to resources and facing a bureaucracy dominated by *yangban,* the late Koryŏ kings and their Mongol consorts sought to enhance the royal prerogative by bringing personnel agencies and the organs of political struggle into the palace and staffing them with such non-*yangban* elements as foreign retainers, eunuchs, and slaves. This became a major source of friction between kings and *yangban,* who made repeated unsuccessful attempts to restore political authority in institutions of the regular bureaucracy. *Yangban* reform efforts focused on abolition of the palace-based Personnel Authority and reversion of control over recruitment and promotion to the Board of Personnel, abolition of the palace *chaech'u* and restoration of policy-making powers to the Todang, and elimination of eunuch and palace *chaech'u* interference in communication between the throne and the bureaucracy and reestablishing regular channels of communication through the document transmission officials of the Security Council. After the decline of Mongol hegemony in the mid-fourteenth century, King Kongmin, in league with reform-minded *yangban* such as Yi Che-hyŏn, attempted to revitalize the dynasty's political system, but the institutional base and prestige of the kingship was already so weakened that Kongmin and his successors found themselves dominated by powerful *yangban* cliques such as the Namyang Hong royal in-laws and the Yi In-im faction. Kongmin and his immediate successor U sought to counterbalance the *yangban* by investing power in such non-*yangban* elements as the slave monk Sin Ton and eunuchs, but they met with no lasting success and the final decades of the dynasty were marked by fierce power struggles among various groups of *yangban*.

The third issue was the question of eligibility to hold office in the central bureaucracy. Because of the way in which the *yangban* had come to identify themselves in terms of traditions of service in the bureaucracy, the problem of qualification for office holding had become, in effect, one of membership in the kingdom's ruling class. The kings' use of eunuchs, slaves, and other non-*yangban* elements was one factor in shaping this issue, but the biggest problem was presented by *hyangni*, whose basic hereditary qualification to hold offices in the central bureaucracy was guaranteed by the dynasty's institutional structure. The arrival in the capital of large numbers of uprooted *hyangni* in the late Koryŏ period swelled the central official class and threatened to undermine the position of the *yangban* at the apex of the social order. Late Koryŏ efforts to deal with this problem revolved around attempts to force *hyangni* to return to the countryside and to limit the number of *hyangni* who could sit for government service examinations. These efforts were stymied by deep-rooted tradition and the recruitment of large numbers of *hyangni*, whom the kings rewarded with supernumerary offices, to fill the ranks of forces fielded to fend off the Wako. As a consequence, the *hyangni* problem continued to fester.

The basic underlying cause of the inability of the late Koryŏ to deal effectively with these institutional problems lay in the weakness of the kingship. The late Koryŏ kings suffered not only from a lack of access to significant amounts of resources, but the royal family had also lost much of its prestige during the military and Mongol periods. In the absence of effective leadership from the throne, the withdrawal of Mongol influence left the field wide open for struggle among *yangban* groups. A secondary factor was the commitment of reform-minded late-Koryŏ *yangban* to restoration and maintenance of the Koryŏ system of governance, which featured their own broad participation at the very highest level at the center and semiautonomous *hyangni* administration in the countryside. Illustrative of this restorationist mentality were repeated attempts to revitalize the Todang and to reinstate *hyangni* as the linchpins of local society.

Given a nearly 500-year history of loyalty to the Koryŏ royal family and the basic restorationist outlook of the late Koryŏ reformers, one wonders why *yangban* abandoned the dynasty at the end of the fourteenth century. We cannot discount the diminished stature of the Koryŏ royal family, which had lost much prestige and authority during the military and Mongol eras, nor can we ignore the incompetence and lack of interest in the daily affairs of governance displayed by such kings as Kongmin and U. Also, it seems almost certain that the late Koryŏ kings' reliance on foreigner retainers, slaves, and eunuchs— which not only limited *yangban* access to power, but also threatened to undermine the status system—must have alienated many *yangban*. Combined, these factors may have created a mind set that made it possible for *yangban* to consider turning against their kings.

It seems to me, however, that a more basic reason was the nature of the Koryŏ polity itself. Although early Koryŏ rulers pursued a policy of centralization that brought the *yangban* class into being, at the same time they made a number of compromises with the locally particularistic indigenous social order that guaranteed a position for *hyangni* as members of the ruling class. In effect, the constitutional foundation of the Koryŏ state was a *hyangni*-based territorial status system that determined who could hold office in the dynastic bureaucracy and how high they could rise. By the end of the thirteenth century, however, the central-official descent groups developed a sense of themselves as constituting a separate social entity, as seen in their use of such terms as *sadaebu*, *sajok*, and *yangban* to distinguish themselves from other social groups. Although the immediate motive for *yangban* use of this terminology was to set themselves apart from the eunuchs and slaves used by the kings to counter *yangban* power, the emphasis on ancestral traditions of service in the dynastic bureaucracy also implied a divergence between central *yangban* interests and the interests of *hyangni* local elites. This meant that there was a fundamental contradiction between interests of the central *yangban* bureaucrat aristocrats and the institutional structure of the Koryŏ state.

By the late fourteenth century, reform-minded *yangban* had come to realize that as members of a class whose power and prestige derived from its status as officials of the dynastic bureaucracy, they were dependent on a strong and effective central regime. This awareness was conditioned by a number of factors, including the inability of the dynasty to defend the country against foreign aggressors or to provide for the well-being of its officials, either in terms of protecting them against competition from other groups or even of providing them with basic material sustenance in the form of salaries. *Yangban* attitudes were also informed by a revitalized Confucian learning, which drew in part from new Chu Hsiist ideas introduced from Yüan China stressing the importance of the moral leadership of the king and his ministers and in part from an older Koryŏ and Northern Sung Ancient Learning tradition emphasizing the role of an activist central government in transforming society. By the late fourteenth century *yangban* had begun to think in terms of a basic overhaul of Korea's social and political institutions.

The reformers, however, were dismayed by the ineptitude of the kings and could see no hope for strong leadership from the throne. Furthermore, they had been alienated by the kings' policy of investing power in slaves and eunuchs. As a consequence, they were open to the possibility of switching allegiance to a new leader who had the power and prestige to effect fundamental changes. Such a candidate was available in Yi Sŏng-gye, who controlled a powerful military force organized around allies from his northeastern homeland and who had gained stature from his successful campaigns against the Red Turbans and Wako.

Yi Sŏng-gye's ability to win the support of the *yangban* reformers was due to more that just his personal power and prestige. His father, Yi Cha-ch'un, had played a key role in bringing the northeastern region under Koryŏ control. After Yi Cha-ch'un and Yi Sŏng-gye arrived at the Koryŏ capital in the mid-fourteenth century, they pursued a policy of building close ties with the central aristocracy by marrying their sons and daughters to the children of such important *yangban* families as the P'yŏngyang Cho and Hwangnyŏ Min. Furthermore, Yi Sŏng-gye's son Yi Pang-wŏn, who was a central figure in eliminating opposition and engineering Yi Sŏng-gye's coronation and who eventually became king himself in 1400, was a graduate of the civil service examinations and shared the reformers' vision of a new order organized on Confucian principles. Thus even though Yi Sŏng-gye was a military leader, he and his family represented something very different from the military officials who had taken control of the dynastic government in the late twelfth century.

Although Yi Sŏng-gye's ascent to the throne in 1392 has often been dismissed as a mere "palace coup," the nature and extent of the reforms that accompanied the change of dynasties indicate that it was an important turning point in Korean institutional history. The Rank Land Law of 1391, although not altering the basic pattern of *yangban* estate ownership, did sharply reduce the amount of land given out as *sajŏn* prebends and greatly increased the amount designated as general revenue *kongjŏn*. The Rank Land Law, in conjunction with confiscation of lands and slaves owned by Buddhist temples, gave the state access to a much greater share of the country's resources. This provided the material basis for the subsequent expansion of state power. While some *yangban* may have been upset at the loss of their old prebendal privileges, the new law contained provisions that protected the interests of the central *yangban* class as a whole, as seen in the granting of regular prebends only to officials who resided in the capital.

Reform in central political institutions, which came only after T'aejong had eliminated the last of the private armies and had concentrated all military control under the throne, was made possible by the overwhelming military might of the new royal family. Abolition of the Todang and dispersal of bureaucratic power among several independent agencies represented a substantial enhancement of the throne's authority and would seem to go against *yangban* interests. Nonetheless, even though some reformers were concerned about preventing the growth of autocracy, many supported T'aejong's restructuring of political institutions, realizing that without a redress of the balance of power between the throne and the bureaucracy, it would not be possible to have a central regime strong and effective enough to enhance their own power and prestige.

Perhaps the greatest difference between Koryŏ and Chosŏn institutions can be found in the area of local governance. The reformers replaced the weak and low-ranking Koryŏ governorship with high-ranking governors who exercised a broad range of control over the provinces. At the same time, the reformers began to bring the entire countryside under direct central control, establishing new prefectureships and magistracies and regularizing the old patchwork system of local administration. This was important to the state's ability to maintain control over land and human resources and was necessitated in part by the disruption of local society and uprooting of *hyangni* that had occurred in the thirteenth and fourteenth centuries.

At the same time reorganization of the system of local governance signaled the formal demise of the old territorial status system that had protected the interests of the *hyangni* class. After 1392 all *hyangni* in the capital, except those few who had passed the government service examination or had extraordinary merit, were forced to return to the countryside. *Hyangni* were no longer guaranteed access to the government service examinations, nor were they given honorary posts and titles. Before long they descended to the status of hereditary clerks and runners in the service of centrally appointed prefects and magistrates. The *yangban* had succeeded in eliminating a major source of competition for power.

Yangban efforts to secure their position at the top of the sociopolitical order did not stop with elimination of the *hyangni*. Reformers enforced provisions preventing descendants of technical officials such as physicians or astronomers—a group that eventually came to be known as "middle people" (*chungin*)—from taking civil service examinations and limiting them to low-ranking offices in the bureaucracy. *Yangban* concerns about maintaining class boundaries also found expression in similar prohibitions against sons of secondary wives, women who were often of servile or commoner origins. *Hyangni*, technical officials, and secondary sons had been able to rise in the Koryŏ bureaucracy; their exclusion represented a definite narrowing of the ruling class. The reformers also succeeded, despite some initial resistance from Yi Sŏng-gye, in removing eunuchs from the center of political power and enforced provisions preventing men of servile, artisan, and merchant backgrounds from sitting for civil service examinations and holding offices in the bureaucracy. As a consequence of these changes, *yangban* now stood alone at the apex of the Korean sociopolitical order.

In sum, the founding of the Chosŏn dynasty entailed a restructuring of Korean political and social institutions around the interests of the central aristocracy that first resulted from the centralizing reforms of early Koryŏ kings. Although central aristocrats suffered some setbacks during the years of military rule and Mongol overlordship, they dominated the country's political life throughout the Koryŏ dynasty. Despite the occasional demise of some descent groups and the addition of others, the central aristocracy displayed a remarkable continuity, in both structure and composition, throughout the Koryŏ period and on into the early Chosŏn. The most significant change in the nature of the central aristocracy during these centuries was the development, in the late thirteenth century, of an awareness of itself as constituting a separate class marked by ancestral traditions of service in the central bureaucracy. The absence of significant urban and commercial groups and erosion of the material and social bases of *hyangni* power in the late Koryŏ meant that there was no other social group with the resources and prestige to challenge the central aristocracy. Although Yi Sŏng-gye and his northeastern cohorts represented a potential new group with substantial power and internal cohesion, they opted to join, rather than replace, the central aristocrats. Indeed, to the extent that Yi and his group needed allies in their quest for power, they had nobody to turn to but the established aristocracy. In order to secure their own position, Yi Sŏng-gye and his immediate successors had no choice but to make concessions to the interests of the great central aristocratic descent groups. Although the new dynasty's political system provided for substantial enhancement of royal authority, those concessions, which included recognition of hereditary birthrights and landed property privileges, ultimately undermined the ability of the Chosŏn kings to rule the kingdom and set the stage for prolonged conflict between kings and *yangban* for control of both resources and political power throughout the Chosŏn dynasty.

The hereditary nature and the landed base of *yangban* power suggests that we should view *yangban* as constituting an aristocracy. We should note, however, that the great central-official descent groups also had bureaucratic characteristics from early on. Evidence from tombstone inscriptions and other sources indicates that men, regardless of their family backgrounds, had to follow a regular career path of spending 15 to 20 years or more in low- and mid-ranking positions before rising to *chaech'u* posts at the top of the bureaucracy. Furthermore, despite the prevalence of the protection privilege throughout the Koryŏ period, the meritocratic government service examinations provided not only initial entry to the central bureaucracy for such prominent descent groups as the Kyŏngwŏn Yi, Haeju Ch'oe, and Ich'ŏn Sŏ, but also an important source of prestige for members of the bureaucracy. The significance of the examination system in the Koryŏ is evidenced by the large numbers of men who chose to take examinations after they had already secured posts in the central bureaucracy and by the high proportion of examination graduates among the top-ranking *chaech'u* officials. The prevalence of these patterns of recruitment and advancement throughout the Koryŏ, in conjunction with evidence for the continuity of central official descent groups, indicates that the origins of the *yangban* as a class of bureaucratic aristocrats dated not from the founding of the Chosŏn, but rather from the late eleventh and early twelfth-century Koryŏ. Seen within the context of substantial continuity within the ruling class, therefore, the 1392 change of dynasties appears to have been less a revolution than the culmination, after more than four centuries, of the tenth-century effort to create a centralized bureaucratic polity.

INTERPRETIVE AND COMPARATIVE IMPLICATIONS

The findings of this study have implications in a number of areas. One, of course, is our understanding of Korea's historical heritage. Another is our perception of the character of historical bureaucratic societies. Yet another, more broadly cast and more tentatively advanced, is the way in which scholars explain historical change.

I believe that what I have presented here conclusively rebuts the "stagnation theory," which has until recently dominated modern explanations of Korean history. We have seen a process of historical change, informed by both external influences and internal dynamics, which by the fifteenth century resulted in a sociopolitical order very different from that of the tenth century. A major feature of this process was the way in which Korean social and political realities conditioned the acceptance of imported political models and cultural values.

In my refutation of the stagnation theory, I share much with mainstream historians in both South and North Korea. But, whereas South Korean advocates of the internal development theory believe the primary motive force of historical change to be the rise to power of new socioeconomic groups, I see historical change in the Koryŏ and early Chosŏn periods as stemming primarily from tension between a drive for centralization, derived in large measure from external models, and a native tradition of local particularism. Thus whereas proponents of the internal theory contend that the Chosŏn dynasty was founded by a "new scholar-official" class of local *hyangni* origins that rose to displace an old Koryŏ central aristocracy, I argue, based on the high degree of continuity in the ruling class between the Koryŏ and Chosŏn and the nature of the reforms that accompanied the founding of the new dynasty, that the founding of the Chosŏn was the ultimate fruition of early Koryŏ efforts to overcome local particularism and establish a centralized bureaucratic political system. From this perspective, the founding of the Chosŏn does not represent the victory of a class of locally based elites of *hyangni* origins over a decadent old central aristocracy; on the contrary, it signifies the ultimate triumph of the central bureaucratic aristocracy over the old locally particularistic, *hyangni*-centered system of the Silla-Koryŏ transition. In this regard, my views come closer to those of North Korean historians, who see the founding of the Chosŏn as a reorganization of the institutions of a centralized feudal system. However, whereas both North and South Korean historians tend to emphasize class conflict as the prime moving force in history, in this work I have placed greater emphasis on questions of institutional stress. In short, I believe that although it is fruitless to try to understand any political system without reference to the social and economic bases of the power of its leading social groups, it is equally fruitless to try to apply a class conflict mode of analysis to a society such as that of Koryŏ and early Chosŏn Korea, where the level of social differentiation was so low as to preclude the rise of social groups that could compete with the landed aristocracy.

Throughout this study I have made frequent reference to Eisenstadt's work on historical bureaucratic societies. I have found his analysis of the relationship between the degree of differentiation of a society and the extent of the bureaucratization of its political system to be most helpful in formulating my own understanding of the Koryŏ and early Chosŏn polities and in grasping the internal dynamics of Korean society.

My findings indicate that the Koryŏ and early Chosŏn clearly belonged to the class of historical bureaucratic societies that featured a combination of free-floating and embedded resources and of bureaucratic and aristocratic tendencies. Within that class, the Koryŏ and early Chosŏn compare most closely to societies such as Sassanid Persia, where the economy was largely undeveloped, society was poorly differentiated, and bureaucratic administration was not yet fully differentiated and organized in autonomous bodies, with the channels of political struggle largely identical with traditional court offices and higher administrative offices.[1] Furthermore, there seems to have been something of a parallel between the rise of the *yangban* in Korea and an aristocratized bureaucracy in Persia, where "the rulers first attempted to establish a royal official-

dom distinct from the old feudal-aristocratic families. Then the upper echelons of this new class developed quickly into a rather closed Aemteraristokratie,
strongly connected with parts of the aristocracy."[2]

It can be argued that the early Chosŏn represented a more highly differentiated social order than did the early Koryŏ. The enhanced authority of the
kingship; the Rank Land Law's expansion of state access to resources; implementation of a stronger, more centralized system of local administration and
the accompanying demise of *hyang, so,* and *pugok* as specially designated areas
for support of specific governmental functions; and the growing importance
of the meritocratic government service examination system all suggest a higher
degree of social differentiation. On the other hand, however, the Korean economy remained overwhelmingly agrarian and there was no other socioeconomic
group that could challenge the *yangban.* Significant resources remained under
yangban control, as seen in the widespread existence of landed estates and the
prevalence of slavery in the fifteenth century. Furthermore, ascriptive principles remained a primary determinant of social status, as seen not only in *yangban,* but also in *chungin* and slaves. Thus although the early Chosŏn may have
represented a more highly differentiated social order than did the early Koryŏ,
even the early Chosŏn remained relatively undifferentiated in comparison with
more complex historical bureaucratic societies.

As useful as I have found Eisenstadt for analyzing the Korean sociopolitical
order and comparing it with other countries, I would be remiss if I did not
point out that Eisenstadt seems to ignore the significance of external elements,
in the form of either threats of invasion or ideal models, for the evolution of
centralized bureaucratic polities in countries such as Korea that developed in
regions adjacent to other bureaucratic empires. The presence of expansionist
and potentially hostile regimes in Manchuria appears to have been an important stimulus toward the creation and maintenance of unified rule on the Korean
Peninsula. Of equally great importance to the evolution of the Korean sociopolitical order during these centuries was the availability of an external institutional model of a centralized polity in China. The T'ang model of centralized
bureaucratic rule, which the tenth-century Koryŏ kings attempted to implement, had to undergo significant modification in Korea, not only because of
the importance of ascriptive privilege but also because of the locally particularistic Korean social order. Thus the evolution of the Korean polity, which
revolved primarily around the internal issues of royal versus aristocratic power
and of central authority versus local autonomy, was nuanced by the complexities
involved in importing and indigenizing an essentially foreign political system.

There has long been a tendency among Western scholars to regard Korea either as a miniature replica of China or, more recently, as a local variant of Chinese civilization. To be sure, there is much that is shared between the two, particularly when seen from a modern Western perspective: both were primarily agrarian, rice-growing economies; both implemented centralized bureaucratic political systems; and both followed Confucian intellectual and cultural traditions. These superficial similarities should not, however, be allowed to obscure significant divergences that are important factors in explaining differences among historical bureaucratic societies. By Sung times the Chinese economy had developed an important commercial sector and society had become more highly differentiated, with significant gentry, merchant, and urban social groups. In contrast, the Korean economy remained almost totally agrarian throughout the Koryŏ and early Chosŏn periods and the landed aristocracy remained the only politically important social group. In China the aristocratic great clans of the interregnum and T'ang periods had by the end of the T'ang ceased to exist as a coherent, self-aware social group. In Korea, however, the great *yangban* bureaucratic aristocrats not only survived the fall of the Koryŏ, but even played the major role in effecting the change of dynasties. Whereas in China Confucianism appears to have contributed to some degree of social mobility and bureaucratization in late imperial times, in Korea, as Martina Deuchler and James Palais have shown, it seems to have upheld the aristocratic tradition.[3] These differences in degree of social differentiation and the persistence of ascriptive privilege do much to explain the rise of autocratic rule in late imperial China in contrast to the perpetuation of a relatively weak kingship in Chosŏn dynasty Korea.

Although I have no desire to engage in an essentializing discourse on the uniqueness of Korean ethnicity and culture, I cannot help but wonder, given the close proximity of Korea and China and the long history of Korean importation of culture from China, why the two countries were not more alike in their basic sociopolitical structures. It has been quite popular in recent years to explain the distinctiveness of Korean culture in terms of a unique underlying shamanic tradition that informed subsequent importation and adaptation of various alien cultures.[4] Although there appears to have been some fusion between shamanic and Buddhist beliefs in Korea, it is difficult to find evidence of shamanic influences on Confucianism.[5] Korean Confucianism did, however, define itself partially in terms of its opposition to shamanic practices. Such Confucian hostility may have reflected the importance of shamanic beliefs and rituals in bolstering, in company with geomantic and Buddhist traditions, the position of strongmen and *hyangni* in local society. Furthermore, there is no doubt about the persistence of shamanic beliefs and practices among women and commoners throughout the Koryŏ and Chosŏn periods. Nonetheless, it seems a far stretch, pending discovery of new evidence of widespread shamanic beliefs among *yangban* and significant shamanic influences on Korean political behavior and institutions, to argue that shamanism was responsible for the social and political differences between Korea and China. The issue is made even more problematic by evidence of significant shamanic influences on early Chinese culture.

One can also argue that Korea did not become more fully sinicized because of the great linguistic differences between the two peoples. Even though Korean elites studied and wrote in literary Chinese for nearly two thousand years, the Korean language is a member of the agglutinative, polysyllabic Tungusic family, whereas Chinese is a tonal, largely monosyllabic Sino-Tibetan tongue. Certainly these linguistic differences, plus the extreme difficulty of learning to read thousands of nonphonetic Chinese characters, must have slowed the penetration of Chinese culture into Korean society, especially among nonelite strata.

It seems to me, however, that geographic considerations are as important as any others. Although Korea and the northern Chinese heartland were relatively close to each other, the region of southern Manchuria that separated the two was a formidable barrier, particularly when Manchuria was under the control of hostile barbarian peoples. Also, whereas China came to constitute a wide area with considerable geographic and climatic diversity that could foster regional economic specialization and economic differentiation, Korea was confined to a small peninsula with a limited range of geographic and climatic differences. Furthermore, as James Palais has pointed out, whereas China was a target for invaders who on several occasions seized control and disrupted Chinese society, replacing Chinese elites at the top of the sociopolitical order and providing opportunities for lower strata to rise, Korea (although it, too, was invaded on a number of occasions) was never the final goal of invaders. Instead, invaders were intent on neutralizing Korea so they could focus their energies on China, with the consequence that foreign invasions usually had little long-range effect on Korean social or political organization.[6] Finally, it may be useful to point out that Korea's location between China and Japan could have enabled the Koreans to dominate seaborne trade in Northeast Asia and thus to develop a more diversified economy, a significant merchant class, and a more highly differentiated social order. This appears to have been precluded, however, by the overthrow of the commoner merchant prince Chang Po-go in the mid-ninth century and the defeat of maritime elements by landed interests in the mid-tenth century. After that time Koreans played only a minor role in Northeast Asian trade.

Finally, I would like to touch on the question of periodization as an explanation of historical change. Advocates of the internal development theory break down the centuries from the Silla-Koryŏ transition through the early Chosŏn into several periods based on their perception of fundamental and sharp changes in the composition and nature of the ruling class. In contrast, I have stressed continuity in institutions and the structure of the ruling class and have portrayed a picture of gradual, evolutionary change. Another recent Western work on premodern Korea, Martina Deuchler's *The Confucian Transformation of Korea,* also depicts slow and gradual change spanning several centuries. This approach might appear to some as a new Orientalism in which the old view of the East—as an unchanging traditional order, presented in contrast to a rapidly modernizing West—has been replaced by one of slow change in marginal areas while basic socioeconomic structures remained unchanged over centuries. Both Deuchler and I, however, are talking about fundamental and far-reaching transformations: in Deuchler's case, from a broadly constituted, horizontally oriented kinship group that included agnates, cognates, and affines to a narrowly defined, vertically-oriented patriarchical system; and in my case, from a decentralized, locally particularistic sociopolitical order to a centralized system organized around the interests of central bureaucratic aristocratic elites. The extent and significance of these changes becomes apparent only when viewed over long periods of time. That does not necessarily mean, however, that a slow process of significant historical change is unique to non-Western societies. Rather, that what we see here is an East Asian corroboration of the principles that Fernand Braudel derived from his study of France and the Mediterranean region: that the historical process is heavily influenced by geographic and, in Korea's case, geopolitical conditions; that the individual event is of little enduring significance; that some trends can be seen in transitional periods of several decades; but that fundamental historical transformations occur very slowly and are visible only in the *longue durée,* only over a span of several centuries.[7]

Notes

Sources included in the Bibliography are listed here in shortened form.

ABBREVIATIONS

HKC   Hŏ Hŭng-sik, ed., *Han'guk kŭmsŏk chŏnmun*
KS   *Koryŏsa*
KSC   *Koryŏsa chŏryo*
MST   *Mansŏng taedongbo*
SG   *Samguk sagi*

INTRODUCTION

1. See Kang Man-gil, "Ilche sidae ŭi pansingmin sahangnon," 233–38 on nationalist historians.

2. A good discussion of the positivist historians is provided by Hong Sŭng-gi, "Silchŭng sahangnon," 39–83.

3. See Paek Nam-un, *Chosen shakai keizaishi* and *Chosen hoken shakai keizaishi*. See also Yi Ch'ŏng-wŏn, *Chosen shakaisha tokuhon* and *Chosen tokuhon*.

4. The official North Korean views are contained in the *Chosŏn t'ongsa* and the massive *Chosŏn chŏnsa*. The *Chosŏn t'ongsa* says, "Although there was a change in dynasties, there was no change in the nature of society. As in the previous period, in the Yi dynasty most of the land, which was the basic means of production, remained in the hands of feudal *yangban* landlords while many commoners and slaves were forced to pay exploitive land rents as tenant farmers. Thus even after the founding of the Yi feudal state, all the feudal systems of exploitation and rule from the previous period were maintained" (p. 314).

5. See No T'ae-don, "Haebang hu minjokchuŭi sahangnon ŭi chŏn'gae," 1–25, on new nationalist historians in post-1945 South Korea.

6. Chŏn Sŏk-tam argued that although Korea did not have a slave-state period, it did have a prolonged feudal period beginning in the Three Kingdoms and lasting until the end of the Chosŏn in his *Chosŏn kyŏngjesa*, 7–35.

7. This awareness is clearly evidenced in the various articles in Han'guk Kyŏngje Sahakhoe, ed., *Han'guksa sidae kubunnon*.

8. Lee Ki-baik's *Han'guksa sillon* was one of two textbooks widely used in Korean colleges and universities in the late 1960s and 1970s. The other was Han

Woo-keun's (Han U-gŭn) *Han'guk t'ongsa,* also translated into English as *The History of Korea.* Although Han remained much closer to the positivist approach and his history is much less schematic than Lee's, even Han shares the basic socioeconomic developmental approach, as seen, for example, in his discussion of the rise of capitalism (English trans., p. 312).

9. The term *minjung* literally means, "people" or "masses." It has generally been used in South Korea, however, to include not only the oppressed masses, but also progressive intellectuals and political activists who have been oppressed by colonial and neocolonial regimes.

10. See Han'guk Yŏksa Yŏn'guhoe, ed., *Han'guksa kangŭi,* 39–41, on the *minjung* historians' criticism of mainstream South Korean historiography.

11. These studies include, for the Koryŏ period, the works of Hugh H. Kang, especially his dissertation, "The Development of the Korean Ruling Class from Late Silla to Early Koryŏ"; Edward J. Shultz's dissertation, "Institutional Development in Korea under the Ch'oe House Rule"; Kim Tang-t'aek, *Koryŏ muin chŏngkwŏn yŏn'gu;* and Pak Yong-un's various studies on the great families of the Koryŏ, including "Koryŏ sidae Haeju Ch'oe-ssi wa P'ap'yŏng Yun-ssi kamun punsŏk," "Koryŏ sidae ŭi Chŏngan Im-ssi, Ch'ŏrwŏn Ch'oe-ssi, Kongam Hŏ-ssi kamun punsŏk," and "Koryŏ sidae Suju Ch'oe-ssi kamun punsŏk." Studies on the Chosŏn period include James B. Palais, *Politics and Policy and Traditional Korea* and "Confucianism and the Aristocratic/Bureaucratic Balance in Korea"; Fujiya Kawashima's dissertation, "Clan Structure and Political Power in Yi Dynasty Korea"; Kim Yong-mo, *Chosŏn chibaech'ŭng yŏn'gu;* and Song June-ho (Song Chun-ho), *Chosŏn sahoesa yŏn'gu.*

12. Donald Clark's "Chosŏn's Founding Fathers: A Study of Merit Subjects in Early Yi Korea" indicates some degree of continuity between the late Koryŏ and the early Chosŏn.

13. See Clark, "Autonomy, Legitimacy, and Tributary Politics," esp. pp. 35–89.

14. Duncan, "The Koryŏ Origins of the Chosŏn Dynasty." A summary version of my findings can be found in "The Social Background to the Founding of the Chosŏn Dynasty."

15. Representative of these older historians is Song June-ho, whose various articles on the traditional *yangban* ruling class have been published collectively in his *Chosŏn sahoesa yŏn'gu.*

16. Kim Kwang-ch'ŏl, *Koryŏ hugi sejokch'ŭng yŏn'gu.*

17. Kim Tang-t'aek, "Ch'ungnyŏl wang ŭi pongnip kwajŏng . . . ," 195–232.

18. Chŏng Tu-hŭi, *Chosŏn Sŏngjongdae ŭi taegan yŏn'gu.*

1. THE KŎRYO POLITICAL SYSTEM

1. The pioneering work on the actual structure and operation of Koryŏ political institutions was done by Pyŏn T'ae-sŏp, whose various articles have been published in his *Koryŏ chŏngch'i chedosa yŏn'gu.*

2. See, for example, Pak Ch'ang-hŭi, "Koryŏ sidae kwallyoje e taehan koch'al," 67–87; and Pak Yong-un's criticism of Pak Ch'ang-hŭi's views in "Kwallyoje wa kwijokche ŭi kaenyŏm kŏmt'o," 141–76.

3. Eisenstadt, *The Political Systems of Empires*, 88–91.

4. Ibid., 225–35.

5. For a fascinating account of how international pressures influenced domestic politics to bring about this shift in orientation, see Michael Rogers, "P'yŏnnyŏn t'ongnok: The Foundation Legend of the Koryŏ State," 3–72.

6. Korean expansionist sentiment seems to have reasserted itself briefly during the final decades of the dynasty in the incorporation of the northeastern reaches of the Korean Peninsula under King Kongmin (r. 1351–74), the Liao-yang expedition of 1370–71, and the abortive 1388 expedition against Liao-tung. See Donald N. Clark "Autonomy, Legitimacy, and Tributary Politics," esp. chap. 1 and 2, on late Koryŏ efforts toward territorial expansion.

7. Lo, *An Introduction to the Civil Service of Sung China*, p. 3.

8. See Ha Hyŏn-gang, "Koryŏ wangjo ŭi sŏngnip kwa hojok yŏnhap chŏnggwŏn," on the nature of the military confederation of the early tenth century.

9. See Lee Ki-baik, *Silla chŏngch'i sahoesa yŏn'gu*, on the strengthening of royal authority and aristocratic resistence in mid- and late Silla.

10. Kang Chin-ch'ŏl, *Han'guk chungse t'oji soyu yŏn'gu*, 13.

11. Ibid., 37–39.

12. See Inoue, "Silla seiji taisei no henten katei," on the resurgence of aristocratic power and reconstitution of the aristocratic council in late Silla.

13. Koryŏ, originally founded by Kungye in 901, went through a number of name changes. Kungye first called his state Later Koguryŏ, before switching to Majin and then T'aebong. The name Koryŏ, a shortened version of Koguryŏ, was finally settled on in 918, when Wang Kŏn ousted Kungye and took the throne for himself.

14. For a concise discussion of the composition of the local strongman class, see Pak Yong-un, *Koryŏ sidaesa*, 25–34.

15. Evidence that maritime trading interests became important political players can be found in the case of Chang Po-go, a commoner merchant prince under whose leadership Silla traders dominated the seaborne trade between China, Japan, and Korea in the ninth Century. Chang's wealth and naval base at Ch'ŏnghaejin on the island of Wando made him an attractive ally for True Bone elements competing for the throne. In return for his support, King Sinmu (reigned briefly in 839) promised to accept Chang's daughter as consort for his son who took the throne in 839 as King Munsŏng (r. 839–57). This provoked strong opposition from True Bone aristocrats, who prevented the marriage from taking place. An aggrieved Chang then rose in revolt but was assassinated in 846. His fate is evidence that the capital-based aristocracy was still able to enforce Bone Rank social strictures. Although Chang's destruction marked the end of Silla dominance of maritime trade in Northeast Asia, other men continued coastal trading.

16. "Koryŏ segye," *Koryŏsa* (hereafter KS) 1a.

17. Takeda, "Korai shoki no kankei," 1–51.

18. Hugh H. Kang, "Wang Kŏn and the Koryŏ Dynastic Order," 161–76.

19. See Ch'oe Byŏng-hŏn, "Han'guk pulgyo ŭi chŏn'gae," 78–99, on the links between various Buddhist schools and social entities in Silla.

20. See Ch'oe Byŏng-hŏn, "Tosŏn's Geomantic Theories and the Foundation of the Koryŏ Dynasty," 65–92.

21. See Lee, *Sourcebook of Korean Civilization* 1:263–66. For a summation of current scholarship on the relationships among Buddhism, geomancy, and various social groups see Pak Yong-un, *Koryŏ sidaesa*, 37–41. For more details, see Ch'oe Byŏng-hŏn, "Namal yŏch'o sŏnjong ŭi sahoe chŏk sŏnggyŏk" and "Tosŏn ŭi saengae wa namal yŏch'o ŭi p'ungsu chirisŏl."

22. Ha Hyŏn-gang, "Koryŏ wangjo ŭi sŏngnip kwa hojok yŏnhap chŏnggwŏn," 53.

23. Members of the Kangnŭng Kim who participated in the founding of the Koryŏ included Kim (Wang) Ye and Kim (Wang) Kyŏng—two top-ranking officials whose daughters became Wang Kŏn's consorts (*KS* 88:6a–b)—along with Kim (Wang) Sun-sik and his sons Su-wŏn and Chang-myŏng, the latter of which provided a force of 600 men to act as a personal guard for Wang Kŏn (*KS* 92:16b). This branch of the Kangnŭng Kim was rewarded with the royal Wang surname by a grateful Wang Kŏn.

24. See Kim Chŏng-suk, "Kim Chu-wŏn segye ŭi sŏngnip kwa kŭ pyŏnch'ŏn," on the early history of the Kangnŭng Kim.

25. Lee Ki-baik, "Silla sabyŏng ko," 43–64.

26. Wang Kŏn's strategy to enlarge the royal family through these marriages is discussed in Deuchler, *The Confucian Transformation of Korea*, 57–58.

27. *KS* 88:1b.

28. Wang Kŏn married two women of the Kangnŭng Kim (Wang), and two of the P'yŏngsan Pak (daughters of Pak Su-mun and Pak Su-gyŏng), as well as the daughter of Kim Ŏng-nyŏm of Kyŏngju, a relative of last Silla king, Kyŏngsun (r. 927–35). See *KS* 88:5b–8a on these marriages.

29. Hugh H. Kang, "The First Succession Struggle of Koryŏ in 945," 411–28. Maritime trading interests in Korea had suffered an early defeat in the Chang Po-go affair of the mid-ninth century.

30. See Kim Tang-t'aek, "Ch'oe Sŭng-no sangsŏmun e poinŭn Kwangjong dae ŭi 'husaeng' kwa Kyŏngjong wŏnnyŏn Chŏnsi kwa," 56–60, on implications of the Slave Investiture Act.

31. *KS* 93:10b.

32. Hugh H. Kang, "The Development of the Korean Ruling Class from Late Silla to Early Koryŏ," 115–22. See also the various articles in Lee Ki-baek, ed., *Koryŏ Kwangjong yŏn'gu.*

33. Ha Hyŏn-gang, "Hojok kwa wanggwŏn," 146.

34. Hugh H. Kang, "Institutional Borrowing," 109–25. Silla did, of course, establish the three-grades reading examination (*toksŏ samp'um kwa*) in the late eighth century. It is unclear, however, to what extent or for how long the examinations were actually used in Silla. Given the Bone Rank system's strict ceilings on upward advancement, it seems unlikely that the Silla examinations could have provided an avenue for upward social mobility.

35. See Pak Yong-un, *Koryŏ sidae ŭmsŏje wa kwagŏje yŏn'gu*, 328–30, for detail.

36. See Kim Yong-dŏk, "Koryŏ Kwangjongjo ŭi kwagŏ chedo munje," 147; and Kim Tu-jin, "Koryŏ Kwangjongdae ŭi chŏnje wanggwŏn kwa hojok," 54–60.

37. At the beginning of the dynasty the central government was essentially a continuation of the Silla system, with the Secretariat (Kwangp'yŏngsŏng) provid-

ing the same kind of forum the Hwabaek Council and the Chŏngsadang had for the Silla True Bone aristocrats, and the Chancellory (Naebongsŏng) fulfilling the administrative duties of the Silla Executive Bureau (Chipsabu). The major difference from Silla was the Military Coordinating Council (Sun'gunbu), where warlord confederates coordinated the activities of their various military forces (see Lee Ki-baik, "Kwijok chŏngch'i ŭi sŏngnip," 8–21). The first significant alteration of this system came under Kwangjong with the abolition of the Military Coordinating Council and the emergence of a new Chancellory (Naeŭisŏng), an organ staffed with Confucian-educated officials whose job was to advise the king on policy matters (see Pyŏn T'ae-sŏp, Koryŏ chŏngch'i chedosa yŏn'gu, 3–5).

38. Eisenstadt, The Political Systems of Empires, 8–9.

39. Ibid., 17–18.

40. See Pyŏn T'ae-sŏp, Koryŏ chŏngch'i chedosa yŏn'gu, 2–82 on the Three Department–Six Board system and the chaesin.

41. See Lo, An Introduction to the Civil Service of Sung China, pp. 42–46, on the differences between the formal and functional organizations of the Sung government. See Ch'ien Mu, "Lun Sung-tai hsiang-ch'üan," 145–50; Chou Tao-chi, "T'ang-tai tsai-hsiang ming-ch'eng yü ch'i shih-ch'üan chih yen-pien," 103–13; and Chou Tao-chi, "Sung-tai tsai-hsiang ming-ch'eng yü ch'i shih-ch'üan chih yen-chiu," 370–77 on the actual functioning of the T'ang and Sung central governments.

42. Lo, An Introduction to the Civil Service of Sung China, 43.

43. See Pak Yong-un, Koryŏ sidaesa, 113–16, on the aristocratic nature of Koryŏ political institutions.

44. Chou Tao-chi, "T'ang-tai tsai-hsiang ming-ch'eng . . . ," 107.

45. The dynastic histories are rife with instances of concurrent appointment of junior second-grade officials of the Security Council to censorial and remonstrance posts in the Koryŏ before 1170. Examples include Sŏ Nul, chungch'uwŏn sa/u san'gi sangsi, in 1022 (Koryŏsa chŏryo [hereafter KSC] 3:44); Yi Tan, usangsi/chi chungch'u sa, in 1026 (KS 5:7a); Hwangbo Yŏng, chungch'u sa/ŏsa taebu (KSC 4:11a); Kim Chŏng-jun, chungch'uwŏn sa/p'an ŏsadae sa, in 1047 (KSC 4:46a); Yi Ui, chi chungch'u sa/chwa san'gi sangsi, in 1081 (KS 9:33b–34a); O Yŏn-ch'ong, chi ch'umirwŏn sa/ŏsa taebu, in 1106 (KS 12:16b); and Wang Cha-ji, Tongji ch'u-mirwon sa/chwa sangs sangsi (KS 14:19b). See Pak Yong-un, Koryŏ sidae taegan chedo yŏn'gu, 228–35, for an overview of chaech'u holding of taegan posts throughout the dynasty.

46. See Pak Yong-un, Koryŏ sidaesa, 99.

47. See Duncan, "The Formation of the Central Aristocracy in Early Koryŏ," 39–61, on how the dynasty's centralization policy created strong competitive pressures in the central bureaucracy.

48. KSC 6:16b.

49. KSC 8:34a.

50. KSC 8:24b; 6:41a; 9:9b.

51. KSC 5:38b. Yi Cha-yŏn's tombstone inscription indicates that he held a Six Boards superintendent post as a junior second-grade official in the pre-1070 period, but this is the only known instance, and cannot be confirmed by the dynastic his-

tories. Perhaps what we see here is a precursor of later trends. See Hŏ Hŭng-sik, ed., *Han'guk kŭmsŏk chŏnmun* (hereafter *HKC*) 2:495.

52. *KSC* 4:45a.
53. *KS* 12:18b.
54. *KS* 13:4a.
55. *KS* 14:41a.
56. *KSC* 9:46b.
57. Pyŏn T'ae-sŏp, *Koryŏ chŏngch'i chedosa yŏn'gu*, 307.
58. Conflict between established central officials and new men recruited through the examination system lay behind much of the political conflict of the twelfth century. See Edward J. Shultz, "Twelfth Century Koryŏ Politics," 3–38, on this conflict.
59. This description of the private political agencies of the military era is based largely on the discussion in Pak Yong-un, *Koryŏ sidaesa*, 429–37. See also, Shultz, "Institutional Development in Korea under the Ch'oe House Rule," on Ch'oe house institutions.
60. See Kim Tang-t'aek, *Koryŏ muin chŏngkwŏn yŏn'gu*, 112–16.
61. Edward Shultz has found that despite a significant infusion of men with military backgrounds into regular dynastic offices, civil officials still accounted for a majority of officials under Ch'oe Ch'ung-hŏn. See Shultz, "Twelfth Century Koryŏ," 15–17.
62. The Chinese scheme of local administration, which began as the *chün-hsien* system under the Ch'in dynasty (221–206 BCE), lost much of its effectiveness during the years of disunity after the fall of the Han, but was revivified in T'ang and Sung times as the *chou-hsien* system. Although the prefecture (*chün/chou*) lost some of its authority, the system that reemerged under the T'ang retained the basic hierarchical structure. See Lo, *An Introduction to the Civil Service of Sung China*, 38–42, for a brief overview of the Sung system. For greater detail, see Shang, *Chung-kuo li-tai ti-fang cheng-chih chih-tu*.
63. *Samguk sagi* (hereafter *SG*) 34:1b.
64. *SG* 40:10b.
65. Hatada, *Chosen chusei shakaishi no kenkyu*, 415–62.
66. See Ha, *Han'guk chungsesa yŏn'gu*, 190–97.
67. See Hatada, *Chosen chusei shakaishi no kenkyu*, 3–40, on the way in which the early Koryŏ system was based on local strongman status.
68. See Kim Yong-dŏk, "Sinbun chedo," for a concise description of the status-based regional administrative system.
69. See Yi Su-gŏn, *Han'guk chungse sahoesa yon'gu*, 9–21. An alternative interpretation argues that the ancestral seat system was imposed from above by the throne. This view holds that there was much wandering among the population during the late Silla and early Koryŏ and that the settling of these people was a major problem for the new dynasty. The dynasty established the ancestral seat system to register the whole population and tie them to specific geographic locations; this was supposedly accomplished before the end of King Kwangjong's reign. According to this interpretation, there are numerous examples of Wang Kŏn's granting surnames and ancestral seats to different individuals, but there are no instances of descent groups' assuming ancestral seats on their own (see

Kim Su-'tae, "Koryŏ pon'gwan chedo ŭi sŏngnip," 41–64). There are, however, some problems with this view. First, it is difficult to imagine how the dynasty could have registered and bound the whole population to specific locales when it was not able to post centrally appointed officials to local offices until late in the tenth century. Second, there is evidence that powerful local descent groups were already identifying themselves by their locale even before the founding of the Koryŏ. Examples include Kim Chu-wŏn, founder of the Kangnŭng Kim, who in the late eighth century migrated to Kangnŭng, where he styled himself "king of Myŏngju (Kangnŭng) Prefecture" (see *Mansŏng taedongbo* [hereafter *MST*] 1:177a); and Kim Hŭng-gwang, the third son of Silla's King Hŏn'gang (875–85), who moved to Kwangsan, where he became "lord of Kwangsan" (Kwangsan *puwŏn kun*) and the founder of the Kwangsan Kim (see *MST* 1:156b). Another example can be found in the P'yŏngsan Pak. According to the twelfth-century tombstones, Pak Chig-yun relocated in the late Silla to P'yŏngju (P'yŏngsan), where he took up residence, built a number of fortresses, and took control of the area, after which his descendents "have been known as P'yŏngju men" (see Hŏ, *HKC* 2:563 and 2:751).

70. See Yi Su-gŏn. *Han'guk chungse sahoesa yŏn'gu*, 111–15, on this practice.

71. See Yi Chong-uk, "940 nyŏndae chŏngch'i seryŏk ŭi punsŏk," 13–15. See also Yi Su-gŏn, *Han'guk chungse sahoesa yŏn'gu*, 227–32.

72. No Myŏng-ho, "Koryŏ sidae ŭi ch'injok kwan'gyemang kwa kajok," 189–90.

73. *KS* 125:22.

74. Whereas the Korean *pugok* was a territorial unit, *pu-ch'ŭ*, the term's equivalent in the interregnum period between the Han and Sui dynasties (220–581) in China, referred to a class of servile agricultural laborers. See Miyazaki Ichisada, "Pu-ch'ŭ kara t'ien-hu e," *Toyoshi kenkyu* 29-4 (1970):30–65 and 30-1; (1971):1–32. See Lien-sheng Yang, *Studies in Chinese Institutional History*, 128, for a brief English-language summary of the *pu-ch'ŭ*.

75. See Park, "Koryŏ T'aejo 23 nyŏn kunhyŏn kaep'yŏn e kwanhan yŏn'gu," 105–31, on the two-level system of local administration in the early Koryŏ.

76. See, for example, Hatada, *Chosen chusei shakaishi no kenkyu*, 57–74; and Kim Yong-dŏk, "Hyang, so, pugok ko," 183–85.

77. See Yi Su-gŏn, *Han'guk chungse sahoesa yŏn'gu*, 450–51, for a general discussion of this issue. More specific studies include Park Jong-ki, "Silla sidae hyang, pugok ŭi sŏnggyŏk e taehan il siron" and "Silla pugokche ŭi kujo wa sŏnggyŏk"; and the original study questioning the conventional interpretation, Yi U-sŏng, "Koryŏ malgi Najumok Kŏp'yŏng pugok e taehayŏ."

78. Peter K. Bol, "*This Culture of Ours*," 36.

79. See Johnson, *The Medieval Chinese Oligarchy*, 20–31.

80. See Pak Yong-un, *Koryŏ sidaesa*, 117–18, on these central emmisaries.

81. Hatada, *Chosen chusei shakaishi no kenkyu*, 105–39.

82. Regarding the hostage system, see Yi Kwang-nin, "Kiin chedo ŭi pyŏnch'ŏn e taehayŏ;" and Kim Sŏng-jun, "Kiin ŭi sŏnggyŏk e taehan koch'al." Recently some scholars have laid more stress on the role of *kiin* as advisors and on the good treatment they received at the hands of Wang Kŏn, arguing that the throne was still

too weak to require unilaterally that local warlords surrender up their sons as hostages (see Ha, *Han'guk chungsesa yŏn'gu,* 80–81).

83. See Pyŏn, *Koryŏ chŏngch'i chedosa yŏn'gu,* 121–31 on this early effort to replicate the T'ang province-system.

84. District shepherds, initially established in 983, were the first permanent representatives (aside from military garrisons) of the dynastic government in the countryside.

85. See Ha, *Han'guk chungsesa yŏn'gu,* 293–345, on the Western Capital's government apparatus.

86. *KS* 77:41a–b.

87. Lee, *Koryŏ pyŏngjesa yŏn'gu,* 162–201.

88. Pyŏn T'ae-sŏp notes the posting of military commandants (*chinsu*) in various strategically important locales and argues that these centrally appointed military officials were the forerunners of the civilian prefects and magistrates posted in the early eleventh century ("Koryŏ ch'ogi chibang chedo," 25–42).

89. See Pyŏn, *Koryŏ chŏngch'i chedosa yŏn'gu,* 141–44.

90. *KSC* 13:20b. Cited in Pyŏn, *Koryŏ chŏngch'i chedosa yŏn'gu,* 172.

91. The T'ang did not create intermediary provincial institutions until the late seventh century, when it first began to appoint commissioners (*an-ch'a shih* or *hsün-ch'a shih*). These commissioners were appointed only sporadically, however, and it wasn't until the mid-eighth century—when the T'ang carried out a major provincial reorganization and began to post inspectors with general supervisory powers over local officials and military governors (*chieh-tu shih*) in the northern frontier areas—that the dynasty can be said to have had a strong system of provincial administration. T'ang governors, especially in the northeast, developed into powerful, largely independent entities after the An Lu-shan rebellion. See Twitchett, "Varied Patterns of Provincial Autonomy in the Late T'ang Dynasty," 91–109, on T'ang local administration.

92. See Pyŏn T'ae-sŏp, *Koryŏ chŏngch'i chedosa yŏn'gu,* 163–80; and Ha, *Han'guk chungsesa yŏn'gu,* 226–58, on the limits of the circuit intendant's role. Ha argues that, based on these limits, intendants cannot be considered to have been heads of circuit administration until very near the end of the dynasty, when the post was upgraded and given additional authority.

93. *KS* 75:45a–b.

94. *KSC* 2:41a.

95. *KS* 75:42b.

96. *KS* 75:47a.

97. See Pak Yong-un, *Koryŏ sidaesa,* 132–37, for a concise discussion of the *hyangni* system. The privileged position of *hyangni* will be discussed at greater length in chapter 2.

98. *SG* 36:4a.

99. *KS* 57:38a.

100. *KS* 56:1b.

101. *KS* 56:15b.

102. *KS* 57:38a–b.

103. Eleven prefectures and counties were reassigned to Naju, nine to Chŏnju,

eight each to Yŏnggwang and Namwŏn, six to Posŏng, and four to Kobu. See *KS* 57:32a–51a.

104. Nineteen prefectures and counties were subordinated to Sangju; 15 to Hongju; 14 to Andong; 12 each to Kyŏngju and Kyŏngsan; 11 to Hapchu; nine to Konju; seven each to Yangju, Suwŏn, and Ch'ŏnan; and six each to Ch'ungju, Kwangju (in modern day Kyŏnggi Province), and Tongju (modern day Ch'ŏrwŏn).

105. *KSC* 2:64a.

106. *KSC* 3:31b. These appointments appear to account for nearly all of the 100 nonsubordinated prefectures and counties of Hyŏnjong's time.

107. *KSC* 7:13a.

108. See Yi Su-gŏn, *Han'guk chungse sahoesa yŏn'gu,* 369–70.

109. These figures were compiled from the "Monograph on Geography," *KS* 56:1a–58:42a.

110. *KS* 57:33b.

111. See Palais, "Land Tenure in Korea," on the welter of competing theories about Koryŏ land tenure.

112. For a description of the provisions of the Field and Woodland Rank system, see Kang Chin-ch'ŏl, "Traditional Land Tenure." A concise discussion of the salary system can be found in Pak Yong-un, *Koryŏ sidaesa,* 173–77.

113. See Hugh H. Kang, "Epilogue," 151.

114. See Kang Chin-ch'ŏl, *Han'guk chungse t'oji soyu yŏn'gu,* 37–39, on the Silla *chŏnjang* estate.

115. Hatada, *Chosen chusei shakaishi no kenkyu,* 176–84.

116. For a summary of the evidence on this point, see Palais, "Land Tenure in Korea," 78–102.

117. For a summary of the village commune theory, see Kang Chin-ch'ŏl, *Han'guk chungse t'oji soyu yŏn'gu,* 73.

118. Kang Chin-ch'ŏl, "Traditional Land Tenure," 55.

119. Ibid., 48.

120. The *Samguk sagi,* for example, contains a story about the wife of the sixth-century Koguryŏ general Ondal, who sold her gold jewelery to buy land, animals, and implements (*SG* 45:8b ff).

121. This argument was first advanced by Kim Yong-sŏp in his article "Koryŏ sidae ŭi yangjŏnje," 86–102.

122. Palais, "Land Tenure in Korea," 155–57, 182–90.

123. See Pak Yong-un, *Koryŏ sidaesa* 158–71, on the provisions and amendments of the Field and Woodland Rank system.

124. Park, *Koryŏ sidae pugokche yŏn'gu,* 135–66.

2. THE RISE OF A CENTRAL BUREAUCRATIC ARISTOCRACY

1. See Johnson, *The Medieval Chinese Oligarchy,* 28–30, on surnames and choronyms in medieval China. See Deuchler, *The Confucian Transformation of Korea,* 84–85, on surnames and ancestral seats in the Koryo. Takeda Yukio argues that in the early Koryŏ only elites had surnames and ancestral seats and that commoners had neither ("Chŏngdusa goso seikito chosei keijiki no kenkyu (1)," 32–37).

2. Johnson, *The Medieval Chinese Oligarchy,* 6.

3. Bol, *"This Culture of Ours,"* 3–4, 32–58. See also Johnson, *The Medieval Chinese Oligarchy,* 5–6.

4. Pak Yong-un, "Yi Sŏng-mu chŏ *Chosŏn ch'ogi yangban yŏn'gu* sŏp'yŏng," 300. Early and mid-Koryŏ usage of the term *sadaebu* almost always is found in formulaic language such as "nobles [*kong,* Ch. *kung*], high ministers [*kyŏng,* Ch. *ch'ing*] and officials [*sadaebu*]." For an example of such usage, see the tombstone inscription for Im Kyŏng-hwa (dated 1159), Hŏ, *HKC* 2:766.

5. See Ho, *HKC* 2:557, 560, 714, 737, and 779, for examples of the use of these terms in the eleventh and twelfth centuries.

6. Deuchler, *The Confucian Transformation of Korea,* 35–39.

7. Ibid., 45–56.

8. Deuchler argues that sometime around the middle of the twelfth century funerary inscriptions of the elite began to list two or three generations of agnatic antecedents (ibid., 39–40). This practice can be found, however, in tombstone inscriptions from the mid-eleventh century, such as the 1051 inscription for Yu Pang-hŏn and the 1075 inscription for Ch'oe Sa-wi, both of which list great-grandfathers, grandfathers, and fathers, along with maternal grandfathers. The most complete collection of Koryŏ tombstone inscriptions is Kim Yong-sŏn, *Koryŏ myojimyŏng chipsŏng.*

9. Fujita, "Yi Cha-yŏn to sono kakei." See also Pak Yong-un, "Koryŏ sidae Haeju Ch'oe-ssi wa P'ap'yŏng Yun-ssi kamun punsŏk"; "Koryŏ sidae ŭi Chŏngan Im-ssi, Ch'ŏrwŏn Ch'oe-ssi, Kongam Hŏ-ssi kamun punsŏk"; "Koryŏ sidae Suju Ch'oe-ssi kamun punsŏk"; and "Koryŏ sidae ŭi Musong Yu-ssi kamun punsŏk."

10. Genealogical records of office holding for the early and mid-Koryŏ periods are highly suspect and must be used with caution. They often claim high-ranking ancestors of whom no trace can be found in the histories or any other source. Granted, the *Koryŏsa* and the *Koryŏsa chŏryo* are somewhat inconsistent in recording official appointments, but I find it difficult to imagine, for example, that men who purportedly rose to the highest post in the government (chancellor, *munha sijung*) would not be mentioned in the histories at least once.

11. The *Koryŏsa* indicates that there were 4,385 civil and military posts in the central government during Munjong's reign, but an undetermined number (from nine to 30 or more) were regularly filled as concurrent appointments, meaning that the actual number of men holding office at any given time was probably somewhat less than 4,358.

12. The number of *chaech'u* posts listed in the "Monograph on Officials" was twelve; we know, however, that in the late eleventh and twelfth centuries it was common practice to make simultaneous multiple appointments to certain posts, meaning that the actual average number of men holding *chaech'u* posts in any given year was somewhat greater than 12. Even if we use 20 as a working estimate of the average number of *chaech'u* posts in early Koryŏ, that still amounts to less than one-half of 1 percent of all posts.

13. See Yi Su-gŏn, *Han'guk chungse sahoesa yŏn'gu,* 5.

14. See Johnson, *The Medieval Chinese Oligarchy,* 33–88, on the great clan lists of interregnum and T'ang China.

15. See Yi Su-gŏn, *Han'guk chungse sahoesa yŏn'gu,* 172–73, 178–79, on the Ich'ŏn Sŏ and Hwangnyŏ Min.

16. See ibid., 143–44, for a speculative estimate of Chŏngju Yu power that puts the number of total officials at nine and the number of *chaech'u* at seven.

17. See ibid., 196–98, on the Kyŏngju Kim in the early Koryŏ.

18. Ibid., 225.

19. Fujita Ryosaku, "Yi Cha-yŏn to sono kakei," *Seikyu gakuso* 15 (1934):121.

20. *KS* 92:16b, 95:26b.

21. Fujita Ryosaku, "Yi Cha-yŏn to sono kakei," *Seikyu gakuso* 13 (1933):1–37; *Seikyu gakuso* 15 (1934):109–35.

22. Sŏng Hyŏn, *Yongjae ch'onghwa* 10:1a

23. These descent-group segments are typically represented in the sources as patrilineages. We know, however, that Koreans of the Koryŏ and early Chosŏn periods also traced descent on the female side, as seen in the several cases where men were known to have been extended the *ŭm* privilege from their maternal grand-fathers or maternal great-grandfathers (see No Myŏng-ho, "Koryŏ sidae ŭi sŭngŭm hyŏljok kwa kwijokch'ŭng ŭi ŭmsŏ kihoe," 363–405) and in the struc-ture of early Chosŏn genealogies such as that of the Andong Kwŏn and the Munhwa Yu (see Wagner, "Two Early Genealogies and Women's Status in Early Yi Dynasty Korea," 23–32.) The treatment of Koryŏ families here focuses on patrilineal descent because of the nature of our source materials: the *Koryŏsa* biographies and the tombstone inscriptions, apparently following Chinese precedents, usually list sev-eral generations of patrilineal ancestors while mentioning only the maternal grandfather. The paucity of information makes it all but impossible to reconstruct matrilineal descent. See Deuchler, *The Confucian Transformation of Korea,* 29–87, on the Koryŏ descent group.

24. The founder of the Ich'ŏn Sŏ, Sŏ Sin-il, appears to have been a local war-lord; his son P'il rose to serve under Kwangjong in the mid-tenth century because of his "literary talent" (*KS* 94:7b, 93:1a). See also *Han'guk chungse sahoesa yŏn'gu,* 172–73, for Yi Su-gŏn's discussion.

25. The Kwangyang Kim also appeared in the central bureaucracy in the mid-tenth century (ibid., 209–10).

26. The Kyŏngwŏn Yi family made its appearance in central officialdom when Yi Cha-yŏn passed the government service examination in 1024 (*KS* 95:9b).

27. See Shultz, "Twelfth Century Koryŏ Politics," 3–39, on the Tanju Han.

28. See Yi Su-gŏn, *Han'guk chungse saehoesa yŏn'gu,* 146–47.

29. See Chŏng Hang's tombstone inscription (*HKC* 2:611 ff) for details regarding his family's *hyangni* origins and the careers of Hang, his father, and his brothers.

30. *KC* 2:775. Confirmation of this line of descent can be found in an earlier tombstone for Ch'oe Sa-wi (*HKC* 2:502).

31. See Yi Su-gŏn, *Han'guk chungse saehosa yŏn'gu,* 166–67, on the status of Ch'oe Ch'ung's father, Ch'oe On, as a local official.

32. See *KS* 95:1a–9a on Ch'oe Ch'ung and his descendents.

33. See Pak Yong-un, *Koryŏ sidae ŭmsŏje wa kwagŏje yŏn'gu,* 328 ff, for details and sources for these men as examination graduates.

34. Yi Su-gŏn gives several examples, including the Ch'oe and Yi of T'osan, the Hŏ and Ch'oe of Yangch'ŏn (Kongam), the Yi and Ch'ae of Inju (Kyŏngwŏn), the Ch'oe and Chŏn of Yŏngam, and the Im and Ko of Okku (*Han'guk chungse sahoesa yŏn'gu*, 231).

35. For discussion of the importance of the Kyŏngwŏn Yi's marriage ties, see Deuchler, *The Confucian Transformation of Korea*, 58–59; and Yi Su-gŏn, *Han'guk chungse sahoesa yŏn'gu*, 153–54.

36. Pak Yong-un, *Koryŏ sidae ŭmsŏje wa kwagŏje yŏn'gu*, 100–101.

37. Kim Yong-sŏn, "Koryŏ sidae ŭi ŭmsŏ chedo e taehan chae kŏmt'o," 275–319.

38. Compiled from the data in ibid., 310–19.

39. See No Myŏng-ho, "Koryŏ sidae ŭi sŭngŭm," 385–86.

40. Kim Kwang-su, "Koryŏ sidae ŭi sŏri chik," 21–25.

41. See Pak Yong-un, *Koryŏ sidae ŭmsŏje wa kwagŏje yŏn'gu*, chap. 3–7, on the organization and operation of the Koryŏ examination system.

42. Pyŏn, *Koryŏ chŏngch'i chedosa yŏn'gu*, 307.

43. Hŏ Hŭng-sik, *Koryŏ sahoesa yŏn'gu*, 352.

44. Pak Yong-un, *Koryŏ sidae ŭmsŏje wa kwagŏje yŏn'gu*, 328–90.

45. The exceptions are the P'yŏngsan Yu, Pongju Chi, and Yŏngch'ŏn Hwangbo.

46. These men include Mun Kong-wŏn and Mun Kŭk-kyŏm of Namp'yŏng, Yun Ŏn-i of P'ap'yŏng, Ch'oe Chŏng of Suju, and Ch'oe Sa-ch'wi of Haeju.

47. See Kim Yŏng-mo, *Chosŏn chibaech'ŭng yŏn'gu*, 439.

48. Han Ch'ung-hŭi, "Koryŏ chŏn'gi sahoe ŭi sŏnggyŏk e taehayŏ," 321–59.

49. *HKC* 2:495. Dates were verified by reference to the *Koryŏsa*.

50. *HKC* 2:505.

51. Sŏ P'il was a first-grade chancellor under King Kyŏngjong; his son Hŭi was chancellor under King Sŏngjong; Hŭi's son Nul also served as chancellor under Kings Tŏkchong (1031–34) and Chŏngjong (1034–46). See KS93:1a, 94:1a–7a. There is some possibility that the Ich'ŏn Sŏ developed two capital-based segments in the mid-eleventh century (see Yi Su-gŏn, *Han'guk chungse sahoesa yŏn'gu*, 172–73), but P'il, Hŭi, and Nul constitute a prime example of father-to-son succession during the tenth and eleventh centuries.

52. Kwak Wŏn was a second-grade state councillor under King Mokchong (997–1009); his son Chŭng held an unspecified position under King Tŏkchong; and Chŭng's son Sang served as state councillor under King Sŏnjong (1083–94). The sources mention Sang's two sons, Yŏ and T'an. T'an is not known to have held office, but Yŏ passed the government service examination and held a series of lower ranking posts (*KS* 94:32b-33a, 97:8a-10a).

53. One line of father-to-son succession in the Kyŏngju Ch'oe clan was that of Ch'oe Sŭng-no, chancellor under King Sŏngjong; his son Suk held a third-grade post under King Hyŏnjong; Suk's son Che-an was chancellor in 1046; and Che-an's son Kye-hun, the last of this line known to hold office, received an eighth-grade post at the time of his father's death (*KS* 93:2a, 93:22b). Another segment was made up of the descendants of Ch'oe Ŏn-wi, an important scholar and official at the beginning of the dynasty; his son Kwang-wŏn held office under King Kwangjong; Kwang-wŏn's son Hang served as assistant chancellor under King

Hyŏnjong; of Hang's two sons, Yu-bu is known to have held high central office as superintendent of the Board of Punishments in 1071, while Yŏng-bu apparently never rose above low-ranking provincial posts (KS 93:31a. See also Yi Sugŏn, Han'guk chungse sahoesa yŏn'gu, 199–202). The Kyŏngju Kim had three identifiable segments in the central officialdom in the early Koryŏ: one deriving from Kim Pu (King Kyŏngsun of Silla); another from Kim In-wi, a high official of the late tenth century; and a third line, which appeared at the beginning of the twelfth century from Kim Kŭn and produced Kim Pu-sik and his brothers (ibid., 196–99.)

54. The details of office holding in these descent group segments are shown in table 2.3. See also Fujita Ryosaku, "Yi Cha-yŏn to sono kakei," for more information on these kinship groups.

55. HKC 2:502.

56. Two of Yi Cha-yŏn's sons can be verified in first- or second-grade positions: Chŏng, who was associate chancellor in 1075; and Ŭi who held a second-grade post in the Security Council in 1091 (KSC 5:31b; KS 9:33b).

57. Two of Ch'oe Ch'ung's sons can be verified as first- and second-grade officials: Yu-sŏn, who died in office as supreme chancellor in 1073; and Yu-gil, who was Finance Commission superintendent in 1077 (KS 9:12b, 9:17b).

58. KS 97:13b.

59. HKC 2:611.

60. KS 98:40b.

61. KS 99:25a.

62. KS 17:19b.

63. For a discussion of how the competition between established capital lines of descent and new arrivals gave rise to political conflict, see Shultz, "Twelfth Century Koryŏ Politics."

64. See ibid. on the conflict between older and newer descent groups in twelfth-century Korea.

65. Pyŏn T'ae-sŏp, Koryŏ chŏngch'i chedosa yŏn'gu, 320.

66. The most influential of several studies on the military ruler's recruitment of hyangni through the examination system is Yi U-sŏng, "Koryŏjo ŭi 'i'e taehayŏ." Yi argues that the recruitment of hyangni under the military represented a new development, but, as we have seen, the rise of hyangni through the examination system was common in the early Koryŏ.

67. See Shultz, "Military Revolt in Koryŏ," 19–48; and "Military-Civilian Conflict of the Koryŏ Dynasty," 5–16. Shultz's findings are confirmed in Kim Tang-t'aek, Koryŏ muin chŏngkwŏn yŏn'gu.

68. Kim Tang-t'aek, Koryŏ muin chŏngkwŏn yŏn'gu, 99–100.

69. If we assume that at any given time roughly 4,000 individuals were holding office and that the average career of all officials was 10 years, 52,800 individuals would have held office between 1260 and 1392. Our 2,660 known officeholders thus represent only about 5 percent of officialdom.

70. Although nearly 70 percent (3,014 of 4,358) of the posts in the central government were bottom-ranking senior and junior ninth-grade slots, officials holding ninth-grade posts make up less than 1 percent (19) of our 2,660 known officials.

In contrast, although the top three grades accounted for slightly over 1 percent (50 of 4,358) of all posts, men holding those posts account for roughly one-fourth (689) of our 2,660 known officials.

71. The numbers used here to define powerful descent groups are greater than those used for the early Koryŏ because of the greater amount of data available on officeholders in the late Koryŏ period.

The *Koryŏsa* indicates 24 *chaech'u* posts in the early Koryŏ, but the number increases during the late Koryŏ to 28 in King Ch'ungnyŏl's reign (1274–1308), 50 in King Kongmin's reign, 70 in King U's reign (1374–88), and as many as 80 at the very end of the dynasty (Pyŏn, *Koryŏ chŏngch'i chedosa yŏn'gu*, 100–102). Since the number is at or below 50 until the final 20 years, 50 seems to be a reasonable working estimate for the 1260–1392 period as a whole.

72. This average of 8.7 was compiled by a random sampling technique in which I arrayed all known *chaech'u* in alphabetical order and looked at every fourth individual's term in second- and first-grade posts. I ran the sample twice, using different starting points, coming up with 8.7 years in the first sample and 8.6 years in the second. Dividing this average of 8.7 into a total of 6,600 *chaech'u* years (132 years times 50 posts), I obtained an estimate of 758 men holding *chaech'u* posts in the late Koryŏ.

73. Members of the Kyŏngwŏn Yi in office in the late Koryŏ include: Yi Chang-yong, chancellor in 1260 (*KS* 27:26b); Yi Yŏng, senior third-grade official in the Security Council in 1277 (*KS* 28:28b); Yi Ik, fourth-grade official in 1363 (*KS* 40:33a); and Yi Wŏn-goeng, fifth-grade censorate official in 1391 (*KS* 46:2a). Sŏ Kyŏn of the Ich'ŏn Sŏ held a fourth-grade censorate post in 1391 (*KS* 46:30a). From the Namp'yŏng Mun, Mun Kyŏng was a third-grade official in the mid-fourteenth century (*KS* 39:27b), while Mun Tar-han held a second-grade state councilor post in 1383 (*KS* 135:7a).

74. Yi Su-gŏn, *Han'guk chungse sahoesa yŏn'gu*, 274.

75. Focusing on the numerically large *chaech'u* descent groups has the disadvantage of excluding small groups that produced one or two very prominent officials, such as Yi Kok and Yi Saek of the Hansan Yi. The existence of such descent groups does not, however, change the large groups' overall domination of upper levels of the bureaucracy.

76. See Yi Su-gŏn, *Yŏngnam sarimp'a ŭi hyŏngsŏng*, 28–32.

77. These progenitors were: Yun Kwan of P'ap'yŏng (Pak Yong-un, "Koryŏ sidae Haeju Ch'oe-ssi wa P'ap'yŏng Yun-ssi kamun punsŏk," 135–37); Yu Kong-kwŏn of Munhwa (Kawashima, "Clan Structure and Political Power in Yi Dynasty Korea," 23–27); Min Yŏng-mo of Hwangnyŏ (Yi Su-gŏn, *Han'guk chungse sahoesa yŏn'gu*, 167–68, 267); Ch'oe Kyun of Chŏnju (ibid., 312); and Hŏ Chae of Kongam (Pak Yong-un, "Koryŏ sidae ŭi Chŏngan Im-ssi, Ch'ŏrwŏn Ch'oe-ssi, Kongam Hŏ-ssi kamun punsŏk," 61.) The Kaesŏng Wang, as putative descendents of Wang Kŏn, are included here. The P'ap'yŏng Yun, Munhwa Yu, Hwangnyŏ Min, and Chŏnju Ch'oe lines of descent are discussed in chapter 4.

78. The Chuksan Pak had one line from Pak Chŏng-su of Injong's reign, which eventually petered out in the fourteenth century, and another, more enduring, line from Pak Hwi, who appeared early in the Mongol era (Yi Su-gŏn, *Han'guk chungse*

sahoesa yŏn'gu, 154–58). The Chuksan Pak are discussed in chapter 3. The Kyŏngju Kim had one line from Kim Han-gong of the early twelfth century and another from Kim In-gwan, who passed the examinations in the early fourteenth century (ibid., 303–4). The P'yŏnggang Ch'ae had one line from Ch'ae Song-nyŏn, who held a mid-level civil office in 1147, and another line, whose relationship with Ch'ae Song-nyŏn is unclear, which appeared in the post-military era (ibid., 299).

79. The capital-based segment of the Namyang Hong was established by Hong Kwan. I have been unable to confirm the clan genealogy's claim that his immediate descendants all held mid- and low-ranking posts (ibid., 272). In the case of the Wŏnju Wŏn, although Wŏn Sŏn-ji's fourteenth-century tombstone inscription (*HKC* 3:1140) traces his forebears back to Wŏn Ching-yŏn of the late tenth century, I have been able to verify only Ching-yŏn (*KS* 2:33b) and Ching-yŏn's son Yŏn (*KS* 5:29a).

80. *KS* 33:24a–b. The 15 *chaesang* families were: Kyŏngju Kim, Ŏnyang Kim, Chŏngan Im, Kyŏngwŏn Yi, Ansan Kim, Ch'angwŏn (Ch'ŏrwŏn) Ch'oe, Haeju Ch'oe, Kongam Hŏ, P'yŏnggang Ch'ae, Ch'ŏngju Yi, Namyang Hong, Hwangnyŏ Min, Hoengsŏng Cho, P'ap'yŏng Yun, and P'yŏngyang Cho.

81. The origins of the P'yŏngyang Cho, Andong Kwŏn, Andong Kim, and Ch'ŏngju Han are discussed in chapter 3. Other newer descent groups with single lines include the Ŏnyang Kim (from Kim Ch'wi-ryŏ) and Sŏngju Yi (Yi Su-gŏn, *Han'guk chungse sahoesa yŏn'gu,* 308).

82. One of the Kwangsan Kim segments descended from Kim Su, another from Kim Chi-suk and a third from Kim Yŏn, each producing two or more late Koryŏ *chaech'u* (Yi Su-gŏn, *Han'guk chungse sahoesa yŏn'gu,* 323–24). The Kim Yŏn segment claimed direct descent from the powerful officials of the early Koryŏ who belonged to the Kwangyang Kim family, but this claim seems doubtful (Hŏ Hŭng-sik, *Han'guk ŭi komunsŏ,* 110–14). Other prominent newer descent groups with multiple segments include the Sunhŭng An, with one from An Hyang and another from An Mun-gae (Yi Su-gŏn, *Han'guk chungse sahoesa yŏn'gu,* 308); and the Kyŏngju Yi, with one from Yi Suk-chin and another from Yi Haek. The Kyŏngju Yi are discussed in chapter 3.

83. *KS* 89:16b, 19a.

84. *KS* 89:16b.

85. *KS* 88:36a, 89:12a.

86. *KS* 89:30b.

87. *KS* 89:16b.

88. *KS* 89:29a.

89. Data for the late Koryŏ marriage relationships of these two descent groups were compiled from their own genealogies, cross-checked, and supplemented with data from tombstone inscriptions and other descent groups' genealogies.

90. Wagner, "Two Early Genealogies and Women's Status in Early Yi Dynasty Korea," 23–32.

91. Kim Yong-sŏn, "Koryŏ sidae ŭi ŭmsŏ chedo," 286–93. There are occasional instances of men gaining office through the *ŭm* privilege of their great-great grandfathers or maternal great-great grandfathers, but Kim Yong-sŏn shows that these cases were limited to the descendents of merit subjects.

92. *KS* 129:33b.

93. Although occasional members of these families chose to pursue military careers, such as Yun Sǔng-nye of P'ap'yǒng, the overwhelming majority opted for the civil branch. See chapter 3 on Hwangnyǒ Min, P'ap'yǒng Yun, and Munhwa Yu officeholders in the late Koryǒ.

94. The exception was the Kyǒngju Ch'oe. Ch'oe central officials of the late Koryǒ included the line of descent that produced Ch'oe Paeg-yun (fl. late 13th cent.), an examination graduate and mid-ranking civil official, and his son Ch'oe Hae (1287–1340), a famous official, scholar, and the author of the *Chǒlgo ch'ǒnbaek* literary collection. (See Yi Kok, *Kajǒng chip* 11:5a for his tombstone inscription; and *KS* 109:27b for his biography.

95. Yi Su-gǒn, *Han'guk chungse sahoesa yǒn'gu*, 341.

96. Han Kang (d. 1303) of Ch'ǒngju passed the civil service examination under King Kojong (1213–59), but didn't rise to high office until King Ch'ungyǒl's reign *KS* 107:1a–b). U T'ak (1263–1342) of Tanyang, who was born after the fall of the military, passed the examinations under Ch'ungyǒl (*KS* 109:20b ff). Yi Chin (1244–1321) of Kyǒngju, father of Yi Che-hyǒn and founder of one of the Kyǒngju Yi segments, passed the examinations probably during Wǒnjong's reign (1259–74) and went on to high office in the civil branch in the early fourteenth century (*KS* 109:3b). There is no mention of the founder of the other Kyǒngju Yi line, Yi Ch'ǒn (fl. 1321–49), passing the examinations, but he held a number of scholarly posts throughout his career, including a concurrent appointment as attending scholar in 1344 (*KS* 37:4b). Yi Cho-nyǒn of Sǒngju passed the examinations under Ch'ungyǒl (*KS* 109:9b). For An Hyang's line of descent in the Sunhǔng An, see *KS* 105:28a ff; for An Sǒk's line, see *KS* 109:21b ff.

97. Cho In-gyu, the first member of the P'yǒngyang Cho known to have risen to high office, had served as an interpreter for the Mongols.

98. Such instances in the early Koryǒ are not unknown. See, for example, the case of Wang Kung-mo, a military official who rose to *chaech'u* posts in the late eleventh century (*KS* 95:26a–b). Nonetheless, such cases seem to have occurred with greater frequency in the late Koryǒ.

99. Kim Yong-sǒn, "Koryǒ sidae ǔi ǔmsǒ chedo e taehan chae kǒmt'o " 315–18.

100. *KS* 105:28a.

101. *KS* 124:32a.

102. *KS* 131:28b.

103. The thirteen civil officials were: Kim Sǔng-yong of Andong, Wǒn Pu of Wǒnju, Kim Pyǒn of Ǒnyang, Hǒ Kong of Kongam, Kwǒn Pu and Kwǒn Tan of Andong, Min Chǒk of Hwangnyǒ, Ch'oe Hae of Haeju, Kim Ku of Puryǒng, Han Kwang-yǒn of Tanju, Yi Ǒn-ch'ung of Chǒnǔi, Kim Tan of Ǔisǒng, and Yi Chon-bi of Kosǒng.

104. The seven military officials were Pae Chǒng-ji of Taegu, Chǒng In-gyǒng of Ch'ǒngju, Wǒn Sǒn-ji of Wǒnju, Yu Cha-u of P'yǒngsan, Kim Yun of Ǒnyang, and Cho Wi and Cho Yǒn-su of P'yǒngyang.

105. Six of these 20 men began their careers in juvenile posts (*yakkwan*). This appears to have been commonplace, at least to the extent that the compilers of the *Koryǒsa* biographies felt constrained to point out that certain individuals had not

held juvenile posts. See, for example, Pak Chŏn-ji's biography (*KS* 109:1a) and Cho Ton's biography (*KS* 111:30a). Such posts were usually palace clerical or guard slots that were outside the regular 18-rank system. In four of these six cases, the inscriptions indicate that the men were protection beneficiaries. All four belonged to our top late Koryŏ families: Kim Sŭng-yong of Andong, Wŏn Sŏn-ji of Wŏnju, and Cho Wi and Cho Yŏn-su of P'yŏngyang. The other two were also probably protection beneficiaries, since they held palace guard posts at young ages and thus match the general profile of their protection-beneficiary counterparts. The widespread usage of juvenile appointments strengthens our sense of the late Koryŏ as an aristocratic order.

106. *HKC* 2:1097.

107. *HKC* 2:1131.

108. See *HKC* 2:1123, 1131, 1112, and 1180 for the careers of these men.

109. Those who followed this path were Han Kwang-yŏn of Tanju (*HKC* 2:1047), Kim Ku of Puryŏng (*HKC* 2:1050), Wŏn Pu of Wŏnju (*HKC* 2:1060), Kim Pyŏn of Ŏnyang (*HKC* 2:1081), Ch'oe Sŏ of Haeju (*HKC* 2:1089), Kim Tan of Ŭisŏng (*HKC* 2:1092), Kwŏn Tan of Andong (*HKC* 2:1109), Kim Sŭng-yong of Andong (*HKC* 2:1136), Min Chŏk of Hwangnyŏ (*HKC* 2:1146), and Yi Ŏn-ch'ung of Chŏnŭi (*HKC* 2:1148).

110. *HKC* 2:1081.

111. *HKC* 2:1092.

112. *HKC* 2:1057, 1063, 1165.

113. *HKC* 2:1165.

114. For example, Yang Chang, lord of Umun (Umun-gun), who is not listed anywhere in the *Koryŏsa* as holding an official position, was ordered by the king to take charge of personnel affairs (*KS* 35:31b).

115. *KS* 133:32b.   •

116. *KS* 38:20a.

117. Yi U-sŏng, "Koryŏjo ŭi 'i' e taehayŏ," 24–25. An alternative interpretation has been offered by Yi Sŏng-mu. Citing a memorial (which had been approved by King Sejong of the Chosŏn dynasty) that said, "We request that officials of the fourth rank and higher be called *taebu* and officials of the fifth rank and lower be called *sa*," Yi argues that *sadaebu* simply denoted officials of the dynastic government. Yi also notes instances, such as a *Koryŏsa* entry regarding the late Koryŏ allotment of stipend lands, where *sadaebu* was used to indicate both civil and military officials. See Yi Sŏng-mu, *Chosŏn ch'ogi yangban yŏn'gu*, 211–12. Both parties agree, however, that widespread use of the term *sadaebu* began in the late Koryŏ.

118. Kim Tang-t'aek, "Ch'ungnyŏl wang ŭi pongnip kwajŏng . . . ," 195–232.

119. See, for example, Min Hyŏn-gu, "Koryŏ hugi ŭi kwŏnmun sejok," 39.

120. *KS* 78:19b.

121. Kim Kwang-ch'ŏl, *Koryŏ hugi sejokch'ŭng yŏn'gu*, 17–47.

122. Yi Sŏng-mu, "Chosŏn ch'ogi sinbunsa yŏn'gu ŭi chae kŏmt'o," 217.

123. *T'aejo sillok* 8:3b.

124. Yi Sŏng-mu, "Chosŏn ch'ogi sinbunsa yŏn'gu ŭi chae kŏmt'o," 217.

125. See Song June-ho, *Chosŏn sahoesa yŏn'gu*, 249–259, on issues in relation to the question of *yangban* status.

126. Johnson, *The Medieval Chinese Oligarchy,* 20.

127. See Pak Yong-un, *Koryŏ sidaesa,* 163–69 for a concise discussion of these revisions.

128. Kim Su-t'ae, "Koryŏ pon'gwan chedo ŭi sŏngnip," 54.

129. See Pak Yong-un, *Koryŏ sidaesa,* 447–48, on the land amalgamation activities of Yi Cha-ryang and Yi Cha-gyŏm.

130. *KS* 79:31a.

131. Palais, *Confucian Statecraft and Korean Institutions,* 213–15.

132. *KS* 78:45a–46b. See Kang Chin-ch'ŏl, *Hanguk chungse t'oji soyu yŏn'gu,* 86–91 for discussion of *cho* as rent.

133. See Song Pyŏng-gi, "Koryŏ sidae ŭi nongjang—12 segi ihu rŭl chungsim ŭro," on the prevalence and size of late Koryŏ *nongjang.*

134. Yi Che-hyŏn, *Yŏgong p'aesŏl* 1:11b.

135. *KS* 46:9b.

136. *KS* 46:29a.

137. Hong Sŭng-gi, *Koryŏ kwijok sahoe wa nobi* and James Palais's review of that book, "Slavery and Slave Society in Koryŏ," 173–80.

138. Song Pyŏng-gi, "Nongjang ŭi paltal," 133–34.

139. The devastating Mongol invasions of the thirteenth century and the Wako raids of the late fourteenth century may also have contributed to the growth of slavery. The countryside in many areas was laid waste, with some districts totally deserted, their fields abandoned and populations killed, scattered, or taken away by the invaders. In 1254 the Mongols in one instance took over 206,800 persons back to the mainland as prisoners and slaughtered countless others (see *KS* 24:20b), while the Wako frequently captured villagers and took them to Japan. The result was an abundance of abandoned land available for confiscation and amalgamation and a severe shortage of people to work it. A similar situation in Europe, where land was widely available and populations low (only 2.2 persons per square kilometer in Germany), stimulated the growth of slavery at the beginning of the medieval period (Duby, *The Early Growth of the European Economy,* 85–87).

140. Sudo, "Korai makki yori Chosen shoki ni ataru nohi no kenkyu."

141. Yi Saek, *Mogŭn chip* 4:5b

142. *KS* 107:12b.

143. *Chŏngjong sillok* 2:16b.

144. Translated by Uchang Kim and Peter Lee in Lee, ed., *Anthology of Korean Literature,* 56–57.

145. See Min Hyŏn-gu, "Koryŏ ŭi Nokkwajŏn," 291–329, for a lucid discussion of the origins, provisions, and significance of the Salary Land system. Limitations of the system are highlighted in Pak Yong-un, *Koryŏ sidaesa,* 566–71.

146. This was due in part to corruption of the Salary Land system as revealed in a 1344 memorial from the Todang that describes the passing of Salary Land system fields from government to private control (*KS* 78:19b), a development typical of the problems that were eroding the dynasty's financial foundations.

147. Palais, "Confucianism and the Aristocratic/Bureaucratic Balance in Korea," 426–68.

148. See Deuchler, *The Confucian Transformation of Korea,* 39–40, on Koryŏ family records.
149. Bol, *"This Culture of Ours,"* 32–36.
150. Johnson, *The Medieval Chinese Oligarchy,* 21–26, 33–44, 121–51.

3. THE *YANGBAN* IN THE CHANGE OF DYNASTIES

1. See, for example, Han Young-woo's treatment of Chŏng To-jŏn in *Chŏng To-jŏn sasang ŭi yŏn'gu.*
2. Chŏng Tu-hŭi, *Chosŏn ch'ogi chŏngch'i seryŏk yŏn'gu,* 54–55.
3. Ibid., 23.
4. *KS* 77:31a.
5. *T'aejo sillok* 7:14a.
6. *Chŏngjong sillok* 3:4a.
7. *Chŏngjong sillok* 4:1a.
8. *T'aejo sillok* 1:45a ff.
9. *Chŏngjong sillok* 4:2b.
10. Wagner, "The Korean Chokpo as a Historical Source," 141–52. Making a strong argument in favor of the reliability of Korean genealogies, Wagner points out that the Confucian value system placed great importance on maintaining correct lines of descent, no claims of elevated status were made for many ancestors, and there is a high degree of correlation between genealogical data and such official sources as examination rosters and census registers.
11. Although greatly diminished in comparison with the early Koryŏ period, the late Koryŏ Kyŏngwŏn Yi still maintained a presence in the central officialdom, with five known officials, including two *chaech'u.*
12. On the late Koryŏ Hamyang Pak, see Yi Su-gŏn, *Han'guk chungse sahoesa yŏn'gu,* 292–93.
13. Min Hyŏn-gu, "Sin Ton ŭi chipkwŏn kwa kŭ chŏngch'ijŏk sŏnggyŏk," 78–92.
14. See Clark, "Chosŏn's Founding Fathers," 17–40, on early Choson merit subjects.
15. *KS* 135:30b.
16. It is possible, perhaps even probable, that members of the P'yŏnggang Ch'ae held low-ranking, unrecorded posts at this time.
17. *KS* 36:16b. See *KS* 108:11b–13b for descent.
18. *KS* 38:20a.
19. Ki T'ak-sŏng was a military official under Ŭijong who rose to high office after the 1170 coup (*KS* 100:14a).
20. *KS* 101:1a–4b.
21. *KS* 126:27a–29a.
22. *KS* 26:13a.
23. Yi Su-gŏn, *Han'guk chungse sahoesa yŏn'gu,* 274.
24. *KS* 126:19b.
25. Ch'ae Se-yong of P'yŏnggang passed the examinations in 1517 and went on to hold a variety of mid-level positions in the mid-sixteenth century, and Ch'ae

Yu-hu passed the examinations in 1623, subsequently rising to the junior second-grade personnel minister post.

26. The famed scholar and official Ki Tae-sŭng was from Haengju, as were several other officials in the sixteenth and seventeenth centuries, such as Ki Tae-hang, Ki Ik-hŏn, and Ki Cha-hŏn.

27. *T'aejo sillok* 12:9b.

28. *Chŏngjong sillok* 4:20a.

29. *T'aejo sillok* 14:28a.

30. Ibid. 13:1b.

31. Ibid. 1:37a, 1:53a.

32. Ibid. 15:2b.

33. *Chŏngjong sillok* 3:13a.

34. *T'aejo sillok* 6:12b; *Mansŏng taedongbo* 2:11.

35. *T'aejo sillok* 2:16b.

36. *T'aejong sillok* 5:29a.

37. *Kukcho pangmok*, 518.

38. *Chŏngjong sillok* 2:16b.

39. Ibid. 2:16b.

40. *T'aejo sillok* 14:29a.

41. Ibid. 11:13b. See *Yŏhŭng Min-ssi sebo* 1:9 for detail on Min Mu-gu.

42. See *KS* 45:23a for Nam Un's earliest known post, a grand generalship (*sang hogun*).

43. *T'aejo sillok* 3:11b.

44. Kim Yŏng-mo, *Chosŏn chibaech'ŭng yŏn'gu*, 439.

45. *Kukcho pangmok*, 528.

46. See Hŏ Hŭng-sik, "Koryŏ kwagŏ chedo ŭi kŏmt'o," 62.

47. Ibid., 52.

48. Ibid., 52–57

49. Pak Yong-un, "Koryŏ sidae ŭmsoje ŭi silche wa kŭ kinŭng," 38.

50. See Wagner, "Two Early Genealogies and Women's Status in Early Yi Dynasty Korea," on distinguishing features of elite descent groups in the early and late Chosŏn.

51. Kawashima, "Clan Structure and Political Power in Yi Dynasty Korea," 25–27.

52. Min Yŏng-mo and his two sons, Sik and Kong-gyu, are in the *Koryŏsa* biographies (*KS* 101:1a–3a). The biographies for Min Chi (*KS* 107:27a) and Min Chŏk (*KS* 108:1a) identify them as fifth-generation descendants without listing intervening ancestors. The lines of descent for both men can be reconstructed, however, using tombstone inscriptions and rosters of examination graduates. See Pak Yong-un, *Koryo sidae ŭmsŏje wa kwagŏje yŏn'gu*, 416 and 429, for detail. The offices held by Min Myŏng-sin and Min Hwi cannot be verified either in the histories or in tombstone inscriptions, but Min In-gyun appears in the *Koryŏsa* (*KS* 73:38a, 74:17b), while Min Hwang's position as a mid-level official is confirmed at two different locations in Ch'oe Hae, *Cholgo ch'ŏnbaek* 2:393, 2:411.

53. *KS* 109:27b ff.

54. *KS* 107:32b.

55. *KS* 108:1a ff.
56. *T'aejo sillok* 11:1a.
57. Chŏng Tu-hŭi, *Chosŏn ch'ogi chŏngch'i seryŏk yŏn'gu*, 10.
58. *Chŏngjong sillok* 4:5a.
59. Chŏng Tu-hŭi, *Chosŏn ch'ogi chŏngch'i seryŏk yŏn'gu*, 41.
60. *KS* 102:19a–b.
61. *KS* 110:13b ff.
62. *T'aejo sillok* 6:6a.
63. Ibid. 10:8b.
64. *Chŏngjong sillok* 2:18a.
65. *T'aejong sillok* 7:22a.
66. *Chŏngjong sillok* 4:14a.
67. Yi Saek, *Mogŭn chip* 18:15a
68. *KS* 37:20b.
69. *KS* 40:21a.
70. *T'aejo sillok* 1:27b.
71. Chŏng Tu-hŭi, *Chosŏn ch'ogi chŏngch'i seryŏk yŏn'gu*, 9.
72. *T'aejo sillok* 15:11a.
73. Ibid. 10:5a.
74. *KS* 105:1a–8b.
75. *T'aejo sillok* 2:15a
76. Ibid. 4:13b.
77. Ibid. 6:15b.
78. Ibid. 11:13b.
79. Ibid. 13:13a.
80. Chŏng Tu-hŭi, *Chosŏn ch'ogi chŏngch'i seryŏk yŏn'gu*, 42.
81. *KS* 35:26b.
82. *KS* 37:10b, 104:31a, 37:7b.
83. *T'aejo sillok* 4:6b.
84. Ibid. 1:50a.
85. Ibid. 13:2a.
86. Ibid. 1:20a.
87. See Yi Su-gŏn, *Han'guk chungse saehosa yŏn'gu*, 158 and 289, for details about this segment of the Chuksan Pak.
88. *KS* 28:2b.
89. *KS* 35:7b.
90. *KS* 35:22a.
91. *KS* 38:25a.
92. *KS* 45:24a.
93. *T'aejo sillok* 3:3b.
94. Ibid. 13:1b.
95. Ibid. 15:7a.
96. *KS* 26:35a.
97. *KS* 36:28a.
98. *KS* 124:25a.
99. *KS* 41:7a.

100. Yi Saek, *Mogŭn chip* 16:3b.

101. Yi Haek's post, the senior second-grade *chwa pogya*, was often given as an honorary post, and could even have been granted to him posthumously in recognition of the merit of his sons.

102. *KS* 109:3a ff.

103. *KS* 37:7b.

104. *KS* 38:15b.

105. *Chŏngjong sillok* 6:5b.

106. Chŏng Tu-hŭi, *Chosŏn ch'ogi chŏngch'i seryŏk yŏn'gu*, 42.

107. *T'aejo sillok* 3:12b.

108. Ibid. 9:3b.

109. *Chŏngjong sillok* 1:17b.

110. See Min, "Cho In-gyu wa kŭ ŭi kamun, sang," 17–24, on the origins of the P'yŏngyang Cho. See Yi Su-gŏn, *Han'guk chungse sahoesa yŏn'gu*, 330–31, for an alternative view that the Cho were local elites.

111. *KS* 37:5a.

112. *KS* 109:42b ff.

113. *KS* 38:24a.

114. *KS* 133:15a.

115. *KS* 105:31b.

116. Chŏng Tu-hŭi, *Chosŏn ch'ogi chŏngch'i seryŏk yŏn'gu*, 9.

117. *T'aejo sillok* 15:1b.

118. Ibid. 13:2a.

119. Ibid. 14:29a.

120. *KS* 107:1a ff.

121. *KS* 107:2a.

122. *KS* 107:2b.

123. *KS* 107:2b.

124. *KS* 42:24a.

125. Chong Tu-hŭi, *Chosŏn ch'ogi chŏngch'i seryŏk yŏn'gu*, 9.

126. *T'aejo sillok* 7:12a.

127. Ibid. 10:4b.

128. Ibid. 6:14a.

129. *Chŏngjong sillok* 4:14a.

130. See Ch'oe Kyun's biography (*KS* 99:41a–42a) for details on these three men.

131. *KS* 108:10a.

132. Pak Yong-un, *Koryŏ sidae umsoje*, 437; and Yi Che-hyŏn, *Ichae nan'go* 7:13b.

133. *KS* 37:7b.

134. *KS* 135:44a.

135. Ch'oe Sŏn appears to have held both military and civil posts (*T'aejo sillok* 11:9a; *Chŏngjong sillok* 4:18a). Ch'oe Koeng held a mid-ranking civil post (*T'aejo sillok* 11:9a).

136. *KS* 34:18b.

137. Yi Saek, *Mogŭn chip* 15:21b

138. *KS* 111:35b–36a.

139. Ch'oe Yu-gyŏng's role in consolidating control over the military is suggested by his promotion to superintendent of the Consolidated Army Command and the gifts he was given in the seventh month of 1400, following the abolition of private armies (*Chŏngjong sillok* 5:1b).

140. *Andong Kwon-ssi songhwa po* 1:4.

141. *P'yŏngyang Cho-ssi sebo* 1:3.

142. Yi Saek's wife was the daughter of Kwŏn Chung-dal (*KMH* 3:222), while Saek's son Chong-sŏn married two women from the Andong Kwŏn, the daughters of Kwŏn Kyun and Kwŏn Kŭn (*Kukcho pangmok,* "U wang," 8th year).

143. *P'yongyang Cho-ssi sebo* 1:9

144. *P'ap'yŏng Yun-ssi sebo* 1:29

145. *T'aejo sillok* 4:8a ff.

146. See Clark, "Chosŏn's Founding Fathers," for a complete list of marriages of children of early Chosŏn kings.

147. Nine of these 11 were well-established Koryŏ descent groups: the Chonŭi Yi, who first appeared in the central officialdom during the military era (Yi Su-gŏn, *Han'guk chungse saehoesa yŏn'gu,* 289); the Chinju Kang and Chinju Yu, both of which established themselves during the military era (ibid., 310); the Hadong Chŏng, with Chŏng Chi-yŏn as an associate chancellor in 1313 (*KS* 34:12b); the Yŏnan Yi, who also rose under the military (Yi Su-gŏn, *Han'guk chungse saehosa yŏn'gu,* 279); the Ch'angnyŏng Cho (with Cho Ik-ch'ŏng and Cho Min-su), who had officials as early as King Ch'ungsuk's reign (*KS* 35:04a, "Cho Kwang-han"); the Yangsŏng Yi, who were active from the late twelfth and early thirteenth centuries and were notorious pro-Yüan elements (Yi Su-gŏn, *Han'guk chungse saehosa yŏn'gu,* 274); the Miryang Pak, who were already well-established by the early fourteenth century (*KS* 33:38a, "Associate Chancellor Pak Ŭi"); and the Hwangnyŏ Yi, who first appeared during the military era and whose members include the famous Yi Kyu-bo (Yi Su-gŏn, *Han'guk chungse saehoesa yŏn'gu,* 267). Two others, the Hansan Yi and Ch'angnyŏng Sŏng, are often cited as representative "new scholar-officials," but, as we have seen in their marriage relations, by the early Chosŏn they had joined the central establishment.

148. These are the Chinju Ha, Tongnae Chŏng, Yŏngil Chŏng (with Chŏng Mong-ju), Kwangju Yi, Kimhae Kim, P'yŏngsan Sin, Yŏnan Kim, Nŭngsŏng Ku, and Sunch'ŏn Pak.

149. These are the Hanyang Cho, Yangju Cho, Kaesŏng Yi, Hayang Hŏ, Hoedŏk Hwang, and Changsu Hwang.

150. See Deuchler, *The Confucian Transformation of Korea,* p. 97, on the roles played by these men in the early Chosŏn.

151. See Hŏ Cho's tombstone inscription in (Yi Sang-ŭn, ed., *Han'guk yŏktae inmuljŏn chipsŏng* 5:4537).

152. *Han'guk yŏktae inmuljŏn* 2:1011, "Haedong myŏngsin-nok." The same information can be found in *Sinch'ang Maeng-ssi sebo* (1937 ed.) 1:2a–3a.

153. Yi Sang-ŭn, ed., *Han'guk yŏktae inmuljŏn chipsŏng* 2:1400, "Kukcho inmulgo."

154. Ibid. 5:4387.

155. *Taejong sillok* 32:26a.

156. *Han'guk yŏktae inmuljŏn chipsŏng* 5:4778.

157. *T'aejo sillok* 8:13a.

158. Yi Saek's son Yi Chong-sŏn held a senior third-grade post in 1396 (*T'aejo sillok* 9:7a) and his grandson Yi Maeng-gyun was a mid-ranking official under T'aejong (*T'aejong sillok* 3:35a).

159. Kim Yŏng-mo, *Chosŏn chibaech'ŭng yŏn'gu,* 439.

160. The two men of the Changsu Hwang in office, Hwang Ch'i-sin and Hwang Su-sin, were sons of the famous Hwang Hŭi. They appear to have gained entry to the bureaucracy due to their father's prestige, and of course, his *ŭm.*

161. Lee Ki-baik, *Han'guksa sillon,* 218–19.

162. Song June-ho, *Chosŏn sahoesa yŏn'gu,* 127–36.

163. *KS* 134:15a.

164. *KS* 114:1a–2b, cited in Pak Un-gyŏng, "Koryŏ hugi chibang p'umgwan seryŏk e kwanhan yŏn'gu," 51.

165. See Kim Yong-sŏn, "Koryŭ chibaech'ŭng ŭi maejangji e taehan koch'al," 269–79.

166. *T'aejong sillok* 8:26a.

167. *KS* 46:4a ff.

168. See Kim Yong-sŏn, "Koryŏ chibaech'ŭng ŭi maejangji e taehan koch'al," 225–79.

169. *T'aejo sillok* 3:2a–3b.

170. Kawashima, "Clan Structure and Political Power in Yi Dynasty Korea," 166–70.

171. The *Wŏnju Wŏn-ssi chokpo* shows that members holding offices in the central government were buried in the Kaegyŏng/Seoul area from the late thirteenth through the mid-fifteenth century; later burial sites are spread throughout the country. The *Ch'ŏngju Han-ssi sebo* shows burial of central official members in the capital region from the fourteenth through sixteenth centuries; tombs appear in the provinces near the end of the sixteenth century.

172. Han Young-woo, "Yŏmal sŏnch'o hallyang kwa kŭ chiwi."

173. Sudo Yoshiyuki, who believed that the great estates of the late Koryŏ marked the beginning of private land ownership in Korea, argued for the continuing existence of those great estates into the early Chosŏn in his article "Raimatsu sensho ni okeru nojo ni tsuite."

174. *T'aejo sillok* 15:8b.

175. *Chŏngjong sillok* 2:16b.

176. Ibid. 3:7b.

177. Sŏng Hyŏn, *Yongje ch'onghwa* 3:19a–b

178. Lee Ki-baik, *Han'guksa sillon,* 248.

179. Sudo Yoshiyuki, "Raimatsu sensho ni okeru nojo ni tsuite"; Yi Sŏng-mu, *Chosŏn ch'ogi yangban yŏn'gu,* 365.

180. *T'aejo sillok* 2:2b.

181. Ibid. 15:7a.

182. Quoted in Yi Su-gŏn, *Yŏngnam sarimp'a ŭi hyŏngsŏng,* 171.

183. Yi Su-gŏn, *Yŏngnam sarimp'a ŭi hyŏngsŏng,* 175–76.

184. In 1850 there were 347,525 slaveholders in the American South, fewer

than 1,800 of whom owned more than 100 slaves (*Encyclopaedia Britannica,* 15th ed. [1978] 18:967–68).

185. Yi Su-gŏn, *Yŏngnam sarimp'a ŭi hyŏngsŏng,* 155–84.
186. Palais, "Slavery and Slave Society in Koryŏ," 174–76
187. Ch'ŏn Kwan-u, "Han'guk t'oji chedo-sa," part 2, 1488.
188. James Palais calculates that in the late Chosŏn the size of one *kyŏl* varied from 2.2 to 8.8 acres depending on the quality of the land (*Politics and Policy in Traditional Korea,* 65). If we apply his calculation to the early Chosŏn, Cho Chun's merit subject grant would increase to approximately 450 acres.
189. *T'aejo sillok* 7:1a–1b.
190. *KS* 46:12a.
191. *T'aejo sillok* 11:11b.
192. Miyakawa, "An Outline of the Naito Hypothesis," 533–52.
193. Ebrey, *The Aristocratic Families of Early Imperial China.*
194. Johnson, *The Medieval Chinese Oligarchy,* 141–45.
195. Bol, *This Culture of Ours,* 48–58.
196. Sŏng Hyŏn, *Yongjae ch'onghwa* 10, cited in Yi Su-gŏn, *Han'guk chungse sahoesa yŏn'gu,* 6.
197. Yang Sŏng-ji, *Nuljae chip,* "sokp'yŏn" 1:10a.
198. Bol, *"This Culture of Ours,"* 327.

4. INSTITUTIONAL CRISIS IN THE LATE KORYŎ

1. E.g., Cho Chun's use of the term *chunghŭng* in his 1389 memorial on fiscal reform (*KS* 78:36b).
2. This point is made by Pyŏn T'ae-sŏp in *Koryŏsa ŭi yŏn'gu,* 84, 86, and 88.
3. Kings removed by the Mongols included Ch'ungsŏn in 1298, Ch'unghye in 1332 and again in 1344, and Ch'ungjŏng in 1351.
4. *KS* 24:36a.
5. *KS* 24:44a.
6. *KS* 25:17b.
7. *KS* 26:12a.
8. *KS* 26:26b–27a.
9. *KS* 26:33b.
10. Ko Pyŏng-il, *Tonga kyosŏpsa ŭi yŏn'gu,* 291–92.
11. Yukkun Ponbu, ed., *Han'guk kunjesa,* 49–50.
12. These two men were Ch'oe Yŏng and Kyŏng Pok-hŭng (*KSC* 28:10a).
13. See Pyŏn T'ae-sŏp, *Koryŏ chŏngch'i chedosa yŏn'gu,* 99–100, on Todang membership.
14. Yi Che-hyŏn, *Yŏgong p'aesŏl* 1:10a–11b; trans. by Hugh H. Kang and Edward J. Shultz (Lee, ed., *A Sourcebook of Korean Tradition,* 295).
15. See Pyŏn T'ae-sŏp's discussion of the expansion of Todang functions in *Koryŏ chŏngch'i chedosa yŏn'gu,* 105–12.
16. *KS* 82:18A ff.
17. *KS* 81:17a.
18. *KS* 110:2b.

19. *KS* 107:7b–8a, 107:30a ff.

20. Yi Che-hyŏn, *Yŏgong p'aesŏl* 1:11b. The translation excerpted here is by Hugh H. Kang and Edward J. Shultz (Lee, ed. *Sourcebook of Korean Tradition,* 293); I have changed the titles of some offices to be consistent with the terms used in this volume.

21. *KSC* 20:14b.

22. *KSC* 22:6a.

23. Pyŏn T'ae-sŏp, *Koryŏ chŏngch'i chedosa yŏn'gu,* 100.

24. Pak Yong-un, *Koryŏ sidae taegan chedo yŏn'gu,* 194–201.

25. Ko Pyŏng-ik, *Tonga kyosŏpsa ŭi yŏn'gu,* 291–92.

26. Eisenstadt, *The Political Systems of Empires,* 115–16.

27. This conflict is detailed in Cheguk's biography (*KS* 89:1a ff).

28. See Kim Sŏng-jun, "Yŏdae Yüan kongju ch'ulsin wangbi ŭi chŏngch'i-jŏk wich'i e taehayŏ," 214–57, on the roles Cheguk and Kyeguk played in late thirteenth-century politics.

29. *KS* 89:24b–25a.

30. The special relationship between the palace and such foreigners as In Hu and Chang Sun-nyong is reflected in the *Koryŏsa* biographies, where those men are included among the "royal favorites" (*p'yehaeng*). See *KS* 123:27b–35b.

31. In the twelfth century King Ŭijong relied heavily on the advice of the eunuch Chŏng Ham, and even had him appointed to low-level (sixth- and seventh-grade) civil posts (Yi Pyong-do, *Han'guksa chungse p'yŏn,* 453–54), but this appears to be an isolated instance of personal favoritism.

32. *KS* 28:22b. In the early Koryŏ eunuchs were allowed to hold offices of the seventh grade or lower, as seen in the case of Chŏng Ham under Ŭijong. What appears to be new here is that Kim Cha-jŏng was appointed to a fourth-grade post.

33. *KS* 30:12a.

34. *KS* 32:24b, 33:8a.

35. *KS* 122:15a.

36. *KS* 124:18b.

37. *KS* 89:24b.

38. The *Koryŏsa* tells us that one of the Ki men, Ch'ŏl, who received the honorary title of king, refused to recognize the Koryŏ king as his lord (*KS* 131:18a).

39. *KS* 131:16b.

40. See *KS* 75:3a ff for a chronological treatment of the Personnel Authority and *KS* 75:3b on its transformation into a palace-based entity. Conventional treatments of the Personnel Authority view it as a bastion of aristocratic (so-called *kwŏnmun sejok*) power (see, for example, Kim Sŏng-jun, *Han'guk chungse chŏngch'i pŏpchesa yŏn'gu,* 210–20). This view, however, stems from two faulty assumptions. One is that the late Koryŏ kings were puppets incapable of acting on their own. The other, closely related, assumption is that the men who staffed the Personnel Authority, including such royal favorites of slave backgrounds as Kang Yun-ch'ung, represented the interests of established official descent groups. See *KSC* 25:58b for Kang's activities in the Personnel Authority; and *KS* 124:9b for his social origins.

41. See Kim Sŏng-jun, "Koryŏ chŏngbang ko," on the Personnel Authority.
42. See *KS* 4:46b on Ch'ungnyŏl's relationship with Kim Chu-jŏng.
43. *KS* 115:32a.
44. *KS* 123:25b.
45. *KS* 104:45b.
46. *KSC* 20:15a–b, 20:20a.
47. *KSC* 22:42b–43a.
48. *KSC* 24:19a.
49. *KSC* 24:45b. See also Ch'oe An-do's biography (*KS* 124:26a).
50. *KS* 89:19b–20a.
51. See table 3.8, this volume.
52. *KS* 111:9a.
53. *KS* 111:27a–28a.
54. Pak Ch'ŏn-sik identifies two major elements in the officialdom during U's reign. One was the group headed by Yi In-im, whose members by and large came from old *yangban* descent groups such as Yi In-im's Sŏngju Yi; the other was a military group—headed by Ch'oe Yŏng and including Yi Sŏng-gye and Pyŏn An-nyŏl—which had grown powerful in the campaigns against the Red Turbans and the Wako of Kongmin's reign. Pak argues that Yi In-im and Ch'oe Yŏng, who joined forces to place U on the throne in 1374, formed an uneasy alliance dominated by Yi that lasted—despite occasional challenges from other *yangban*—almost until the end of U's reign, when Ch'oe purged the Yi In-im group in the first month of 1388 and established himself as the kingdom's supreme power broker (Pak Ch'ŏn-sik, "Koryŏ Uwang dae ŭi chŏngch'i seryŏk kwa kŭ ch'ui," 1–48).
55. *KS* 122:24b.
56. *KS* 122:27a. Kim Sa-haeng later reemerged as an important figure in the early years of the Chosŏn.
57. The eunuchs were Yi Tŭk-pun and Kim Sil (*KS* 134:19a).
58. *KSC* 32:21b–22a.
59. *KS* 137:27b.
60. *KS* 30:10a.
61. *KSC* 31:5b.
62. *KSC* 32:5a–b.
63. *KSC* 28:12a.
64. *KSC* 31:9a
65. *KS* 126:20a, cited in Pyŏn t'ae-sŏp, *Koryŏ chŏngch'i chedosa yŏn'gu*, 103. "Transmittal of edicts" is a rendering of the Sino-Korean term *ch'ullap*, which in modern Korean is used almost exclusively for monetary receipts and disbursements. In traditional Korea, however, it included the transmission of royal documents such as edicts and proclamations. See, for example, *KS* 76:10b for the usage in the description of Security Council functions.
66. See, for example, *KSC* 32:21b and 32:26b for discussions of U's profligacy and *KS* 135:40b for complaints of the eunuchs.
67. *KS* 126:27b–28a.
68. Pak Ch'ŏn-sik, "Koryŏ Uwangdae . . . ," 41–43.

69. Ibid., 42–44.
70. Yi Che-hyŏn, *Yŏgong p'aesŏl* 1:9a.
71. See *KS* 84:22a–23b for the text of Hong Cha-bŏn's memorial.
72. See Yi Ki-nam, "Ch'ungsŏn wang ŭi kaehyŏk kwa Sarimwŏn ŭi sŏlch'i," esp. 94–96, on staffing of the Sarimwŏn. Yi argues that Ch'ungsŏn's reforms were the result of "new scholar-official" influence.
73. Kim Sŏng-jun, "Yŏdae Yüan kongju ch'ulsin wangbi ŭi chŏngch'ijŏk wich'i e taehayŏ," 214–57.
74. Kim Sŏng-jun, *Han'guk chungse chŏngch'i pŏpchesa yŏn'gu*, 216.
75. See Min Hyŏn-gu, "Chŏngch'i Togam ŭi sŏnggyŏk," for the most comprehensive study of the Chŏngch'i Togam. While I do not agree with Min's "new scholar-official" versus "old aristocracy" frame of analysis, I found this study very useful in understanding the nature and activities of the directorate.
76. *KS* 109:30b.
77. *KS* 84:27a.
78. *KS* 110:34a.
79. *KSC* 26:7b–8a.
80. *KSC* 26:9b.
81. *KSC* 26:10a.
82. Noguk may have been a main source of strength and ambition for Kongmin. She was, from all accounts, a remarkably strong individual. During the retreat south from the Red Turbans in 1361, she abandoned the royal palanquin and led the way on horseback, and at the time of Kim Yong's attempt to assassinate Kongmin in 1363, she hid the king in her room and faced down the plotters until help arrived. It is no wonder, then, that after she died Kongmin found himself at loose ends (*KS* 89:26b).
83. *KS* 132:3a–b.
84. Among the victims of Sin Ton's purges were such members of the Namyang Hong as Hong In-gye (*KS* 41:6a).
85. See Min Hyŏn-gu, "Sin Ton ŭi chipkwŏn kwa kŭ chŏngch'ijŏk sŏnggyŏk," on Sin Ton's term of office.
86. *KS* 43:5b.
87. *KS* 75:18b.
88. *KS* 82:8a.
89. *KS* 113:15a.
90. *KS* 84:20a–b.
91. *KS* 43:10a.
92. *KS* 84:40a.
93. *KS* 111:14b, 113.26a.
94. *KS* 82:21b.
95. *KS* 133:2b.
96. *KS* 133:25a.
97. *KS* 81:26a ff.
98. *KS* 135:27a, 29b, 30a, 40b.
99. *KS* 75:8a.
100. *KS* 113:45b.

101. *KS* 24:20a.
102. *KS* 78:18b.
103. See Yi Kyŏng-sik, *Chosŏn chŏn'gi t'oji chedo yŏn'gu*, 59–61, for evidence and discussion of the persistence of the Field and Woodland Rank system.
104. See Min Hyŏn-gu, "Koryŏ ŭi Nokkwajŏn," 291–329, for a detailed discussion of the Salary Rank Land system.
105. Yi Pyŏng-do, *Han'guksa chungse p'yŏn*, 581.
106. Min Hyŏn-gu, "Koryŏ ŭi Nokkwajŏn," 315.
107. *KS* 80:17a.
108. *KS* 78:19a.
109. *KS* 78:18b.
110. *KS* 80:18a.
111. *KS* 80:20a.
112. *KS* 80:1b ff.
113. *KS* 133:28b.
114. *T'aejo sillok* 2:5a.
115. *KS* 46:3a.
116. *KS* 80:18–19b.
117. Park Jong-ki, *Koryŏ sidae pugokche yŏn'gu*, 183–88.
118. *KS* 28:22a.
119. *KS* 28:36a, cited in Yi Kyŏng-sik, *Chosŏn chŏn'gi t'oji chedo yŏn'gu*, 49.
120. *KS* 84:25b.
121. *KS* 78:20b.
122. An Ch'uk, *Kŭnjae chip* 1:20a
123. Yi Kok, *Kajŏng chip* 20:6a
124. Wŏn Ch'ŏn-sŏk, *Un'gok sisa* 1:6b–7a
125. *KS* 41:5a, 19a; 43:15a; 133:10b, 24b, 35b.
126. Yi Sŏng-mu, for example, says, "The dispersal of the people and disorder in the status system in the late Koryŏ resulted in a shaky economic foundation for the state. In order to restore its shattered economic foundations, beginning with the reign of Wŏnjong the state on several occasions launched projects to determine the status of lands and peoples, but each time, due to the opposition of powerful families, it was unable to achieve much success" (Yi Sŏng-mu, *Chosŏn ch'ogi yangban yŏn'gu*, 176).
127. Min, "Sin Ton ŭi chipkwŏn kwa kŭ chŏngch'ijŏk sŏnggyŏk," part 2, 63–70.
128. Min, "Koryŏ ŭi Nokkwajŏn," 297
129. Im, "Nobi munje," 138.
130. *KS* 77:27a.
131. *KS* 32:10a.
132. *KS* 38:5a–b.
133. *KS* 132:6b.
134. *KS* 77:27a.
135. See Sudo Yoshiyuki, "Sensho ni okeru nuhi no bentei to shusatsu to ni tsuite," 11–61, on slavery litigation in the early Chosŏn.
136. *KS* 78:18b.
137. *KS* 82:39b.

138. *KS* 78:20b.

139. *KSC* 32:25b.

140. *KS* 43:11a.

141. *KS* 136:32a.

142. See Sudo Yoshiyuki, "Koraicho yori Richo shoki ni itaru oshitsu zaisei," 95–102.

143. See Song Pyŏng-gi, "Nongjang ŭi paltal," 62–65 on land amalgamation by state agencies in the late Koryŏ. Song argues that although this ostensibly provided for agency operating expenses, in fact it provided pay for agency officials.

144. See *KS* 85:27a on the functions of the *sun'gun.*

145. See Pak Yong-un, *Koryŏ sidaesa,* 545–46 and 552, on aspects of these reform movements that pertained to the countryside.

146. Yi Kok, *Kajŏng chip* 20:6a

147. *KS* 75:47b.

148. *KS* 75:48a.

149. *KSC* 22:5a.

150. *KS* 73:11b.

151. See Yi Sŏng-mu, *Chosŏn ch'ogi yangban yŏn'gu,* esp. chaps. 1 and 2. Much of what follows is based on Professor Yi's research. He, however, conducts his analysis within the framework of the conventional *kwŏnmun sejok/sadaebu* dichotomy, whereas I emphasize tension between the traditional Koryŏ institutional structure and interests of central official families.

152. See Yi T'ae-jin, "Koryŏ hugi ŭi in'gu chŭngga yoin saengsŏng kwa hyangyak ŭisul paltal," 203–79.

153. Hŏ Hŭng-sik, *Koryŏ kwagŏ chedosa yŏn'gu,* 145–64.

154. Whereas local official eligibility for the regular civil service examinations was limited to the sons of only the top two local officials (headman and assistant headman), sons of lower-ranking local officials were eligible to sit for the technical examinations (Yi Sŏng-mu, *Chosŏn ch'ogi yangban yŏn'gu,* 57).

155. *KS* 105:28a.

156. This tendency is noted by Yi Sŏng-mu (*Chosŏn ch'ogi yangban yŏngu,* 26 n 91), who draws his conclusions from the *Koryŏsa* biographies. Hŏ Hŭng-sik, basing himself on examination rosters, makes a similar observation (*Koryŏ kwagŏ chedosa yŏn'gu,* 159–61).

157. *KS* 28:24b.

158. *KS* 75:47b.

159. Yi Sŏng-mu, *Chosŏn ch'ogi yangban yŏn'gu,* 138–39.

160. Kim Kwang-su, "Koryŏ sidae ŭi tongjŏng chik," 119.

161. *Kŏmgyo* appointees were given both stipends and prebends, while *tongjŏng* recipients received prebends only.

162. The waiting period for *tongjŏng* appointees varied from five years for examination graduates to eight years for men of clerk origins (*KS* 75:1b).

163. See Pak Yong-un, *Koryŏ sidaesa,* 105, on honorary offices.

164. See Yi Sŏng-mu, *Chosŏn ch'ogi yangban yŏn'gu,* 140–42 on new restrictions placed on honorary office holders.

165. *KS* 104:35b ff.

166. See Yi Sŏng-mu, *Chosŏn ch'ogi yangban yŏn'gu*, 148 *n* 410, for a calculation of the number of supernumerary posts given out at this time.

167. *KS* 75:38a–b.

168. Yi Sŏng-mu, *Chosŏn ch'ogi yangban yŏn'gu*, 148–49.

169. *KS* 75:38b.

170. Yi T'ae-jin, "Sarimp'a ŭi yuhyangso pongnip undong," in his *Han'guk sahoesa yŏn'gu: nongŏp kisul paltal kwa sahoe pyŏndong*, 136–43.

171. Hŏ Hŭng-sik, "*Kukpo hojok* ŭro pon Koryŏ malgi ŭi sahoe kujo," 51–147, esp. tables on pp. 112–13.

172. See Yŏng-ho Ch'oe, "Commoners in Early Yi Dynasty Civil Examinations," 611–31, *The Civil Service Examination System and the Social Structure in Early Yi Dynasty Korea;* and Han Young-woo, "Chosŏn ch'ogi sahoe kyech'ung yŏn'gu e taehan chaeron," 305–58.

173. Song June-ho, *Chosŏn sahoesa yŏn'gu*, 208–12.

174. *KS* 75:48b.

175. Strange though it may seem, slaves, artisans, and merchants may have had much better opportunities to rise than did ordinary peasants. Public slaves and slaves belonging to the royal family were in many cases already close to centers of political power, while the economic activities of artisans and merchants, many of whom were quite wealthy, brought them into close contact with government agencies and powerful individuals.

176. This provision is found in the biography of Ŏm Su-an, a man of local official origins who passed the government service examination during Wŏnjong's reign (*KS* 106:36b).

177. Yi Sŏng-mu, *Chosŏn ch'ogi yangban yŏn'gu*, 57.

178. *KS* 33:5a.

179. *KS* 38:6a.

5. REFORM AND DYNASTIC CHANGE

1. See, for example, Chai-sik Chung, "Chŏng To-jŏn."

2. For a discussion of Cho Chun's background, reform activities, and thought, see Chang Tŭk-chin, "Cho Chun ŭi chŏngch'i hwaltong kwa kŭ sasang," 159–212.

3. See *KSC* 33:35a ff for the complete text of Cho Chun's memorial.

4. These various reform proposals can be found in the "Food and Money Monograph" (*KS* 78:20b ff). A Korean-language summary can be found in Han Young-woo, *Chosŏn chŏn'gi ŭi sahoe sasang yŏn'gu*, 115–25; an English-language discussion of Chŏng to-jŏn's proposal can be found in Palais, "Han Yŏng-u's Studies of Early Chosŏn Intellectual History," 201–3.

5. Lee Ki-baik, *Han'guksa sillon*, 223–24.

6. Yi Kyŏng-sik, "Chosŏn chŏn'gi t'oji kaehyŏk nonŭi," 217–46.

7. Yi Sang-baek, *Yijo kŏn'guk ŭi yŏn'gu.*

8. *T'aejong sillok* 9. Cited in Yi Kwan-hui, "Koryŏmal Chosŏnch'o chŏnhyŏnggwan," 96 *n*10.

9. Han Young-woo, "Yŏmal sŏnch'o ui hallyang," 33–75. The provisions of the Rank Land Law allowed *hallyang* from five to ten *kyŏl* of Soldiers' Land, the amount to be determined based on the amount of land they had been receiving under the old system. Yi Sŏng-mu argues that the Soldiers' Land grants were in fact merely recognition of tax exemption on a part of the of lands that these people already held, the majority of which was restored to tax-paying status. See Yi Sŏng-mu, *Chosŏn ch'ogi yangban yŏn'gu*, 221.

10. A recent article on land grants and military service contends that only top-ranking former officials were given rank lands and that former officials below the junior second grade (even those living in the capital) were given soldiers' fields and incorporated into the capital guards. This argument is based on limited, indirect evidence and is highly speculative, but it is interesting to note that the junior second grade was the highest rank granted to supernumerary appointees. This suggests that even supernumerary officials who managed to remain in the capital were excluded from the official class and were, in effect, reclassified as ordinary soldiers. See Yi Kwan-hŭi, "Koryŏmal Chosŏnch'o chŏnhyŏnggwan/ch'ŏmsŏlgwan e taehan t'oji pun'gŭp kwa kunyŏk pugwa," 91–124.

11. *KS* 78:41b.

12. See Shin, "Land Tenure and the Agrarian Economy in Yi Dynasty Korea: 1600–1880," 12–13, on changes made in the prebend system during the fifteenth and sixteenth centuries.

13. See *KS* 78:41a–42b for these provisions of the Rank Land Law. They are also laid out in Yi Pyong-do, *Han'guksa chungse p'yŏn*, 698.

14. *T'aejong sillok* 12:35b, cited in Yi Kyŏng-sik, "Chosŏn chŏn'gi t'oji kaehyŏk nonŭi," 221.

15. *T'aejong sillok* 12:36a.

16. Yi Kyŏng-sik, "Chosŏn chŏn'gi t'oji kaehyŏk nonŭi," 221.

17. Ibid., 224–27.

18. See Yi Sŏng-mu, *Chosŏn ch'ogi yangban yŏn'gu*, 181–185 on household registers. Yi, linking this reform with the extensive litigation over slave ownership in the early Chosŏn, argues that the primary goal of household register revision was to increase the number of commoner households available for service to the state. His argument seems valid as far as it goes, but when this reform is considered within the larger contest of the chaotic rural situation of the late fourteenth century and the new dynasty's efforts to regularize local administration, it can also be seen as an integral part of the dismantling of the old decentralized Koryŏ system and its replacement with a stronger system of direct central control over the countryside.

19. Kim Hak-sik, *Chosŏn sidae pon'gŏn sahoe ŭi kibon kujo*, 95–96.

20. Yi Sŏng-mu, *Chosŏn ch'ogi yangban yŏn'gu*, 183.

21. Lee Ki-baik, *Han'guksa sillon*, 248–49.

22. *Chosenshi* 15:580. This came about because of the need for people to reclaim idle lands in the northern provinces.

23. Yi Su-gŏn tabulates nearly 200 *pugok*, *hyang*, and *so* in the Koryŏ period (*Han'guk chungse sahoesa yŏn'gu*, 338).

24. Ibid., 437.

25. See Palais, *Politics and Policy in Traditional Korea,* on the long-term effects of the struggle between state and *yangban* over control of resources.

26. See Pyŏn T'ae-sŏp, *Koryŏ chŏngch'i chedosa yŏn'gu,* 181–94, for a thorough discussion of intermediary provincial administration in the late Koryŏ.

27. Takeda Yukio, "Korai richo jidai no zokken," 33. Takeda's figures for 1450 are compiled from the *Sejong sillok chiriji.*

28. Yi Sung-in's family seat was Kyŏngsan (Sŏngju), Chŏng Mong-ju's Yŏnil, and Kil chae's Sŏnsan. Although Yi Saek's family seat was at Hansan in Ch'ungch'ŏng Province, he had close ties with Ulsan through his maternal line (Yi Sugŏn, *Yŏngnam sarimp'a ŭi hyŏngsŏng,* 42).

29. *KS* 57:5a.

30. Ko Sŭng-je, *Han'guk ch'ollak sahoesa yŏn'gu,* 211–12.

31. *KS* 75:14a.

32. *KS* 75:16a.

33. Yi Sŏng-mu, "Chosŏn ch'ogi ŭi hyangni," 68.

34. Ko Sŭng-je, *Han'guk ch'ollak sahoesa yŏn'gu,* 212.

35. Quoted in Yi Sŏng-mu, "Chosŏn ch'ogi ŭi hyangni," 67.

36. *Sejo sillok,* 5:23a.

37. Ibid.

38. Yi Su-gŏn, *Han'guk chungse sahoesa yŏn'gu,* 392–93.

39. *KSC* 33:36b.

40. *KS* 75:48b.

41. *KS* 75:39b.

42. See Yi Sŏng-mu's discussion of the process leading to the abolition of supernumerary appointments in the early Chosŏn in his *Chosŏn ch'ogi yangban yŏn'gu,* 149–51.

43. Yi Sŏng-mu, "Chosŏn ch'ogi ŭi hyangni," 40–42.

44. See Yi Sŏng-mu, *Chosŏn ch'ogi yangban yŏn'gu,* 57–59, on legal and extralegal limitations on local clerks seeking to take government service examinations in the Chosŏn period. Limitations included exclusion of incumbents, limits on the number of sons who could sit for the examinations, requirement that prospective candidates from local clerk families obtain written authorization from their magistrate or prefect, and a series of rigorous preliminary examinations not required of other candidates. These restrictions were much heavier than those for commoners and could mean that local clerks of the early Chosŏn occupied a lower rung on the social ladder. Yi Sŏng-mu argues, correctly I believe, that in fact the opposite was true: local clerks presented a much greater threat to *yangban* and thus were burdened with more restrictions.

45. Yi Sŏng-mu, "Chosŏn ch'ogi ŭi hyangni," 34–35.

46. Yi Sŏng-mu, "Chungin ch'ŭng ŭi sŏngnip munje." See also Kim Yŏng-mo, *Chosŏn chibaech'ŭng yŏn'gu,* 28–33.

47. *T'aejo sillok* 2:17b.

48. Ibid. 15:9b.

49. *Chŏngjong sillok* 5:8b.

50. See Song June-ho, *Chosŏn sahoesa yŏn'gu*, 453–56, on the Chosŏn *yangban*'s unyielding opposition to allowing men of suspect social origins, such as merchants and artisans, to hold office.

51. Yi Sang-baek, *Chosŏn munhwasa yŏn'gu non'go*, 193–228.

52. Yi Sŏng-mu, *Chosŏn ch'ogi yangban yŏn'gu*, 52–54.

53. Deuchler, *The Confucian Transformation of Korea* 270–71.

54. *KSC* 33:35a–37a.

55. *T'aejo sillok* 2:20a.

56. Ibid. 15:5b.

57. *Chŏngjong sillok* 3:2a;3:3b.

58. *T'aejo sillok* 11:15b; 5:1a; 12:1b.

59. Ibid. 13:12b.

60. Ibid. 1:40a ff.

61. Ibid. 2:4a.

62. Ibid. 15:6b.

63. *Chŏngjong sillok* 1:5a.

64. Ibid. 2:19b.

65. There was a complaint in 1451 about eunuchs limiting officials' access to the throne and interfering with the flow of information to the king (Yi Sang-baek, *Han'guksa kŭnse chŏn'gi p'yŏn*, 50 *n4*). On the whole, however, from the reign of T'aejong on, the Chosŏn period was remarkable for the lack of eunuch participation in politics, especially when compared with the late Koryŏ and with Chinese dynasties.

66. See Yi Sang-baek, *Chosŏn munhwasa yŏn'gu non'go*, 63–88, on the complications Yi Sŏng-gye's Buddhist faith caused between Yi and the officials.

67. *T'aejo sillok* 14:28b.

68. We should note, however, that late in Sejong's reign that devoutly Buddhist monarch did appoint one more preceptor—Sinmi, who bore the title *chonja*, the appellation used for preceptors during the years of Mongol domination (*Munjong sillok* 2:25a–b).

69. Chŏng Tu-hŭi, "Chosŏn kŏn'guk ch'ogi t'ongch'i," 53–75.

70. *KS* 137:31b.

71. *KS* 45:8a.

72. *Chŏngjong sillok:* 6:10a.

73. See *Chŏngjong sillok* 5:9a.260.

74. *T'aejo sillok* 14:19b.

75. *Chŏngjong sillok* 2:15b.

76. Ibid. 3:7b.

77. Ibid. 4:8a.

78. *T'aejo sillok* 6:16b.

79. Ibid. 2:1b.

80. It should be noted that a Security Council–like entity was reestablished in 1432 under the same name used in the early Koryŏ, the Chungch'uwŏn, but this agency was charged only with palace security.

81. *T'aejong sillok* 2:2b.

82. The last appointments to top Secretariat/Chancellery posts came in 1401,

when Cho Chun was made superintendent of the Chancellery (*p'an* Munhabu *sa*). See *T'aejong sillok* 3:28b.

83. See Yi Sang-baek, *Han'guksa kŭnse chŏn'gi p'yŏn*, 175.

84. The new institutional structure did still allow for concurrent appointment of state councillors to posts in a number of outside agencies, including the Crown Prince Tutorial Office, Office of Examinations, Royal Confucian Academy, Office of Royal Lectures, and Office of Special Counselors. For the most part, however, these agencies were charged with specialized functions and lay outside the regular flow of bureaucratic power. It is possible, of course, that concurrent appointments outside those provided for by the statutes may have been given to such key agencies as the Six Boards or the Office of the Inspector General, but I did not find any such examples in my study of office holding during Sejong's and Sejo's reigns.

85. See Ch'oe Sŭng-hŭi, "Yangban yugyo chŏngch'i ŭi chinjŏn," 137–44, on the Six Boards, State Council, and throne in the early Chosŏn.

86. The importance attached to the chief of personnel is discussed by Kim Yŏng-mo, *Chosŏn chibaech'ŭng yŏn'gu*, 455–57.

87. Chŏng Tu-hŭi, "Chosŏn kŏn'guk ch'ogi t'ongch'i" 75

88. Wagner, *The Literati Purges*, 1–2.

89. See Farquhar, "Structure and Function in the Yüan Imperial Government," 25–55, on Yüan political institutions.

90. This discussion of Ming institutions is based on Hucker, *The Ming Dynasty*.

91. Hucker, *The Ming Dynasty*, 45–46.

92. Chosŏn *yangban* use of the tributary relationship between Korea and China to curb the authority of the throne has been laid out by Sohn Pow-key in his dissertation, "Social History of the Early Yi Dynasty, 1392–1592." A shorter version of Sohn's argument can be found in his article "Power versus Status," 209–53.

6. THE IDEOLOGY OF REFORM

1. For a thorough critique of this interpretation, see Palais, "Han Yŏng-u's Studies of Early Chosŏn Intellectual History," 199–224.

2. Kim Ch'ung-nyŏl, *Koryŏ yuhaksa*, 409.

3. Deuchler, *The Confucian Transformation of Korea*, 92.

4. Ibid., 24–27.

5. De Bary and Haboush, *The Rise of Neo-Confucianism in Korea*, 34–37.

6. For a concise presentation of this view, see Reischauer and Fairbank, *East Asia*, 220–22 and 235–41. This view seems to have been largely informed by Naito Konan's depiction of fundamental sociopolitical change between the T'ang and the Sung, and by Feng Yu-lan's studies on Chinese intellectual history, which focused on Ch'eng-Chu philosophical thought and its origins.

7. Tillman, *Confucian Discourse and Chu Hsi's Ascendency*.

8. Bol, *"This Culture of Ours,"* 333.

9. Deuchler, *The Confucian Transformation of Korea*, 127.

10. Han Young-woo, *Chosŏn chŏn'gi ŭi sahoe sasang yŏn'gu*, esp. part 2, chap. 1 and 2.

11. Yi T'ae-jin, *Chosŏn yugyo sahoeron*, 74–75.

12. The most detailed argument for an early development of Nature and Principle Learning in Korea can be found in Kim Ch'ung-nyŏl, *Koryŏ yuhaksa*, 87–97.

13. The various texts used for royal lectures in the early twelfth century are specified in Kim Ch'ung-nyŏl, *Koryŏ yuhaksa*, 110–12. Kim lists forty-one separate lectures during the years 1105–70; *The Doctrine of the Mean* was used on four occasions.

14. Yi Pyŏng-do, *Han'guksa chungse p'yŏn*, 227.

15. Pak Sŏng-hwan, "Yugyo," 257–61.

16. See, e.g., the discussions of the Koryŏ literary tradition in Yi Ka-wŏn, *Han'guk hanmunhak sa*, 74–75.

17. See Ch'oe Sŭng-no's views on the roles of Confucianism and Buddhism, in Lee, *Sourcebook of Korean Civilization*, 1: 289–92.

18. The intellectual climate of Yejong's reign is discussed in Shultz, "Twelfth Century Koryŏ." See also Cho Tong-il, *Han'guk munhak t'ongsa*, 1: 377–80.

19. Cho Tong-il, *Han'guk munhak t'ongsa* 1: 348.

20. Quoted in ibid., 1: 382–83.

21. *KS* 73:9a–b. See Bol, "Examinations and Orthodoxies," 5–6 for a discussion of Fan's reform.

22. *KS* 73:10a–b.

23. Although the *KS* "Monograph on Recruitment" does not mention this change, that it happened is certain because the next recorded modification (after 1154) in the content of the examinations, which occurred in 1320, was the elimination of poetry and rhyme-prose in favor of policy essays. See *KS* 73:11a.

24. See Bol, "*This Culture of Ours*", chap. 8, for a discussion of Su Shih's intellectual outlook.

25. Yu Ch'ang-gyu, "Koryŏ muin chŏnggwŏn sidae ŭi munin Pak In-sŏk," 171–93.

26. Kim Tang-t'aek, *Koryŏ muin chŏngkwŏn yŏn'gu*, 202–21.

27. Ch'oe Cha, *Pohan chip*, "Sŏ" (Introduction), 1a–2b.

28. Ibid., 1:9b.

29. See Yi Wŏn-myŏng, "Koryŏ sŏngnihak suyong ŭi sasang chŏk paegyŏng," 53–55, for discussion of Ch'oe Cha's critical attitude toward *changgu* scholars.

30. Ch'oe Cha, *Pohan chip* 1:1a.

31. For Kim Ku's biography, see *KS* 106:12a ff.

32. Ch'oe Cha, *Pohan chip* 1:4a

33. Ibid., 1:6a.

34. Ibid., 1:10a.

35. Ibid., 1:1a–2b.

36. It is interesting to note in this regard that Yun So-jong also brought up the issue of Ch'oe Ŭng's remarks in his late-fourteenth-century tirade against Buddhism. See *KS* 120:14a.

37. *KS* 74:31b.

38. See Chŏng To-jŏn's preface to Yi Sung-in's literary collection in *Toŭn chip* 1:2a. Chŏng actually states that Yi Che-hyŏn was the first in Korea to practice the Ancient Style. It seems unlikely that Chŏng was unaware of earlier Korean

Ancient Style practitioners; perhaps he engaged in rhetorical flourish to emphasize the significance of Yi Che-hyŏn's contributions.

39. See, e.g., Chŏng Ok-cha, "Yŏmal Chuja Sŏngnihak ŭi toip e taehan sigo,"
29–54.

40. Yi Che-hyŏn, *Yŏgong p'aesŏl*, part 1, 1:13a–b. It was common practice in
the late Koryŏ for young men aspiring to take the government service examinations to study belles lettres under Buddhist monks. See Duncan, "The Late
Koryŏ," on this practice.

41. Yi Che-hyŏn, *Yŏgong p'aesŏl*, "Sŭbyu" (Addendum), 4a.

42. Yi Che-hyŏn, *Ikchae nan'go* 3:11a.

43. *KS* 110:41a.

44. Kwŏn Kŭn, "Haengjang" (Achievements of Yi Saek), in Yi Saek, *Mogŭn
chip*, 3b–4a.

45. Tillman, *Utilitarian Confucianism*, 45.

46. Yi Saek, *Mogŭn chip* 9:4a–b.

47. Ha Yun, "P'oŭn sŏnsaeng si kwŏn sŏ" (Preface to volume of Chŏng Mong-
ju's poetry), in Chŏng Mong-ju, *P'oŭn chip* 1:a.

48. Kim Chong-jik, *Chŏmp'iljae chip* 1:46a–b.

49. Yi Pyŏng-hyu argues that Kim Chong-jik's interest in literature means that
Kim Chong-jik was a transitional figure with one foot in the belletrist camp and
the other in the classicist (*kyŏnghak*) (Yi, *Chosŏn chŏn'gi kiho sarimp'a yŏn'gu*,
29–30). Kim Chong-jik may very well have been a transitional figure, but not
between the T'ang style belletrists and the Ch'eng-Chu Learning scholars represented by Cho Kwang-jo; rather, Kim Chong-jik seems to represent a transition
from Ancient Style Learning to a more purely Ch'eng-Chu intellectual style.

50. *Sejo sillok* 34:9a.

51. Cho Tong-il, *Han'guk munhak t'ongsa*, 3:346–55; quotation, p. 354.

52. Yang Sŏng-ji, *Nuljae chip* 4:31a–b.

53. Cited in Han Young-woo, *Chosŏn chŏn'gi ŭi sahoe sasang yŏn'gu*, 167.

54. If leading members of both the rusticated literati and meritorious elite groups
shared commitments to Ch'eng-Chu Learning and Ancient Style Learning ideas
about literature, how do we distinguish between the two groups intellectually? Were
rusticated literati contentions that the meritorious elite were belletrists simply polem-
ical attempts to discredit the meritorious elite by trying to associate them with the
old T'ang style? It seems possible that by the early sixteenth century, when the
conflict between the two groups was the sharpest, the rusticated literati had evolved
toward a more orthodox Ch'eng-Chu Learning that no longer tolerated the kinds
of ideas expressed by Kim Chong-jik.

55. This view is summarized in Lee Ki-baik, *Han'guksa sillon*, 268.

56. See Yi Sang-baek, *Chosŏn munhwasa yŏn'gu non'go;* and Han Woo Keun's
two articles "Yŏmal sŏnch'o ŭi pulgyo chŏngch'aek" and "Sejongjo e issŏsŏ ŭi
tae pulgyo si'chaek."

57. Although the P'algwan Festival has conventionally been regarded as a
Buddhist ceremony, perhaps because its name derived from the Buddhist doctrine
of Eight Prohibitions (P'algwan Chaegye), the ceremony actually centered on the

worship of the various spirits of heaven, mountains, and rivers. Such content suggests links with the shamanist tradition.

58. Hŏ Hŭng-sik, *Koryŏ pulgyosa yŏn'gu,* esp. chap. 1, "Koryŏ sahoe ŭi pul-
gyojŏk kiban" (The Buddhist basis of Koryŏ society). See also Deuchler, *The
Confucian Transformation of Korea,* 29–87.

59. Duncan, "The Late Koryŏ," 42–46.

60. Wagner, *The Literati Purges.* The evidence here appears mostly in terms of
official attempts to limit the influence of Buddhism and the difficulties these attempts
encountered. See, e.g., pp. 34–35 on reversals of anti-Buddhist measures in 1492.

61. See Han Woo-keun, "Yŏmal sŏnch'o ŭi pulgyo chŏngch'aek."

62. The complexity of early Chosŏn religious life is also noted in Deuchler, *The
Confucian Transformation of Korea,* 175.

63. Hŏ Hŭng-sik, *Koryo pulgyosa yŏn'gu,* 416–17.

64. Yi Sang-baek, *Chosŏn munhwasa yŏn'gu non'go,* 104–82.

65. *Sejong sillok* 127:13b.

66. *Munjong sillok* 2:25a–b.

67. Ibid. 3:8a.

68. *Sejong sillok* 123:1a.

69. Kalton, "The Writings of Kwŏn Kŭn," 95, 122 n. 10.

70. *Andong Kwŏn-ssi songhwa po* 1:4a. That Kwŏn Kŭn's brother was a monk
is also noted in Kalton, "The Writings of Kwŏn Kŭn," 101.

71. Yi Saek, *Mogŭn chip* 17:4b.

72. *Munjong sillok* 7:20a.

73. *T'aejo sillok* 4:1b.

74. Sŏng Hyŏn, *Yongjae ch'onghwa* 1:18.

75. Ibid. 1:195.

76. *Sejong sillok* 23:30a.

77. Ibid. 114:7a ff.

78. Ibid. 121:6b.

79. See Kalton, "The Writings of Kwŏn Kŭn," 94–98.

80. Ibid., 101.

81. Yi Sŏng-mu, "The Influence of Neo-Confucianism on Education," 140.

82. *Sejong sillok* 83:7a.

83. Ibid. 100:2b.

84. Ibid. 100:15b.

85. For Kim Su-on's discussion of the unity of principle and the variety of its
manifestations, see *Sigu chip* 2:16b–17b.

86. Ibid., 2:4a.

87. Bol, "Chu Hsi's Redefinition of Literati Learning," 151–85.

88. *KS* 73:43a.

89. *KS* 73:11a.

90. *KS* 73:11b.

91. For a listing of this series of reversals, with virtually no explanatory discussion, see *KS* 73:11b–12b.

92. Yi Sung-in, *Toŭn chip* 4:12b–13a.

93. Yi Sŏng-mu, "The Influence of Neo-Confucianism on Education," 148–49.

94. Ibid., 152–53, and 160 n.144.

95. *Sejong sillok* 49:21b.

96. We should note, however, that the sides were not always so clearly drawn between Ancient Learning–Ch'eng-Chu adherents and T'ang belletrists. One of the early advocates of the written test was Kwŏn Kŭn, who had perhaps the most sophisticated understanding of Ch'eng-Chu Learning among all early Chosŏn thinkers. In 1407 Kwŏn argued for the written test on the grounds that literary scholarship was necessary for the writing of diplomatic documents and for hosting Chinese envoys. (For Kwŏn's lengthy memorial on the examination system, see *T'aejong sillok* 13:14a–15b.) This kind of thinking may help to explain why the literary licentiate examination was continued even after the first-stage written examinations were eliminated from the higher government-service examination in 1450. It also indicates that the arguments made by Korean thinkers in these years were not always reflective solely of ideological positions, but often were informed by practical social and political considerations.

97. See, e.g., Hwang, *Chosŏnjo chonggyo sahoesa yŏn'gu,* 32–34.

98. Bol, *"This Culture of Ours,"* 333.

99. Ibid., 338–39.

100. Chung, "Chŏng To-jŏn," 67–72.

101. See Tillman, *Utilitarian Confucianism,* 86–87.

102. Ibid., 203–4.

103. Wakeman, *The Fall of Imperial China,* 149.

104. Chung, "Chŏng To-jŏn," 68–69.

105. Deuchler, *The Confucian Transformation of Korea.*

106. Eisenstadt, *The Political Systems of Empires,* 62–65.

107. Deuchler attributes the revolutionary impulse in Korean Ch'eng-Chu Learning to a belief in the perfectability of man, which could be achieved through guidance from without and which "demanded the creation of an appropriate environment in which human nature could be realized to its fullest" (*The Confucian Transformation of Korea,* 24–25).

108. De Bary, *East Asian Civilizations,* 60.

109. Eisenstadt notes close ties between literati and gentry in China, but he argues that the gentry were not a hereditary class. See Eisenstadt, *The Political Systems of Empires,* 328–331.

110. Palais, "Confucianism and the Aristocratic/Bureaucratic Balance in Korea," 455–57.

111. See de Bary, *Neo-Confucian Orthodoxy and the Learning of the Mind-and-Heart,* 16, for discussion of the antagonism felt by the Ch'eng-Chu school for Su Shih. De Bary notes that the cleavage between followers of Su Shih and followers of Chu Hsi persisted into Yüan times (p.43).

7. SOME FINAL CONSIDERATIONS

1. For a discussion of less-differentiated societies, see Eisenstadt, *The Political Systems,* 105–9.

2. Ibid., 163.

3. See Palais, "Confucianism and the Aristocratic/Bureaucratic Balance in Korea"; and Deuchler, *The Confucian Transformation of Korea,* esp. 295–300.

4. See, for example, Huntley, *Korea,* 3.

5. See Hideo Inoue, "The Reception of Buddhism in Korea and Its Impact on Indigenous Culture," 43–71.

6. Palais, "Confucianism and the Aristocratic/Bureaucratic Balance in Korea," 430–31.

7. Braudel, *On History,* 25–52.

Korean Dynasties and Kings

(Includes only Silla kings mentioned in text)

Muryŏl	武烈	(654–61)
Kyŏngdŏk	景德	(742–65)
Hyegong	惠恭	(765–80)
Sinmu	神武	(839)
Munsŏng	文聖	(839–857)
Hyŏn'gang	憲康	(875–85)
Kyŏngsun	敬順	(927–35)

LATER KOGURYŎ/MAJIN/T'AEBONG

Kungye	弓裔	(901–18)

LATER PAEKCHE

Kyŏnhwŏn	甄萱	(892–935)
Sin'gŏm	神劍	(935–36)

KORYŎ

T'aejo	太祖	(918–43)
Hyejong	惠宗	(943–45)
Chŏngjong	定宗	(945–49)
Kwangjong	光宗	(949–75)

Kyŏngjong   景宗 (975–81)

Sŏngjong   成宗 (981–97)

Mokchong   穆宗 (997–1009)

Hyŏnjong   顯宗 (1009–31)

Tŏkchong   德宗 (1031–34)

Chŏngjong   靖宗 (1034–46)

Munjong   文宗 (1046–83)

Sunjong   順宗 (1083)

Sŏnjong   宣宗 (1083–94)

Hŏnjong   獻宗 (1094–95)

Sukchong   肅宗 (1095–1105)

Yejong   睿宗 (1105–22)

Injong   仁宗 (1122–46)

Ŭijong   毅宗 (1146–70)

Myŏngjong   明宗 (1170–97)

Sinjong   神宗 (1197–1204)

Hŭijong   熙宗 (1204–11)

Kangjong   康宗 (1211–13)

Kojong   高宗 (1213–59)

Wŏnjong   元宗 (1259–74)

Ch'ungnyŏl   忠烈 (1274–1308)

Ch'ungsŏn   忠宣 (1298, 1308–13)

Ch'ungsuk   忠肅 (1313–30, 1332–39)

Ch'unghye   忠惠 (1330–32, 1339–44)

Ch'ungmok   忠穆 (1344–48)

Ch'ungjŏng   忠定 (1348–51)

Kongmin   恭愍 (1351–74)

U   (1374–88)

Ch'ang   昌   (1388–89)

Kongyang   恭讓   (1389–92)

EARLY CHOSŎN

T'aejo   太祖   (1392–98)

Chŏngjong   定宗   (1398–1400)

T'aejong   太宗   (1400–18)

Sejong   世宗   (1418–50)

Munjong   文宗   (1450–52)

Tanjong   端宗   (1452–55)

Sejo   世祖   (1455–68)

Yejong   睿宗   (1468–69)

Sŏngjong   成宗   (1469–94)

Glossary of Korean, Chinese, and Japanese Terms

ch'ansŏng 贊成

ch'ansŏngsa 贊成事

chapkwa 雜科

Chejudo 濟州島

Chekiang 浙江

Ch'eng-Chu Hsüeh (K. Chŏngjuhak) 程朱學

Ch'eng-ming (K. Sŏngmyŏng) 誠明

chesul kwa 製述科

chi 至

chi chu sa 知州事

chi Ch'umirwŏn *sa* 知樞密院使

chi Chungch'u *sa* 知樞中使

chi kun sa 知郡事

chi Munha 知門下

chi Munhasŏng *sa* 知門下省事

chi Ŭijŏngbu *sa* 知議政府事

chibae ch'ŭng 支配層

chieh-tu shih (K. *chŏltosa*) 節度使

chien-chiao (K. *kŏmgyo*) 檢校

chigonggo 知貢考

Chikchŏn 職田

Chikkwan chi 職官志

Chin (Jurchen dynasty) 金

chin (encampment, fort) 鎮

chin (ferry station) 津

Chinch'ŏn 鎮川

Chindo 珍島

ch'ing (K. *kyŏng*) 卿

Chin'gang 晉康

Chin'gol 真骨

ching-shu (K. *kyŏngsul*) 經術

Chinju 晉州

Chinju Ha 晉州河

Chinju Kang 晉州姜

chinsa (Ch. *chin-shih*) 進士

chinsa kwa 進士科

chin-shih (K. *chinsa*) 進士

chinsu 鎮守

Chinwi 振威

Chiphyŏnjŏn 集賢殿

Chipsabu 執事府

Ch'irwŏn Yun 漆原尹

chisinsa 知申事

Chiu-p'in Chung-cheng 九品中正

cho (land tax, rent) 租

cho (local tribute tax) 調

ch'o 初

ch'ŏ 處

ch'ŏgan 處干

Ch'ogye Chŏng 草溪鄭

ch'ŏkpul sungyu 斥佛崇儒

Cholgo ch'ŏnbaek 拙稿千百

chŏljesa 節制使

Chŏlla 全羅

ch'ollak kongdongch'e 村落 共同體

chŏlli 田里

chŏltosa (Ch. *chieh-tu shih*) 節度使

ch'ŏmsŏljik 添設職

Ch'ŏmŭibŭ 僉議府

chŏn kwŏn 田券

Ch'ŏnan 天安

Chŏngan Im 定安任

Chŏngbang 政房

Chŏngch'i Togam 整治都監

chongch'in changgun 從親將軍

Chŏngch'on 井村

Chŏngdong Haengsŏng 征東行省

chŏngdang munhak 政當文學

ch'onggwan 摠管

Ch'ŏnghaejin 清海鎮

ch'ŏngjŏng 清淨

Chŏngju 貞州

Ch'ŏngju 清州

Ch'ŏngju Chŏng 清州鄭

Ch'ŏngju Han 清州韓

Ch'ŏngju Kwak 清州郭

Ch'ŏngju Kyŏng 清州慶

Ch'ŏngju Yi 清州李

Chŏngju Yu 貞州柳

Chŏngjuhak (Ch. Ch'eng-Chu Hsüeh) 程朱學

chongsa 宗師

Chŏngsadang 政事堂

Ch'ŏngsong Sim 青松沈

chŏngsŭng 政丞

Chŏngŭp 井邑

chŏnho 佃戶

ch'ŏnho 千戶

chonja 尊者

chŏnjang 田莊

Chŏnju 全州

chŏnju 田主

ch'onju 村主

Chŏnju Ch'oe 全州崔

Chŏnju Yi 全州李

Chŏnmin Pyŏnjŏng Togam 田民 辨整都監

Chŏnsi Kwa 田柴科

Ch'ŏnsu 天授

Chŏnŭi Yi 全義李

Ch'ŏrwŏn (Ch'angwŏn, Tongju) 鐵原 (昌原, 東州)

Ch'ŏrwŏn (Ch'angwŏn) Ch'oe 鐵原 (昌原) 崔

Chosŏn 朝鮮

chou (K. *chu*) 州

Chou Tun-i 周敦頤

chou-hsien (K. *chuhyon*) 州縣

Chou-li 周禮

chu (Ch. *chou*) 州

chü-ching ch'iung-li (K. *kǒgyǒng kungni*) 居敬窮理

Ch'udong 秋洞

chugun 主郡

chuhyon (Ch. *chou-hsien*) 州縣

chuhyǒn 主縣

Chujahak (Ch. Chu-tzu Hsüeh) 朱子學

ch'ujingsaek 追徵色

Chuksan An 竹山安

Chuksan Pak 竹山朴

ch'ullap 出納

Ch'umirwǒn 樞密院

chün (K. *kun*) 郡

Ch'ungch'ǒng 忠清

Chungch'u *sa* 中樞使

Chungch'uwǒn 中樞院

Chungch'uwon *sa* 中樞院使

chunghǔng 中興

chungin 中人

Ch'ungju 忠州

Ch'ungju Chi 忠州池

Ch'ungju Yu 忠州劉

Chungnim Kohoe 竹林高會

chungsǒ munha sirang 中書門下侍郎

chungsǒ munha sirang p'yǒngjangsa 中書門下侍郎平章事

Chungsǒ Munhasǒng 中書門下省

chungsǒ sirang p'yǒngjangsa 中書侍郎平章事

Chungsǒsǒng 中書省

Chungyong (Ch. *Chung-yung*) 中庸

Chung-yung (K. *Chungyong*) 中庸

chün-hsien (K. *kunhyǒn*) 郡縣

chun-t'ien 均田

ch'usin 樞臣

Chu-tzu Hsüeh (K. Chujahak) 朱子學

chwa ch'amch'an 左參贊

chwa ch'ansǒng 左贊成

chwa san'gi sangsi 左散騎常侍

chwa ǔijong 左議政

chwa u 左右

Hadong Chǒng 河東鄭

Haeju 海州

Haeju Ch'oe 海州崔

Haeju O 海州吳

haengjang 行狀

Haengju Ki 幸州奇

Haep'yǒng Kil 海平吉

Haep'yǒng Yun 海平尹

Hallimwǒn (Ch. Han-lin Yüan) 翰林院

hallyang 閑良

Hamgil (province) 咸吉

Hamgyŏng (province) 咸慶

Hamyang Pak 咸陽朴

hanjŏn 限田

Han-lin Yüan (K. Hallimwŏn)
翰林院

Hansan Yi 韓山李

Hansŏngbu *p'anyun* 漢城府判尹

Hanyang 漢陽

Hanyang Cho 漢陽趙

Hapchu 陝州

Hapchu Yi 陝州李

Hayang Hŏ 河陽許

Hobu 戶部

hogu tanja 戶口單子

hojang 戶長

Hojo 戶曹

hojok 豪族

hojŏk 戶籍

hojŏng 戶正

Hoeamsa 檜嚴寺

Hoedŏk Hwang 懷德黃

Hoengsŏng Cho 橫城趙

hoesi 會試

Hongju 洪州

Hongju Yi 洪州李

hop'ae 號牌

hou (K. *hu*) 候

hsiang (K. *hyang*) 鄉

Hsiao-ching 孝經

Hsiao-hsüeh (K. *sohak*) 小學

hsien (K. *hyŏn*) 縣

hsien-hsing (K. *hyŏnsŏng*) 縣姓

hsien-ling (K. *hyŏllyŏng*) 縣令

hsing 姓

Hsing-li Hsüeh (K. Sŏngnihak)
性理學

hsü (K. *sŏ*) 序

hsün-ch'a shih (K. *sunch'alsa*)
巡察使

hu (Ch. *hou*) 候

Hu Koguryŏ 後高句麗

Hu Paekche 後百濟

huang-ti (K. *hwangje*) 皇帝

Hua-yen 華嚴

Hŭian 喜安

Hullyangmae 欣良買

Hŭngch'ŏnsa 興天寺

Hŭngdŏksa 興德寺

hun'gu 勳舊

Hunyo Sipcho 訓要十條

Hwabaek 和白

hwangdo 皇都

Hwanghae 黃海

hwangje (Ch. *huang-ti*) 皇帝

Hwangju Hwangbo 黃州皇甫

Hwangnyŏ (Yŏju) Min 黃驪
（驪州）閔

Hwangnyǒ (Yǒju) Yi 黃驪（驪州）李

Hwaǒm 華嚴

hyang (Ch. *hsiang*) 鄉

hyanggong 鄉貢

hyangni 鄉吏

hyǒllyang kwa 賢良科

hyǒllyǒng (Ch. *hsien-ling*) 縣令

hyǒn (Ch. *hsien*) 縣

hyǒn' gam 縣監

Hyǒngbu 刑部

Hyǒngjo 刑曹

hyǒnsǒng (Ch. *hsien-hsing*) 縣姓

hyǒnwi 縣尉

i (clerk, Ch. *li*) 吏

i (principle, Ch. *li*) 理

i (righteousness, K. *ǔi*) 義

Ibu 吏部

Ich'ǒn Sǒ 利川徐

Ijo 吏曹

Ikchae nan'go 益齋亂藁

ilban yangin 一般良人

I-li 儀禮

in (Ch. *jen*) 仁

Inch'ǒn (Inju, Kyǒngwǒn) Yi 仁川（仁州，慶原）李

ingsok 仍屬

Inju (In'chǒn, Kyǒngwǒn) Yi 仁州（仁川，慶原）李

Iphak tosǒl 入學圖譜

jen (K. *in*) 仁

ju (K. *yu*) 儒

Jurchen 汝真

Kaegyǒng 開京

Kaehwa 皆火

Kaesǒng Wang 開城王

Kaesǒng Yi 開城李

kammu 監務

Kanghwado 江華島

Kangnǔng (Myǒngju) 江陵（溟州）

Kangnǔng Ch'oe 江陵崔

Kangnǔng (Myǒngju) Kim 江陵（溟州）金

Kangnǔng Wang (Kim) 江陵王（金）

kan'gwan 諫官

Kangwǒn 江原

kanji 墾地

kap'ung 家風

Khitan 契丹

kiin 其人

Kimhae Kim 金海金

kizoku (K. *kwijok*, Ch. *kueï-tsu*)
貴族

Kobu 古阜

Koguryŏ 高句麗

kŏgyŏng kungni (Ch. *chŭ-ching ch'iung-li*) 居敬窮理

Kohŭng Yu 高興柳

kohyang 故鄉

Koi 高伊

kŏjok 鉅族

Koksan Han 谷山韓

kŏmgyo (Ch. *chien-chiao*) 檢校

Komun (Ch. Ku-wen) 古文

komunsŏ 古文書

kong (Ch. *kung*) 公

Kongam (Yangch'ŏn) Hŏ 孔巖
（陽川）許

Kongbu 工部

Kongjo 工曹

kongjŏn 公田

Kongju 公州

kongsin 功臣

kongsinjŏn 功臣田

kongŭm chŏnsi 功陰田柴

Koryŏ 高麗

Koryŏsa 高麗史

Koryŏsa choryŏ 高麗史節要

Kosaburi 古沙夫里

Kosŏng Yi 固城李

Koyang 高陽

kuan-ch'a shih (K. *kwanch'alsa*)
觀察使

kuei-tsu (K. *kwijok*, J. *kizoku*)
貴族

Kukchagam 國子監

kukche 國制

Kukpo hojŏk 國寶戶籍

kuksa 國師

kun (Ch. *chün*, prefecture) 郡

kun (lord) 君

kung (K. *kong*) 公

Kungsŏng Sugwibu 宮城宿衛部

kunhyŏn (Ch. *chün-hsien*) 郡縣

Kunhyŏn pyŏnghap samok 郡縣
併合事目

kunsa 軍士

Ku-wen (K. Komun) 古文

Kwajŏn Pŏp 科田法

Kwan-ch'a shih (K. *Kwanch'alsa*)
觀察使

kwanch'alsa (Ch. *kwan-ch'a shih*)
觀察使

Kwanggun 光軍

Kwangju (in modern Chŏlla
Province) 光州

Kwangju (in modern Kyŏnggi
Province) 廣州

Kwangju An 廣州安

Kwangju Yi 廣州李

Kwangp'yŏngsŏng 廣評省

Kwangsan Kim 光山金

Kwangyang Kim 光陽金

kwanhakchŏk kyŏngsehak 官學的 經世學

kwijok (Ch. kuei-tsu, J. kizoku) 貴族

kwŏnmun sejok (hereditary families) 權門世族

kwonmun sejok (powerful families) 權門勢族

kwŏnsega 權勢家

kwŏnsin 權臣

kyegŭp 階級

Kyoha No 交河盧

Kyojong Togam 教定都監

Kyoju 交州

kyŏl 結

kyŏng (Ch. ch'ing) 鄉

Kyŏngguk taejŏn 經國大典

kyŏnghak 經學

Kyŏnggi 京畿

Kyŏngju (Tonggyŏng) 慶州 （東京）

Kyŏngju Ch'oe 慶州崔

Kyŏngju Kim 慶州金

Kyŏngju Yi 慶州李

kyŏngnyŏksa 經歷司

Kyŏngsan 京山

Kyŏngsang 慶尙

kyŏngsehak 經世學

kyŏngsul (Ch. ching-shu) 經術

Kyŏngwŏn (Inch'ŏn, Inju) Yi 慶原 （仁川，仁州）李

lei-shu hsüeh (K. yusŏhak) 類書 學

li (clerk, K. i) 吏

li (principle, K. i) 理

Liao 遼

Li-chi 禮記

Lun-yü 論語

Majin 摩震

manho 萬戶

men-fa (K. munbŏl, J. monbatsu) 門閥

milchik pusa 密直副使

Milchiksa 密直司

min 民

Ming 明

ming-tsu (K. myŏngjok) 明族

Ming-tsung 明宗

minjok 民族

minjokchuŭi sahak 民族主義 史學

minjung 民眾

minjung sahak 民眾史學

Miryang Pak 密陽朴

Miryang Pyŏn 密陽卞

mok 牧

moksa 牧使

monbatsu (K. *munbŏl*, Ch. *men-fa*) 門閥

muban 武班

muhangsan 無恆產

mun (Ch. *wen*) 文

mun kwa 文科

munban 文班

munbŏl (Ch. *men-fa*, J. *monbatsu*) 門閥

mundŏk (Ch. *wen-te*) 文德

munha sijung 門下侍中

munha sirang p'yŏngjangsa 門下侍郎平章事

Munhasŏng 門下省

Munhwa Yu 文化柳

munjang (Ch. *wen-chang*) 文章

munsin 文臣

musin 武臣

Musong Yu 茂松庚

myŏnggyŏng kwa 明經科

myŏngjok (Ch. *ming-tsu*) 明族

Myŏngju (Kangnŭng) Kim 溟州 (江陵) 金

nae chaech'u 內宰樞

Naebongsŏng 內奉省

naejaejŏk palchŏn non 內在的發展論

naesang 內相

naesi 內侍

naesok 來屬

Naeŭisŏng 內議省

Naju 羅州

Naju Na 羅州羅

Naju O 羅州吳

namban 南班

Namgyŏng (Yangju) 南京 (陽州)

Namp'yŏng Mun 南平南

Namwŏn 南原

Namwŏn Yang 南原梁

Namyang Hong 南陽洪

nangjang 郎將

nangsa 郎士

Nobi An'gŏm Pŏp 奴婢按檢法

nogŭp 綠邑

Nokkwajŏn 祿科田

nokpong 祿俸

noksa 錄士

nong 農

nongjang 農莊

nongmin 農民

Nuljae chip 訥齋集

nŭngmun nŭngni 能文能吏

Nŭngsŏng Cho 綾城曹

Nŭngsŏng Ku 綾城具

oegwan 外官

Oeyokchŏn 外役田

Ogya 沃野

Okku Im 沃溝林

Okku Ko 沃溝高

Ŏnyang Kim 彦陽金

ŏsa taebu 御事大夫

Ŏsadae 御事臺

p'a 派

P'aegangjin 浿江鎮

paek (Ch. *po*) 伯

Paekche 百濟

Paekch'ŏn Cho 白川趙

Paekkwan chi 百官志

paeksŏng 百姓

P'algŏ To 八莒都

P'algwan Chaegye 八關齋戒

P' algwanhoe 八關會

p'an Ŏsadae *sa* 判御事臺事

p'an Samsa *sa* 判三司事

p'an Ŭijŏngbu *sa* 判議政府事

p'an Yukpu *sa* 判六部事

p'an'gwan 判官

Pannam Pak 潘南朴

p'ansa 判事

p'ansŏ 判書

P'ap'yŏng Yun 坡平尹

Parhae (Ch. Po-hai) 渤海

P'iltoji 必闍赤

Pisŏsŏng 秘書省

po (K. *paek*) 伯

Poan 保安

Po-hai (K. Parhae) 渤海

Pohan chip 補閑集

Pokkung 福宮

Po-ling Ts'ui 博陵崔

pon'gwan 本貫

Ponghwa Chŏng 奉化鄭

Pongju Chi 鳳州智

Pongsŏng Yŏm 峰城廉

ponju 本主

pu hojang 副戶長

pu-ch'ü (K. *pugok*) 部曲

pugok (Ch. *pu-ch'ü*) 部曲

Pukkye 北界

puldang 佛堂

Puryŏng 扶寧

Puryŏng Kim 扶寧金

Pusan (Koguryŏ county) 富山

pusil ho 富實戶

p'yehaeng 嬖幸

pyŏlchang 別將

pyŏlch'ŏng chaech'u 別廳宰樞

p'yŏng 坪

Pyŏngbu 兵部

P'yŏnggang Ch'ae 平康蔡

Pyŏngjo 兵曹

pyŏngmasa 兵馬使

P'yŏngsan Pak 平山朴

P'yŏngsan Sin 平山申

P'yŏngsan Yu 平山庾

P'yŏngt'aek Im 平澤林

P'yŏngyang (Sŏgyŏng) 平壤
 (西京)

P'yŏngyang Cho 平壤趙

P'yŏnnyŏn t'ongnok 編年通祿

sa (Ch. shih) 士

sabyŏng 私兵

Sach'ŏn Mok 泗川睦

sadaebu (Ch. shih-ta-fu) 士大夫

saengwŏn (Ch. sheng-yüan) 生員

Saganwŏn 司諫院

sahoe kyŏngje sahakcha 社會經濟
 史學者

Sahŏnbu 司憲府

sajok (Ch. shih-tsu) 士族

sajŏn 私田

samgong 三公

Samguk sagi 三國史記

Samguk yusa 三國遺事

Samgunbu 三軍部

samsa (finance commissioners)
 三使

samsa (preceptors) 三師

Samsa sa 三使司

Samsŏng 三省

Samsŏng Yukpu 三省六部

sang changgun 上將軍

Sangch'il 尚柒

Sangjil 尚質

Sangju 尚州

Sangnak kun 尚洛君

sangsŏ 尚書

Sangsŏsa 尚瑞司

Sangsŏsŏng 尚書省

san-li 三禮

sanwŏn 散員

sarim 士林

Sarimwŏn 詞林院

sasimgwan 事審官

Sasŏ (Ch. Ssu-shu) 四書

Sayŏgwŏn 司譯院

Sega (Annals) 世家

sega (hereditary families) 世家

Segye 世係

sejok 世族

senjinkoku (K. *sŏnjin'guk*) 先進國

serokchŏn 世祿田

sheng-yüan (K. *saengwŏn*) 生員

shih (poetry; K. *si*) 詩

shih (scholar; K. *sa*) 士

shih-ta-fu (K. *sadaebu*) 士大夫

shih-tsu (K. *sajok*) 士族

shinhŭng sadaebu 新興士大夫

si (examination) 試

si (poetry, Ch. *shih*) 詩

Sigu chip 拭疣集

sigŭp 食邑

Sikhwa chi 食貨志

silchŭng sahak 實證史學

Silla 新羅

Sillok 實錄

Sinch'ang Maeng 慎昌孟

Sinch'ŏn Kang 信川康

Sinmunsaek 申聞色

sim 心

Sirhak 實學

so (local administrative unit) 所

sŏ (non-official, commoner) 庶

sŏban 西班

sogyŏng (lesser capital) 小京

Sŏgyŏng (P'yŏngyang) 西京
　　（平壤）

sŏgyŏng (ratification) 署經

Sŏhae 西海

Sohak (Ch. *Hsiao-hsüeh*) 小學

sŏk 石

sokhyŏn 屬縣

sokkun 屬郡

sŏkto 釋道

Sŏn (Ch. Ch'an, J. Zen) 禪

Sŏn Kyo chong to ch'ongsŏp 禪教
　　宗都總攝

Sŏnggol 聖骨

Sŏnggyun'gwan 成均館

Songhak (Ch. Sung Hsüeh) 宋學

sŏngju 城主

Sŏngju Pae 星州裴

Sŏngju Yi 星州李

sŏngjung aema 成眾愛馬

Sŏngmyŏng (Ch. Ch'eng-ming)
　　誠明

Sŏngnihak (Ch. Hsing-li Hsüeh)
　　性理學

Sŏn'gŏ chi 選舉志

sŏnjin'guk (J. *senjinkoku*) 先進國

sŏp 攝

sŏri 胥吏

Ssu-shu (K. Saso) 四書

sŭbyu 拾遺

Sugun Manhobu 水軍萬户府

Suju 水州

Suju (Suwŏn) Ch'oe 水州（水原）崔

Suju Yi 樹州李

sunch' alsa (Ch. *hsün-ch'a shih*) 巡察使

Sunch'ang Sŏl 淳昌薛

Sunch'ŏn Pak 順天朴

Sŭngch'ubu 承樞府

Sŭngjŏngwŏn 承政院

sŭngsŏn 承宣

sun'gun 巡軍

Sun'gun Manhobu 巡軍萬戶府

Sunhŭng An 順興安

Sung 宋

Sung Hsüeh (K. Songhak) 宋學

Sun'gunbu 巡軍府

Susŏng 水城

Suwŏn 水原

Ta-chung (K. Taejung) 大中

tae tohobu 大都護府

taesagan 大司諫

taesahŏn 大司憲

T'aebong 奉封

taebu 大夫

taedŭng 對等

taega sejok 大家世族

taegan 臺諫

taejok (Ch. *ta-tsu*) 大族

Taejung (Ch. Ta-chung) 大中

Taesan 大山

t'aesu (Ch. *t'ai-shou*) 太守

t'ai-shou (K. *t'ae-su*) 太守

T'ang 唐

tang taedŭng 當對等

Tanju Han 端州韓

Tanyang U 丹陽禹

Tao Hsüeh (K. Tohak) 道學

ta-tsu (K. *taejok*) 大族

to (circuit/province) 道

to anmu sa 都按撫使

to chihwi sa 都指揮使

to ch'ongje 都摠制

Tobang 都房

Todang 都當

todokpu 都督府

Tohak (Ch. Tao Hsüeh) 道學

tohobu 都護府

Tollyŏngbu 敦寧府

tong chigonggo 同知貢考

tongban 東班

Tonggye 東界

Tonggyŏng (Kyŏngju) 東京（慶州）

tongji Ch'umirwŏn sa 同知樞密院事

tongji Chungch'uwŏn sa 同知中樞院事

tongjong (Ch. *t'ung-cheng*) 同正

Tongju (Ch'angwŏn) 東州（昌原）

Tongmunsŏn 東文選

Tongnae Chŏng 東萊鄭

Top'yŏngŭisasa 都評議事司

T'osan Ch'oe 兔山崔

T'osan Yi 兔山李

t'osŏng 土姓

Tsu-chih t'ung-chien 資治通鑑

Tsushima 對馬島

t'ung-cheng (K. *tongjŏng*) 同正

tup'um 頭品

u ch'amch'an 右參贊

u ch'ansŏng 右贊成

u pu taeŏn 右副代言

u san'gi sangsi 右散騎常侍

u sangsi 右常侍

u ŭijŏng 右議政

Ubong Ch'oe 牛峰崔

ŭihap 議合

Ŭijŏngbu 議政府

Ŭiryŏng Nam 宜寧南

Ŭisŏng Kim 義城金

ŭm (Ch. *yin*) 蔭

Umun-gun 佑文君

ŭi (Ch. *i*) 義

ŭi kwa 醫科

ŭmyang (Ch. *yin-yang*) 陰陽

Wako (K. Waegu) 倭寇

Wando 莞島

wang 王

wangsa 王師

wangt'o sasang 王土思想

wen (K. *mun*) 文

wen-chang (K. *munjang*) 文章

wen-te (K. *mundŏk*) 文德

Wŏnak Hyangni Ch'ŏbŏl Pŏp 元惡鄉吏處罰法

Wŏnju Pyŏn 原州邊

Wŏnju Wŏn 原州元

yakkwan 弱官

yangban 兩班

yangbu 兩府

Yangch'ŏn (Kongam) Hŏ 陽川（孔嚴）許

Yanggwang 楊廣

Yanggye 兩界

Yangju (Namgyong) 陽州（南京）

Yangju Cho 陽州趙

yangmin 良民

Yangsŏng Yi 陽城李

Yebu 禮部

Yejo 禮曹

yin (K. *ŭm*) 蔭

yin-yang (K. *ŭmyang*) 陰陽

yŏk 驛

Yŏju (Hwangnyŏ) Min 驪州閔

Yŏju (Hwangnyŏ) Yi 驪州李

Yŏnan Kim 延安金

Yŏnan Yi 延安李

Yŏndŭnghoe 蓮燈會

yong 庸

yŏng Samsa *sa* 領三司事

yong to Ch'ŏmŭisa *sa* 領都
僉議使事

Yongch'ŏn Hwangbo 永川皇甫

Yongch'ŏn Yi 永川李

Yonggung Kim 龍宮金

Yŏnggwang 靈光

Yŏnggwang Kim 靈光金

yonghu 龍喉

yŏnghyŏn 領縣

Yŏngil Chŏng 迎日鄭

Yongin 龍仁

Yongjae ch'onghwa 慵齋叢話

Yŏngju 寧州

yŏngŏpchŏn 永業田

yongsa 勇士

Yŏngsan Puwŏn Kun 永山
府院君

Yŏngsan Sin 靈山辛

yŏngŭijŏng 領議政

yu (Ch. *ju*) 儒

Yüan 元

yuhak 儒學

Yukcho 六曹

yukcho p'ansŏ 六曹

Yukpu 六部

yukpu sangsŏ 六部尙書

yuŏp 儒業

yusaeng 儒生

yusŏhak (Ch. *lei-shu hsüeh*) 類書學

zen (K. Sŏn, Ch. Ch'an) 禪

PERSONAL NAMES

An Chong-wŏn 安宗源

An Ch'uk 安軸

An Hyang (An Yu) 安向
（安裕）

An Mok 安牧

An Mun-gae 安文凱

An No-saeng 安魯生

An Pu 安浮

An Sŏk 安碩

An Wan-gyŏng 安完慶

Chach'o 自超

Ch'ae Ch'ŏl 蔡哲

Ch'ae Ch'ung-sun 蔡忠順

Ch'ae Ha-jung 蔡河中

Ch'ae Hong-ch'ŏl 蔡洪哲

Ch'ae Se-yŏng 蔡世英

Ch'ae Song-nyŏn 蔡松年

Ch'ae Yu-hu 蔡裕後

Chang Po-go 張保皐

Chang Sa-gil 張思吉

Chang Sun-nyong 張舜龍

Cheguk taejang kongju 齊國大長公主

Ch'en Liang 陳亮

Ch'eng Yi 程頤

Chi Yun 池奫

Cho Chun 趙浚

Cho Ch'ung-sin 趙忠臣

Cho Ho 趙瑚

Cho Hu 趙煦

Cho Hwa 趙禾

Cho Ik-ch'ŏng 曺益清

Cho Il-sin 趙日新

Cho In-byŏk 趙仁璧

Cho In-gyu 趙仁規

Cho In-ok 趙仁沃

Cho Kon 趙琨

Cho Kong 趙珙

Cho Kwang-han 曺光漢

Cho Kyŏn 趙狷

Cho Min-su 曺敏修

Cho On 趙溫

Cho Pak 趙璞

Cho Sa- gyŏm 趙思謙

Cho Si-jŏ 曺時著

Cho Sŏk 曺碩

Cho Sun 曺旬

Cho Tae-rim 趙大臨

Cho Tŏg-yu 趙德裕

Cho Ton 趙暾

Cho Wi 趙瑋

Cho Wi-ch'ong 趙位寵

Cho Yŏn 趙璉

Cho Yŏng-mu 趙英武

Cho Yŏn-su 趙延壽

Cho Yun-sŏn 趙允瑄

Ch'oe Cha 崔慈

Ch'oe Chae 崔梓

Ch'oe Che-an 崔濟顏

Ch'oe Ch'i-wŏn 崔致遠

Ch'oe Ch'ŏk-kyŏng 崔陟卿

Ch'oe Chŏn 崔佺

Ch'oe Chŏng-sin 崔正臣

Ch'oe Ch'ung 崔沖

Ch'oe Ch'ung-hŏn 崔忠獻

Ch'oe Hae 崔瀣

Ch'oe Hang (10th cent.) 崔沆

Ch'oe Hang (13th cent.) 崔沆

Ch'oe Ho 崔虎

Ch'oe I (Ch'oe U) 崔怡（崔瑀）

Ch'oe Koeng 崔宏

Ch'oe Kwang-wŏn 崔光遠

Ch'oe Kyun 崔均

Ch'oe Mun-do 崔文度

Ch'oe Nam-bu 崔南敷

Ch'oe On 崔昷

Ch'oe Ŏn-bu 崔彥父

Ch'oe Ŏn-wi 崔彥撝

Ch'oe Paeg-yun 崔伯胤

Ch'oe Pi-il 崔毗一

Ch'oe Po-sun 翟甫淳

Ch'oe Sa-ch'u 崔思諏

Ch'oe Sa-gang 崔士康

Ch'oe Sa-gyŏm 崔士謙

Ch'oe Sa-gyu 崔士規

Ch'oe Sa-ryang 崔思諒

Ch'oe Sa-ŭi 崔士儀

Ch'oe Sa-wi (12th cent.) 崔士威

Ch'oe Sa-wi (14th cent.) 崔思威

Ch'oe Se-yŏn 崔世延

Ch'oe Sŏ 崔瑞

Ch'oe Sŏn 崔詵

Ch'oe Sŏng-ji 崔誠之

Ch'oe Suk 崔肅

Ch'oe Sung 崔崇

Ch'oe Sŭng-no 崔承老

Ch'oe Sun-jak 崔純爵

Ch'oe Tam 崔灊

Ch'oe Tŭk-p'yŏng 崔得枰

Ch'oe U (Ch'oe I) 崔瑀（崔怡）

Ch'oe Ŭi 崔竩

Ch'oe Ŭng 崔凝

Ch'oe Ŭr-ŭi 崔乙儀

Ch'oe Yak 崔渝

Ch'oe Yong 崔勇

Ch'oe Yŏng 崔瑩

Ch'oe Yŏng-bu 崔永浮

Ch'oe Yŏng-ji 崔永沚

Ch'oe Yu 崔濡

Ch'oe Yu-bu 崔有孚

Ch'oe Yu-gil 崔惟吉

Ch'oe Yu-gyong 崔有慶

Ch'oe Yun-ch'ing 崔允偁

Ch'oe Yun-ŭi 崔倫儀

Ch'oe Yu-sŏn 崔惟善

Chogu 祖丘

Ch'ŏk Chun-gyŏng 拓俊京

Chŏn Nok-saeng 田祿生

Chŏn Yŏng-bo 全英甫

Chŏng Chi-yŏn 鄭之衍

Chŏng Chŏm 鄭漸

Chŏng Ch'ong 鄭摠

Chŏng Chun 鄭崔

Chŏng Chung-bu 鄭仲夫

Chŏng Hang 鄭沆

Chŏng Hŭi-gye 鄭熙啓

Chŏng In-bo 鄭寅普

Chŏng In-gyŏng 鄭仁卿

Chŏng Mok 鄭穆

Chŏng Mong-ju 鄭夢周

Chŏng Nam-jin 鄭南晉

Chŏng Pae-gŏl 鄭倍傑

Chŏng T'aek 鄭澤

Chŏng T'ak 鄭擢

Chŏng To-jŏn 鄭道傳

Chu Hsi 朱熹

Fan Chung-yen 范仲庵

Ha Sŭng-hae 河承海

Ha Yun 河崙

Ham Pu-rim 咸傅霖

Ham Yu-il 咸有一

Han Ak 韓渥

Han An-in 韓安仁

Han An-jung 韓安中

Han Ch'ŏn 韓巚

Han Chong-yu 韓宗愈

Han Hŭi-yu 韓希愈

Han I 韓理

Han Kang 韓康

Han Ki 韓起

Han Kong-ŭi 韓公義

Han Kwang-yŏn 韓光衍

Han Kyu 韓圭

Han Myŏng-hoe 韓明澮

Han Ŏn-gong 韓彥恭

Han Sa-gi 韓射奇

Han Sang-dŏk 韓尙德

Han Sang-gyŏng 韓尙敬

Han Sang-hang 韓尙恒

Han Sang-jil 韓尙質

Han Su 韓修

Han Tae-sun 韓大淳

Han Yu 韓愈

Han Yu-ch'ung 韓惟忠

Hŏ Chae 許載

Hŏ Cho 許稠

Hŏ Chong 許琮

Hŏ Hae 許垓

Hŏ Hyŏn 許玄

Hŏ Kong 許珙

Hŏ Kwi-ryong 許貴龍

Hŏ Kyong 許慶

Hŏ Si 許時

Hŏ Wŏn 許元

Hŏ Yun-ch'ang 許允昌

Hong Cha-bŏn 洪子潘

Hong Chung-sŏn 洪仲宣

Hong Kwan 洪灌

Hong Kyŏng 洪敬

Hong Kyu 洪奎

Hong Ŏn-bak 洪彦博

Hong Sang-bin 洪尙賓

Hong Yŏng-t'ong 洪永通

Hsü Ching 徐兢

Hwang Ch'i-sin 黃致身

Hwang Hŭi 黃喜

Hwang Su-sin 黃守身

Hwangbo Yŏng 皇甫潁

Im Ch'un 林椿

Im Kun-bo 任君輔

Im Kyŏn-mi 林堅美

Im Ŏn-su 林彦修

Im Sŏng-mi 林成美

Im Ŭi 任懿

Im Wŏn-gae 任元凱

Im Wŏn-jun 任元濬

Im Wŏn-suk 任元淑

Im Yŏn 林衍

Im Yu-mu 林惟茂

In Hu 印侯

In Tang 印璫

Iryŏn 一然

Isa 二巳

Kang Cho 康兆

Kang Hoe-baek 姜淮伯

Kang Kam-ch'an 姜邯贊

Kang Min-ch'ŏm 姜民瞻

Kang Si 姜蓍

Kang Yun-ch'ung 康允忠

Ki Cha-hŏn 奇自獻

Ki Cha-o 奇子敖

Ki Ch'ŏl 奇轍

Ki Ik-hŏn 奇益獻

Ki Sam-man 奇三萬

Ki Tae-hang 奇大恆

Ki Tae-sŭng 奇大升

Kil Chae 吉再

Kim An-guk 金安國

Kim Ch'aek 金策

Kim Cha-jŏng 金子廷

Kim Chang 金蓴

Kim (Wang) Chang-myŏng 金（王）長命

Kim Chi 金䃼

Kim Chin 金縝

Kim Chin-yang 金震陽

Kim Chi-suk 金之淑

Kim Ch'ŏk 金惕

Kim Ch'ŏn 金薦

Kim Chong-jik 金宗直

Kim Chŏng-jun 金廷俊

Kim Chu-jŏng 金周鼎

Kim Chun (Kim In-jun) 金俊（金仁俊）

Kim Chung-gu 金仲龜

Kim Chu-wŏn 金周元

Kim Ch'wi-ryŏ 金就礪

Kim Haeng 金荇

Kim Han-gong 金漢功

Kim Hŭng-gwang 金興光

Kim Hwang-wŏn 金黃元

Kim Hyo-in 金孝印

Kim Hyu 金休

Kim Ik-chŏng 金益精

Kim In-ch'an 金仁贊

Kim In-gwan 金仁琯

Kim In-jon 金仁存

Kim In-jun (Kim Chun) 金仁俊（金俊）

Kim In-wi 金仁渭

Kim Kil 金吉

Kim Ko 金沽

Kim Ku 金坵

Kim Kŭn 金覲

Kim Ku-yong 金九容

Kim Kwang-ch'ŏl 金光轍

Kim Kwang-ni 金光利

Kim Kwan-ŭi 金寬毅

Kim (Wang) Kyŏng 金（王）景

Kim Nan 金蘭

Kim No 金輅

Kim Ŏng-nyŏm 金億廉

Kim Pang-gyŏng 金方慶

Kim Po-dang 金甫當

Kim Pong-mo 金鳳毛

Kim Pu 金溥

Kim Pu-ch'ŏl (Kim Pu-ŭi) 金富轍（金富儀）

Kim Pu-il 金富佾

Kim Pu-p'il 金富弼

Kim Pu-sik 金富軾

Kim Pu-ŭi (Kim Pu-ch'ŏl) 金富儀（金富哲）

Kim Pyŏn 金胼

Kim Sa-haeng 金師幸

Kim Sa-hyŏng 金士衡

Kim Sang-gi 金上琦

Kim Sa-ryŏm 金士廉

Kim Sŏn 金愃

Kim Song-myŏng 金續命

Kim Su (Andong) 金綏

Kim Su (Kwangsan) 金須

Kim Sun 金恂

Kim Sŭng 金陞

Kim Sŭng-yong 金承用

Kim (Wang) Sun-sik 金（王）順式

Kim Su-on 金水溫

Kim (Wang) Su-wŏn 金（王）守元

Kim Tam 金潭

Kim Tan (12th cent.) 金端

Kim Tan (14th cent.) 金但

Kim Ton-jung 金敦中

Kim Ŭi-wŏn 金義元

Kim Yag-on 金若溫

Kim Yak-ch'ae 金若采

Kim Yang-gam 金良鑑

Kin (Wang) Ye 金（王）乂

Kim Yŏn 金璉

Kim Yong 金鏞

Kim Yŏng-bu 金永夫

Kim Yŏng-don 金永敦

Kim Yŏng-hu 金永煦

Kim Yŏng-hwi 金永暉

Kim Yun 金倫

Kungye 弓裔

Kwak Ch'u 郭樞

Kwak Chŭng 郭拯

Kwak Ch'ung-bo 郭忠輔

Kwak Sang 郭尙

Kwak Sŭng-u 郭承佑

Kwak T'an 郭坦

Kwak Won 郭元

Kwak Yŏ 郭輿

Kwŏn Chae (Wang Hu) 權載 （王煦）

Kwŏn Cha-yŏ 權子與

Kwŏn Chin 權軫

Kwŏn Chŏk 權適

Kwŏn Chŏng 權精

Kwŏn Chŏng-ju 權定柱

Kwŏn Chun 權準

Kwŏn Ch'ung 權衷

Kwŏn Chung-hwa 權仲和

Kwŏn Chung-si 權仲時

Kwŏn Han-gong 權漢功

Kwŏn Ho (son of Kwŏn Pu) 權昊

Kwŏn Ho (son of Kwŏn Yŏm) 權鎬

Kwŏn Hong 權弘

Kwŏn Hŭi 權僖

Kwŏn Hŭi-dal 權稀達

Kwŏn Hŭi-jŏng 權稀正

Kwŏn Hun 權壎

Kwŏn Hwa 權和

Kwŏn Hyŏk 權奕

Kwŏn Kŭn 權近

Kwŏn Kyŏm 權謙

Kwŏn Kyun 權鈞

Kwŏn Nam 權擥

Kwŏn Po 權堡

Kwŏn Pu 權傅

Kwŏn Su 權鏞

Kwŏn Su-hong 權守洪

Kwŏn Su-p'yŏng 權守平

Kwŏn Tan 權旽

Kwŏn Tam 權湛

Kwŏn U 權遇

Kwŏn Wi 權韙

Kwŏn Yang-jun 權良俊

Kwŏn Yŏm 權濂

Kwŏn Yong 權鏞

Kwŏn Yong-il 權用一

Kyeguk *taejang kongju* 薊國大長公主

Kyŏng Pok-hŭng 慶復興

Kyŏnhwŏn 甄萱

Liu Tsung-yüan 柳宗元

Maeng Hŭi-do 孟希道

Maeng Sa-sŏng 孟思誠

Manu 卍雨

Min An-in 閔安仁

Min Che 閔霽

Min Chi 閔漬

Min Chi-saeng 閔智生

Min Chŏk 閔頔

Min Chong-yu 閔宗儒

Min Chung-ni 閔中理

Min Hwang 閔滉

Min Hwi 閔暉

Min Hyŏn 閔玹

Min In-gyun 閔仁鈞

Min Kae 閔開

Min Ka-gŏ 閔可舉

Min Kong-gyu 閔公珪

Min Kong-saeng 閔公生

Min Kyŏng-saeng 閔慶生

Min Kŭn 閔瑾

Min Mu-gu 閔無咎

Min Mu-hyul 閔無恤

Min Mu-jil 閔無疾

Min Myŏng-sin 閔命莘

Min Pyŏn 閔忭

Min Sang-baek 閔祥白

Min Sang-jŏng 閔祥正

Min Sa-p'yŏng 閔思平

Min Sik 閔湜

Min Sim-ŏn 閔審言

Min Sŏn 閔璿

Min Su-saeng 閔壽生

Min Yak-son 閔若孫

Min Yŏ-ik 閔汝翼

Min Yŏng-mo 閔令謨

Min Yu 閔愉

Mok In-gil 睦仁吉

Mun Ik 文翼

Mun Ik-chŏm 文益漸

Mun Kong-mi 文公美

Mun Kong-wŏn 文公元

Mun Kong-yu 文公裕

Mun Kŭk-kyŏm 文克謙

Mun Kyŏng 文璟

Mun Tar-han 文達漢

Myoch'ŏng 妙清

Myŏngdŏk *t'aehu* Hong-ssi 明德太后洪氏

Nam Chae 南在

Nam Chi 南智

Nam Ŭn 南誾

No Ch'aek 盧頤

No Yŏng-sŏ 盧英瑞

Noguk *taejang kongju* 魯國大長公主

O Mong-ŭl 吳蒙乙

O Yŏn-ch'ong 吳延寵

Ondal 溫達

Ou-yang Hsiu 歐陽修

Pae Chŏn 裴佺

Pae Chŏng-ji 裴廷芝

Pae Kŭng-nyŏm 裴克廉

Paek I-jŏng 白頤正

Paek Mun-bo 白文寶

Pak Cha-hŏ 朴子虛

Pak Cha-ryang 朴子良

Pak Chig-yun 朴直胤

Pak Chi-wŏn 朴趾源

Pak Ch'ong 朴叢

Pak Chŏn-ji 朴全之

Pak Ch'ung-jwa 朴忠佐

Pak Chung-yong 朴仲容

Pak Hwi 朴暉

Pak Hyŏng 朴形

Pak Ik 朴翊

Pak Il-lyang 朴寅亮

Pak In-sŏk 朴仁碩

Pak Ko 朴翺

Pak Kyŏng-baek 朴景伯

Pak Kyŏng-in 朴景仁

Pak Kyŏng-san 朴景山

Pak Mun-sŏn 朴文琁

Pak Mun-su 朴門秀

Pak P'o 朴苞

Pak Sang-ch'ung 朴尙衷

Pak Si-ja 朴時滋

Pak Su-gyŏm 朴守謙

Pak Su-gyŏng 朴守卿

Pak Su-mun 朴守文

Pak Sun 朴純

Pak Tŏk-kong 朴德公

Pak Tŏng-nyong 朴德龍

Pak Ŭi 朴義

Pak Ŭi-ji 朴宜之

Pak Ŭn-sik 朴殷植

Pak Wŏn 朴遠

Pak Yŏng-ch'ung 朴永忠

Pyŏn An-nyŏl 邊安烈

Pyŏn Chung-nyang 卞仲良

Pyŏn Kye-ryang 卞季良

Sin Ch'ae-ho 申采浩

Sin Ton 辛旽

Sin'gŏm 神劍

Sinmi 信眉

Sŏ Hŭi 徐熙

Sŏ Kyŏn 徐甄

Sŏ Kyŏng-dŏk 徐敬德

Sŏ Kyun-hyŏng 徐均衡

Sŏ Mok 徐穆

Sŏ Nul 徐訥

Sŏ P'il 徐弼

Sŏl Kong-gŏm 薛公儉

Son Ki 孫琦

Sŏng Hyŏn 成俔

Ssu-ma Kuang 司馬光

Su Shih (Su Tung-p'o) 蘇軾
（蘇東坡）

To Sŏng-gi 陶成器

To Kil-bu 都吉敷

Tŏngnyŏng *taejang kongju* 德寧
大長公主

Tu Fu 杜甫

U Hyŏn-bo 禹玄寶

U T'ak 禹倬

Wang An-shih 王安石

Wang Cha-ji 安字之

Wang (Kim) Chang-myŏng 王
（김）長命

Wang Kŏn 王建

Wang Kung-mo 王國髦

Wang (Kim) Kyŏng 王（金）景

Wang Kyu 王規

Wang (Kim) Sun-sik 王（金）順式

Wang (Kim) Su-wŏn 王（金）
守元

Wang (Kim) Ye 王（金）乂

Wi Kye-jong 魏繼宗

Wi Su-yŏ 韋壽餘

Wŏn Ching-yŏn 元徵衍

Wŏn Ch'ŏn-sŏk 元天錫

Wŏn Kwan 元瓘

Wŏn Pu 元傅

Wŏn Sŏn-ji 元善之

Yang Chang 梁將

Yang Sŏng-ji 梁誠之

Yang Wŏn-jun 梁元俊

Yi Cha-ch'un 李子春

Yi Cha-gyŏm 李資謙

Yi Cha-hyŏn 李資玄

Yi Cha-in 李資仁

Yi Ch'ang-no 李彰路

Yi Chang-yong 李藏用

Yi Cha-ryang 李資諒

Yi Cha-sang 李子詳

Yi Cha-ŭi 李資義

Yi Cha-yŏn 李子淵

Yi Che 李濟

Yi Che-hyŏn 李齊賢

Yi Chi-bo 李之甫

Yi Chi-jŏ 李之氐

Yi Chik 李稷

Yi Chi-mi 李之美

Yi Chin 李瑱

Yi Ching-ok 李澄玉

Yi Chi-ŏn 李之彥

Yi Chip 李集

Yi Chi-ran (Yi Tu-ran) 李之蘭
  (李豆蘭)

Yi Chi-wŏn 李之元

Yi Chi-yun 李之允

Yi Chŏ 李宇

Yi Chŏk 李頔

Yi Chon 李存

Yi Chŏn 李傅

Yi Chon-bi (Yi In-song) 李尊庇
  (李仁成)

Yi Ch'ŏn 李蒨

Yi Chŏng 李頲

Yi Chŏng-bo 李廷俌

Yi Chong-dŏk 李種德

Yi Chŏng-gong 李靖恭

Yi Chŏng-gyŏn 李廷堅

Yi Chong-hak 李種學

Yi Chong-sŏn 李種善

Yi Chon-o 李存吾

Yi Chon-sŏng 李存性

Yi Cho-nyŏn 李兆年

Yi Ch'un 李椿

Yi Chun-yang 李俊陽

Yi Haek 李核

Yi Hang-nim 李學林

Yi Ho 李顥

Yi Hong-jik 李弘稙

Yi Hwa 李和

Yi Hwang 李滉

Yi Hye 李惠

Yi I 李珥

Yi Ik 李益

Yi Il-lo 李仁老

Yi In-bok 李仁復

Yi In-im 李仁任

Yi In-mi 李仁美

Yi In-min 李仁敏

Yi In-sŏng (Yi Chon-bi) 李仁成
  (李尊庇)

Yi Kil-sang 李吉祥

Yi Kŏ-i 李居易

Yi Kŏ-in 李居仁

Yi Kok 李穀

Yi Kyŏng-jung 李敬中

Yi Kyu-bo 李奎報

Yi Maeng-gyun 李孟畇

Yi Nae 李來

Yi O 李顙

Yi Ŏn-ch'ung 李彥沖

Yi Pang-bŏn 李芳蕃

Yi Pang-gan 李芳幹

Yi Pang-gwa 李芳果

Yi Pang-sŏk 李芳碩

Yi Pang-ŭi 李芳毅

Yi Pang-wŏn 李芳遠

Yi Pon 李本

Yi Pyŏng-do 李丙燾

Yi Saek 李穡

Yi Se-gi 李世基

Yi Sŏk 李碩

Yi Son-bo 李孫寶

Yi Song 李竦

Yi Sŏng-gye 李成桂

Yi Su 李壽

Yi Suk (12th cent.) 李壽

Yi Suk (14th cent.) 李淑

Yi Suk-chin 李淑真

Yi Suk-pŏn 李叔蕃

Yi Sung-in 李崇仁

Yi Sŭng-sang 李昇商

Yi Tal-chon 李達尊

Yi Tal-ch'ung 李達衷

Yi Tam 李檐

Yi Tan 李端

Yi Tang 李堂

Yi Tu-ran (Yi Chi-ran) 李豆蘭
(李之蘭)

Yi Ŭi 李顗

Yi Ŭi-bang 李義方

Yi Ŭi-min 李義旼

Yi Wi 李瑋

Yi Wŏn-goeng 李元紘

Yi Ye (Kyŏngju Yi) 李芮

Yi Ye (Kyŏngwŏn Yi) 李預

Yi Yŏng 李穎

Yi Yuk 李毓

Yŏm Che-sin 廉悌臣

Yŏm Chŏng-su 廉廷秀

Yŏm Hŭng-bang 廉興邦

Yŏm Sŭng-ik 廉承益

Yu An-t'aek 柳安澤

Yu Cha-u 庚自愚

Yu Chin 柳鎮

Yu Ch'ong 柳總

Yu Chŏng-hyŏn 柳廷顯

Yu Ch'ŏng-sin 柳清臣

Yu Ch'ŏn-gung 柳天弓

Yu Hong 柳洪

Yu Im 柳臨

Yu In-gi 柳仁琦

Yu Kong-gwŏn 柳公權

Yu Kwan 柳寬

Yu Kye-jo 柳繼祖

Yu Kyŏng (Kangnŭng Yu)
劉敬

Yu Kyŏng (Munhwa Yu) 柳璥

Yu Man-su 柳曼珠

Yu Ŏn-ch'im 柳彦沈

Yu Pang-hŏn 柳邦憲

Yu Po-bal 柳甫發

Yu Sa-nul 柳思訥

Yu Sik 柳湜

Yu Sŏng-bi 柳成庇

Yu Sŏng-wŏn 柳誠源

Yu Sun 柳淳

Yu Sŭng 柳陞

Yu T'aek 柳澤

Yu T'ak 柳濯

Yu Ton 柳敦

Yu Ŭn-ji 柳殷之

Yu Wŏn- hyŏn 柳原顯

Yu Wŏn-ji 柳原之

Yu Yang 柳亮

Yu Yŏn-ji 柳衍之

Yun Am 尹諳

Yun An-ch'ŏk 尹安蹄

Yun An-suk 尹安淑

Yun Chang 尹將

Yun Ch'ŏk 尹陟

Yun Hae 尹侅

Yun Ho 尹虎

Yun Hwan 尹桓

Yun Hyang 尹向

Yun Kon 尹坤

Yun Kwan 尹瓘

Yun Kyu 尹珪

Yun Mok 尹穆

Yun Ŏn-i 尹彦頤

Yun Ŏn-min 尹彦旼

Yun Ŏn-sik 尹彦植

Yun Po (son of Yun An-ch'ŏk) 尹輔

Yun Po (son of Yun Pog-wŏn) 尹

Yun Po-gung 尹寶弓

Yun Pog-wŏn 尹復元

Yun Pŏn 尹璠

Yun Po-ro 尹普老

Yun Sang-gye 尹商季

Yun So-jong 尹紹宗

Yun Sŭng-nye 尹承禮

Yun Sŭng-sun 尹承順

Yun Ton-sin 尹惇信

Bibliography

PRIMARY SOURCES

An Ch'uk. *Kŭnjae chip* (Collected works of An Ch'uk). In *Koryŏ myŏnghyŏn chip*, vol. 2 (q.v.).

Andong Kim-ssi taedongbo (Andong Kim genealogy). N.d.

Andong Kwŏn-ssi songhwa po (Andong Kwŏn genealogy). 1476.

Ch'oe Cha. *Pohan chip* (Collected works of Ch'oe Cha). In *Koryŏ myŏnghyŏn chip*, vol. 2 (q.v.).

Ch'oe Hae. *Cholgo ch'ŏnbaek* (Collected works of Ch'oe Hae). In *Koryŏ myŏnghyŏn chip*, vol. 2 (q.v.).

Chŏng Mong-ju, *P'oŭn chip* (Collected works of Chŏng Mong-ju). In *Koryŏ myŏnghyŏn chip*, vol. 4 (q.v.).

Chŏng To-jŏn. *Sambong chip* (Collected works of Chŏng To-jŏn). Seoul: Kuksa P'yŏnch'an Wiwŏnhoe [National Historical Compilation Committee], 1961.

Chŏngjong sillok (Veritable records of King Chŏngjong). In *Chosŏn Wangjo Sillok*.

Ch'ŏngju Han-ssi sebo (Ch'ŏngju Han genealogy). 1865.

Chosŏn Wangjo Sillok (Veritable Records of the Chosŏn dynasty). 48 vols. Seoul: Kuksa P'yŏnch'an Wiwŏnhoe, 1955–58.

Chuksan Pak-ssi Ch'unghŏn'gong p'abo (Genealogy of Ch'unghŏn'gong branch of the Chuksa Pak). 1975.

Chŭngbo munhon pigo (Expanded encyclopedia of Korea). Seoul: Tongguk Munhwa-sa, 1957.

Hanyang Cho-ssi taebo (Hanyang Cho genealogy). 1935.

Hŏ Hŭng-sik, ed. *Han'guk chungse sahoesa charyo chip* (Collected materials on medieval Korean social history). Seoul: Asea Munhwasa, 1976.

————. *Han'guk kŭmsŏk chŏnmun* (Complete Korean epigraphy). 3 vols. Seoul: Asea Munhwasa, 1984.

Hsü Ching. *Kao-li t'u-ching* (Report on the Koryŏ). Seoul: Asea Munhwasa, 1972.

Im Ch'un, *Sŏha chip* (Collected works of Im Ch'un). In *Koryŏ myŏnghyŏn chip*, vol. 2 (q.v.).

Inch'ŏn Yi-ssi chokpo (Inch'ŏn [Kyŏngwŏn] Yi genealogy). 1954.

Kim Chong-jik. *Chŏmp'iljae chip* (Collected works of Kim Chong-jik). In *Yijo myŏnghyŏn chip*, vol. 2.

Kim Pyŏn, *Chip'o chip* (Collected works of Kim Pyŏn). In *Koryŏ myŏnghyŏn chip,* vol. 2 (q.v.).

Kim Su-on. *Sigu chip* (Collected works of Kim Su-on). In *Yijo myŏnghyŏn chip,* vol. 2 (q.v.).

Kim Yong-sŏn, ed. *Koryŏ myojimyŏng chipsŏng* (Collection of Koryŏ tombstone inscriptions). Ch'unch'on: Hallim Taehakkyo Asia Munhwa Yŏn'guso, 1993.

Koryŏ myŏnghyon chip (Collected works of famous Koryŏ worthies). 5 vols. Seoul: Sŏnggyun'gwan Taehakkyo Taedong Munhwa Yŏn'guwŏn, 1986.

Koryŏsa (History of the Koryŏ). 3 vols. Seoul: Yŏnhŭi Taehakkyo, 1955.

Koryŏsa chŏryo (Essentials of Koryŏ history). Seoul: Asea Munhwasa ed., 1976.

Kukcho pangmok (Roster of examination graduates). Seoul: Kukhoe Tosŏgwan, 1971.

Kwŏn Kŭn. *Yangch'on chip* (Collected Works of Kwŏn Kŭn). Seoul: Asea Munhwasa, 1974.

Kyŏngguk taejŏn (Great code of administration). Keijo: Chosen Sotokufu, 1934.

Kyŏngju Yi-ssi sebo (Kyŏngju Yi genealogy). 1931.

Mansŏng taedongbo (Comprehensive genealogy). 3 vols. Seoul: Myŏngmundang, 1983.

Munhwa Yu-ssi sebo (Munhwa Yu genealogy). N.p.: 1565.

Munjong sillok (Veritable records of King Munjong). In *Chosŏn wangjo sillok.*

P'ap'yŏng Yun-ssi sebo (P'ap'yŏng Yun genealogy). N.p.: 1959.

P'yŏngyang Cho-ssi sebo (P'yŏngyang Cho genealogy). N.p.: 1791.

Samguk sagi (History of the Three Kingdoms). Seoul: Kyŏngin Munhwasa, 1976.

Sejo sillok (Veritable records of King Sejo). In *Chosŏn wangjo sillok.*

Sejong sillok (Veritable records of King Sejong). In *Chosŏn wangjo sillok.*

Sinch'ang Maeng-ssi sebo (Sinch'ang Maeng genealogy) (1937).

Sŏng Hyŏn. *Yongjae ch'onghwa* (Collected tales of Sŏng Hyŏn). In *Taedong yasŭng* (Korean literary miscellanea) Keijo: Chosen Kosho Kankokai, 1911.

Sunhŭng An-ssi chokpo (Sunhŭng An genealogy). 1864.

T'aejo sillok (Veritable records of King T'aejo). In *Chosŏn wangjo sillok.*

T'aejong sillok (Veritable records of King T'aejong). In *Chosŏn wangjo sillok.*

Tanjong sillok (Veritable records of King Tanjong). In *Chosŏn wangjo sillok.*

Wŏn Ch'ŏn-sŏk. *Un'gok sisa* (Collected works of Wŏn Ch'ŏn-sŏk). In *Koryŏ myŏnghyŏn chip,* vol. 5 (q.v.).

Wonju Wŏn-ssi chokpo (Wŏnju Wŏn genealogy). N.p.: 1988.

Yang Sŏng-ji. *Nuljae chip* (Collected works of Yung Sŏng-ji). Seoul: Asea Munhwasa, 1973.

Yi Che-hyŏn. *Ikchae nan'go* (Random jottings of Yi Che-hyŏn). In *Koryŏ myŏnghyŏn chip,* vol. 2 (q.v.).

———. *Yŏgong p'aesŏl* (Lowly jottings by Old Man Oak). In *Koryŏ myŏnghyŏn chip,* vol. 2 (q.v.).

Yi Kok. *Kajŏng chip* (Collected works of Yi Kok). In *Koryŏ myŏnghyŏn chip,* vol. 3 (q.v.).

Yi Saek. *Mogŭn chip* (Collected works of Yi Saek). In *Koryŏ myŏnghyŏn chip,* vol. 3 (q.v.).

Yi Sang-ŭn, ed. *Han'guk yŏktae inmuljŏn chipsŏng* (Collection of Korean historical biographies). Seoul: Minch'ang Munhwasa, 1990.

Yi Sung-in, *Toŭn chip* (Collected works of Yi Sung-in), in *Koryŏ myŏnghyŏn chip*, vol. 4.

Yijo myŏnghyŏn chip (Collected works of famous Chosŏn worthies). 6 vols, Seoul: Sŏnggyun'gwan Taehakkyo Taedong Munhwa Yŏn'guwŏn, 1977.

Yŏhŭng Min-ssi sebo (Hwangnyŏ Min genealogy). N.p.: 1973.

SECONDARY SOURCES — ASIAN LANGUAGES

An Kye-hyŏn. "Chogye-jong kwa ogyo yangjong" (The Ch'ogye Order and the Five Schools and Two Orders). In *Han'guksa* (History of Korea), vol. 7. Seoul: Kuksa P'yŏnch'an Wiwŏnhoe, 1981.

Chang Suk-kyŏng. "Koryŏ muin chŏnggwŏnha munsa ŭi tongt'ae wa sŏnggyŏk" (The situation and nature of the literati under the Koryŏ military regime). *Han'guksa yŏn'gu* 34 (1981).

Chang Tong-ik. *Koryŏ hugi oegyosa yŏn'gu* (Studies on the diplomatic history of the late Koryŏ). Seoul: Ilchogak, 1994.

Chang Tŭk-chin. "Cho Chun ŭi chŏngch'i hwaltong kwa kŭ sasang" (Cho Chun's political activity and his thought). *Yŏksahak yŏn'gu* 38 (1984).

Ch'ien Mu. "Lun Sung-tai hsiang-ch'üan" (On the power of chief ministers in the Sung dynasty). *Chung-kuo wen-hwa yen-chiu hui-kan* 2 (1942).

Cho In-sŏng. "Kungye ŭi ch'ulsaeng kwa sŏngjang" (The birth and childhood of Kungye). *Tonga yŏn'gu* 17 (1989).

Cho Tong-il. *Han'guk munhak t'ongsa* (History of Korean literature). 5 vols. Seoul: Chisik Sanŏpsa, 1982–1988.

Ch'oe Byŏng-hŏn (Ch'oe Pyŏng-hŏn). "Han'guk pulgyo ŭi chŏn'gae" (The development of Korean Buddhism). *Han'guk sasang ŭi simch'ŭng yŏn'gu* (Studies in Korean thought). Seoul: Tosŏ Ch'ulp'an Usŏk, 1982.

———. "Namal yŏch'o sŏnjong ŭi sahoe chŏk sŏngygŏk" (Social nature of Sŏn Buddhism in the late Silla and early Koryŏ). *Sahak yŏn'gu* 25 (1975).

———. "Tosŏn ŭi saengae wa namal yŏch'o ŭi p'ungsu chirisŏl: sŏnjong kwa p'ungsu chirisŏl ŭi kwan'gye rŭl chungsim ŭro" (Tosŏn's life and geomancy in late Silla and early Koryŏ: The relationship between geomancy and meditational Buddhism). *Han'guksa yŏn'gu* 11 (1975).

Ch'oe Kŭn-yŏng. *T'ongil Silla sidae ŭi chibang seryŏk yŏn'gu* (Studies of local power in the unified Silla period). Rev. ed. Seoul: Tosŏ Ch'ulp'an Sinsŏwŏn, 1993.

Ch'oe Sŭng-hŭi. "Yangban yugyo chŏngch'i ŭi chinjŏn" (The advance of *yangban* Confucian politics). In *Han'guksa* (Korean history). vol. 9. Seoul: Kuksa P'yonch'an Wiwŏnhoe, 1981.

Chŏn Hae-jong. "Tae Song oegyo ŭi sŏnggyŏk" (The nature of Koryŏ's Sung diplomacy). *Han'guksa* 4 (1974).

———. "Yŏ-Wŏn muyŏk ŭi sŏnggyŏk" (The nature of trade between the Koryŏ and the Yüan). *Tongyang sahak yŏn'gu* 12–13 (1978).

Ch'ŏn Kwan-u. "Han'guk t'oji chedo-sa" (History of Korean land systems). Part 2. In *Han'guk munhwasa taegye* (Survey of Korean Cultural History), vol. 2. Seoul:, Koryŏ Taehakkyo, 1965.

Chŏn Sŏk-tam. *Chosŏn kyŏngjesa* (Economic history of Korea). Seoul: Pangmunsa, 1949.

Chŏng Chae-hun. "Haeju O-ssi chokto ko" (Examination of the Haeju O descent diagram). *Tonga yŏn'gu* 17 (1989).

Chŏng Chŏng-hwan. *Koryŏ-Chosŏn sidae nokbongje yŏn'gu* (Studies on the salary system of the Koryŏ and Chosŏn periods). Taegu: Kyŏngbuk Taehakkyo, 1991.

Chŏng Ku-bok. "Ssangmaedang Yi Ch'ŏm ŭi yŏksa sŏsul" (The historical writings of Yi Ch'ŏm). *Tonga yŏn'gu* 17 (1989).

Chŏng Ok-cha. "Yŏmal Chuja Sŏngnihak ŭi toip e taehan sigo" (A preliminary examination of the introduction of Chu Hsi's Nature and Principle Learning in the late Koryŏ). *Chindan hakpo* 51 (1981).

Chŏng Tu-hŭi. *Chosŏn ch'ogi chŏngch'i seryŏk yŏn'gu* (Studies in the political power of the early Chosŏn dynasty). Seoul: Ilchogak, 1983.

———. "Chosŏn kŏn'guk ch'ogi t'ongch'i ch'eje ŭi sŏngnip kwajŏng kwa kŭ yŏksa chŏk ŭimi" (The process of establishing the system of rule at the beginning of the Chosŏn and its historical significance). *Han'guksa yŏn'gu* 67 (1989).

———. *Chosŏn Sŏngjongdae ŭi taegan yŏn'gu* (Studies in the censorial officials in the reign of King Sŏngjong of the Chosŏn dynasty). Seoul: Han'guk yŏn'gu-wŏn, 1989.

Chosŏn chŏnsa (Complete history of Korea). P'yŏngyang: Sahoe Kwahagwŏn, 1979.

Chosŏn t'ongsa (History of Korea). P'yŏngyang: Sahoe Kwahagwŏn, 1977.

Chosenshi (History of Korea). Keijo: Chosen Sotokufu, 1932–40.

Chou Tao-chi. "T'ang-tai tsai-hsiang ming-ch'eng yü ch'i shih-ch'üan chih yen-pien" (Nomenclature of T'ang dynasty chief ministers and changes in their authority). *Ta-lu tsa-chih* 16:4 (1952).

———. "Sung-tai tsai-hsiang ming-ch'eng yü ch'i shih-ch'üan chih yen-chiu" (A study in the nomenclature of Sung dynasty chief ministers and their authority). *Ta-lu tsa-chih* 17:12 (1954).

Fujita Ryosaku. "Yi Cha-yŏn to sono kakei" (Yi Cha-yŏn and his kin group). *Seikyu gakusho* 13–15 (1933–34).

Ha Hyŏn-gang. *Han'guk chungsesa yŏn'gu* (Studies in medieval Korean history). Seoul: Ilchogak, 1988.

———. "Hojok kwa wanggwŏn" (Strongmen and royal power). *Han'guksa* 4 (1981).

———. *Koryŏ chibang chedo ŭi yŏn'gu* (Studies in Koryŏ local administration). Seoul: Han'guk Yŏn'guwŏn, 1977.

———. "Koryŏ wangjo ŭi sŏngnip kwa hojok yŏnhap chŏnggwŏn" (The founding of the Koryŏ dynasty and the strongman alliance). *Han'guksa* 4 (1974).

Han Ch'ung-hŭi, "Chosŏn ch'ogi yukcho yŏn'gu" (Studies on the Six Boards at the beginning of the Chosŏn). Ph.D. diss. Koryŏ Taehakkyo, 1992.

———. "Koryŏ chŏn'gi sahoe ŭi sŏnggyŏk e taehayŏ" (On the nature of early Koryŏ society). In Kim Ŭi-gyu, ed., *Koryŏ sahoe ŭi kwijokchesŏl kwa kwally-ojeron*.

Han Woo-keun (Han U-gŭn). *Han'guk t'ongsa* (History of Korea). Seoul: Ŭryu munhwasa, 1970. Transl. into English by Kyung-shik Lee as *The History of Korea* Honolulu: University of Hawaii Press, 1974.

———. *Kiinje yŏn'gu* (Studies in the hostage system). Seoul: Ilchisa, 1992.

———. "Sejongjo e issŏsŏ ŭi tae pulgyo sich'aek" (Policies toward Buddhism in Sejong's reign). *Chindan hakpo* 25–27 (1964).

———. "Yŏmal sŏnch'o ŭi pulgyo chŏngch'aek" (Policy toward Buddhism in the late Koryŏ and early Chosŏn). *Seoul tae nonmunjip, inmun sahoe kwahak* 6 (1957).

——— and Yi T'ae-jin, eds. *Saryo ro pon Han'guk munhwasa, Chosŏn chŏn'gi p'yŏn* (Sources of Korean cultural history, early Chosŏn volume). Seoul: Ilchisa, 1984.

Han Young-woo (Han Yŏng-u) *Chŏng To-jŏn sasang ŭi yŏn'gu* (Studies in the thought of Chŏng To-jŏn). Seoul: Han'guk Munhwa Yŏn'guso, 1973.

———. "Chosŏn ch'ogi sahoe kyech'ŭng yŏn'gu e taehan chaeron" (A reconsideration of research on early Chosŏn social strata). *Han'guk saron* 12 (Feb. 1985).

———. "Chosŏn ch'ogi sinbun kyech'ŭng yŏn'gu ŭi hyŏnhwang kwa munje chŏm" (Status and problems of research on status strata in the early Chosŏn). *Sahoe kwahak p'yŏngnon* 1 (1982).

———. *Chosŏn chŏn'gi sahoe kyŏngje yŏn'gu* (Studies in Early Chosŏn society and economy). Seoul: Ŭryu Munhwasa, 1983.

———. *Chosŏn chŏn'gi ŭi sahoe sasang yŏn'gu* (Studies on the social thought of the early Chosŏn). Seoul: Han'guk Ilbosa, 1976.

———. "Koryŏ sidae yuga sasang ihae ŭi munje chŏm" (Problems in understanding the Confucian Thought of the Koryŏ period). In Han'guk Ch'ŏrhak Yŏn'guhoe (Korean Philosophy Research Society), ed., *Han'guk ch'ŏrhak yŏn'gu* (Studies in Korean philosophy). Seoul: Tongmyŏngsa, 1977.

———. "Yŏmal sŏnch'o hallyang kwa kŭ chiwi" (The Hallyang of the late Koryŏ and early Chosŏn and their status). *Han'guksa yŏn'gu* 4 (1969).

Han'guk Kyŏngje Sahakhoe (Korean Economic History Society), ed. *Han'guksa sidae kubunnon* (Theories on the periodization of Korean history). Seoul: Ŭryu Munhwasa, 1970.

Han'guk Yŏksa Yŏn'guhoe (Korean History Research Society), ed. *Han'guksa kangŭi* (Lectures on Korean history). Seoul: Hanul Ak'ademi, 1989.

Han'guksa T'ŭkkang P'yŏnch'an Wiwŏnhoe (Committee for Editing Seminar on Korean History), ed. *Han'guksa t'ŭkkang* (Seminar on Korean History). Seoul: Seoul Taehakkyo, 1990.

Hatada, Takashi. *Chosen chusei shakaishi no kenkyu* (Studies on the social history of medieval Korea). Tokyo: Hosei Daigaku, 1972.

Hŏ Hŭng-sik. *Han'guk ŭi komunsŏ* (Old documents of Korea). Seoul: Minŭsa, 1988.

———. "Koryŏ kwagŏ chedo ŭi kŏmt'o" (An examination of the Koryŏ government service examination system). *Han'guksa yŏn'gu* 10 (1974).

———. *Koryŏ kwagŏ chedosa yŏn'gu* (Studies on the Koryŏ examination system. Seoul: Ilchogak, 1981.

———. *Koryŏ pulgyosa yŏn'gu* (Studies on Koryŏ Buddhist history). Seoul: Ilchogak, 1986.

———. *Koryŏ sahoesa yŏn'gu* (Studies on Koryŏ social history). Seoul: Ilchogak, 1980.

———. "Koryŏ ŭi kukchagam si wa i rŭl t'onghan sinbun yudong" (The Koryŏ Royal Confucian Academy examination and social mobility). *Han'guksa yŏn'gu* 12 (1976).

———. "*Kukpo hojŏk* ŭro pon Koryŏ malgi ŭi sahoe kujo" (The structure of late Koryŏ society as seen through the National Treasure Household Register). *Han'guksa yŏn'gu* 16 (1977).

Hong Sŭng-gi. "Koryŏ hugi sasimgwan chedo ŭi unyong kwa hyangni ŭi chinch'ul" (The operation of the local inspector system and the rise of *hyangni* in the late Koryŏ). *Tonga yŏn'gu* 17 (1989).

———. *Koryŏ kwijok sahoe wa nobi* (Koryŏ aristocratic society and slaves). Seoul: Ilchogak, 1983.

———. ed., *Koryŏ muin chŏngkwŏn yŏn'gu* (Studies on the military regime of Koryŏ). Seoul: Sŏgang Taehakkyo Ch'ulp'anbu, 1995.

———. *Koryŏ T'aejo ŭi kukka kyŏngyŏng* (Administration of the state by King T'aejo of Koryŏ). Seoul: Seoul Taehakkyo Ch'ulp'anbu, 1996.

———. "Silchŭng sahangnon" (Positivist historiography). In Hallim Kwahagwŏn, ed., *Hyŏndae han'guk sahak kwa sagwan* (Contemporary Korean historiography and views of history). Seoul: Ilchogak, 1991.

Hsiao Kung-ch'üan. *Chung-kuo cheng-chih ssu-hsiang shih* (History of Chinese political thought). Taipei: Chung-hua Wen-hua Ch'u-pan-she, 1954.

Hwang Sŏn-myŏng. *Chosŏnjo chonggyo sahoesa yŏn'gu* (Studies on Chosŏn religious and social history). Seoul: Ilchisa, 1985.

Im Yŏng-jŏng. "Nobi munje" (The slave problem). In *Han'guksa*. Vol. 8. Seoul: Kuksa P'yŏnch'an Wiwŏnhoe, 1981.

———. "Yŏmal sŏnch'o ŭi sabyŏng" (Private military forces in the late Koryŏ and early Chosŏn). *Han'guk saron* 7 (1981).

Inoue, Hideo. "Silla seiji taisei no henten katei" (The Process of change in the Silla political system). *Kodaisi kozo* 4 (1962).

Kang Chin-ch'ŏl. *Han'guk chungse t'oji soyu yŏn'gu* (Studies on land ownership in medieval Korea). Seoul: Ilchogak, 1989.

———. *Han'guk sahoe ŭi yŏksasang* (Historical aspects of Korean society). Seoul: Ilchisa, 1992.

———. "Koryŏ ch'ogi ŭi kuninjon" (Soldiers' land in the early Koryŏ). *Sungmyŏng taehakkyo nonmun chip* 3 (1963).

———. "Koryŏ sidae ŭi chidae e taehayŏ" (On land rents in the Koryŏ period). *Chindan hakpo* 53–54 (1982).

———. "Koryŏ sidae ŭi nongŏp kyŏngyŏng hyŏngt'ae" (Forms of agricultural management in the Koryŏ period). *Han'guksa yŏn'gu,* 12 (1977).

———. *Koryŏ t'oji chedosa yŏn'gu* (Studies in Koryŏ land systems). Seoul: Koryŏ Taehakkyo, 1980.

Kang Man-gil. "Ilche sidea ŭi pansingmin sahangnon" (Anticolonialist historiography of the Japanese imperialist era). In Han'guksa Yŏn'guhoe, ed., *Han'guk sahaksa ŭi yŏn'gu* (Studies on Korean historiography). Seoul: Ŭryu Munhwasa, 1985.

Kim Ch'ang-hyŏn. "Koryŏ hugi Chŏngbang yŏn'gu" (Studies on the Personnel Authority of the late Koryŏ). Ph.D. diss. Koryŏ Taehakkyo, 1996.

Kim Ch'ang-su. "Sŏngjung aema ko" (An examination of palace guards). *Tongguk sahak* 9–10 (1966).

Kim Chŏng-suk. "Kim Chu-wŏn segye ŭi sŏngnip kwa kŭ pyŏnch'ŏn" (Establishment and evolution of Kim Chu-wŏn's line of descent). *Paeksan hakpo* 28 (1984).

Kim Ch'ung-nyŏl. *Koryŏ yuhaksa* (History of Koryŏ Confucian learning). Seoul: Koryŏ Taehakkyo, 1984.

———. "Sŏngnihak ŭi suip kwa hyŏngsŏng kwajong" (The process of the introduction and formation of Nature and Principle Learning). In Taedong Munhwa Yŏn'guwŏn, ed., *Han'guk sasang taegye* (Outline of Korean thought). Seoul: Sŏnggyun'gwan Taehakkyo, 1983.

Kim Hak-sik. *Chosŏn sidae pon'gŏn sahoe ŭi kibon kujo* (Structure of feudal society in the Chosŏn period). Seoul: Pagyŏngsa, 1981.

Kim Han-gyu. "Koryŏ Ch'oe-ssi chŏnggwŏn ŭi Chin'gangbu" (The Chin'gang estate administration of the Koryŏ Ch'oe house). *Tonga yŏn'gu* 17 (1988).

Kim Kwang-ch'ŏl. *Koryŏ hugi sejokch'ŭng yŏn'gu* (Studies on late Koryŏ hereditary descent groups). Pusan: Tonga Taehakkyo, 1991.

Kim Kwang-su. "Koryŏ sidae ŭi sŏri chik" (The clerical offices of the Koryŏ period). *Han'guksa yŏn'gu* 4 (1969).

———. "Koryŏ sidae ŭi tongjŏng chik" (Honorary offices of the Koryŏ period). *Yŏksa kyoyuk* 11/12 (1969).

Kim Nam-gyu. *Koryŏ yanggye chibangsa yŏn'gu* (Studies on the local history of the two border regions of the Koryŏ). Seoul: Saemunsa, 1989.

Kim Pok-sun. "Ch'oe Ch'i-wŏn ŭi pulgyo kwan'gye chŏsŏ e tae han kŏmt'o." (An examination of Ch'oe Ch'i-wŏn's writings related to Buddhism). *Han'guksa yŏn'gu* 43 (1983).

Kim Sang-gi. *Koryŏ sidaesa* (History of the Koryŏ period). Seoul: Tongguk Munhwasa, 1966.

Kim Sŏng-jun. *Han'guk chungse chŏngch'i pŏpchesa yŏn'gu* (Studies on Korean medieval political and legal history). Seoul: Ilchogak, 1985.

———. "Kiin ŭi sŏnggyŏk e taehan koch'al" (Examination of the nature of hostages). *Yŏksa hakpo* 10–11 (1958–59).

———. "Koryŏ chŏngbang ko" (An examination of the Koryŏ personnel authority). *Yŏksa hakpo* 13 (1962).

———. "Yŏdae Yüan kongju ch'ulsin wangbi ŭi chŏngch'ijŏk wich'i e taehayŏ" (On the political position of Yüan princess royal consorts in the Koryŏ period). In Ewha Yŏja Taehakkyo, ed. *Han'guk yŏsŏng munhwa non'chong* (Studies in Korean women's culture) Seoul: Ewha Yŏja Taehakkyo, 1958.

Kim Su-t'ae. "Koryŏ pon'gwan chedo ŭi sŏngnip" (The establishment of the Koryŏ ancestral seat system). *Chindan hakpo* 52 (1981).

Kim T'ae-uk. "Koryŏ Hyŏnjongdae ŭi chaech'u" (The *chaech'u* of the reign of Koryŏ King Hyŏnjong). *Yŏksa hakpo* 144 (1994).

Kim T'ae-yŏng. "Kwajŏn pŏp ch'ejeha ŭi t'oji saengsannyŏk kwa yangjŏn" (Land productivity and land surveys under the Rank Land Law system). *Han'guksa yŏn'gu* 35 (1981).

Kim Tang-t'aek. "Ch'oe Sŭng-no sangsŏmun e poinŭn Kwangjong dae ŭi 'husaeng' kwa Kyŏngjong wŏnnyŏn Chŏnsi kwa" (The 'new men' of Kwangjong's reign seen in Ch'oe Sŭng-no's memorial and the Field and Woodland Ranks of Kyŏngjong's first year). In Lee Ki-baik, ed., *Koryŏ Kwangjong yŏn'gu* (Studies on Koryŏ King Kwangjong). Seoul: Ilchogak, 1981.

————. "Ch'ungnyŏl wang ŭi pongnip kwajŏng ŭl t'onghae pon ch'ŏn'gye ch'ulsin kwallyo wa 'sajok' ch'ulsin kwallyo ŭi chŏngch'i chŏk kaltŭng: 'sadaebu' kaenyŏm e taehan kŏmt'o," (Political conflict between officials of mean origins and officials of *sajok* origins as seen in the reenthronement of King Ch'ungnyŏl: An examination of the *sadaebu* concept). *Tonga yŏn'gu* 17 (1989).

————. *Koryŏ muin chŏngkwŏn yŏn'gu* (Studies on the Koryŏ military government). Seoul: Saemunsa, 1986.

Kim Tu-jin. "Koryŏ Kwangjongdae ŭi chŏnje wanggwŏn kwa hojok" (Royal autocracy and the strongmen in the reign of King Kwangjong of the Koryŏ). *Han'guk hakpo* 15 (1979).

Kim Ŭi-gyu. "Koryŏ muin chipkwŏn'gi munin ŭi chŏngch'i hwaltong" (Political activities of the literati during the Koryŏ military period). *Han Woo-Keun paksa chŏngnyŏn kinyŏm sahak nonch'ong* (Festschrift in honor of Dr. Han Woo-Keun). Seoul: n.p.: 1981.

————, ed. *Koryŏ sahoe ŭi kwijokchesŏl kwa kwallyojeron* (Aristocratic and bureaucratic theories on Koryŏ Society). Seoul: Chisik Sanŏpsa, 1985.

Kim Yong-dŏk. "Hyang, so, pugok ko" (A study of the *hyang, so,* and *pugok*). In *Paek Nak-chun hwan'gap kukhak kinyŏm nonch'ong* (Festschrift in honor of Paek Nak-chun). Seoul: Sasanggye, 1955.

————. "Koryŏ Kwangjongjo ŭi kwagŏ chedo munje" (Problems in the examination system of the reign of Koryŏ King Kwangjong). *Chungangdae nonmunjip* 4 (1959).

————. "Sinbun chedo" (Social status system). *Han'guk saron* 2 (1977).

Kim Yŏng-mo. *Chosŏn chibaech'ŭng yŏn'gu* (Studies on the ruling stratum of the Chosŏn dynasty). Seoul: Ilchogak, 1977.

Kim Yong-sŏn. "Koryŏ chibaech'ŭng ŭi maejangji e taehan koch'al" (An examination of the burial sites of the Koryŏ ruling stratum). *Tonga yŏn'gu* 17 (1988).

————. "Koryŏ sidae ŭi ŭmsŏ chedo e taehan chae kŏmt'o" (A reexamination of the protection system of the Koryŏ period). In Kim Ŭi-gyu, ed., *Koryŏ sahoe ŭi kwijokchesŏl kwa kwallyojeron* (q.v.).

————. *Koryŏ ŭmsŏ chedo yŏn'gu* (Studies on the Koryŏ protection system). Seoul: Ilchogak, 1991.

Kim Yong-sŏp, "Koryŏ sidae ŭi yangjŏnje" (The land survey system of the Koryŏ period). *Tongbang hakchi* 16 (1976).

Kim Yun-gon. "Sinhŭng sadaebu ŭi taedu" (The advent of the "New scholar-officials"). In *Han'guksa,* vol 8. Seoul: Kuksa P'yŏnch'an Wiwŏnhoe, 1981.

Ko Pyŏng-ik. *Tonga kyosŏpsa ŭi yŏn'gu* (Studies on East Asian international relations). Seoul: Seoul Taehakkyo, 1970.

Ko Sŭng-je. *Han'guk ch'ŏllak sahoesa yŏn'gu* (Studies on the social history of rural Korea). Seoul: Ilchisa, 1977.

Lee Ki-baik (Yi Ki-baek). *Han'guksa sillon* (A new history of Korea). Rev. ed. Seoul: Ilchogak, 1990. The 1976 edition has been translated into English by Edward W. Wagner as *A New History of Korea.* Cambridge: Harvard University Press, 1984.

———. *Koryŏ kwijok sahoe ŭi hyŏngsŏng* (The formation of Koryŏ aristocratic society). Seoul: Ilchogak, 1990.

———. *Koryŏ pyŏngjesa yŏn'gu* (Studies on the Koryŏ military system). Seoul: Ilchogak, 1968.

———. "Koryŏ sahoe esŏ ŭi sinbun ŭi sesŭp kwa pyŏndong," (Succession to and change in status in Koryŏ Society). In Minjok Munhwa Yŏn'guso (Korean Cultural Research Center) ed., *Han'guk ŭi chŏnt'ong kwa pyŏnch'ŏn* (Tradition and change in Korea). Seoul: Koryŏ Taehakkyo, 1973.

———. "Kwijok chŏngch'i ŭi sŏngnip" (The establishment of aristocratic politics). *Han'guksa* 5 (1981).

———. *Silla chŏngch'i sahoesa yŏn'gu* (Studies in Silla Sociopolitical history). Seoul: Ilchogak, 1974.

———. "Silla sabyŏng ko" (An examination of private military forces in Silla). *Yŏksa hakpo* 9 (1958).

———, ed. *Koryŏ Kwangjong yŏn'gu* (Studies on Koryŏ King Kwangjong). Seoul: Ilchogak, 1981.

——— and Min Hyŏn-gu, eds. *Saryo ro pon Han'guk munhwasa, Koryŏ p'yŏn* (Sources of Korean cultural history, Koryŏ volume). Seoul: Ilchisa, 1984.

Min Hyŏn-gu. "Cho In-gyu wa kŭ ŭi kamun, sang" (Cho In-gyu and his family, part 1). *Chindan hakpo* 42 (1976).

———. "Chŏngch'i togam ŭi sŏnggyŏk" (The nature of the General Directorate for Political Reform). *Tongbang hakchi* 23–24 (1980).

———. *Chosŏn ch'ogi kunsa chedo wa chŏngch'i* (Early Chosŏn military insitutions and politics). Seoul: Han'guk Yŏn'guwŏn, 1983.

———. "Kongminwang chŭgwi paegyŏng" (The background to Kongmin's enthronement). *Han Woo-Keun paksa chŏngnyŏn kinyŏm sahak nonch'ong* (Fetschrift in honor of Dr. Han Woo-Keun). Seoul: N.p., 1981.

———. "Koryŏ hugi ŭi kwŏnmun sejok" (Late Koryŏ powerful families). In *Han'guksa.* Vol. 8. Seoul: Kuksa P'yŏnch'an Wiwŏnhoe, 1981.

———. "Koryŏ ŭi Nokkwajŏn" (Koryŏ stipend lands) *Yŏksa hakpo* 53–54 (1972).

———. "Min Chi wa Yi Che-hyŏn" (Min Chi and Yi Che-hyŏn). In *Yi Pyŏng-do kusu kinyŏm han'guk sahak nonch'ong* (Fetschrift in honor of Yi Pyŏng-do). Seoul: Chisik Sanŏpsa, 1987.

———. "Sin Ton ŭi chipkwŏn kwa kŭ chŏngch'ijŏk sŏnggyŏk" (The rule of Sin Ton and its political nature) Parts 1 and 2. *Yŏksa hakpo* 38 (1968) and 40 (1970).

———. "Yi Chang-yong sogo" (A brief study of Yi Chang-yong). *Han'gukhak nonch'ong* 3 (1980).

Miyazaki, Ichisada. "Pu-ch'ü kara t'ien-hu e" (From servile labor to tenancy). *Toyoshi kenkyu* 29-4 (1970) and 30-1 (1971).

Mun Ch'ŏr-yŏng. "Yŏmal sinhŭng sadaebu tŭl ŭi sin yuhak suyong kwa kŭ t'ŭkch-ing" (acceptance of Neo-Confucianism by the "new scholar-officials" of the late Koryŏ and its features). *Han'guk munhwa* 3 (1982).

Mun Hyŏng-man. "Yŏdae kwihyang-go" (A study of men returning to their native districts in the Koryŏ period). *Yŏksa hakpo* 23 (1964).

Nam In-guk. "Ch'oe-ssi chŏnggwŏn-ha munsin chiwi ŭi pyŏnhwa" (Change in the position of civil officials under the Ch'oe regime). *Taegu sahak* 22 (1983).

No Kye-hyŏn. *Koryŏ oegyosa* (Diplomatic history of Koryŏ). Seoul: Kabin Ch'ulp'ansa, 1994.

No Myŏng-ho. "Koryŏ sidae ŭi ch'injok kwan'gyemang kwa kajok" (Kinship relations and the family in the Koryŏ period). *Han'guk saron* 19 (1988).

———. "Koryŏ sidae ŭi sŭngŭm hyŏljok kwa kwijokch'ŭng ŭi ŭmsŏ kihoe" (Scope of protection privilege kinship and aristocratic opportunities for protection privilege). In Kim Ŭi-gyu, ed., *Koryŏ sahoe ŭi kwijokchesŏl kwa kwallyojeron.*

No T'ae-don. "Haebang hu minjokchuŭi sahangnon ŭi chŏn'gae" (Evolution of nationalist historiography after liberation). In Hallim Kwahagwŏn, ed., *Hyŏndae han'guk sahak kwa sagwan.* Seoul: Ilchagak, 1991.

Paek Nam-un. *Chosen hoken shakai kezaishi* (Feudal socioeconomic history of Korea). Tokyo: Kaijosha, 1937.

———. *Chosen shakai kezaishi* (Socioeconomic history of Korea). Tokyo: Kaijosha, 1933.

Pak Ch'ang-hŭi. "Koryŏ sidae 'kwallyoje e taehan koch'al" (An examination of the bureaucratic system of the Koryŏ period). In Kim Ui-gyu, ed., *Koryŏ sahoe ŭi kwijokchesŏl kwa kwallyojeron* (q.v.).

———. "Musin chŏngkwŏn sidae ŭi munin," (Literati of the military period). In *Han'guksa.* Vol. 7. Seoul: Kuksa P'yŏnch'an Wiwŏnhoe, 1981.

Pak Ch'ŏn-sik. "Koryŏ Uwangdae ŭi chŏngch'i seryŏk kwa kŭ ch'ui" (Political power and trends in the reign of Koryŏ King U). *Chŏnbuk sahak* 4 (1980).

Pak Kyŏng-ja. "Koryŏ hyangni chedo ŭi sŏngnip" (The establishment of the Koryŏ *hyangni* system). *Yŏksa hakpo* 63 (1974).

Pak Sŏng-bong. "Kukchagam kwa sahak" (The Royal Confucian Academy and the private schools). In *Han'guksa.* Vol. 6. Seoul: Kuksa P'yŏnch'an Wiwŏnhoe, 1981.

Pak Sŏng-hwan. "Yugyo" (Confucianism). *Han'guk saron* 2 (1977).

Pak Un-gyŏng. "Koryŏ hugi chibang p'umgwan seryŏk e kwanhan yŏn'gu" (A study of the power of officials in the provinces in the late Koryŏ). *Han'guksa yŏn'gu* 44 (1984).

Pak Yong-un. "Koryŏ sidae Haeju Ch'oe-ssi wa P'ap'yŏng Yun-ssi kamun pun-sŏk" (Analysis of the Haeju Ch'oe and P'ap'yŏng Yun descent groups in the Koryŏ period). *Paeksan hakpo* 23 (1977).

———. "Koryŏ sidae Suju Ch'oe-ssi kamun punsŏk" (Analysis of the Suju Ch'oe descent group in the Koryŏ period). *Sach'ong* 26 (1983).

———. *Koryŏ sidae taegan chedo yŏn'gu* (Studies on the censorial officials of the Koryŏ period). Seoul: Ilchisa, 1980.

———. "Koryŏ sidae ŭi Chŏngan Im-ssi, Ch'ŏrwŏn Ch'oe-ssi, Kongam Hŏ-ssi kamun punsŏk" (Analysis of the Chŏngan Im, Ch'orwŏn Ch'oe, and Kongam Hŏ descent groups in the Koryŏ period). *Han'guksa nonch'ong* 3 (1978).

———. "Koryŏ sidae ŭi Musong Yu-ssi kamun punsŏk" (Analysis of the Musong Yu descent group in the Koryŏ period). In *Yi Pyŏng-do kusun kinyŏm sahak nonch'ong* (Festschrift in honor of Yi Pyŏng-do). Seoul: Chisik Sonŏpsa, 1987.

———. "Koryŏ sidae ŭmsoje ŭi silche wa kŭ kinŭng" (The reality and function of the Koryŏ era protection system). *Han'guksa yŏn'gu* 37 (1982).

———. *Koryŏ sidae ŭmsŏje wa kwagŏje yŏn'gu* (Studies on the protection system and examination system of the Koryŏ period). Seoul: Ilchisa, 1990.

———. *Koryŏ sidaesa* (History of the Koryŏ period). 2 vols. Seoul: Ilchisa, 1987.

———. "Kwallyoje wa kwijokche ŭi kaenyŏm kŏmt'o" (Examination of the concepts of bureaucracy and aristocracy). In Kim Ŭi-gyu, ed., *Koryŏ sahoe ŭi kwijokchesŏl kwa kwallyojeron* (q.v.).

———. "Yi Sŏng-mu chŏ *Chosŏn ch'ogi yangban yŏn'gu* sŏp'yŏng" (Review of Yi Sŏng-mu, *Studies on the early Chosŏn yangban*). *Asea yŏn'gu* 66 (1981).

Park Jong-ki (Pak Chong-gi). *Koryŏ sidae pugokche yŏn'gu* (Studies in the *pugok* system of the Koryŏ period). Seoul: Seoul Taehakkyo, 1990.

———. "Koryŏ t'aejo 23 nyŏn kunhyŏn kaep'yŏn e kwanhan yŏn'gu" (A study on the realignment of counties and prefectures in the 23rd year of Koryŏ King T'aejo). *Han'guk saron* 19 (1988).

———. "Silla pugokche ŭi kujo wa sŏnggyŏk" (The structure and nature of Silla's *pugok* system). *Han'guk saron* 10 (1984).

———. "Silla sidae hyang, pugok ŭi sŏnggyŏk e taehan il siron" (An essay on the nature of the *hyang* and *pugok* of the Silla period). *Han'guk saron* 10 (1984).

Pyŏn T'ae-sŏp, "Koryŏ ch'ogi chibang chedo" (Local administration at the beginning of Koryŏ). *Han'guksa yŏn'gu* 57 (1987).

———. *Koryŏ chŏngch'i chedosa yŏn'gu* (Studies on the history of Koryŏ political institutions). Seoul: Ilchogak, 1971.

———. "Koryŏ ŭi chŏngch'i chedo wa kwŏllyŏk kujo" (Political insitutions and power structure in the Koryŏ). *Han'guk hakpo* 4 (1976).

———. *Koryŏsa ŭi yŏn'gu* (Studies on the *Koryŏsa*). Seoul: Samyŏngsa, 1982.

———. ed. *Koryŏsa ŭi chemunje* (Various problems in Koryŏ history). Seoul: Samyŏngsa, 1986.

Shang Wen-li. *Chung-kuo li-tai ti-fang cheng-chih chih-tu* (History of Chinese local government). Taipei: Cheng-chung Shu-chu, 1981.

Sin Ho-chŏl. "Kyŏnhwŏn ŭi ch'ulsin kwa sahoe chŏk chinch'ul" (The origins and rise in society of Kyŏnhwŏn). *Tonga yŏn'gu* 17 (1989).

Sŏgang Taehakkyo Inmun Kwahak Yŏn'guso (Center for Humanities Research, Sŏgang University), ed. *Koryŏmal Chosŏnch'o t'oji chedo ŭi chemunje* (Various problems in land systems of the late Koryŏ and early Chosŏn). Seoul: Sŏgang Taehakkyo, 1987.

Song June-ho (Song Chun-ho). *Chosŏn sahoesa yŏn'gu* (Studies on Chosŏn social history). Seoul: Ilchogak, 1987.

Song Pyŏng-gi. "Koryŏ sidae ŭi nongjang—12 segi ihu rŭl chungsim ŭro" (Landed estates of the Koryŏ period with focus on the twelfth century and later). *Han'guksa yŏn'gu* 3 (1969).

———. "Nongjang ŭi paltal" (The development of estates). *Han'guksa*, Vol. 8 (Seoul: Kuksa P'yŏnch'an Wiwŏnhoe, 1981),

Sudo Yoshiyuki. "Korai makki yori Chosen shoki ni ataru nuhi no kenkyu" (Studies on slaves in the late Koryŏ and early Chosŏn). *Rekishigaku kenkyu* 9 (1939).

———. "Koraicho yori Richo shoki ni itaru oshitsu zaisei: Tokuni shizoko no kenkyu" (Royal finances in the Koryŏ and early Chosŏn: Particularly private warehouses). *Toho gakuho* 10–1 (1939).

———. "Raimatsu sensho ni okeru nojo ni tsuite" (On the estates of the late Koryŏ and early Chosŏn). *Seikyu gakusho* 17 (1934).

———. "Sensho ni okeru nuhi no bentai to shusatsu to ni tsuite" (On the investigation and adjudication of slaves in the early Chosŏn period). *Seikyu kakusho* 22 (1935).

Takeda Yukio. "Chŏngdusa goso seikito chosei keijiki no kenkyu (1)—Yangmokkun no kozo" (A study on the inscription for the erection of a five-story pagoda at Chŏngdu Temple (1): The structure of Yangmok County). *Chosen gakuho* 25 (1962).

———. "Korai jidai no hyakujo" (Village chiefs of the Koryŏ period). *Chosen gakuho* 28 (1963).

———. "Korai richo jidai no zokken" (Subordinate counties of the Koryŏ and Chosŏn periods). *Shigaku zasshi* 72–8 (1963).

———. "Korai shoki no kankei: Korai ocho kakuritsu katei no ichi kosatsu" (Official ranks in the early Koryŏ: A study of the process of establishing the Koryŏ dynasty). *Chosen gakuho* 41 (1966).

Yi Chang-u. "Chosŏn ch'ogi ui chŏnse chedo wa kukka chaejŏng" (The land tax system and state finance at the beginning of the Chosŏn). Ph.D. diss., Sŏgang Taehakkyo, 1993.

Yi Chin-han. "Koryŏ chŏn'gi kwanjik kwa nokpong ui kwan'gye yŏn'gu" (Studies on the relationship between offices and salaries in the early Koryŏ). Ph.D. diss., Koryŏ Taehakkyo, 1998.

Yi Chŏng-sin. "13 segi nongmin/ch'ŏnmin ponggi" (Uprisings of common and servile people in the thirteenth century). In *Song Kap-ho kyosu chŏngnyŏn t'oeim kinyŏm nonmunjip* (Fetschrift in honor of Professor Song Kap-ho). Seoul: Koryŏ Taehakkyo, 1993.

Yi Chong-uk. "940 nyŏndae chŏngch'i seryŏk ŭi punsŏk" (An analysis of political power in the 940s). In Lee Ki-baik, ed., *Koryŏ Kwangjong yŏn'gu* (q.v.)

Yi Ch'ŏng-wŏn. *Chosen shakaishi tokuhon* (Reader in Korean social history). Tokyo: Hakuyosha, 1936.

———. *Chosen tokuhon* (Reader on Korea). Tokyo: Gakugeisha, 1937.

Yi Hong-jik, ed. *Kuksa taesajŏn* (Dictionary of national history). Seoul: Chimungak, 1962.

Yi Hŭi-dŏk. *Koryŏ yugyo chŏngch'i sasang ŭi yŏn'gu* (Studies on the Confucian thought of the Koryŏ period). Seoul: Ilchogak, 1984.

Yi Hyŏng-u. "Uwang ŭi wangkwŏn kanghwa noryŏk kwa kŭ chwajŏl" (King U's effort to strengthen royal power and its failure). *Yŏksa wa hyŏnsil* 23 (1997).

Yi Ka-wŏn. *Han'guk hanmunhak sa* (History of Chinese literature in Korea). Seoul: Minjung Sŏgwan, 1961.

Yi Ki-nam. "Ch'ungsŏn wang ŭi kaehyŏk kwa Sarimwŏn ŭi sŏlch'i (King Ch'ungsŏn's reforms and the establishment of the Sarimwŏn). *Yŏksa hakpo* 52 (1971).

Yi Kwan-hŭi. "Koryŏmal Chosŏnch'o chŏnhyŏnggwan/ch'ŏmsŏlgwan e taehan t'oji pun'gŭp kwa kunyŏk pugwa" (Allocation of land and levying of military service on former officials and supernumerary officials in the late Koryŏ and early Chosŏn). In Sŏgang Taehakkyo Inmun Kwahak Yon'guso, ed, *Koryŏmal Chosŏnch'o t'oji chedosa ŭi chemunje.*

Yi Kwang-nin. "Kiin chedo ŭi pyŏnch'ŏn e taehayŏ" (On changes in the hostage system). *Yŏksa hakpo* 3 (1954).

Yi Kyŏng-sik. *Chosŏn chŏn'gi t'oji chedo yŏn'gu* (Studies on the land system of the early Chosŏn). Seoul: Ilchogak, 1986.

———. "Chosŏn chŏn'gi t'oji kaehyŏk nonŭi" (The debate over land system reform in the early Chosŏn). *Han'guksa yŏn'gu* 61–62 (1988).

Yi Pŏm-jik. "Chosŏn chŏn'gi yugyo kyoyuk kwa hyanggyo ŭi kinŭng" (Early Chosŏn Confucian education and the role of local schools). *Yŏksa hakpo* 20 (1976).

Yi Pyong-do. *Han'guksa chungse p'yŏn* (History of Korea: The medieval era). Seoul: Ŭryu Munhwasa, 1961.

———. *Han'guksa taegwan* (Overview of Korean history). Seoul: Ilchogak, 1964.

Yi Pyŏng-hyu. *Chosŏn chŏn'gi kiho sarimp'a yŏn'gu* (Studies on the Kiho *sarim* of the early Chosŏn). Seoul: Ilchogak, 1984.

Yi Sang-baek. *Chosŏn munhwasa yŏn'gu non'go* (Studies on Korean cultural history). Seoul: Ŭryu Munhwasa, 1947.

———. *Han'guksa kŭnse chŏn'gi p'yŏn* (History of Korea: Early modern period). Seoul: Ŭryu Munhwasa, 1962.

———. *Yijo kŏn'guk ŭi yŏn'gu: Yijo ŭi kŏn'guk kwa chŏnje kaehyŏk munje* (A study on the founding of the Chosŏn dynasty: The founding of the Chosŏn and the land reform problem). Seoul: Ŭryu Munhwasa, 1949.

Yi Sŏng-mu. "Chosŏn ch'ogi sinbunsa yŏn'gu ŭi chae kŏmt'o" (A reexamination of the history of status in the early Chosŏn). *Yŏksa hakpo* 102 (1984).

———. "Chosŏn ch'ogi ŭi hyangni" (Hyangni of the early Chosŏn). *Han'guksa yŏn'gu* 5 (1970).

———. *Chosŏn ch'ogi yangban yŏn'gu* (Studies on the early Chosŏn *yangban*). Seoul: Ilchogak, 1980.

———. "Chungin ch'ŭng ŭi sŏngnip munje" (The problem of the formation of the *chungin* stratum). *Tongyanghak* 8 (1978).

Yi Su-gŏn. *Han'guk chungse sahoesa yŏn'gu* (Studies in the social history of medieval Korea). Seoul: Ilchogak, 1984.

———. *Yŏngnam sarimp'a ŭi hyŏngsŏng* (Formation of the Yŏngnam *sarim*). Taegu: Yŏngnam Taehakkyo, 1979.

Yi Suk-kyŏng. "Koryŏ sidae chibang kwanch'ŏng pusokchi e taehan il koch'al" (An examination of lands belonging to local government agencies in the Koryŏ period). *Tonga yŏn'gu* 17 (1989).

Yi T'ae-jin. *Chosŏn yugyo sahoeron* (On the Confucian society of the Chosŏn). Seoul: Chisik Sanŏpsa, 1989.

———. *Han'guk sahoesa yŏn'gu: nongŏp kisul ŭi paltal kwa sahoe pyŏndong* (Studies in Korean social history: Advances in agricultural technology and social change). Seoul: Chisik Sanŏpsa, 1986.

———. "Koryŏ hugi ŭi in'gu chŭngga yoin saengsŏng kwa hyangyak ŭisul paltal" (The production of factors for population growth in the late Koryŏ and the development of medicial technology). *Han'guk saron* 19 (1988).

———. "Sarimp'a ŭi yuhyangso pongnip undong" (The Rusticated Literati faction's movement to restore the local governance body). *Chindan hakpo* 34–35 (1973).

Yi U-sŏng. "Koryŏ malgi Najumok Kŏp'yŏng pugok e taehayŏ" (On Kŏp'yŏng *pugok* in Naju at the end of the Koryŏ). *Chindan hakpo* 29–30 (1966).

———. "Koryŏjo ŭi 'i' e taehayŏ" (On the "clerks" of the Koryŏ dynasty). *Yŏksa hakpo* 21 (1964).

———. "Yijo sadaebu ŭi kibon sŏnggyŏk" (The basic nature of the Chosŏn dynasty scholar-officials). In Yi U-sŏng, *Han'guk ŭi yŏksa sang* (Korea's historical aspects). Seoul: Ch'angjak Kwa Pip'yŏngsa, 1982.

———. "Yŏdae paeksŏnggo" (An examination of Koryŏ village chiefs). *Yŏksa hakpo* 14 (1961).

Yi Ŭr-ho. "Koryŏ ŭi yugyo ch'ŏrhak" (The Confucian philosophy of the Koryŏ). In Han'guk Ch'ŏrhak Yŏn'guhoe (Korean Philosophy Research Society), ed., *Han'guk ch'ŏrhak yŏn'gu* (Studies in Korean philosophy). Seoul: Tongmyŏngsa, 1977.

Yi Wŏn-myŏng. "Koryŏ sŏngnihak suyong ŭi sasangjŏk paegyŏng" (The intellectual background to the Koryŏ reception of Nature and Principle Learning). Ph.D. diss., Koryŏ Taehakkyo, 1992.

Yu Ch'ang-gyu. "Koryŏ muin chŏnggwŏn sidae ui munin Pak In-sŏk: Komun chonjung/kyesŭng kwa kwallyŏn hayŏ" (The literatus Pak In-sŏk of the Koryŏ military regime period: In relation to the preservation of the Ancient Learning style). *Tonga yŏn'gu* 17 (1989).

Yu Kyŏng-a. "Koryŏ Kojong Wŏnjong sidae ŭi millan ŭi sŏnggyŏk" (Nature of popular uprisings during the years of Koryŏ Kings Kojong and Wonjong). *Yidae sawŏn* 22–23 (1988).

Yukkun Ponbu (Republic of Korea Army Headquarters), ed. *Han'guk kunjesa— kŭnse Chosŏn chŏn'gi p'yŏn* (History of Korean military institutions: Early Chosŏn). Seoul: Yukkun Ponbu, 1968.

Yun Han-t'aek. *Koryŏ chŏn'gi sajŏn yŏn'gu* (Studies on the *sajŏn* of the early Koryŏ). Seoul: Koryŏ Taehakkyo Minjok Munhwa Yŏn'guso, 1995.

Yun Kyŏng-jin. "Koryŏ T'aejodae kunhyŏnje kaep'yŏn ŭi sŏnggyŏk" (Nature of the reform of the prefecture-county system in the reign of King T'aejo of Koryŏ). *Yŏksa wa hyŏnsil* 22 (1996).

Yun Nam-han. "Yugyo ŭi sŏnggyŏk" (The nature of Confucianism). *Han'guksa*. Vol. 6. Seoul: Kuksa P'yŏnch'an Wiwŏnhoe, 1981.

SECONDARY SOURCES—ENGLISH LANGUAGE

Bol, Peter K. "Chu Hsi's Redefinition of Literati Learning." In John W. Chaffee and Wm. Theodore deBary, eds., *Neo-Confucian Education: The Formative Stage*. Berkeley and Los Angeles: University of California Press, 1989.

———. "Examinations and Orthodoxies: 1070 and 1313 Compared." Paper presented at the workshop "Culture and the State in Late Imperial China: The

Political and Cultural Construction of Norms," University of California at Irvine, June 1992.

———. *"This Culture of Ours": Intellectual Transitions in T'ang and Sung China.* Stanford: Stanford University Press, 1992.

Braudel, Fernand. *On History.* Sarah Matthews, trans. Chicago: University of Chicago Press, 1980.

Chafee, John W. *The Thorny Gates of Learning in Sung China.* Cambridge: Cambridge University Press, 1985.

———, and Wm. Theodore de Bary, eds. *Neo-Confucian Education: The Formative Stage.* Berkeley and Los Angeles: University of California Press, 1989.

Ch'oe Byŏng-hŏn. "Tosŏn's Geomantic Theories and the Foundation of the Koryŏ Dynasty." *Seoul Journal of Korean Studies* 2 (1989).

Ch'oe, Yŏng-ho. *The Civil Service Examination System and the Social Structure in Early Yi Dynasty Korea.* Seoul: Korean Research Center, 1987.

———. "Commoners in Early Yi Dynasty Civil Examinations: An Aspect of Korean Social Structure." *Journal of Asian Studies* 33 (1974).

Chung, Chai-sik. "Chŏng To-jŏn: Architect of Yi Dynasty Government and Ideology." In Wm. T. de Bary and JaHyun Kim Haboush, ed., *The Rise of Neo-Confucianism in Korea* (q. v.).

Clark, Donald N. "Autonomy, Legitimacy, and Tributary Politics: Sino-Korean Relations in the Fall of the Koryŏ and the Founding of the Yi." Ph.D. diss. Harvard University, 1978.

———. "Chosŏn's Founding Fathers: A Study of Merit Subjects in Early Yi Korea." *Korean Studies* 6 (1982).

Dardess, John W. *Confucianism and Autocracy: Professional Elites in the Founding of the Ming Dynasty.* Berkeley: University of California Press, 1983.

———. *Conquerors and Confucians.* New York: Columbia University Press, 1973.

de Bary, Wm. T. *East Asian Civilizations: A Dialogue in Five Stages.* Cambridge: Harvard University Press, 1988.

———. "Introduction." In Wm. T. de Bary and JaHyun Kim Haboush, ed., *The Rise of Neo-Confucianism in Korea* (q.v.).

———. *Neo-Confucian Orthodoxy and the Learning of the Mind-and-Heart.* New York: Columbia University Press, 1981.

de Bary, Wm. T., and JaHyun Kim Haboush, eds. *The Rise of Neo-Confucianism in Korea,* New York: Columbia University Press, 1986.

de Bary, Wm. T., et al., eds. *Sources of Chinese Tradition.* New York: Columbia University Press, 1961.

Deuchler, Martina. *The Confucian Transformation of Korea: A Study of Society and Ideology.* Cambridge: Harvard University Council on East Asian Studies, 1992.

———. "NeoConfucianism: The Impulse for Social Action in Early Yi Dynasty Korea." *Journal of Korean Studies* 2 (1980).

Duby, Georges. *The Early Growth of the European Economy.* Howard B. Clarke, trans. Ithaca: Cornell University Press, 1974.

Duncan, John B. "Confucianism in the Late Koryŏ and Early Chosŏn." *Korean Studies* 18 (1994).

———. "The Formation of the Central Aristocracy in Early Koryŏ." *Korean Studies* 12 (1988).

———. "The Koryŏ Origins of the Chosŏn Dynasty: Kings, Aristocrats, and Confucianism." Ph.D. diss. University of Washington, 1988.

———. "The Late Koryŏ: A Buddhist Aristocracy?" Paper presented at the annual meeting of the Association for Asian Studies, Washington, D.C., 1992.

———. "The Social Background to the Founding of the Chosŏn Dynasty: Change or Continuity?" *Journal of Korean Studies* 6 (1988–89).

Ebrey, Patricia. *The Aristocratic Families of Early Imperial China: A Case Study of the Po-ling Tsui Family.* Cambridge: Cambridge University Press, 1978.

Eisenstadt, S. N. *The Political Systems of Empires.* New York: Glencoe Press, 1963.

Farquhar, David M. "Structure and Function in the Yüan Imperial Government." In John Langlois, ed., *China under Mongol Rule.* Princeton, N.J.: Princeton University Press, 1981.

Hucker, Charles. O. "The Ming Dynasty: Its Origins and Evolving Insitutions." *Michigan Papers in Chinese Studies* 34 (1978).

Huntley, James Grayson. *Korea: A Religious History.* Cambridge, England: Clarendon Press, 1988.

Hymes, Robert. *Statesmen and Gentlemen: The Elite of Fu-chou, Chiang-hsi, in Northern and Southern Sung China.* Cambridge, England: Cambridge University Press, 1986.

Inoue, Hideo. "The Reception of Buddhism in Korea and Its Impact on Indigenous Culture." In Lewis E. Lancaster and C. S. Yu, eds., *Introduction of Buddhism to Korea: New Cultural Patterns.* Berkeley: Asian Humanities Press, 1987.

Johnson, David. *The Medieval Chinese Oligarchy.* Boulder: Westview Press, 1977.

Kalton, Michaël. "The Writings of Kwŏn Kŭn: The Context and Shape of Early Chosŏn Neo-Confucianism" In Wm. T. de Bary and Ja Hyun Kim Haboush, eds., *The Rise of Neo-Confucianism in Korea* (q.v.).

Kang Chin-ch'ŏl. "Traditional Land Tenure." In Hugh H. Kang, ed., *The Traditional Culture and Society of Korea* (q.v.).

Kang, Hugh H. "The Development of the Korean Ruling Class from Late Silla to Early Koryŏ." Ph.D. diss., University of Washington, 1964.

———. "Epilogue." In *The Traditional Culture and Society of Korea* (q.v.).

———. "The First Succession Struggle of Koryŏ in 945: A Reinterpretation." *Journal of Asian Studies* 36:3 (1977).

———. "Insitutional Borrowing: The Case of the Chinese Civil Service Examination System in Early Koryŏ." *Journal of Asian Studies* 34 (1974).

———. "Wang Kŏn and the Koryŏ Dynastic Order." *Han'guk munhwa* 7 (1986).

———, ed. *The Traditional Culture and Society of Korea: Thought and Institutions.* Occasional Papers of the Center for Korean Studies 5. Honolulu: University of Hawaii, 1975.

Kawashima, Fujiya. "Clan Structure and Political Power in Yi Dynasty Korea— A Case Study of the Munhwa Yu Clan." Ph.D. diss., Harvard University, 1972.

———. "The Local Gentry Association in Mid-Yi Dynasty Korea: A Preliminary Study of the Ch'angnyŏng Hyangan, 1600–1838." *Journal of Korean Studies* 2 (1980).

Lancaster, Lewis E., and C. S. Yu, eds. *Introduction of Buddhism to Korea: New Cultural Patterns*. Berkeley: Asian Humanities Press, 1987.

Langlois, John D. "Political Thought in Chin-hua Under Mongol Rule." In Langlois, ed., *China Under Mongol Rule*. Princeton: Princeton Univ. Press, 1981.

Lee, Peter H., ed. *Anthology of Korean Literature*. Honolulu: University of Hawaii Press, 1981.

———. *Sourcebook of Korean Civilization*. Vol 1. New York: Columbia University Press, 1993.

Lo, Winston. *An Introduction to the Civil Service of Sung China: With Emphasis on Its Personnel Administration*. Honolulu: University of Hawaii Press, 1987.

McMullen, David L. *State and Scholars in T'ang China*. Cambridge, England: Cambridge University Press, 1988.

Miyakawa Hisayuki. "An Outline of the Naito Hypothesis and Its Effects on Japanese Studies of China." *Far Eastern Quarterly* 14:4 (1955).

Palais, James B. *Confucian Statecraft and Korean Institutions: Yu Hyŏngwŏn and the Late Chosŏn Dynasty*. Seattle: University of Washington Press, 1996.

———. "Confucianism and the Aristocratic/Bureaucratic Balance in Korea." *Harvard Journal of Asiatic Studies* 44-2 (1984).

———. "Han Yŏng-u's Studies of Early Chosŏn Intellectual History." *Journal of Korean Studies* 2 (1980).

———. "Land Tenure in Korea: Tenth to Twelfth Centuries." *Journal of Korean Studies* 4 (1982–83).

———. *Politics and Policy in Traditional Korea*. Cambridge, Mass.: Harvard University Press, 1975.

———. "Slavery and Slave Society in Koryŏ." *Journal of Korean Studies* 5 (1984).

Reischauer, Edwin O., and John K. Fairbank. *East Asia: The Great Tradition*. Boston: Houghton Mifflin Company, 1960.

Rogers, Michael. "P'yŏnnyŏn t'ongnok: The Foundation Legend of the Koryŏ State." *Journal of Korean Studies* 4 (1982–83).

Salem, Ellen. "Slavery in Medieval Korea." Ph.D. diss., Columbia University, 1978.

Shin, Susan. "Land Tenure and the Agrarian Economy in Yi Dynasty Korea: 1600–1800." Ph.D. diss., Harvard University, 1973.

Shultz, Edward J. "Institutional Development in Korea Under the Ch'oe House Rule." Ph.D. diss., University of Hawaii, 1976.

———. "Military Revolt in Koryŏ: The 1170 Coup d'etat." *Korean Studies* 3 (1979).

———. "Military-Civilian Conflict of the Koryŏ Dynasty." In David McCann et al., eds., *Studies on Korea in Transition*. Honolulu: University of Hawaii Press, 1979.

———. "Twelfth Century Koryŏ: Merit and Birth." Paper presented at the annual meeting of the Association for Asian Studies, Washington, D.C., 1993. Forthcoming in *Journal of Korean Studies* 9.

———. "Twelfth Century Koryŏ Politics: The Rise of Han An-in and His Partisans." *Journal of Korean Studies* 6 (1988–89).

Sohn Pow-key (Son Po-gi). "Power versus Status: The Role of Ideology during the Early Yi Dynasty." *Tongbang hakchi* 10 (1969).

———. "Social History of the Early Yi Dynasty, 1392–1592. Ph.D. diss., University of California at Berkeley, 1963.

Song Ch'an-sik. "Genealogical Records." *Korea Journal,* January 1977.

Tillman, Hoyt Cleveland. *Confucian Discourse and Chu Hsi's Ascendency.* Honolulu: University of Hawaii Press, 1992.

———. *Utilitarian Confucianism: Ch'en Liang's Challenge to Chu Hsi.* Cambridge: Harvard University Press, 1982.

Twitchett, Denis. "Varied Patterns of Provincial Autonomy in the Late T'ang Dynasty." In John Curtis Perry and Bardwell L. Smith, ed., *Essays on T'ang Society: The Interplay of Social, Political, and Economic Forces.* Leiden: E. J. Brill, 1976.

Wagner, Edward W. "The Korean Chokpo as a Historical Source." In Spencer Palmer, ed., *Studies in Asian Genealogy.* Provo: Brigham Young University, 1974.

———. *The Literati Purges: Political Conflict in Early Yi Korea.* Cambridge: Harvard University Press, 1974.

———. "Two Early Genealogies and Women's Status in Early Yi Dynasty Korea." In Laurel Kendall and Mark Peterson, ed., *Korean Women: View from the Inner Room.* New Haven: East Rock Press, 1983.

Wakeman, Frederic. *The Fall of Imperial China.* New York: Free Press, 1975.

Yang, Lien-sheng. *Studies in Chinese Institutional History.* Harvard-Yenching Institute Series. Cambridge, Mass.: Harvard University, 1961.

Yi Sŏng-mu. "The Influence of Neo-Confucianism on Education and the Civil Service Examination System in Fourteenth and Fifteenth Century Korea." In Wm. T. de Bary and JaHyun Kim Haboush, ed., *The Rise of Neo-Confucianism in Korea* (q.v.).

Index

An Chong-wŏn, 226
An Ch'uk, 175, 186
An Hyang, 77, 81, 140
An Mok, 148
An No-saeng, 150
An Pu, 193
ancestral seats, 31, 52–53, 144, 290*n*69
Ancient Style Learning, 239, 241;
    beginnings in Korea, 242; setback
    of, 243–44; revival of, 244–46;
    adherents of, 247; and Ch'eng-Chu
    Learning, 258–60; and reform,
    261–62, 264, 265
an-ch'a shih. See commissioners
anch'alsa. See commissioners
Andong, 32, 41, 42, 56, 146
Andong Chang, 105, 109–11
Andong Kim, 73–74, 77–78, 83, 121;
    examination graduates of, 80, 143;
    use of *ŭm* privilege, 81; in bureau-
    cracy, 105, 108–9, 110, 139;
    lineage chart, 126–27; marriage
    relations of, 134–35
Andong Kwŏn, 32, 73–74, 76–78,
    122–24, 132; marriage relations
    of, 76, 133–35; examination grad-
    uates of, 80, 142–43; use of *ŭm*
    privilege, 81; economic founda-
    tions of, 93; in bureaucracy, 105–
    6, 108–9, 110, 120, 137, 139;
    hyangni branch groups, 121; lin-
    eage chart, 122–23
Ansan Kim, 57, 60, 69, 133
aristocracy, 21, 53. *See also* central

aristocratic bureaucrats; civil
    aristocrats
artisans, 210, 220–21
Asiatic mode of production, 4
assistant magistrates, 43

Bad Local Official Punishment Law,
    219
belles lettres, 237, 239, 249–50;
    revived after 1170 military coup,
    241, 243–44; 256. *See also* parallel
    prose; poetry; regulated verse;
    rhyme-prose
Bol, Peter K., 97, 152, 239, 257
Bone Rank system, 15, 31, 267; lin-
    gering influence of, 17–19, 21
Braudel, Fernand, 283
Buddhism, 17–18, 49, 238, 239, 242–
    43, 245–46; royal patronage of,
    224–25, 251–53, 255; opposition
    to, 224, 237, 238, 245–46, 251,
    253, 255; Yi Che-hyŏn on, 247;
    among *yangban*, 252–57; and
    shamanism, 281. *See also* Hwaŏm
    Buddhism; Sŏn Buddhism
Buddhist monks: and officeholding,
    171, 220–21; and Rank Land Law,
    210; in palace, 255; as teachers of
    yangban, 254–56
Buddho-Confucian tradition, 237,
    239, 242, 244, 256
bureaucratic societies. *See* historical
    bureaucratic societies
burial sites, 144–46, 308*n*171

maternal relatives, 76, 295*n*23; in late Koryŏ, 78, 80–81; in early Chosŏn, 119–20; and scholar-officials, 140–41. *See also* protection privilege

village commune theory, 45–46

Wagner, Edward W, 106, 223, 252
Wakeman, Frederic, 261
Wako, 73, 116, 158, 160, 175, 188, 205; and fiscal difficulties, 183–84
Wang An-shih, 257, 261, 262
Wang Hu, 123. *See also* Kwŏn Chae
Wang Kŏn, 14, 16–19, 267; family background of, 16, 18; Ten Injunctions of, 17–18; marriages of, 19. *See also* T'aejo
Wang Kung-mo, 58
wangsa. See royal preceptors
warlord confederation, early Koryŏ, 18–20, 267. *See also* local strongmen
Weber, Max, 11
Wihwa Island, 116, 226
Wŏn Ch'ŏn-sŏk, 186
Wŏn Kwan, 77
Wŏn Sŏn-ji, 83
Wŏnak Hyangni Ch'ŏbŏl Pŏp. *See* Bad Local Official Punishment Law
Wŏnjong (Koryŏ king), 79, 157, 166
Wŏnju Wŏn, 73–75, 83, 146, 299*n*79; marriage relations of, 76–77, 134; examination graduates of, 80; use of ŭm privilege, 81; decline of, 114; in bureaucracy, 139, 143; burial sites of, 308*n*171

Yalu River, 14
Yang Sŏng-ji, 149, 153, 250
yangban, 8–9, 98, 99, 106, 108–9, 111, 113, 116, 120, 129, 131, 271–74, 276; meaning of term, 88–89, 152–53; economic foundations of, 88–94, 135, 271;

residence patterns of, 144–47; in provinces, 147; domination of bureaucracy, 160, 164; and inner palace politics, 173, 181; and reform efforts, 174, 175, 273; and *hyangni*, 197; as central elite, 199; and Rank Land Law, 208; exclusion of others by, 220–21; sons as Buddhist monks, 254; and late Koryŏ kings, 273; as aristocracy, 277; formation of, 278. *See also* central aristocratic bureaucrats; civil aristocrats
yangbu, 24–25
Yangch'ŏn, 186
Yanggu, 186
Yanggwang circuit, 37
Yangju, 36
Yangju Cho, 139, 143
Yangsŏng Yi, 139
Yejong (Koryŏ king), 42, 242–44
Yi Cha-ch'un, 135
Yi Cha-gyŏm, 67, 90
Yi Cha-hyŏn, 67, 242
Yi Cha-in, 67
Yi Ch'ang-no, 128
Yi Chang-yong, 157
Yi Cha-ryang, 67, 90
Yi Cha-sang, 67
Yi Cha-ŭi, 28, 58, 67
Yi Cha-yŏn, 28, 59, ,64, 67
Yi Che, 112, 135, 148, 227
Yi Che-hyŏn, 93, 128–29, 132, 272; on Todang, 161–62; on abuses of Personnel Authority, 173–74; as reform leader, 174–76, 177; and Ch'eng-Chu Learning, 247; and Ancient Style Learning, 247–48, 257; retirement of, 248; and examination reforms, 257–58
Yi Chi-bo, 67
Yi Chi-jŏ, 166
Yi Chik, 140
Yi Chi-mi, 67
Yi Chin, 128, 174